ENTREPRENEURIAL ECONOMICS

AN INDEPENDENT INSTITUTE BOOK

ENTREPRENEURIAL ECONOMICS

Bright Ideas from the Dismal Science

Edited by Alexander Tabarrok

UNIVERSITY PRESS

2002

OXFORD
UNIVERSITY PRESS

Oxford   New York
Athens   Auckland   Bangkok   Bogotá   Buenos Aires   Cape Town
Chennai   Dar es Salaam   Delhi   Florence   Hong Kong   Istanbul   Karachi
Kolkata   Kuala Lumpur   Madrid   Melbourne   Mexico City   Mumbai   Nairobi
Paris   São Paulo   Shanghai   Singapore   Taipei   Tokyo   Toronto   Warsaw

and associated companies in
Berlin   Ibadan

Copyright © 2002 by The Independent Institute

Published by Oxford University Press, Inc.
198 Madison Avenue, New York, New York 10016

Oxford is a registered trademark of Oxford University Press

Library of Congress Cataloging-in-Publication Data
Entrepreneurial economics: bright ideas from the
dismal science / edited by Alexander Tabarrok.
    p.   cm.
Includes bibliographical references and index.
ISBN 0-19-515028-7 (cloth); ISBN 0-19-514503-8 (pbk.)
1. Entrepreneurship.   2. Economics.   I. Tabarrok, Alexander.
HB615 .E5967 2002
338'.04—dc21   2001045841

9 8 7 6 5 4 3 2 1

Printed in the United States of America
on acid-free paper

Acknowledgments

The contributors appreciate permission to reprint the following:

Aghion, P., O. Hart, and J. Moore. 1994. Improving Bankruptcy Procedure. *Washington University Law Quarterly* 72 (3):849–72. Reprinted here as chapter 11. Reprinted with permission of Washington University Law Quarterly. © 1994 Washington University Law Quarterly. All rights reserved.

Athanasoulis, S., R. Shiller, and E. van Wincoop. 1999. Macro Markets and Financial Security. *Federal Reserve Bank of New York: Economic Policy Review* 5 (1):21–39. Reprinted here as chapter 2. Reprinted with permission of S. Athanasoulis, R. Shiller, and E. van Wincoop. © 1999 Federal Reserve Bank of New York and Economic Policy Review. All rights reserved.

Barnett, A. H., R. D. Blair, and D. L. Kaserman. 1996. A Market for Organs. *Society* 33 (6):8–17. Reprinted here as chapter 6. Reprinted with permission of Transaction Publishers. © 1996 by Transaction Publishers. All rights reserved.

Cochrane, J. H. 1995. Time-Consistent Health Insurance. *Journal of Political Economy* 103 (3):445–73. Reprinted here as chapter 4. Reprinted with permission of the Journal of Political Economy and J. H. Cochrane. © 1995 The University of Chicago. All rights reserved.

Friedman, D. 1996. More Justice for Less Money. *Journal of Law and Economics* XXXIX (April):211–40. Reprinted here as chapter 10. Reprinted with permission of the Journal of Law and Economics. © 1996 by The University of Chicago. All rights reserved.

Hanson, R. D. 1999. Decision Markets. *IEEE Intelligent Systems* (May/June): 16–19. Reprinted here as chapter 5. © 1999 IEEE. Reprinted with permission from IEEE Intelligent Systems and R. D. Hanson.

Klein, D. B., A. T. Moore, and B. Reja. 1997. Curb Rights: Eliciting Competition and Entrepreneurship in Urban Transit. *The Independent Review* II (1):29–54. Reprinted here as chapter 14. Reprinted with permission of the publisher. © Copyright 1997, The Independent Institute, 100 Swan Way, Oakland, California 94621-1428; http://www.independent.org.

Kremer, M. 1998. Patent Buyouts: A Mechanism for Encouraging Innovation. *Quarterly Journal of Economics* 113 (November):1137–67. Reprinted here as chapter 13. Reprinted with permission of Michael Kremer. © 1998 by the President and Fellows of Harvard College and the Massachusetts Institute of Technology. All rights reserved.

Landsburg, S. 1993. Selection from *The Armchair Economist*. pp. 148–51, The Free Press, New York. Reprinted here as chapter 8. Reprinted with the permission of the Free Press, a Division of Simon & Schuster, Inc. Copyright © 1993 by Steven E. Landsburg.

Romano, R. 1998. Empowering Investors: A Market Approach to Securities Regulation. *Yale Law Journal* 107 (8):2359–430. Reprinted here with editing for length as chapter 12. Reprinted by permission of The Yale Law Journal Company and William S. Hein Company.

Tabarrok, A. 1997. Trumping the Genetic Tarot Card: Insurance against Bad Genes. *Contingencies* 9 (4):20–23. Reprinted here as chapter 3. Reprinted with permission of A. Tabarrok. © 1997 Contingencies. All rights reserved.

Contents

Contributors

David Friedman is Professor of Law at the University of Santa Clara School of Law and the author of, most recently, *Hidden Order* and *Law's Order*.

Robin D. Hanson is Assistant Professor of Economics at George Mason University.

Oliver Hart is the Andrew E. Furer Professor of Economics at Harvard University.

David L. Kaserman is the Torchmark Professor of Economics at Auburn University.

Daniel B. Klein is Associate Professor of Economics at Santa Clara University.

Michael Kremer is Senior Fellow at the Brookings Institution and Professor of Economics at Harvard University.

Steven Landsburg is the author of, most recently, *The Armchair Economist* and *Fair Play*. He is adjunct Associate Professor of Economics at the University of Rochester.

Adrian T. Moore is Director of Privatization and Government Reform at Reason Public Policy Institute (RPPI) in Los Angeles.

John Moore is Professor of Economics at the London School of Economics.

Binyam Reja is an evaluation officer for the World Bank.

Morgan Reynolds is Professor of Economics at Texas A&M University and Director of the Criminal Justice Center of the National Center for Policy Analysis.

Roberta Romano is the Allen Duffy/Class of 1960 Professor of Law at Yale University.

Robert Shiller is the Stanley B. Resor Professor of Economics at Yale University.

Eric van Wincoop is a senior economist at the Federal Reserve Bank of New York.

Contributors

Alexander Tabarrok is Vice President and Research Director dent Institute and Assistant Editor of *The Independent Rev* his Ph.D. in economics from George Mason University, at at the University of Virginia and Ball State University. Sch Dr. Tabarrok have appeared in *The Journal of Law and Ec Choice, Economic Inquiry, The Journal of Health Econon of Theoretical Politics, Theory and Decision*, and many o coeditor (with D. Beito and P. Gordon) of the Independer *The Voluntary City*, Dr. Tabarrok has also contributed to th *lative Term Limits* and *Women and Liberty*, among others. by Dr. Tabarrok have appeared in many magazines and ne

Philippe Aghion is Professor of Economics at Harvard Unive

Stefano Athanasoulis is Visiting Assistant Professor of Econon versity.

Andy H. Barnett is Professor of Economics and Chair of the Economics, International Studies, and Public Administratic can University of Sharjah.

Roger D. Blair is the Huber Hurst Professor of Business and the University of Florida.

John H. Cochrane is the Sigmund E. Edelstone Professor of University of Chicago Graduate School of Business.

Foreword

STEVEN LANDSBURG

Would you rather live in a world without blood transfusions or a world without maritime insurance? Blood transfusions are dramatic and memorable (which is why we see them on prime-time hospital shows), while the facilitation of commerce through risk sharing is routine and easily taken for granted. But I'd be willing to bet that by almost any measure, three centuries of organized insurance markets have contributed more to human happiness than three centuries of transfused blood.

Would you rather live in a world without personal computers or a world without junk bonds? It is both obvious and true that your computer runs wonderful software. It's less obvious but equally true that a lot of that software was developed only because some entrepreneur was able to finance a risky venture. The unprecedented prosperity of the past two decades is due partly to innovations in information technology and partly to innovations in the organization of financial markets. I don't know which has contributed more. (The question is very much complicated by the fact that each kind of innovation feeds off the other.) The obvious lower bounds offer no guidance: In the late 1980s, Microsoft's annual economic profit and Michael Milken's annual income were both in the same neighborhood at about $600 million.

Invention is the engine of prosperity, but inventions come in many forms. The internal combustion engine is an invention, and so is the system of just-in-time inventory management. Economists study the causes and effects of both. But nobody turns to economists to design a better car, so why should anybody turn to economists to design a better market?

Many economists would answer that there is no good answer. Their position is that we, as a profession, have no more business designing markets than we have designing cars; our job is to understand existing institutions, not to improve them. We are scientists, not engineers.

But if economists don't design better markets, who will? The mantra of positive economics is that we can't give advice on improving efficiency because anything that's efficient has already been adopted. But that mantra founders on two counts, both of which will be obvious to anyone who glances more than casually at the articles in this volume. First, a lot of market innovations yield benefits that are difficult to capture privately, so even if we can rely on the entrepreneurs to invent just-in-time inventory management, we can't rely on them to invent markets for everything. Second, and more to the point, economists can be very good at thinking about markets. Electric light was inefficient until Thomas Edison had a good idea. Private patent markets were inefficient until Michael Kremer figured out how to organize them (see chapter 13 in this volume); if Edison can change the world, why can't Kremer?

Economists have a lot of socially useful tasks to perform. One of those tasks is to translate our understanding and appreciation for markets into innovative proposals for making the world run more efficiently. The chapters in this book prove that at least some of us can do that.

We can do that partly because we are in the habit of thinking hard about the design of incentives and the assignment of property rights. Some of these chapters are about how governments can assign property rights more efficiently; others suggest new ways for entrepreneurs to create and sell new kinds of property rights.

I learned a lot reading *Entrepreneurial Economics*, and I'll surely steal some of the ideas for use in future books and columns. I hope others steal them for use, not just entertainment. Unfortunately, there are no property rights in the ideas themselves. That suggests we're not getting enough of them. Let's cherish the ones we've got.

ENTREPRENEURIAL ECONOMICS

1

Introduction

ALEXANDER TABARROK

No one goes to the barricades for efficiency. For liberty, equality, or frater-
nity, perhaps, but never for efficiency. Efficiency's failure as a revolutionary
battle cry is rather puzzling, at least to an economist. Efficiency is the one
thing *everyone* should go to the barricades for. Will the chapters in this
volume therefore inspire marches on city hall? It's doubtful, but even modest moves toward more efficient policies can be highly valuable. Ronald
Coase, the 1991 winner of the Nobel Prize in economics, argued that an
economist who delays a bad policy from being implemented by as little as
a week has earned his salary for a lifetime. Presumably an economist who
encourages a good policy has done the same. Coase's own contribution to
more efficient public policy, his 1959 proposal to auction off the radio spectrum, was not adopted until 1993.[1] Coase, however, was not disappointed
by the nearly forty years of delay. The first nine spectrum auctions alone
raised over $20 billion in revenue and reduced deadweight costs by close
to $1 billion.[2]

James Buchanan ([1959] 1987), another Nobel Prize winner, has argued
that the job of the political economist "is that of locating possible flaws in
the existing social structure and in presenting possible 'improvements'."[3]
Where then lies the difference between the political economist and the
myriad others who try to steer public policy? The political economist is
disciplined. She must offer up for judgment only those policies she believes
are Pareto improvements—policies capable, at least in principle, of bene-
fiting some while harming none. This is no easy task. The vast majority of
political proposals fail this goal miserably. In contrast, the chapters in this
volume take the task of political economy seriously. The authors offer up
for judgment potentially genuine improvements in social institutions.

Steven Landsburg's chapter on the bail system is a good example of the difference between an economist's approach to policy issues and that of other policy entrepreneurs. Conservatives often argue that judges are too lenient on criminal defendants and that more defendants should be locked up prior to trial. Liberals respond that every defendant must be considered "innocent until proven guilty" and thus bail should not be made prohibitive. On this question, Landsburg offers no opinion. Instead he offers a principle that should be agreeable to conservatives and liberals alike: Whether many or few defendants are released on bail, those released should be the ones *least likely* to commit crimes. Economists can't say whether many or few defendants should be released, but they can tell us that people generally work harder and smarter when they have an incentive to work harder and smarter. Landsburg proposes that we increase the incentives of judges to choose the least dangerous defendants to release. Landsburg's clever method for doing this is discussed in chapter 8 and further described in the next section. The point here is that whether or not his scheme works, it is not a mere argument for making some better off at the expense of others. Landsburg's proposal is a genuine potential Pareto improvement.

Overview of the Chapters

Wealth and Health Insurance

Since the seminal essay on options pricing by Black and Scholes (1973), the pace of financial innovation has exploded. With the help of "financial engineers," firms today can buy, sell, and control risk better than ever before. Unfortunately, individuals still have difficulty managing the largest economic risks they face. Individuals have some control over their income through choices about work effort, education, and job, but the largest economic risks stem from factors outside of the individual's control, such as the health of the macroeconomy. A rising tide lifts all boats and a falling tide drops them all, too. Over long time periods, some nations grow while others stagnate, pulling individual incomes up or down. In chapter 2, Stefano Athanasoulis, Robert Shiller, and Eric van Wincoop (ASvW) explain how new markets could give individuals greater control over their income streams by letting them hedge national income risk.

To see how these markets would work, consider an analogy. The income of General Motors (GM) workers is in part determined by their work effort and skills and in part by how well GM performs in the world market. When GM performs poorly, dividends on GM stock will be low and so will worker income, since hours and wages are likely to be reduced (and vice versa when GM performs well). Dividends on GM stock and the income of GM

workers are correlated. Workers can therefore reduce their income risk by purchasing shares in a well-diversified portfolio with money they earn from selling borrowed GM shares (shorting GM). Selling borrowed shares may sound peculiar, but individuals who "short" GM have, in effect, borrowed money at an interest rate that is tied to GM dividends. (Someone who borrows and sells GM shares must pay the lender GM dividends.) This is exactly what GM workers wish to do since their own incomes are correlated with GM dividends. When GM is performing poorly, labor income is low but so are GM dividends, and thus the interest rate on the worker's borrowed shares is low. When GM is performing well, labor income is high but so are GM dividends, and thus the interest rate on the worker's borrowed shares is high. In either case, workers offset the required interest payments with their labor income, and they take home instead the dividends from their portfolio of owned stocks. Take-home pay is stabilized because the dividends flow from a well-diversified portfolio. Amazingly, this stabilization of income can be had virtually for nothing because workers buy their stock portfolios with money they earn from shorting GM stock. On net, therefore, workers need only pay the transaction costs of buying and selling some shares.

National income markets, as proposed by ASvW, would let individuals buy and sell shares in a country in the same way they buy and sell shares in GM today.[4] Workers would thus be able to hedge away some of their national income risk. United States workers are currently in the same position as the GM workers discussed above. Some of their income comes from their own efforts and skills, and some of it comes from the fact that they work in the United States and are subject to swings in the national economy. By shorting "USA" shares and using the proceeds to purchase shares in a portfolio of world incomes, U.S. workers could significantly reduce the riskiness of their personal incomes.

The idea of macro markets is quite general. Markets in state or regional income, for example, could let individuals hedge away personal income risks not well correlated with national income. Markets in aggregate occupational income could be created and hedged against (e.g., a dentist could hedge in the dental income market against the risk that a scientific discovery eliminates the possibility of cavities). A judicious combination of national, regional, and occupational hedging could create an effective form of private unemployment insurance, thereby eliminating the inefficiencies of the current public system.

Macro markets could also be useful for nonhedging purposes. Once these markets are created they will become powerful indicators of the effectiveness of government policy. Just as the price of a corporation represents the expected sum of discounted future dividends, the price of a national security represents the expected sum of discounted future national income. In an efficient market, the expected effects of government policy would in-

stantly be visible in the prices of national income securities. (Robin Hanson explores this idea more generally in his contribution to this volume discussed below.)

The existence of national income securities could even improve government policy. It is often argued that politicians won't support policies with short-term costs even if the long-term benefits are large, because they fear voters will penalize them for the costs and reward future politicians for the eventual benefits. Even worse, politicians with short time horizons might support policies with greater costs than benefits if the benefits come early and the costs late. Such short-term thinking might decline if politicians could point to the prices of national income securities to indicate the long-run impact of their policies.

Chapters 3 and 4 propose two ways of making the health insurance market more efficient and more equitable. In "Gene Insurance," Alexander Tabarrok proposes that firms sell insurance against the possibility of possessing a bad gene. By reading your genetic code, medical practitioners are increasingly able to predict your future health. Genetic testing and sophisticated imaging, for example, can predict Alzheimer's twenty years before the onset of any obvious symptoms. The new genetic knowledge has many potential benefits, including earlier detection and treatment of disease and more focused investigation into cures. Many people fear, however, that health and life insurance companies will raise premiums or deny insurance altogether if a test indicates the presence of a disease-associated gene. Gene insurance can alleviate many of these fears.

Gene insurance is insurance against a change in health insurance premiums due to the revelation of genetic information. Before taking a genetic test, an individual would have the option of buying insurance. If the test reveals a "bad" gene, gene insurance pays the policyholder a lump-sum amount capable of funding the actuarially sound increase in future health premiums associated with that gene. Under this system, individuals would always have enough money to purchase health and life insurance at the actuarially sound rates. Insurers, instead of shunning so-called bad risks, would eagerly compete to offer policies to all individuals regardless of their genetic makeup.

Whenever long-term information about health is revealed, whether by genetic test or otherwise, consumers may legitimately worry that insurance premiums will skyrocket or that they will lose their health insurance altogether. Even individuals who buy insurance through a large group may lose their insurance if they or their spouses lose their jobs. Fears like this play a large role in contemporary proposals to reform the U.S. health care system. Most of these reforms involve more government regulation and intervention into health care markets, and voters have been rightly skeptical about the value of these plans. In chapter 4, John Cochrane shows how markets can solve the problem of unexpected premium increases. The idea

is similar in flavor to that of gene insurance. In the same way that gene insurance insures against a change in health insurance premiums due to new genetic knowledge, Cochrane shows that it is possible to insure against unexpected changes in premiums due to any cause.

Cochrane uses a potentially imposing mathematical model to make his arguments, but the flavor of the argument is quite easy to understand. In essence, insurance companies would sell two contracts, one for health insurance and the other for premium insurance. If a person's health gets unexpectedly worse, premiums on the health insurance contract increase, but premium insurance pays a lump-sum amount large enough to make future premiums affordable. Would premium insurance be expensive? No—with one modification we can make premium insurance available for free! Suppose that the contract is made symmetrical so that if an individual's health unexpectedly improves, he must pay a lump-sum amount to the premium insurance company. In this case, it can be shown that the net value of the contract is zero, so a risk-neutral competitive firm will be willing to sell premium insurance for as little as the transaction costs of writing the policy![5]

Although they appear to be very different, Cochrane's idea, which he calls "time-consistent health insurance," is fundamentally similar to the "macro markets" proposed by ASvW in chapter 2.[6] Another way of describing time-consistent health insurance is that a market is created for an asset that pays dividends according to an individual's health insurance premiums. The price of this "health asset" is the discounted sum of expected future health insurance premiums. To insure against changes in these premiums, the individual buys a perpetual future on the health asset, and the insurance firm takes the opposite side of the contract.[7] At the time of sale, the futures price is set such that the contract has zero value, that is, it can be bought for nothing. When the asset price (i.e., the expected sum of discounted future health insurance premiums) rises above the futures price (perhaps because the individual is diagnosed with cancer), the seller pays the buyer the difference. If health improves and the discounted sum of future premiums falls below the futures price, the buyer pays the difference to the seller. Because the price of the asset falls (rises) only when the individual's expected premiums fall (rise), the individual is insured against changes in the costs of health insurance. Furthermore, by cashing out the contract, the individual can transfer health insurance to another firm without ever having to worry about not having enough cash to pay actuarially sound premiums.

It's not possible or desirable to create an actual market in an individual's health insurance premiums because trading would be too thin to establish competitive equilibrium prices—the only person interested in buying a future on the value of my expected future health premiums is me! To avoid these problems and also issues of liquidity, Cochrane presents his idea in the form of a contract rather than a market. The contract, however, can be thought of as a contract on an "ideal" security, a security that would exist if markets were perfectly competitive and liquid.

The Use of Information in Markets

In the great socialist calculation debate of the 1930s and 1940s, Friedrich Hayek argued that information about preferences, abilities, resources, and technology, which economists take as "given" in their models, is in fact not given to anyone but rather exists only in dispersed form in millions of independent minds. The economic problem is thus not so much the mathematical problem of finding an optimal solution, given knowledge of preferences, abilities, resources, and technology, but rather the problem of making use of highly dispersed information that is never known to anyone in even a fraction of its totality. Markets, Hayek (1945) pointed out, are a "marvelous" means of solving just such a problem.

Research since Hayek's time has confirmed that markets aggregate information remarkably well—so well that forecasts made by markets tend to be more accurate than any other forecasts.[8] Forecasts based upon market prices are more accurate than other forecasts because markets aggregate information from thousands (sometimes millions, and potentially billions) of highly motivated consumers, producers, and investors. In a complicated process that is still not well understood, individual forecasts feed into market prices through buying and selling and market prices feed back into individual forecasts, which in turn reignites buying and selling. The result of this process is prices that efficiently aggregate large quantities of information.

In the past twenty years, economists have become accustomed to extracting forecasts and other information from raw market data, but few markets have been created explicitly for the purpose of generating information. This is what Robin Hanson proposes in chapter 5.

There is one well-known market that was created to generate information, the Iowa Political Stock Market. The Iowa market lets anyone in the world invest real money in shares that have been designed so that their prices reveal the probabilities that market participants attach to various political and financial events.[9] On average, the Iowa market has predicted election results better than polls. A few pioneering corporations have also established markets for the purpose of information creation. Hewlett-Packard (HP), for example, wanted to improve sales forecasts. Hewlett-Packard believed that collectively their sales forces "knew" more about the probability of future printer sales than management was able to ascertain from surveys or other methods. Thus, they created a market in which sales-contingent securities could be bought and sold. A typical security would pay out $1 if and only if future sales were, say, between 10,000 and 15,000 units. By examining prices on a large set of these securities, HP was able to get a good picture of the potential distribution of future sales. Moreover, in sixteen trials, the mean market prediction was never further from actual sales than the official prediction, and in fifteen out of sixteen runs, it was significantly closer (Plott 2000).[10]

Hanson proposes that information-aggregation (IA) markets be used to improve public policy. Consider the 1993 debate over the North American Free Trade Agreement (NAFTA). During the NAFTA debate, some politicians predicted that if NAFTA passed, thousands of manufacturing plants would be closed and as many as five million U.S. jobs would be lost to low-wage Mexican workers. Almost all economists disagreed with this prediction but it was difficult to transmit the breadth and depth of their disagreement to citizens. In order to appear unbiased, news organizations like to present "both sides" of every issue. The media debate on NAFTA, therefore, appeared much more balanced than was expert opinion. It was difficult for a citizen to know that one "half" of the debate represented perhaps 2 percent of expert opinion while the other "half" represented 98 percent. It was also difficult for citizens to distinguish a Ravi Batra from a Jagdish Bhagwati, even though experts knew that the latter was by far the more important and respected contributor to the theory of international economics.

An IA market might help to alleviate some of these problems. As with the HP sales-contingent market, job-contingent securities could be created whose prices would represent the probability that if a trade deal passed, job loss (gain) would be between −10,000 and 0, 1 and 10,000, 10,001 and 20,000, etc.[11] With many thousands of people participating and with significant incentives for participants to be informed, prices would represent the best of expert opinion much more accurately than the media.

Much work remains to be done in implementing these sorts of markets and in understanding under exactly what conditions markets are able to efficiently aggregate information (Plott 2000). Is it necessary, for example, to trade real money or will fantasy markets also predict well?[12] Hanson's chapter discusses in more detail some of the benefits of IA markets in answering public policy questions and some of the difficulties of creating such markets. If Hanson is right about the benefits, then perhaps one day, instead of quoting an expert, the *New York Times* editorial section will refer to the latest quote on "health care plan A" available in the business pages.

The Shortage of Human Organs

Thousands of people die every year while waiting for an organ transplant. At the same time, organs that could save their lives are being buried or burned. Few examples more poignantly illustrate the welfare losses that occur when government intervention forces a mismatch between demand and supply. To restore equilibrium, Barnett, Blair, and Kaserman (BBK) suggest eliminating current laws that forbid the sale of human organs. The same idea has been advocated by Nobel Prize winner Gary Becker (1997) and lawyers Richard Epstein (1993, 1997) and Lloyd Cohen (1989). The idea has become so common among economists that in their popular textbook, Pindyck and Rubinfeld (1998) use the organ shortage to illustrate the effects of price controls more generally. Barnett, Blair, and Kaserman's chapter 6 is particularly good at confronting objections to a futures market in human organs and also in describing the superiority of the market approach to what superficially looks like a similar proposal, compensating donor families.

Pricing is not the only way in which the market for organs can be made to clear. In chapter 7, Tabarrok discusses some possible problems with using price as a clearing mechanism and instead suggests that we consider restricting organ transplants to those who previously agreed to be organ donors—in short, a "no-give, no-take" rule. The no-give, no-take rule has the advantage of being supported by strong moral intuitions. Why should someone who was not willing to give an organ be allowed to take an organ?

The no-give, no-take rule can also be defended on grounds of economic efficiency. Current United Network for Organ Sharing policy treats organs like a common pool. Anyone is allowed to fish from the pool, regardless of whether or not they offer to restock it. As usual, free riders take but do not donate and the commons becomes depleted. From this perspective, the organ shortage is a classic tragedy of the commons problem (rather than a classic price control problem as suggested in BBK). The solution to a commons problem is enclosure—reserve entry to those willing to donate. Signing your organ donor card should thus be thought of as entry into a club, the club of potential organ recipients. Being willing to give up an organ, should it no longer be of use to you, is the premium to be paid for the right to receive someone else's organ if one of yours fails. Chapter 7 discusses the no-give, no-take rule in further detail and explains why the market clears under this rule.

Efficient Justice

Even simple economic ideas can have dramatic implications when consistently applied. In chapter 8, already discussed briefly above, Steven Landsburg takes the simple idea of incentives and applies it to judges who must decide whether or not to release a criminal defendant on bail. Landsburg proposes that judges be fined for every criminal defendant they release who commits a crime while out on bail. To balance incentives, bounties are paid when released defendants do not commit crimes. By adjusting the fines and bounties, society can choose how strict or lenient it wants the bail system to be while maintaining strong incentives to release only those defendants least likely to commit future crimes. In addition to creating better incentives, Landsburg's plan will tend to select for better judges because judges who are good at figuring out which defendants will commit future crimes,

and which will not, will make more money than their less perceptive colleagues. Although some judges will make more and others less, Landsburg's
plan need not cost the taxpayer anything because fines and bounties can be
uniformly raised or lowered so that, on average, judicial salaries do not
change.

Landsburg's proposal is perhaps more appropriately applied to the probation and parole systems rather than to the bail system because, as discussed by Morgan Reynolds in chapter 9, the bail system is already remarkably efficient. Most defendants do not have enough cash to post bail and
therefore turn to the bail bondsman (almost half of "bondsmen" are
women). If the defendant fails to show up in court, the bondsman sacrifices
his bond and his lending fee. Bondsmen, therefore, bear significant losses
if defendants fail to appear, and they have evolved a number of strategies,
such as monitoring defendants and requiring that members of the defendant's family put up assets as collateral, to minimize the chances that the
defendant will skip bail. When defendants do skip bail, highly effective
bounty hunters step in to bring them back to justice. As a result, fugitive
rates are very low. Thus, although judges may not have optimal incentives
to set bail amounts, bail bondsmen do have very good incentives to make
sure that the defendants show up in court. The situation, however, is quite
different in the probation and parole systems.

Few agents in the parole and probation systems have strong incentives
to make the system work well. Moreover, since the system is underfunded
and monitoring is only sporadic, parolees have few incentives to keep the
conditions of their parole. As a result, 38 percent of the people arrested for
felonies are already on probation, parole, or pretrial release for some other
crime! To improve these abysmal figures, Reynolds suggests that we require
parolees to post bail as a condition of parole. Violation of parole conditions
would result in a forfeiture of the parolee's bond.

The bond system improves incentives in two ways. First, it raises the
costs of crime to the parolee because in addition to running the risk of
further incarceration, the parolee is now threatened with the loss of his
bond. Second, the bond system gives bondsmen a strong incentive to help
their charges stay honest and thus pay off their bonds. In a privatized parole
and probation system, we might even see innovative plans in which bondsmen provided job training and counseling to parolees and probationers.
Bondsmen would have a much better incentive to find training plans that
work than the current correctional bureaucracies.[13]

Class-action suits often involve thousands of plaintiffs. Even when liability to the class can be determined in a single trial, a problem arises when
determining damages. Letting each plaintiff have his day in court is time
consuming and expensive. Judge Robert Parker, facing this problem in *Cimino et al. v. Raymark Industries, Inc., et al.* (751 F. Supp. 649), came up
with an innovative solution. Parker resolved over two thousand cases by
grouping them into categories, trying a subset of each category, and award-

ing every other claimant the average amount awarded in the tried subset. Parker's procedure works well when the plaintiffs can be broken down into a small number of reasonably homogeneous groups. But if the plaintiffs are heterogeneous in relevant ways—perhaps they have different injuries or are comparatively negligent in different degrees—then justice is not served when the award received is based upon a small subset of all cases or when every claimant in the nontried subset receives the same award.

David Friedman suggests a better version of Parker's procedure in chapter 10. In Friedman's procedure, the plaintiffs' lawyer makes a claim for damages on behalf of each plaintiff. The defense lawyer chooses which, let's say 5 percent, of cases will be litigated. Plaintiffs with cases that go to trial receive the trial award. Plaintiffs with nontried cases receive their claimed amount multiplied by the ratio of awarded damages to claimed damages in the tried subset. Intuition for Friedman's procedure comes from the well-known method of dividing a cake fairly—you slice and I choose which half I would like. Since I will choose the larger half, leaving you with less than half if you slice the cake unfairly, you have an incentive to slice the cake fairly. In this context, lawyers for the defense will choose to litigate those cases with the most overclaimed damages, thereby driving down damages in the nontried subset. Knowing this, the plaintiffs' lawyer will try to make fair claims, that is, the lawyer will try to set claims equal to what a jury would actually award in a trial. A number of fine points and alternative designs are explored at greater length in chapter 10.

Bankruptcy and Securities Regulation

Bankruptcy is no more than a transfer of ownership from one set of a firm's investors (the equityholders) to another (the bondholders). In principle, it should be easy to make this transfer. In practice, however, bankruptcy procedures are very costly. Firms often spend years in Chapter 11 and a significant percentage of the firm's already low value is depleted in lawyers' fees and other transaction costs.[14] Chapter 7, in which the firm is auctioned off to the highest bidder, appears much simpler than Chapter 11 but is also costly when capital markets are imperfect.

Building on work by Bebchuk (1988), Aghion, Hart, and Moore (AHM) offer a bankruptcy procedure that promises to considerably lower the costs of transferring ownership rights. The AHM proposal has four important elements. First, all debt claims are extinguished and 100 percent of the equity is transferred to the senior creditors. Second, under the supervision of a judge, cash and noncash bids are solicited for the firm both from insiders (management) and from any interested outside parties. Third, junior creditors are given options to buy out the equity of the senior creditors at a price equal to the debt owed to the senior creditors. Similarly, ex-shareholders are given options that allow them to repurchase the firm if they repay the debts they owe to the senior and junior creditors. Fourth, the new equityholders—who may be some combination of senior and junior debtholders and initial shareholders, depending on how different people evaluate the bids—vote on which offer to accept.

The AHM plan offers several advantages over competing bankruptcy procedures. First, the elimination of debt in favor of a single class of equity means that every person who participates in the final vote has exactly the same interest—maximizing total firm value. By contrast, in "Chapter 11" proceedings, the voters may include senior and junior debtholders with conflicting interests (and none of the voters may be interested in maximizing total firm value). Second, allowing for cash and noncash offers reduces problems with imperfect capital markets. Sometimes it's not possible to raise enough cash quickly enough to buy a firm at its fundamental value. Problems of asymmetric information also suggest that the current bondholders and shareholders may be in a better position to buy the firm (by accepting stock) than outsiders. Third, letting management submit bids allows for a more nuanced disciplining of management as compared to Chapter 7 (where the tendency is to always turf management) or Chapter 11 (where the tendency is to maintain the current managers). Under the AHM proposal, the owners of the firm can accept bids from management when they believe the firm's difficulties are not due to management error, and they can reject them otherwise, thus providing fairness and sound ex-ante incentives.

Is the AHM procedure the best procedure for all times and places? Of course not. Thus, AHM's most important argument may be that bankruptcy codes are best produced by laissez-faire.[15] Currently, the federal system is mandatory; AHM suggest that firms should be able to offer shareholders and lenders their own codes. Some firms might offer a code based on the ideas of AHM, other firms might choose the federal code, and others may choose something else entirely. Competition, AHM implicitly argue, will produce good bankruptcy codes just as it produces good blue jeans.

Roberta Romano's chapter (chapter 12) argues for something similar to laissez-faire in securities regulation. Currently, the federal government offers a one-size-must-fit-all system. Romano argues convincingly in favor of competitive federalism; each state should be able to offer its own securities regulations that should be respected by every other state. At first, the idea of competitive regulation or letting firms make their own bankruptcy codes seems incoherent. Won't firms offer codes that unfairly favor the interests of management over those of shareholders and lenders? Won't a race to the bottom cause states to offer the most meager of securities regulations? Ronald Coase (1960), however, shows that such thinking is wrong. When transaction costs are low and both sides to an exchange have good information, the market produces good law just as it produces good tennis shoes.

For an exchange to take place, both the buyer and the seller must expect to benefit, otherwise one or the other would not make the exchange. If both the buyer and the seller have good information, then neither can expect to benefit at the expense of the other. In particular, sellers can't benefit from exploiting buyers when buyers have good information. It follows that if sellers are to make themselves better off, they must produce products at prices that also improve the lot of buyers. The argument is unremarkable. Holding all else equal, McDonald's can't increase its profits by reducing the amount of beef in its hamburgers—if it does so, fewer people will buy McDonald's hamburgers and they won't be willing to pay as high a price as they did formerly.[16]

The application to bankruptcy codes and securities regulation is straightforward but to many people surprising. A firm that tried to offer its lenders a bankruptcy code biased in favor of management would have to compensate the lenders for the bias. Because lenders are compensated, the firm would bear any losses produced by a less efficient code. Firms that wish to increase profits, therefore, must do so by producing better codes. The same argument applies to securities regulation. Firms will choose a state with "tough" regulation as long as the benefits to the buyer of the regulation exceed the costs to the seller (just as firms will produce a higher quality tennis shoe as long as the benefits to the buyer exceed the costs to the seller). In an area like securities regulation where it's not obvious what the optimal regulations are, and the optimal regulations may differ for different firms or at different times, competition among regulators is the best method of finding good regulatory systems at reasonable prices. Romano elaborates in chapter 12.

Patents without Monopoly

In chapter 13, Michael Kremer presents an innovative plan to improve the U.S. patent system. For hundreds of years, the debate over patents has raged. Are patents grants of monopoly power? Or are they a necessary spur to invention? The answer, of course, is that they are both. Because it costs more to invent a new product or process than it does to copy it, invention would be a losing proposition if inventors didn't have some method of capturing the benefits of their ideas. Patents prevent copiers from using an inventor's ideas free of charge and, in this way, they increase the incentive to invent. Patents, however, work only imperfectly. Ex-ante inducements to invention become ex-post grants of market power. Firms with patent protection charge higher than competitive prices, and consumers who are willing to pay the competitive price but not willing to pay the monopoly price bear losses not matched by increases in the monopolist's profits. Figure 1.1 shows this "dead weight loss" as area DWL.

It's often thought that dead weight loss is "the" patent problem, but this is incorrect. Once patent protection ends, prices will fall to competitive levels, so this loss is only temporary. More serious is the fact that inventors never capture the full value of their ideas and so never have an incentive to invest as much in research and development as would be optimal. Re-

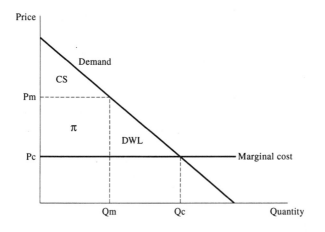

Fig. 1.1 Patents and two problems with monopoly.

turning to figure 1.1, the total value of the inventor's invention is area CS + π + DWL. Area DWL is lost in the short run and flows to consumers in the long run. Area CS, the consumer surplus, flows to consumers in both the short and long runs. Area π flows to inventors, but only in the short run. Patents, therefore, give inventors too little incentive to invent. Perhaps to overcome this problem, most modern governments subsidize research. Government-subsidized research, however, has a woeful record of producing valuable consumer products despite its evident success in producing weaponry.

If governments know the size of CS + π + DWL, then the solution to the patent problem is simple. Buy the patents at price CS + π + DWL and place them into the public domain. By doing so, the dead weight loss caused by monopoly pricing is eliminated and the incentive to invent is raised to its optimal level. Of course, governments have no idea what the true value of an invention is and standard estimation procedures are liable to abuse. To overcome this problem, Kremer proposes that patent holders be invited to tender their rights in an open auction. Competitive bidders will be willing to pay up to area π for the patent. The government will also bid on the patent, but its bid will be some multiple of the highest bid. The multiple would reflect the social benefits of the innovation, that is, (CS + π + DWL)/ π. Obviously, if the nongovernment bidders never win the auction, they have no incentive to bid accurately—the very motivation for the auction—so Kremer suggests that in randomly chosen auctions, the patent should go to the highest nongovernment bidder rather than to the government.

One virtue of Kremer's idea is that it can be tried in small doses. Indeed, it is not even necessary that the government be involved. Today, consumers and foundations contribute billions of dollars directly to medical research.

Perhaps some of these contributions would be better spent supporting research indirectly through a patent auction.

Urban Transit

Klein, Moore, and Reja (KMR) present an innovative plan to improve urban transit in chapter 14. Public transportation systems have an unenviable record of achievement. In many cities, they are poorly maintained, infrequently used, and expensive (to the taxpayer if not always to the rider). Private systems, however, have also faced their share of problems. The main difficulty of private systems is the conflict between scheduled, fixed route transport and jitney transport. Scheduled systems operating on fixed routes offer the consumer daily dependability. Jitneys—essentially shared-ride cabs traveling along quasi-fixed routes—provide flexibility, speed, and convenience. In an ideal setting, jitneys would complement fixed route transport, but in practice, jitneys impede fixed route transport by swooping in just before scheduled service to grab up waiting customers. When such claim jumping becomes common, jitneys can drive scheduled transportation out of the market. But without scheduled service, claim jumping no longer works and the market for jitneys also declines.

Some cities have "resolved" this transit dilemma by making jitneys illegal. Other cities, often in developing countries where police and court systems are already strained, have let jitneys run free. Neither response is optimal. In addition to losing their advantages, cities that make jitneys illegal often end up with monopolized transit systems unresponsive to consumers. Cities that let them run wild lose all the benefits of scheduled service.

Klein, Moore, and Reja get to the heart of the dilemma—creators of scheduled, fixed route systems must invest resources to get customers to the bus stop, but because of interloping jitneys, they don't have property rights to the fruits of their labor. The solution is to create a system of property rights, but not any system will do. In effect, making jitneys illegal gives the owners of the fixed route system a property right, but to all public transport—a larger right than their investments warrant. Letting jitneys run free effectively also gives the fixed-route owners a property right, but only to customers who enter their system—a smaller right than the owner's investments warrant. Too large a property right leads to monopoly; too small a property right leads to "cut-throat" competition.

KMR would resolve this dilemma by creating "curb rights," the right to use a certain section of the curb to pick up and drop off transit passengers. Curb rights could be auctioned off to the highest bidder and could be split up according to both time and location so that one firm might "own the curb" between 9:00 and 9:15 AM while another might own it between 9:30 and 9:45 AM. Curb rights give owners of scheduled services incentives to invest in getting customers to the curb, yet they avoid monopoly and allow jitneys to retain their place in the transit system. Whether KMR have structured their system of property rights correctly remains to be seen, but what is valuable to other reformers—in many areas other than transit policy—is their careful attention to the matching of investments and property rights.

Conclusions

We have become accustomed to the thought of new ideas in science, medicine, and business. But we are less accustomed to the thought of new markets, institutions, and economic practices. One sometimes hears, for example, that new institutions can't be any good, because if they were, they would have been invented already (what is, is efficient, so the slogan goes). This argument, however, is no different than the suggestion that the latest AIDS drug can't be any good, because if it were, someone would have invented it already! New ideas in institutional design are just as possible as new ideas in drug design.

It would be remarkable if our present-day institutions for producing and allocating transplantable human organs, for insuring against declines in health, or for encouraging innovation were the best of all such possible institutions. The authors of this volume are convinced that we do not live in the best of all possible worlds and thus can do better. The editor is convinced that some of the ideas and institutions discussed in this book are among the better institutions. Like William H. Lever—who said that half of his advertising budget was wasted, he just wasn't sure which half—I am unsure which of the chapters in this volume are genuine breakthroughs and which are beset by unseen difficulties. Time, I hope, will tell.

Notes

I'd like to thank my initial editor at Oxford University Press, Ken MacLeod, for his enthusiasm and quick understanding of the concept behind *Entrepreneurial Economics*. The skills of Mia McIver, Robin Miura, and other staff at Oxford have also been much appreciated. At *The Independent Institute*, Carl Close, Lowell Britson, and Priscilla Busch all provided great assistance. I thank Tyler Cowen and Bryan Caplan for their comments on the introduction.

1. The idea had also been proposed a few years earlier by Herzel (1951).

2. Coase's comments about the value of delaying a bad policy can be found in Coase ([1975] 1994); his reflections on selling the spectrum are in Coase (1998). The October 1998 issue of the *Journal of Law and Economics* is devoted to the issue of spectrum policy. The revenue and deadweight losses figures are from Hazlett (1998), in that issue.

3. It would be remiss of me not to mention the inspiration on this book of Milton Friedman, the most entrepreneurial of all twentieth-century economists. A partial list of the policy-relevant ideas to which Friedman has contributed to as theoretician or advocate would include education vouchers, monetary rules, uniform-price auctions for government securities, floating exchange rates, the

negative income tax, and the voluntary army. Amazingly, Friedman's advocacy efforts have not been restricted to writing but have included political entrepreneurship, especially with regard to the voluntary army and education vouchers. All of this, needless to say, comes on top of his contributions to economic theory for which he received the Nobel Prize in 1976.

4. To be precise, what would be bought and sold would be rights to income streams based upon indices of national income. Someone who bought a "USA" share would own the right to receive a dividend based upon U.S. national income statistics. Someone who shorted a "USA" share would have bought the obligation to pay a dividend based upon U.S. national income.

5. For further intuition on this point, see below, read chapter 3 on gene insurance, and of course see Cochrane's chapter in this volume.

6. This paragraph and the next are more technical and can be skipped without lost of continuity.

7. The model in chapter 4 simplifies by assuming an infinitely lived individual; such an individual would wish to purchase a perpetual future. In the appendix to his essay (not included here), Cochrane reworks the model assuming finite lives. A finitely lived individual would want to buy a future that expired when the individual died (an uncertain expiration day). This change does not affect anything of importance in the model.

8. Hundreds of essays examine the "efficient markets hypothesis" as applied to financial markets. Malkiel (2000) is a popular introduction; Elton and Gruber (1991) is a good textbook introduction. The evidence is less developed in other areas. Plott (2000) surveys the experimental results; Plott, Wit, and Yang (1997) look at the evidence from pari-mutuel betting markets; and Berg, Forsythe, and Rietz (1996) look at election markets.

A good example of markets versus "experts" as predictors comes from Paul Heyne's (1997) introductory textbook, *The Economic Way of Thinking*. Heyne points out that in December of 1991, the United Nations Food and Agriculture Organization and the WorldWatch Institute predicted a shortage of wheat in the coming year. On the day the forecasts were published, wheat was selling at $4.05 a bushel for immediate delivery, $3.87 on the March 1992 futures market, $3.33 on the July futures market, and $3.51 on the December 1992 futures market. Clearly, unlike the United Nations and the WorldWatch Institute, the market was not forecasting a shortage. Heyne asks his students, In which forecast should we place more confidence?

9. For more information and to trade in this market, see http://www.biz.uiowa.edu/iem/index.html. A market for European political events has also been created in Germany at http://www.wahlstreet.de/ (in German).

10. Ortner (1998) discusses a similar market designed for Siemens and Kumo Inc. to predict delays in the launch of a new product.

11. The definition of "job loss" and the procedure or judge for determining such loss would have to be specified as part of the definition of the contingent claim (see chapter 5). Commodity and asset markets must also specify exactly what commodity or asset will satisfy the contract (e.g., a "wheat" futures contract might specify No.2 Hard Kansas Wheat delivered in Chicago between March 15 and April 1). The payoff to so-called exotic securities may be a very complicated function of a number of events—all of this must be spelled out as part of the definition of the claim. Thus, defining a public policy contingent

claim is not in principle different from that of defining a commodity or financial-asset contract.

12. A number of Internet markets trade in fantasy dollars. The Foresight Exchange (http://www.ideosphere.com), based on Robin Hanson's work, lets traders buy and sell securities in all manner of contingent events. The Hollywood Exchange (http://www.hsx.com) lets traders buy and sell securities, including shares, options, mutual funds, and bonds, in the box office receipts of forthcoming movies and music. Trading may start years before a project is completed.

It's unclear whether IA markets that use fantasy money will generate the same accuracy as real-money IA markets. One reason to think not is that most traders in election markets exhibit some information biases such as wish fulfillment (the tendency to overestimate the probability of events the agent wishes to occur). Election markets are nonetheless remarkably accurate because the minority of nonbiased traders exert a disproportionate influence on prices (Forsythe et al., 1999). Nonbiased traders may be more concerned with money returns than biased players (nonbiased traders do in fact earn significantly higher returns than biased traders). If so, fantasy markets are unlikely to motivate the minority of nonbiased traders who in real markets help to generate efficient predictions.

The Hollywood Exchange claims that the results of its markets are used by producers and executives to help them make decisions. But neither the Hollywood Exchange nor the Foresight Exchange has published data on the accuracy of their market forecasts.

13. It's unlikely that the same number of defendants would be released under a bond system as under the current system, so Reynold's proposal raises issues of distribution in addition to those of efficiency. Even low bail amounts, however, could improve the efficiency of the current system, so distribution issues may not be large. Further research should be aimed at developing Landsburg incentive systems and bail-parole systems in enough detail so that small-scale trials could be developed.

14. Chapter 11 is the United States' structured bargaining approach to bankruptcy. Chapter 7 is their cash auction approach. For definitions of these terms and a brief discussion of bankruptcy procedures in other countries, see chapter 11 in this volume.

15. This argument is made briefly in note 6 of their chapter.

16. If the price of beef increases, McDonald's might increase its profits by decreasing the amount of beef in its patties, but only because at the higher price of beef, consumers prefer smaller patties at lower prices to larger patties at higher prices. Notice that this statement is an application of the insight in the text and not a counterargument.

References

Bebchuk, Lucian A. 1988. A New Approach to Corporate Reorganization. *Harvard Law Review* 101:775–804.

Becker, G. 1997. How Uncle Sam Could Ease the Organ Shortage. *Business Week* 3510 (20 Jan.):18.

Berg, J., R. Forsythe, and T. A. Rietz. 1996. What Makes Markets Predict Well? Evidence from the Iowa Electronic Markets. In *Understanding Strategic Inter-*

action: Essays in Honor of Richard Selten, ed. W. Albers et al., 444–63. New York: Springer.

Black, F., and M. Scholes. 1973. The Pricing of Options and Corporate Liabilities. *Journal of Political Economy* 81(3):637–654.

Buchanan, J. 1959. Positive Economics, Welfare Economics, and Political Economy. *Journal of Law and Economics* 2:124–38. Reprinted in R. D. Tollison and V. J. Vanberg (eds), 1987.

Coase, R. H. 1960. The Problem of Social Cost. *Journal of Law and Economics* 3:1–44.

———. [1975] 1994. Economists and Public Policy. In *Essays On Economics and Economists*, 47–63. Chicago: University of Chicago Press.

———. 1998. Comment on Thomas W. Hazlett: Assigning Property Rights to Radio Spectrum Users. *Journal of Law and Economics* XLI (2) (pt.2):577–80.

Cohen, L. R. 1989. Increasing the Supply of Transplant Organs: The Virtues of a Free Market. *George Washington Law Review* 58 (1):1–51.

Elton, E. J., and M. J. Gruber. 1991. *Modern Portfolio Theory and Investment Analysis*. 4th ed. New York: John Wiley and Sons. Chapter 15: pp. 405–17.

Epstein, R. A. 1993. Organ Transplants: Is Relying on Altruism Costing Lives? *The American Enterprise* 4(6):50–57.

———. 1997. *Mortal Peril*. New York: Addison-Wesley Publishing Co.

Forsythe, R., T. A. Rietz, and T. W. Ross. 1999. Wishes, Expectations and Actions: A Survey on Price Formation in Election Stock Markets. *Journal of Economic Behavior and Organization* 39:83–110.

Hayek, F. A. 1945. The Use of Knowledge in Society. *American Economic Review* XXXV (4):519–30.

Hazlett, T. W. 1998. Assigning Property Rights to Spectrum Users: Why Did the FCC License Auctions Take 67 Years? *Journal of Law and Economics* XLI (2) (pt.2):529–76.

Herzel, L. 1951. 'Public Interest' and the Market in Color Television Regulation. *University of Chicago Law Review* 18:802–16.

Heyne, P. 1997. *The Economic Way of Thinking*. 8th ed. Upper Saddle River, N.J.: Prentice-Hall.

Malkiel, B. 2000. *A Random Walk Down Wall Street*. 7th ed. New York: W.W. Norton & Co.

Ortner, G. 1998. Forecasting Markets—An Industrial Application. Working paper, TU Vienna Dep. of Managerial Economics and Industrial Organization. Available at http://ebweb.tuwien.ac.at/apsm/fmaia2.pdf, accessed Sept. 15, 2000.

Pindyck, R. S., and D. L. Rubinfeld. 1998. *Microeconomics*. 4th ed. Upper Saddle River, N.J.: Prentice-Hall.

Plott, C. R. 2000. Markets as Information Gathering Tools. *Southern Economic Journal* 67 (1):1–15.

Plott, C. R., J. Wit, and W. C. Yang. 1997. Pari-mutuel Betting Markets as Information Aggregation Devices: Experimental Results. Social Science Working Paper No. 986, California Institute of Technology.

PART I

WEALTH AND HEALTH INSURANCE

2

Macro Markets and Financial Security

STEFANO ATHANASOULIS, ROBERT SHILLER,
AND ERIC VAN WINCOOP

Today, people have a rich set of investment options, ranging from low-risk money market instruments to high-risk growth stocks. They can choose to invest in mutual funds, hedge funds, and pension plans. They can hedge themselves with options and other derivatives while investing both at home and across the globe. Plenty of opportunities are available for diversifying their portfolios and avoiding excess exposure to sectoral or geographic risk. Nonetheless, there is good reason to believe that most people's wealth is not well diversified. For example, although investors can diversify through equity markets, corporate profits account for less than 10 percent of national income. That figure suggests that about 90 percent of an average person's income is sensitive to sectoral, occupational, and geographic uncertainty.

Shiller (1993) has proposed a new set of markets that could in theory provide much better diversification opportunities. These so-called macro markets would be large international markets trading, in the form of futures contracts, long-term claims on major components of incomes shared by a large number of people or organizations. For example, in a macro market for the United States, an investor could buy a claim on the U.S. national income and then receive, for as long as the claim is held, dividends equal to a specified fraction of U.S. national income. Such a claim is comparable to a share in a corporation, except that the dividend would equal a share of national income rather than a share of corporate profits. Such markets might exist for entire countries (e.g., the United States, Japan, and Brazil) or for regions (such as the European Union and North America). Even a market for claims on the combined incomes of the entire world could be formed. Prices would rise and fall in these markets as new information about national, regional, or global economies became available, just as

23

prices rise and fall in the stock market as new information about corporate profits is revealed.

The potential future importance of these markets is supported by the most basic principle of finance—diversification. People could use macro markets to hedge their own national income risks and to invest in the rest of the world. This investment strategy would reduce income growth uncertainty and lead to a more secure financial future.

We address several questions in this chapter. First, how could macro markets be useful to the average person? Second, how large are the potential benefits from diversification if these markets were to be introduced and used optimally? Third, can existing financial markets achieve a similar degree of diversification when used optimally? Fourth, why don't these markets already exist?

How Would Investors Use Macro Markets?

The basic idea behind macro markets is a simple one. Consider the case of claims on national income. If macro markets existed for every country of the world, people could take short positions in their country's market, thereby hedging their own country's risk, and long positions in the markets of all other countries in proportion to each country's size, thereby completely hedging themselves. The short positions in their home country would exactly offset the long positions that they hold by virtue of living there, and the long positions in the world would mean that they were completely diversified. If everyone hedged risk in this way, it would all add up, that is, for every long in every country there would be a short, and demand would equal supply in each macro market. The dividends paid on the securities for each country would be paid by the people who live in that country and hold short positions. By definition, these people can always make the payments because they are earning the national income upon which the dividends are drawn.

Taking such positions in these markets is the best way for an individual to achieve diversification. After hedging, everyone earns a share of global income. It would be impossible for individuals to lower their risks any further. It is impossible for everyone to diversify away uncertainty about global income, because total income earned across all individuals equals global income itself.

Retail Institutions

Of course, most people are not accustomed to hedging. Thus, it would probably be unrealistic to expect the average person to hedge through macro markets without the assistance of intermediaries. Most people are familiar with insurance, and they readily buy insurance against other risks. Retail institutions, such as pension funds or insurance companies, could offer people contracts to hedge their aggregate income risk. These insurance companies and pension funds would trade in macro markets to sell off the risk incurred by writing the contracts in retail markets. These institutional investors would be hedging, much as institutions now hedge in stock index futures markets.

An Average Investor

We will now give an example of how these markets and retail institutions could serve the individual investor. Consider a person who earns income from wages and from returns on financial assets (such as stocks and bonds). The individual cares about the uncertainty of the future value of his *total wealth*, which is the sum of the future value of financial assets and the future value of "human capital." The value of human capital is equal to the present value of the stream of future wages earned by the individual. The value of the person's wealth can thus be written as $Wealth = PDV(\pi) + PDV(W)$, where PDV is present discounted value, π represents the annual dividends and interest earned from financial assets, and W is wages plus noncorporate business income. Even if the individual were well diversified in the equity and bond markets, he would still be exposed to uncertainty associated with wages earned. Because wages plus noncorporate profits are at least nine times as great as corporate profits (in national income accounts), the largest component of wealth remains undiversified.

Let us further assume that the wealth of the individual is "average"—the value of the individual's financial assets is average and his wages are equal to the average wage rate in the country plus an idiosyncratic component. The idiosyncratic component of wages depends on individual-specific effort as well as a dose of good or bad luck. Insuring against the idiosyncratic component is impossible because of moral hazard problems. If an individual were insured against all uncertainty about future wages, he would have little incentive to work hard and to put effort into a successful career. Given these assumptions, the value of wages is written as $W = W_c + W_I$, where W_c is the average wage rate in the country and W_I is the idiosyncratic component. The sum of the idiosyncratic component over all individuals is zero. Moral hazard problems do not apply to insuring oneself against uncertainty about W_c because the individual has little control over the average wage rate earned in the country as a whole.

We also assume that the individual invests only in domestic stocks and bonds and that he is well diversified domestically. The absence of international diversification is not far from current practice: Japanese and U.S. investors hold at least 90 percent of their equity portfolio in domestic assets.[1] Because the individual's financial assets are average, the dividends earned on these assets, π, are equal to the per capita value of total corporate profits in the country. We can then write the individual's wealth as

Wealth = *PDV*(*GDP*) + *PDV*(*W$_I$*), where *GDP* is per capita gross domestic product, which equals $\pi + W_c$. Wealth is therefore equal to the present discounted value of future per capita GDP plus the present discounted value of the idiosyncratic component of wages. Macro markets can be used to insure the uncertainty associated with per capita GDP.

As a matter of simplification, assume that the expected future per capita GDP of the country in which the individual resides is equal to that for the world as a whole (*GDP$_W$*) and that the "riskiness" of the country's future GDP is average. We will be more precise about what that means in a moment. Insurance companies and pension funds can allow people to hedge uncertainty about the country's per capita GDP by offering a hedging instrument with a yearly payoff of *GDP$_W$* – *GDP*. As we explain below, the price of this hedging instrument is zero. Although the expected payoff is zero, the actual payoff can be both positive or negative. If it is negative, the individual must make a payment. If the hedging instrument is offered by a pension fund, the payment could be made through a debit on the individual's account at the pension fund. This contract is attractive to a risk-averse individual because he will lose on the hedging contract only when the domestic economy is doing unexpectedly well. The individual will receive positive payments from the contract when the economy's performance is unexpectedly poor. If the individual opts to use this instrument, his net wealth will be *Wealth* = *PDV*(*GDP$_W$*) + *PDV*(*W$_I$*). The individual clearly gains by hedging in macro markets to the extent that less uncertainty surrounds the growth rate of world output than the growth rate of the home country's output.

Notice that in our example the individual invests only in domestic financial assets, then hedges uncertainty about both domestic financial returns and domestic wages through the hedging instrument. This investment strategy is attractive because it avoids the need to make decisions about investment in foreign financial assets. The problem of asymmetric information means that domestic investors are at a disadvantage relative to foreign investors when evaluating foreign stocks and bonds. Foreign investors tend to be better informed about companies trading in their own stock markets, particularly in the case of smaller companies. They can therefore adjust their portfolio more rapidly than domestic investors as new information becomes available to them. Gehrig (1993) shows that investors are reluctant to invest abroad if foreign investors receive a more precise price signal about foreign stock returns than domestic investors. Asymmetric information is one of the most common explanations for the lack of observed international diversification in equity and bond markets. In macro markets, which are tied to aggregate incomes, asymmetric information is much less of a concern. Japanese investors are not likely to predict Japanese GDP growth rates more accurately than U.S. investors because the information needed to make such predictions is publicly available.

The diversification strategy outlined above is different from the type of diversification most investors are accustomed to. Most individual stock market investors diversify by investing their money in a wide basket of assets. With macro markets, diversification is achieved instead through a hedging contract.

Pricing in Macro Markets

So far we have left two issues unaddressed. First, the institutional investors that offer the hedging contract we just described will themselves be exposed to risk when offering the instrument. Second, we have yet to explain why the price of the contract will be zero. To understand how institutional investors will lay off the risk and what factors determine prices, we describe in more detail the macro markets on which the hedging instruments are based. These markets trade perpetual claims on a GDP index. Trade can take place either over the counter or on an exchange like the Chicago Board of Trade.

Existing theoretical research has laid out exactly what will determine prices in markets like these.[2] As with any asset, the price of a claim on a country's per capita GDP depends on two factors—expected payoff and risk. The expected payoff is the expected present discounted value of future per capita GDP. Risk is measured by the covariance between the present discounted value of a country's per capita GDP and the present discounted value of the world's GDP.

First consider a simple example in a symmetric world. Two countries have an equal number of residents. Assume that expected future per capita GDP is the same in both markets. If we also assume that the variance of the present discounted value of GDP is the same for both countries, then the covariance with the world claim will be identical for the two countries. Claims on the per capita GDP of both countries therefore will have the same price.

Let us say for the sake of simplicity that the only traders in these markets are pension funds, and let N be the size of the population in both markets. Domestic pension funds will sell $\frac{1}{2}N$ perpetual claims on domestic per capita GDP and buy $\frac{1}{2}N$ perpetual claims on foreign per capita GDP. Because these claims have the same price, the net cost will be zero. Foreign pension funds take the other side of the market. The per capita GDP of the world, GDP_W, equals $\frac{1}{2}GDP + \frac{1}{2}GDP^*$, where GDP^* is foreign per capita GDP. Through their operations in the macro markets, domestic pension funds have effectively purchased N perpetual claims on $GDP_W - GDP$. Because the pension funds also sell N perpetual claims on $GDP_W - GDP$ to domestic individuals through the hedging instrument, domestic pension funds break even. The same is true for the foreign pension funds. The two countries have effectively agreed to swap a claim on half of each other's

GDP. Under this arrangement, there is no cost or "insurance premium" to reducing risks. After risk sharing, the residents of both countries will hold claims on half the domestic country's per capita GDP plus half the foreign country's per capita GDP, which together add up to world per capita GDP. Residents' expected average income is the same as it was before, but the variability of income is lower.

So far everything in the example is very symmetric. Now suppose that the domestic country is much larger than the foreign country: Its population N is a hundred times that of the foreign country. Accordingly, the covariance between domestic GDP and world GDP will be higher than the covariance between foreign GDP and world GDP, even if the variance of per capita GDP in both countries is the same. The price of a perpetual claim on the foreign country's per capita GDP will therefore be higher than the price of a claim on the domestic country's per capita GDP.

If the prices of claims on the per capita GDP of both countries were still equal—as they were when both countries had the same population—then people in the larger country would want to swap half their income for half the per capita income of the people in the smaller country. But there are not enough people in the smaller country to take the other side of these transactions. Therefore, the price of a perpetual claim on the foreign country's per capita GDP will be higher than the price of a claim on the domestic country's per capita GDP. Consequently, the people in the larger country will be discouraged from demanding so many claims on the foreign country, and market clearing can take place.

In more technical terms, a claim on domestic per capita GDP can be exchanged for α claims on world per capita GDP, with $\alpha < 1$. Through trade in macro markets, domestic pension funds will buy N claims on $\alpha(GDP_W) - GDP$ (with a net price of zero) and sell those claims as hedging instruments to domestic individuals. After the hedge, domestic residents have a perpetual claim on times per capita world GDP. Foreign pension funds will take the other side of the market by selling N claims on $\alpha(GDP_W) - GDP$, which is equivalent to buying $N/100$ (the foreign population) claims on $\beta GDP_W - (GDP)^*$. Here, $\beta = 101 - 100\alpha > 1$. Foreign pension funds will sell these claims as hedging instruments to foreign individuals, who will then own a perpetual claim on β times per capita world GDP. The higher price of a claim on the foreign country's output leads to larger claims on world per capita GDP by foreign residents after risk sharing.

In the example above, we have assumed for simplicity that all individuals within a country have the same exposure to their country's national income risk. In reality, some individuals' income is more sensitive to national growth rates than other people's income. The optimal hedge position that an investor takes through pension funds or insurance companies depends on his exposure to national risk. Because people's exposure to national income risk differs, macro markets would still be beneficial even if trade in claims on a country's national income were limited to the residents

of that particular country. Although this limitation would eliminate international risk sharing, it would allow individuals to share their exposures to national income risk. Ultimately, through the appropriate retail institutions, those individuals with high exposure to national income risk could sell perpetual claims indexed to national income to those individuals with low exposure to national income risk.

The Potential Risk-Sharing Benefits

Individuals are exposed to many types of aggregate risk. The most common risks are specific to a sector (occupational risk), to an age cohort (demographic risk), or to a geographic area in which someone works (geographic risk). For example, an auto worker is subject to auto industry risk. A decline in demand for automobiles will affect the entire industry. Geographic risk can be linked to a specific neighborhood or to a whole continent. To measure the potential diversification benefits of macro markets, we restrict our analysis to national income risk, abstracting from other types of aggregate risk. Because we limit ourselves to national risk, the measure of hedgeable aggregate income risk derived in this section is lower than the level achievable through aggregate income markets generally.

Because individuals cannot diversify away global income growth uncertainty, we focus on country-specific growth, that is, the difference between a country's growth rate and the world growth rate. As explained in the previous section, macro markets allow individuals to eliminate the country-specific component of their income growth uncertainty. We now quantify the size of this uncertainty.[3]

A Regression Model of Country-Specific
Growth Uncertainty

To identify country-specific growth uncertainty, we estimate the following regression for each horizon s: $g_{i, t, t+s} - g^W_{t, t+s} = \lambda'_s(z_{it} - z^W_t) + u_{i, t, t+s}$. The left-hand side of the equation represents country i's growth in real per capita GDP from year t to $t+s$ minus global growth in real per capita GDP over the same period. The first term on the right-hand side of the equation is the predictable component of the deviation of country growth from world growth. This component depends on the relevant information set available to the market, which is captured by the vector z_{it}, in deviation from its global counterpart. The term u is the unpredictable component of the country-specific deviation from world growth. We also refer to country-specific growth uncertainty as residual risk.

We apply this regression for various horizons using panel data for the postwar period (1955–90) from the Penn World Tables and the Barro and Lee (1994) data set.[4] In our application, we consider two different sets of

countries that engage in risk sharing (and therefore make up our artificial "world"): a set of twenty-one Organization for Economic Cooperation and Development (OECD) countries and a more comprehensive set of forty-nine countries (see chapter appendix). The OECD countries are of interest because they would likely be the first countries to experiment with macro markets. Their income risk, however, is likely to fall below that of developing countries. The larger set of forty-nine countries provides us with an estimate of the potential risk-sharing benefits in the event that a broader array of countries introduced macro markets. Because we have only one growth observation per country for long horizons, we are unable to estimate country-specific growth uncertainty for each country separately. Thus, the results from the regressions, which combine data from all the countries in the sample, reflect "average" growth uncertainty across countries.

In choosing the variables that make up the information set, we draw on a large empirical and theoretical literature on economic growth.[5] Our base information set consists of thirteen variables: the log of per capita GDP; the most recent one- and five-year growth rates of per capita GDP; the most recent five-year population growth rate; the ratio of private consumption to GDP; the ratio of government consumption to GDP; the ratio of investment to GDP; openness as measured by exports plus imports as a fraction of GDP; gross enrollment ratios for primary, secondary, and higher education; the fertility rate; and life expectancy at birth.[6] We also consider a smaller information set consisting of the three variables with the most predictive power, that is, they led to the lowest estimated standard deviation of residual risk at a thirty-five-year horizon. For the set of forty-nine countries, these variables are the log of per capita GDP, the fertility rate, and the investment rate. For the OECD country set, the investment rate is replaced by enrollment in higher education.

Diversifiable Country-Specific Risk

Figures 2.1 and 2.2 show the standard deviation of residual risk as a function of the time horizon. For the base information set, the standard deviation of the growth rate at a thirty-five-year horizon is 16.4 percent for the set of OECD countries and 33 percent for the set of forty-nine countries. These numbers are very large, implying a 95 percent confidence interval of 66 percent for OECD countries and 132 percent for the forty-nine countries. The figures also show that the results for the smaller information set are almost the same as the results for the full information set. This similarity implies that adding more variables does not significantly help in predicting long-term growth rates.

To get a better sense of the amount of uncertainty involved here, we perform a simple experiment. We take 10,000 draws from the distribution of residual risk for each country,[7] assuming that the draws are independent across countries and that each country's standard deviation of residual risk

Standard Deviation

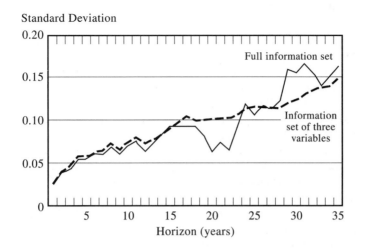

Fig. 2.1 Growth uncertainty in the OECD countries. The figure shows the standard deviation of the unpredictable component of the difference between the per capita GDP growth of a representative OECD country and that of the world. The full information set used to predict growth consists of thirteen variables (see text). The information set of three variables consists of the log of per capita GDP, the fertility rate, and enrollment in higher education. Source: Authors' calculations.

Standard Deviation

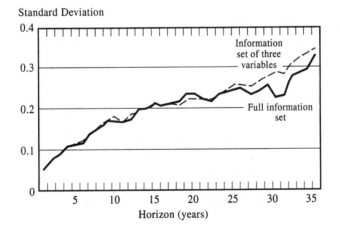

Fig. 2.2 Growth uncertainty in the set of forty-nine countries. The figure shows the standard deviation of the unpredictable component of the difference between the per capita GDP growth of a representative country and that of the world. The full information set used to predict growth consists of thirteen variables (see text). The information set of three variables consists of the log of per capita GDP, the fertility rate, and the investment rate. Source: Authors' calculations.

is the same. For the set of forty-nine countries, we use the results to compute the probability that per capita GDP of the best performing country will
unexpectedly double, triple, quadruple, or quintuple relative to that of the
worst performing country over the specified time horizon. The results are
shown in figure 2.3. The probability that the best performing country's per
capita GDP doubles or triples relative to that of the worst performing country is practically 100 percent at the thirty-five-year horizon. The probability
that the best performing country's per capita GDP quadruples or quintuples
relative to that of the worst performing country is 81 percent and 44 percent, respectively. These results are striking. They suggest that, after controlling for the growth that had already been expected, per capita GDP of
the best performing country is likely to rise by a factor of five relative to
that of the worst performing country! Even at the short ten-year horizon, the
probability that the per capita GDP of the best performing country would
unexpectedly double relative to the per capita GDP of the worst performing
country is 84 percent.

For the set of OECD countries, we report the probability that the per
capita GDP for the best performing country rises by 30 percent, 50 percent,
70 percent, or 100 percent relative to that of the worst performing country
(fig. 2.4). At a thirty-five-year horizon, the probabilities are 99.99 percent,
99.9 percent, 61 percent, and 13 percent, respectively. Although less spectacular, these numbers are still significant. Indeed, the best performing
country's per capita GDP is likely to rise by 70 percent relative to the worst
performing country's over a period of thirty-five years.

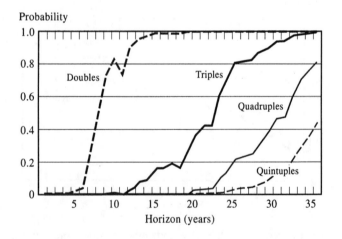

Fig. 2.3 Per capita GDP: best performing country versus worst performing country—
forty-nine countries. The figure shows the probability that the per capita GDP of the
best performing country will unexpectedly double, triple, quadruple, or quintuple
relative to that of the worst performing country. These probabilities depend on the
growth horizon. Source: Authors' calculations.

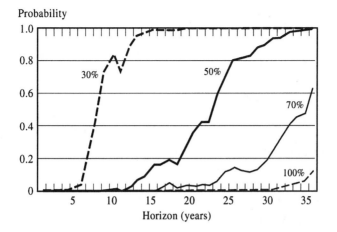

Fig. 2.4 Per capita GDP: best performing country versus worst performing country—
OECD countries. The figure shows the probability that the per capita GDP of the best
performing country will unexpectedly rise by 30 percent, 50 percent, 70 percent, or
100 percent relative to that of the worst performing country. These probabilities
depend on the growth horizon. Source: Authors' calculations.

Because these figures only consider the very extremes, that is, the worst
compared with the best performing countries, we also compute the probability that the unweighted average per capita GDP of the seven best performing countries doubles, triples, quadruples, or quintuples relative to the
unweighted average of per capita GDP of the seven worst performing countries. For the set of forty-nine countries, at the thirty-five-year horizon, the
probabilities are 99.9 percent, 89.4 percent, 29 percent, and 3 percent, respectively. These results suggest that, contrary to expectation, the per capita GDP of the seven best performing countries as a group is likely to triple
relative to that of the seven worst performing countries over thirty-five
years. For the set of OECD countries, we find a probability of 88 percent
that the unweighted average of per capita GDP of the three top-performing
countries in the sample rises by 50 percent relative to that of the three worst
performers. Note that in both of these cases we look at the best performing
one-seventh and worst performing one-seventh of the countries in our
sample.

To illustrate further that these numbers are not unrealistic, figure 2.5
shows the expected deviation from world growth in 1955 for the thirty-five-
year period 1955–90 (according to the information set of three variables)
compared with the actual deviation from world growth over the same period. For the set of forty-nine countries, the best performing countries relative to the expectation in 1955 were Thailand and Japan. Several African
and South American countries were the worst performers. Note that Thailand was expected to grow slightly less than Uruguay in 1955. In fact, how-

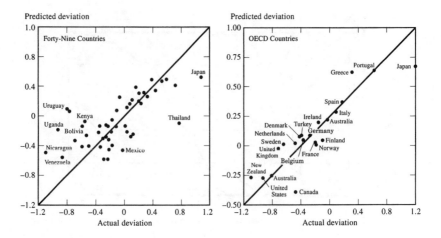

Fig. 2.5 Predicted and actual deviation from world growth, 1955–90. These figures show the actual and predicted deviation of individual countries' per capita GDP growth from world per capita GDP growth. Here, "world" is defined as the sum of the countries in the sample. Countries below the 45-degree line performed better than expected. Countries above the 45-degree line performed worse than expected. Source: Authors' calculations.

ever, Thailand's per capita GDP rose by a factor of 5.1 relative to that of Uruguay! Per capita GDP of the worst performing country in the sample, Nicaragua, dropped 22 percent over the period 1955–90. Some countries that are not in our sample performed even worse. Extreme cases include Nigeria, whose real per capita GDP declined 59 percent from 1976 to 1990, and Guyana, whose real per capita GDP dropped 59 percent from 1976 to 1990. For the world's poorest countries, hedging national income risks may truly be a matter of life and death for some citizens. In these countries, declines in national income have seriously harmed the quality of health care, nutrition, environmental protection, and law enforcement.

These results might leave the impression that only nations in Africa, South America, and East Asia are subject to large income shocks. Although these countries have experienced the most dramatic changes in per capita GDP during the past several decades, what matters today is uncertainty about *future* income. It is quite possible that over the next fifty years the biggest income surprises will come from other parts of the world. Large gains from risk sharing are therefore not necessarily limited to the set of countries that has faced the largest income shocks in recent years.

We see from figure 2.5 that in our sample of OECD countries the best performing countries were Japan and Canada. In 1955, based on various indicators such as low investment, low school enrollment, high per capita income, and low recent growth rates, Canada was not expected to grow as fast as the average OECD country. Nonetheless, its growth rate turned out to be almost average. The worst performing countries were Greece, the United Kingdom, and New Zealand. Japan's per capita GDP grew 80 percent more than that of Greece, even though the two countries' expected growth rates were very similar in 1955. These results are suggestive of the significant uncertainty of relative performance among OECD countries. Of course, we caution against taking the results for individual countries too literally. The figures are somewhat sensitive to the precise information set and the countries considered. Nonetheless, this exercise provides a good sense of the degree of diversifiable uncertainty of future income.

Although our sample ends in 1990, a very recent and large growth surprise surfaced in Ireland. Ireland's economy stagnated during the first half of the 1980s. In 1987, its per capita GDP was 63 percent of Britain's. But only nine years later, in 1996, Ireland's per capita GDP surpassed Britain's. The economy expanded 10 percent in 1995 and 7 percent in 1996. Relative to expectations in the mid-1980s, this remarkable growth episode was clearly unexpected. Foreign direct investment contributed to growth, but even now it is hard to fully explain Ireland's spectacular growth performance.[8]

Individual-Specific Risk

In addition to aggregate income uncertainty, individuals must contend with income variations that are specific to their situation. Individual-specific risk cannot be shared through macro markets. Indeed, no institution can completely eliminate this type of risk because of moral hazard problems. How important are these individual risks? How much income variation is left after people have completely hedged their aggregate risks?

Fortunately, individual-specific income risk appears to amount to less than half of total income risk. Shiller and Schneider (1998), using 1968–87 U.S. data from the Panel Study of Income Dynamics, estimate the variance of income changes that are not under the control of individuals. They categorize individuals into seven occupational groupings according to objective factors such as retirement, employment, and educational status. They then compute an index of labor income for the United States for each grouping. The results show that between one-half and three-quarters of the variance of five-year income changes can be explained by the aggregate indexes. Most of people's income risk could therefore be managed through macro markets, assuming that they were opened not just on national incomes but, within that, on occupational incomes.

Can Existing Financial Markets Do the Job?

In theory, existing financial markets could achieve most of the potential benefits from diversification if the aggregate return on domestic financial

assets were highly correlated with the return of a claim on the present discounted value of aggregate income. This is the case when the return on
human capital is highly correlated with the return on domestic financial
assets. Consider an average individual whose current wealth consists of
$900,000 in nontraded assets. Nontraded assets include both human capital
and noncorporate business assets, but, for simplicity, we will simply refer
to both as human capital. An additional $100,000 of the individual's wealth
is in financial assets, including pension funds. Now assume that the return
on domestic financial capital is perfectly correlated with the return on domestic human capital. The individual can then achieve full diversification
as follows. First, if the financial return has the same standard deviation as
the human capital return, selling short domestic financial assets by
$900,000 eliminates all domestic risk. After that, $1 million is invested
globally ($100,000 of financial wealth plus the $900,000 of revenue from
selling short domestic assets).

The correlation between the return on human capital and the return on
financial capital, however, is much smaller than one. Bottazzi, Pesenti, and
van Wincoop (1996) compute this correlation using data for the years
1970–92 for OECD countries. The return on human capital is defined as the
innovation in the present discounted value of wages divided by the current
value of human capital.[9] The innovation is computed using the results from
a vector autoregressive process for the wage rate and the profit rate or for
the wage rate and a broad measure of return on domestic financial capital.
A trend is extracted from both the wage rate and the profit rate. Three measures of the return on domestic financial capital are used: the profit rate
(profits divided by the capital stock); the present discounted value of the
profit rate, again using the results from the vector autoregressive process;
and the weighted average of returns on stocks, long-term bonds, and short-
term deposits (a broad measure of financial returns). Across countries, the
average of the estimated correlation between the return on human capital
and the return on financial capital for the three measures is 0.26, –0.34, and
–0.43, respectively—the correlations are all much smaller than one.

It is important to note that these correlations are based on wages and
profits after extracting a trend. A common stochastic growth trend is likely
to exist across countries.[10] Because such a common trend represents global
risk, it cannot be shared among countries. Therefore, controlling for such a
trend is appropriate for our purposes. It is useful to note, however, that the
negative correlation for two of the measures is not inconsistent with a positive correlation between the "raw" returns on human capital and domestic
assets. An improvement in global technology raises both profits and wages.

There are many possible explanations for the absence of a strong positive
correlation. First, shocks to the bargaining power of labor or a change in
government can significantly affect the income distribution. Second, if
wages are less flexible than prices, positive demand shocks will affect real
wages and profits asymmetrically. Third, standard trade theory predicts

that the wage rate and return to capital move in opposite directions in response to terms of trade shocks (Stolper-Samuelson).

An important question that we do not address is how much of the country-specific income growth uncertainty documented in the preceding section can be shared through existing financial markets. No research has yet been done to address that question. Nonetheless, the low correlations between the return on human capital and financial assets reported above suggest that macro markets have an important role to play in the diversification of aggregate income growth uncertainty, a role that existing financial markets cannot completely fill.

Macro markets would also allow individuals to invest in firms and companies that are not traded publicly. Stock indexes only include companies after they have become successful. But productivity growth is influenced by private firms and start-ups at least as much as by public companies. Thus, investment in stock indexes cannot capture the growth of these smaller companies. For an individual who wants to invest in a country because the fundamentals of the country are strong, buying a share of GDP would be more appropriate than buying a stock index.

Why Don't Macro Markets Exist?

If the potential benefits of aggregate income markets are so large, and the underlying risk management concepts are apparently so simple, why have they not already developed in the private sector? Surely, significant commissions could be earned if a large demand for these securities developed. Surely, there ought to be some niche for these securities somewhere in the world. And yet there is no evidence that markets like these have ever existed. In principle, macro markets would not be difficult to introduce. In 1997, the U.S. Treasury introduced inflation-indexed bonds. The only essential difference is that in macro markets the coupons would be indexed to a measure of aggregate income rather than to the consumer price index (CPI). It is important, therefore, to try to understand what barriers stand in the way of the creation of macro markets.

Not So Obvious

The first thing to note is that while the concept of risk management is very basic, the idea of markets that share income risks is not so obvious as to occur immediately to most people. The idea of markets in aggregate incomes is like other important inventions in the history of technology that have seemed extremely simple after they were implemented—simple, that is, from the vantage point of people viewing the final invention and not the idea that preceded it. For example, rejecting a proposal for investment in radio technology in the 1920s, David Sarnoff's Associates wrote, "The wireless music box has no imaginable commercial value. Who would pay for a message sent to nobody in particular?" Between 1939 and 1944, more than twenty companies rejected the idea of Chester Carlson, inventor of the Xerox machine, to copy a document on plain paper. Although the idea was considered useless at the time, today Rank Xerox Limited earns annual revenues of about $1 billion, and it is hard to imagine life without the machine. Establishing markets for long-term claims on flows of income aggregates is no more obvious than other recent financial innovations. Even the concept of national income itself is a relatively new invention that has been perfected over many years. Developed earlier in this century by Kuznets (1937), Stone (1947), and others, the concept of national income as we know it did not become widely accepted until after World War II.

Similarly, many risk-management institutions that are now commonplace have gotten off to slow starts. For example, markets in foreign currency swaps—which now account for about half the gross turnover in the foreign exchange market—did not develop until the early 1980s. A futures market in stock price indexes also did not develop until 1982. An even more recent innovation is the creation of indexed bonds. Economists have been pointing out the dangers of long-term nominal contracting for more than 100 years, and yet in the United States long-term debt has been almost exclusively nominal. Indexed federal government debt did not exist in the United States until 1997, and it still only accounts for less than 1 percent of the federal debt.[11] Brainard and Dolbaer (1971) have long pointed out the advantages of creating contracts that allow people to share occupational income risks, but serious discussion of such contracts has only just begun.

Potential for Failure

Not only do market innovations take a long time to start, but also they often fail. Those who contemplate taking the time and effort to establish such markets may be deterred by past failures. A good example of such a failure is the CPI futures market, which bears some resemblance to the macro markets described here.

A CPI futures market allows an investor to hedge against a change in real income that occurs when nominal income is rigid and the price level changes. Consumer price index markets were proposed in the 1970s by Lovell and Vogel (1974) at a time when U.S. inflation was high. The Lovell-Vogel proposal launched a discussion of the benefits of the CPI market, attracting endorsements from such prominent economists as Milton Friedman and Paul Samuelson. Despite this interest, it took a dozen years before the CPI market was established in the United States at the Coffee, Sugar, and Cocoa Exchange in 1985. Unfortunately, by the time the market was established, the inflation rate (as well as inflation uncertainty) had fallen to a fairly low level. As a result, the relatively short-term contracts had virtually no hedging function. Despite some early activity, the market was essentially dead by 1986.

The failure of the CPI futures market in the United States is often cited as evidence that the idea behind the market was flawed. A CPI market did succeed, however, in Brazil. The market started around the same time as in the United States, 1986, but inflation uncertainty was much higher in Brazil. The Brazilian market flourished until it was shut down by the Brazilian government as an anti-inflation measure.[12] The lesson that can be learned from the CPI futures market is not that such markets cannot succeed, but that they are slow to get started. Moreover, they must be started while the risks that the market is designed to manage are prominent.

Lack of Investor Awareness

It may be that people simply are not aware of long-term income growth uncertainty and the exposure of their own incomes to aggregate risk. Investors frequently emphasize short-term over long-term portfolio performance. One potential factor behind such a short-term focus is the agency problem associated with the delegation of financial market decisions. The difficulty in monitoring decisions carried out by an outside agency naturally leads to an overemphasis on easily observable short-term performance.

Individuals might not be aware of their exposure to aggregate income growth uncertainty because short-run fluctuations in their own income often appear to be independent of fluctuations in aggregate incomes. This narrow focus could lead them to underestimate the long-term correlation between individual income and aggregate income. Most people are probably not aware that over longer time intervals, individuals' incomes tend to rise and fall with aggregate income. As we mentioned above, even at the relatively short five-year horizon, most of an individual's income growth uncertainty can be attributed to aggregate risk. Nonetheless, many people attribute these income fluctuations to their own efforts and abilities as well as to luck. This lack of awareness raises doubts about whether large-scale demand in macro markets would ultimately materialize, even though in principle the diversification benefits are high.

Lack of Price History

We have yet to find a single example of a mutual fund that advertises a low or negative correlation of its returns with income aggregates as one of its selling points—even though finance theory suggests that such a correlation is one of the most important things to advertise. One explanation for the failure of mutual funds to advertise such a correlation is that claims on income aggregates have no market price and therefore no observable return. No one knows how volatile the price of aggregate income claims would be. Only the history of the income movements themselves is observable. Consider the case of investors who own corporate stock. If individuals could observe only dividend announcements and not the price, no one would know the amount of volatility present in stock prices.[13]

The Importance of Public Debate and Leadership

One reason aggregate income markets do not exist is that there has been very little public debate about the potential goals of such markets. Kennickell, Starr-McCluer, and Sundén (1996) find that friends and relatives are the most important source of financial advice. Others' actions clearly provide an important signal for most people. Thus, a broad consensus on the value of macro markets among financial advisors, writers, commentators, lawyers, regulators, and lawmakers is very important if risk-management contracts are to be sold to the public. Historical evidence suggests that professional leadership is an important factor in making risk-management institutions a success. Consider, for example, disability risk insurance. In the early part of this century, private disability insurance was available but the public showed little interest in it. Only through the work of economists—notably John R. Commons, a cofounder of the American Economic Association—did the state-government institution of Workers' Compensation become established in the United States in all but six states by 1920.[14] Since then, disability insurance has become common among private employers as well. Today, disability insurance is a well-established institution that is not exclusively governmental, even though relatively little disability insurance is sold directly to individuals by insurance companies.

A Public Goods Problem

Another reason why these securities may not exist is that market innovators typically capture a very small fraction of the benefits and almost all of the costs of introducing a new market. Financial instruments or ways of doing business usually cannot be patented. Evidence indicates that when a firm successfully issues a new financial product, a competitor typically introduces a similar product within a period of less than two or three months.[15] At the same time, the introduction of aggregate income assets requires substantial initial investments from the innovator, including collecting data, publicizing the product, experimenting with different types of contracts, and educating the public on how to use these markets.

Measurement Problems

What these contracts should cash-settle on is a serious issue that poses significant measurement problems. Per capita income measures can change based on shifting demographics alone. One solution may be to keep track of the incomes of a large group of individuals. Changes in quality are also notoriously hard to measure. Beyond such measurement issues is the question of how to deal with revisions. Shiller (1993) advances the theory of index numbers to address these questions. He proposes several kinds of chain indexes that are relatively robust to revision problems; adjustments to national income measures could be made along these lines. Attempts to generate labor income indexes that are less sensitive to the changing composition of the labor force are reported in Shiller and Schneider (1998). The standardization of the indexes is essential to creating liquidity in these markets. A related problem is that governments collect most of the data to compute these indexes. If countries sell short claims on their own income, which they should do for the purpose of risk sharing, governments have an incentive to underreport GDP. It is not immediately clear how to resolve the problem of underreporting, although similar problems have not stopped the development of markets in indexed bonds and CPI futures.

Problems of Enforcement

Enforceability may also be a significant obstacle. In the formation of macro markets, contract designers need to avoid incentives for investors to renege on contracts. Consider the hedging instruments discussed earlier, which yield an annual payoff of $GDP_W - GDP$. Domestic residents buy such securities from pension funds to eliminate their exposure to country-specific aggregate risk. But when per capita output in their own country unexpectedly grows faster than per capita world output, they lose on the contract. In order to guarantee their ability to pay, domestic residents must put up margin. These margin calls can be very large because the expected present discounted value of a country's per capita GDP can fluctuate widely. The amount of margin required shrinks as the margin is adjusted more frequently, because at shorter time intervals the uncertainty about asset price changes is smaller. Nonetheless, as we saw in October 1987 and October 1997, sometimes very large asset price changes are observed even over very short periods of time. High levels of margin may push individuals who do not have sufficient liquid assets out of the market. One advantage of arranging these contracts through pension funds is that the money already invested in the fund can be applied as margin. Very young investors—whose pension accounts are still small—may not be able to fully diversify against aggregate income risk. This problem gradually improves as an investor gets older. Most middle-aged people have accumulated sufficient wealth to take full advantage of the option to hedge aggregate risk. But as an investor gets older, the horizon for hedging becomes shorter and the benefits from risk sharing decrease.

Macro Market Bubbles

An additional problem is that the price of the macro securities may be even more volatile than the underlying fundamentals. Asset price bubbles cannot be ruled out. An asset price bubble occurs when increasing optimism causes investors to bid up prices to unsustainable levels, eventually resulting in a bursting of the bubble and a sudden crash. By some accounts, bubbles are caused in part by individuals who overreact to past positive returns and flock into a bull market. Investors who enter the market because of excessive optimism typically choose to depart once they find that their optimism is unfounded and can cause a market to crash.

Stock market crashes have sometimes had significant repercussions on economic performance. The worldwide stock market crash of 1929, for example, appears to have triggered a public sense of great uncertainty and a desire to postpone expenditures until the economic outlook grew clearer (see Romer [1990]). This reaction may have been a factor in bringing on the Great Depression. The consequences of such price swings in macro markets, and safety measures to protect against such shocks, need to be considered and addressed.

Portfolio Management Problems

Finally, we would like to address a very practical question. Given the uncertainties surrounding a person's future income, future employment, and future career developments, how will he know what positions to take in these markets? In our earlier example, we assumed that the individual's wages are equal to the per capita wage rate plus an idiosyncratic component unrelated to aggregate risk. But in reality, some people's income is more exposed to the national business cycle than others'. This exposure depends on the location of someone's work as well as the sector in which he works. In general, the optimal positions in the aggregate income markets depend on how much one's future income is correlated with measures of aggregate income over long-term horizons. Depending on the sector and location of someone's work, information about long-term income fluctuations can be obtained from historical data. But what happens when someone moves to another part of the country or to another sector, or when someone changes careers altogether? Of course, every person's career has a significant idiosyncratic component. What is really needed, however, is a good estimate of the aggregate component of a person's future income that takes into consideration characteristics such as age, education, location, and the sector in which he works. Financial advisors can use this information, which can be obtained from longitudinal data sources, to determine optimal hedging strategies. Obtaining such measures of covariances is a very difficult task. We do not want to exaggerate this difficulty, however. Over longer horizons, which matter most for diversification purposes, people's incomes are more correlated than they are over short horizons. In the end, almost all people are sensitive to the growth performance of the aggregate economy, no matter where or in what sector they work.

Conclusion

We have outlined how macro markets can be beneficial to the average person interested in long-term financial security. The introduction of such markets allows pension funds to offer a hedging instrument that can be used to reduce, or even eliminate, exposure to country-specific growth performance. We have found that the benefits of eliminating exposure to such country-specific risk are large. Over a period of thirty-five years, the per capita GDP of one industrialized country relative to that of another industrialized country could unexpectedly double. For a broader group of countries, the risks are much larger. While not documented in this chapter, large gains are likely to be achieved by trading other forms of aggregate income claims, particularly those associated with occupational risks. We have also pointed out that existing financial markets are not a good substitute for macro markets that cash-settle on a measure of national income.

Given that macro markets can provide substantial improvements in long-term financial security—improvements that cannot be achieved in existing markets—it may seem peculiar that these markets have not yet developed. We offer several explanations for the absence of macro markets. Investors tend to be focused on short-term financial performance and may not consider the benefits of long-term financial security. Moreover, research has shown that for most people, friends and family represent the main source of financial advice. It is therefore unlikely that investors will consider the benefits of protecting themselves from country-specific risks until a broad consensus develops on the value of macro markets among financial advisors, writers, lawyers, the media, regulators, and lawmakers.

Before aggregate income contracts can be introduced, many practical hurdles must be overcome. Rules for settlement need to be developed, and decisions must be made about income measures, contract size, and margin requirements. Circuit breakers or other measures that deal with the possibility of sudden booms or crashes in the macro markets will be necessary. An array of regulatory and tax issues will need to be resolved. Perhaps most important, methods for evaluating the aggregate income risk exposure of individual households and businesses will need to be developed so that people will know how to use the markets. Given the costs of introducing such markets, it is also important to think about where the first markets should be created and whether initial markets should be for individual countries or for aggregates of countries.[16]

Some of the hurdles to a wide-scale use of macro markets could turn out to be too large. Margin requirements to enforce the contracts may be too big for many individuals. It may also be difficult to determine optimal exposure to aggregate income risk for individual people and to convince investors of the benefits of hedging this risk. Even if these markets are eventually introduced, they may be used more narrowly than has been suggested here.

The presence of these obstacles, however, does not mean that we should avoid serious debate about the creation of aggregate income markets. Aggregate income growth uncertainty represents the largest macroeconomic risk incurred by households all over the world. The benefits from trading in macro markets are potentially very large. Factors that are essential to the start of such markets—including well-functioning financial exchanges, a sophisticated technology of trading, and the intellectual appreciation of the importance of risk management—are already in place. Eventually, portfolio managers and individuals could routinely hedge aggregate income risks in macro markets.

Appendix: Two Sets of Countries

We use two sets of countries in the regression analysis—a set of forty-nine countries and a smaller set of twenty-one OECD countries.

The forty-nine countries are Kenya, Mauritius, Uganda, Canada, Costa Rica, the Dominican Republic, El Salvador, Guatemala, Honduras, Mexico, Nicaragua, Panama, Trinidad and Tobago, the United States, Argentina, Bolivia, Brazil, Chile, Colombia, Ecuador, Paraguay, Peru, Uruguay, Venezuela, India, Japan, Pakistan, the Philippines, Sri Lanka, Thailand, Austria, Belgium, Cyprus, Denmark, Finland, France, Germany, Greece, Ireland, Italy, the Netherlands, Norway, Portugal, Spain, Sweden, Turkey, the United Kingdom, Australia, and New Zealand.

The twenty-one OECD countries are Canada, the United States, Japan, Austria, Belgium, Denmark, Finland, France, Germany, Greece, Ireland, Italy, the Netherlands, Norway, Portugal, Spain, Sweden, Turkey, the United Kingdom, Australia, and New Zealand.

Notes

The authors thank Phil Strahan and two anonymous referees for many useful comments and suggestions.

1. See Kang and Stulz (1997), French and Poterba (1991), and Tesar and Werner (1994, 1997).

2. See Shiller and Athanasoulis (1995) and Athanasoulis and Shiller (1997); for related work, see also Demange and Laroque (1995) and Allen and Gale (1994).

3. The country-specific growth uncertainty can also be transformed into a measure of welfare gains from international risk sharing. See Athanasoulis and van Wincoop (1997) and van Wincoop (1994, 1996, 1999).

4. See Athanasoulis and van Wincoop (1997) for details on the estimation procedure. For each horizon s, we use data for all nonoverlapping intervals with that length, starting with the most recent interval ending in 1990.

5. See Barro and Sala-i-Martin (1995) and Levine and Renelt (1992).

6. We experimented with additional variables: political instability; terms of trade growth over the past five years; percentage of primary, secondary, and higher education attained; the most recent one- and five-year growth rates of private consumption; and the investment rate averaged over the past five years. None of these variables improved predictive power substantially.

7. The residual risk is based on the three variables that have the most predictive power.

8. See *The Economist*, May 17–23, 1997, pp. 21–24, for a discussion of Ireland's recent growth.

9. The wage rate is the average real wage per employee using national data on employee compensation divided by the number of employees and the consumer price index.

10. Plenty of evidence suggests that technological convergence occurs across industrialized countries, leading to a common stochastic growth trend.

11. See Shiller (1997) for a discussion of public resistance to indexation.

12. Similar markets were reintroduced twice in the late 1980s. However, each time they were eventually shut down by the government.

13. This problem is not insurmountable. Initial public offerings face the same problem.

14. See Moss (1995).

15. See Tufano (1992).

16. Shiller and Athanasoulis (1995) find that a U.S.-Japan swap of national incomes may be the best single contract to recommend, with a U.S.-Europe swap being important as well. Athanasoulis and Shiller (1997) find that an important market to develop early would be a market for the entire world, a market that would trade claims on the aggregated incomes of all countries.

References

Allen, F., and D. Gale. 1994. *Financial Innovation and Risk Sharing*. Cambridge: MIT Press.

Athanasoulis, S. G., and E. van Wincoop. 1997. "Growth Uncertainty and Risk-sharing." *Federal Reserve Bank of New York Staff Reports*, no. 30 (October).

Athanasoulis, S. G., and R. J. Shiller. 1997. "The Significance of the Market Portfolio." NBER Technical Working Paper no. 209.

Barro, R. J., and J. Lee. 1994. "Sources of Economic Growth." *Carnegie Rochester Conference Series on Public Policy* 40: 1–46.

Barro, R. J., and X. Sala-i-Martin. 1995. *Economic Growth*. New York: McGraw-Hill.

Bottazzi, L., P. Pesenti, and E. van Wincoop. 1996. "Wages, Profits and the International Portfolio Puzzle." *European Economic Review* 40, no. 2 (February): 219–54.

Brainard, W., and F. T. Dolbaer. 1971. "Social Risk and Financial Markets." *American Economic Review* 61, no. 2: 360–70.

Demange, G., and G. Laroque. 1995. "Optimality of Incomplete Markets." *Journal of Economic Theory* 65, no. 1 (February): 218–32.

French, K. R., and J. M. Poterba. 1991. "Investor Diversification and International Equity Markets." *American Economic Review* 81, no. 2 (May): 222–

266. Papers and Proceedings of the 103rd Annual Meeting of the American Economic Association, December 1990.

Gehrig, T. P. 1993. "An Information Based Explanation for the Domestic Bias in International Equity Investment." *Scandinavian Journal of Economics* 95, no. 1: 97–109.

Kang, J., and R. M. Stulz. 1997. "Why Is There a Home Bias? An Analysis of Foreign Portfolio Equity Ownership in Japan." *Journal of Financial Economics* 46, no. 1: 3–28.

Kennickell, A. B., M. Starr-McCluer, and A. E. Sundén. 1996. "Financial Advice and Household Portfolios." Working paper, Board of Governors of the Federal Reserve System.

Kuznets, S. 1937. *National Income and Capital Formation.* New York: National Bureau of Economic Research.

Levine, R., and D. Renelt. 1992. "A Sensitivity Analysis of Cross Country Growth Regressions." *American Economic Review* 82, no. 4: 942–63.

Lovell, M. C., and R. C. Vogel. 1974. "A CPI-Futures Market." *Journal of Political Economy* 81, no. 1: 9–12.

Moss, D. A. 1995. *Socializing Security: Progressive Era Economists and the Origin of American Social Policy.* Cambridge: Harvard University Press.

Romer, C. 1990. "The Great Crash and the Onset of the Great Depression." *Quarterly Journal of Economics* 105, no. 3: 597–624.

Shiller, R. J. 1993. *Macro Markets: Creating Institutions for Managing Society's Largest Economic Risks.* New York: Clarendon Press.

———. 1997. "Public Resistance to Indexation: A Puzzle." *Brookings Papers on Economic Activity*, no. 1: 159–211.

Shiller, R. J., and S. Athanasoulis. 1995. "World Income Components: Measuring and Exploiting International Risk Sharing Opportunities." NBER Working Paper no. 5095.

Shiller, R. J., and R. Schneider. 1998. "Labor Income Indices Designed for Use in Contracts Promoting Income Risk Management." *Review of Income and Wealth* 44, no. 2: 163–82.

Stone, R. 1947. "Definition and Measurement of the National Income and Related Totals." In Subcommittee on National Income Statistics of the League of Nations Committee of Statistical Experts, Studies and Reports on Statistical Methods no. 7, *Measurement of National Income and the Construction of Social Accounts*, 21–116. Geneva: United Nations.

Tesar, L. L., and I. M. Werner. 1994. "International Equity Transactions and U.S. Portfolio Choice." In J. A. Frankel, ed., *The Internationalization of Equity Markets.* Chicago: University of Chicago Press.

———. 1997. "The Internationalization of Securities since the 1987 Crash." Working paper, University of Michigan.

Tufano, P. 1992. "Financial Innovation and First Mover Advantage." *Journal of Applied Corporate Finance* 5: 83–87.

van Wincoop, E. 1994. "Welfare Gains from International Risksharing." *Journal of Monetary Economics* 34, no. 2 (October): 175–200.

———. 1996. "A Multi-Country Real Business Cycle Model with Heterogeneous Agents." *Scandinavian Journal of Economics* 98, no. 2: 233–51.

———. 1999. "How Big Are the Potential Welfare Gains from International Risksharing?" *Journal of International Economics* 47, no. 1: 109–35.

3

Gene Insurance

ALEXANDER TABARROK

Not so long ago, the only way to get a glimpse of your future health was to take a trip to the local psychic for a tarot card reading. Now, thanks to advances in genetic research, medical practitioners are increasingly able to read your health future from a much more reliable source—your individual genetic code. The correlation between specific genes and some diseases is now well established, and further discoveries are announced almost weekly.

This knowledge permits you to better understand your vulnerability to disease and so attempt to minimize the effect of genetic conditions. However, accurate genetic information also brings fear that health insurance could become unaffordable or even unavailable to those with genetic predisposition to disease. And because most individuals are insured through their employer, some people worry that knowledge of genetic traits might lead to employment discrimination. Solutions that would maintain access to health insurance have been proposed, but most would almost inevitably lead to antiselection and a disruption of the underwriting process, with potentially dire impact on the solvency of insurers.

Adam Smith's invisible hand points to a better approach: By designing and encouraging products that take advantage of free-market incentives, we can retain individual access to the health insurance market within the present system of risk classification. One such product is genetic insurance (see Tabarrok 1994).

Insuring Your Genes

For a small premium cost, genetic insurance would insure against possessing a "bad" gene. Policies would be sold to all individuals *before* they un-

47

derwent genetic testing. If a test came back positive, the customer would be paid a sum of money large enough to cover the expected costs of the disease or an equivalent amount of money to purchase health insurance at the new, higher premiums. For example, if a woman is found to be carrying BRCAI (the gene related to a higher probability of breast cancer), she would be paid enough to purchase actuarially sound risk premiums. We are used to thinking of insuring against sickness; genetic insurance makes it equally possible to insure against a high *probability* of sickness.

All the benefits of genetic testing, such as improved treatment and health planning targeted to offset a genetic vulnerability, could be exploited because the discovery of a bad gene would not cause an individual to lose health insurance coverage. Thus, genetic insurance would cure a chronic condition that can have serious health consequences: fear of taking a genetic test.

The single ground rule of mandatory purchase would avoid the problem of adverse selection. Enforcement should not be difficult. First, most people do not carry serious genetic defects, so the expected gain from concealing a positive result, and thereby cheating an insurer, is small. A small penalty will deter this type of action. Second, enforcement would be carried out through medical institutions rather than by individuals. Genetic tests are complicated; their performance and interpretation typically requires expensive lab equipment and trained technicians and physicians. The requirement to buy genetic insurance can be enforced by making it illegal for physicians and laboratories to run tests without proof that genetic insurance has been bought.

Legislation to mandate genetic insurance could be drafted by the National Association of Insurance Commissioners for adoption by the states. Although the idea is too new to permit speculation about the prospects for such legislation, a genetic insurance requirement would likely win support from both insurers and consumers. Companies would stand to reap a reasonable profit on the product, and consumers would benefit because insurance coverage takes the fear out of genetic testing.

In the near future, genetic testing is likely to be fully integrated into the medical process. A battery of tests done on a single blood or tissue sample will become standard procedure at or before birth. Genetic insurance could become part of the normal testing procedure, making serious enforcement problems unlikely.

Genetic insurance would make it profitable for insurers to insure everyone, regardless of genetic status or potential future health problems. Insurance firms, under this proposal, would no longer have an incentive to drop customers with genetic defects. Indeed, insurance firms would actively seek out such customers because of the profits to be made from the higher premiums. Individuals with serious genetic defects would buy their insurance individually (or as part of a special genetic group) rather than through their employer. Employers also would have far fewer incentives to genetically discriminate.

Life Insurance Uses

Genetic insurance also could improve the life insurance market. Life insurance contracts usually are written for much longer terms than health insurance contracts. Surprisingly, lengthy life insurance contracts could make the impact of genetic testing either more or less serious on life insurers than on health insurers.

If insurance companies have access to information from genetic tests, many people will want to buy long-term life insurance before the tests are taken. Under this scenario, genetic tests will not cause great difficulties for the life insurance market. But if legislation makes genetic information "private," very serious adverse selection problems could occur. Precisely because life insurance is a long-term contract, adverse selection problems could be more serious than in the health insurance market.

Genetic information should be accessible by life insurance companies along with other types of health information. If all information is accessible, most individuals will be willing to buy life insurance before taking any genetic tests. Problems will arise, however, if genetic tests reveal information about probable health status for time periods beyond the typical tenure of a life insurance contract.

Genetic insurance, however, will allow you to insure against increases in life insurance premiums just as it allows you to insure against increases in health insurance premiums. You may want to be tested early in life. If you're uncertain at the time of testing about the appropriate amount of life insurance to buy, "life-insurance options" could be sold to give you the right to buy a given amount of coverage at a set price at some point in the future. Thus, genetic insurance and full access to information can improve the life and health insurance markets.

What Will it Cost?

Genetic insurance can be sold in private competitive markets just as are other types of insurance. But will it be affordable? It seems likely that everyone who today purchases health insurance also will be able to purchase genetic insurance. Genetic insurance cannot raise the total cost of health insurance because today's health insurance already covers the possibility of possessing a defective gene, but it does so implicitly, and given today's technology, inefficiently. Today's health insurance is a combination of insurance against genetic disease and insurance against nongenetic disease or accident. Included in the premium cost is a price for genetic insurance. By making use of new gene technologies to separate the genetic and nongenetic aspects of health insurance, we are simply making explicit an existing implicit market.

Separating the genetic and nongenetic health insurance markets cannot raise the total price of health insurance because the same product is being sold. Thus, whoever can afford today's health insurance package will also be able to afford genetic insurance and health insurance when priced separately.

In fact, the total price of health insurance will fall under this proposal. Individuals who gain early knowledge of a genetic defect can seek earlier treatment, which is usually cheaper and more effective. In addition, factors that complement the adverse effects of the defective gene, such as a high-fat diet, can be avoided, thereby reducing the probability of ever contracting the disease. These cost savings will be passed on to insurance customers.

Delta Insurance

Genetic insurance insures against unexpected changes in the price of health insurance caused by information from a genetic test. A 1995 essay by economist J. H. Cochrane, reprinted in this volume, has shown how this idea may be extended so that unexpected changes in the price of health insurance from any source can be insured.

Cochrane's approach is quite technical but, as with genetic insurance, the essence of the idea is to sell two contracts. The first contract covers health expenses in the next year; the second insures against any changes in expected future health expenses. To see how this second contract, called delta insurance, works, and how it is priced, consider this highly simplified example.

Assume that individuals live forever and the expected cost of health care is $2,000 per year. At the beginning of Year 1, an individual (let's call him Barney) pays $2,000 to a risk-neutral firm to cover any health expenses that may occur during the first year. Barney is worried that in Year 2 his health insurance might rise in price, so he buys a delta contract from the firm. During Year 1, Barney discovers that he has cancer. His doctors hope that the cancer may be cured, but Barney's expected future health expenses rise to $10,000, and so does the price of his health insurance, so the insurer can cover its costs.

But Barney bought a delta contract. It pays him just enough so that he can afford the higher rates. Assuming a yearly interest rate of 10 percent, a lump-sum payment to Barney of $80,000 will give him enough so that every year he can pay the higher rate (since $80,000 × 0.1 = $8,000).

How much would delta insurance cost? Surprisingly, with minor modification, delta insurance can be sold for free. To see how, imagine that Barney's cancer is cured in Year 2 and that his expected health care costs fall back to $2,000 per year. This means that the price of his health insurance goes down to $2,000. Barney's insurance costs are no higher than they were in Year 1, but now he has an extra $80,000 in the bank. Assuming that Barney wants insurance against changes in the price of health insurance and not an opportunity to gamble, he won't complain too much if he must pay the $80,000 back to the insurance company.

Let's then rewrite the delta insurance contract so that whenever Barney's health care costs rise, the insurance company pays Barney a lump-sum fee, but whenever Barney's health care costs fall, Barney pays the insurance a lump-sum fee. But recall that when delta insurance is bought at the beginning of Year 1, the best estimate of Barney's lifetime health care costs in Year 2 is exactly the same as in Year 1: $2,000 per year.

In other words, the expected change in Barney's health care cost is zero, so the insurance firm is just as likely to gain as to lose from a delta insurance contract. A risk-neutral firm will be happy to offer such a contract for the price of the paperwork that it takes to write the contract.

More generally, delta insurance works as follows: In Year 1, the insurance company makes an estimate of the individual's total lifetime health expenses (not including expected expenses for the current year). Competition will force each insurer to make an unbiased estimate of these expenses. In Year 2, the insurance company reestimates lifetime health expenses. If lifetime health expenses have risen, the insurance company makes a payment to the individual. If health expenses have fallen, the individual makes a payment to the insurance company.

In Year 2, the insurance company has an incentive to indicate that health expenses have fallen. Several things can be done to control this problem.

First, contracts can be written so that revisions in expected health expenses must be made on the basis of publicly observable information and must be made according to a publicly stated formula. Thus, a positive genetic test result would lead to a contractually obligated payment. The discovery of HIV or cancer could be handled similarly, with due changes made for factors such as age and severity of the disease. The insurance industry already uses much of this information in standardized form for the computation of premiums.

Second, lump-sum payments can be made a function of changes in health insurance premiums by Year 2. By requiring consistency between premiums charged to new insurees and premiums implicitly charged to holders of delta insurance, this type of plan can be made compatible with incentives.

Genetic insurance is just one possible solution to the problems posed by our rapidly expanding understanding of human genetics. A dynamic free market will undoubtedly create other products to ensure the availability of insurance. Far from spelling new restrictions on insurance consumers, knowledge gained through genetic tests will offer enhanced choices and greater opportunity to maintain good health.

References

Tabarrok, A. 1994. "Genetic testing: an economic and contractarian analysis." *Journal of Health Economics* 13:75–91.

4

Time-Consistent Health Insurance

JOHN H. COCHRANE

Currently available health insurance contracts do not fully insure many long-term illnesses, such as AIDS, cancer, senile dementia, heart disease, or organ failure. Many people who get such diseases face ruinous increases in premiums. Others lose their health insurance by losing their job or their spouse or by exceeding a lifetime cap on benefits. Some are bankrupted by health expenses; some are unable to get further medical care. Many other kinds of insurance do not cover long-term risks in the same way, for example, medical malpractice and product liability insurance.

The absence of effective long-term health insurance is perhaps *the* most important issue driving health care regulation proposals, including the Clinton plan and congressional proposals. To the voting, insured middle class, the plans offer "health insurance that *can't be taken away.*" This absence is also a central motivation for plans offered by academics (see Enthoven and Kronick 1989, 34–35; Himmelstein et al. 1989; Pauly et al. 1991, 14–15; and esp. Diamond 1992, 1238–39).

Neither the authors of health regulation plans nor their critics have focused on the standard question for a proposed regulation: What, precisely, is the market failure? Or is the absence of effective long-term health insurance due instead to regulation or poor court enforcement and ex-post reinterpretation of long-term contracts? Plan authors typically just assume that markets cannot provide long-term health insurance, or they make anecdotal reference to textbook asymmetric information stories. Critics have focused on the distortionary side effects of the plans and their financing provisions (see, e.g., the *Journal of Economic Perspectives* "Health Care Reform" symposium; Newhouse 1994; Cutler 1994; Aaron 1994; Pauly 1994; Zeckhauser 1994; Diamond 1994; Poterba 1994). But these and other critics have not answered the planners' central challenge: How can long-term insurance be provided *without* intrusive and distorting regulation?

Here, I try to answer this question. I show why current health insurance contracts cannot provide long-term insurance in a competitive environment. I describe *time-consistent* contracts that can provide long-term insurance, and I discuss how time-consistent contracts might be implemented in practice. I anticipate some objections, and I offer an explanation for the fact that they have not already been implemented. The bottom line of the analysis is that markets can provide long-term health insurance, and *de*-regulation is the likely policy route to achieve it.

Overview

A long-term standard insurance contract should provide insurance for long-term illness. In its simplest form, the consumer agrees to pay a constant premium and the insurer promises to pay health expenses, cross-subsidizing the expenses of those who turn out to be sick from the premiums of those who turn out to be healthy. (For the purposes of this chapter, it doesn't matter whether the "consumer" is an individual or an employer-based or other group; whether the consumer pays for insurance directly or whether the employer does so on his behalf; or whether the "insurer" is a health insurance company or an insurer-provider such as a health maintenance organization.)

But suppose the consumer gets a long-term illness. He is now a long-term liability of the insurer, so the insurer has a strong incentive to get rid of him. Current contracts are not, in fact, long-term contracts, because the insurer can respond to this incentive. It can increase an individual's premiums or deny a renewal of the contract. Devices such as lifetime caps on health expenditures and preexisting conditions clauses further limit coverage of long-term illness.

It is tempting to simply shore up insurers' obligations in long-term contracts—outlaw premium increases and preexisting conditions clauses, mandate renewability, and so forth. This change will not solve the problem, however, because *consumers* cannot be held to long-term contracts. Suppose a consumer turns out to be *healthier* than average. This consumer now owes the insurer a long-term stream of net payments—the prearranged premium is higher than his expected health costs. The insurer needs to bind him to the contract to pay the expenses of the sick, but the courts will not and arguably cannot force healthy consumers to stay with the original insurer forever or pay damages for leaving. A competing insurer can woo the healthy consumer away at a lower premium, so the original insurer is left with the lemons. The original insurer is then forced to limit coverage of the sick or it will go bankrupt.

Furthermore, long-term contracts require *lifetime* ties in order to insure long-term illness. Consumers cannot change insurers, even for reasons unrelated to health, such as a move, marriage or divorce, job change, retirement, or changing preferences over quality and convenience of care. If sick, a consumer depends on the lifetime commitment of *one* insurer, because no other will take him. If well, he must be bound to his insurer to cross-subsidize the sick.

For these and other reasons, the health insurance literature recognizes that long-term contracts are poor vehicles for insuring long-term health risks (see Diamond 1992, 1238–39). Contract theory also recognizes the defects of long-term contracts. Fortunately, it finds that in many situations (including some with moral hazard), a long-term contract can be replaced by a sequence of carefully crafted short-term contracts (see Malcomson and Spinnewyn 1988; Fudenberg, Holmstrom, and Milgrom 1990; Rey and Salanie 1990). The sequence of short-term contracts must be *time consistent*, or *renegotiation-proof*. They must satisfy a *participation constraint*: Each party must be willing to sign the next contract, no matter what happens. (Kocherlakota [1994] shows how participation constraints can result in suboptimal contracts.) A sequence of short-term contracts with this feature constitutes a *self-enforcing* long-term contract. Typically, Pareto-optimal, time-consistent contracts require a series of state-contingent *severance payments*. The methods in this chapter are taken from finance, where replacing long-term contingent claims with dynamic trading in short-term securities is a fundamental technique.

For example, suppose the long-term debts between insurer and consumer are periodically settled or marked to market. If the consumer has gotten sick, the insurer pays him the increased present value of his expected lifetime health costs and is now free to charge an actuarially fair premium. If the consumer has gotten healthier, he pays the insurer the decreased present value of lifetime health costs and is free to leave or demand a lower premium. Now, both sides are happy to sign a new contract, because the premiums are actuarially fair. Whether the consumer stays or changes to a new insurer, long-term illness is insured, because the severance payment exactly compensates for changes in premiums.

Since long-term debts are periodically settled, the contract is *time consistent* and can provide long-term health insurance. It implements the Pareto-optimal or contingent-claim outcome. Furthermore, consumers do not depend on the long-term commitment of a single insurer, they are not stuck in jobs, and they do not face termination of insurance or disastrous rises in out-of-pocket expenses if they lose their jobs, get divorced, move, or change insurers for any reason. This freedom to change insurers should enhance competition and product variety. Finally, the improvement is free: The consumer's total payments are exactly the same as in an enforced long-term contract. In the place of a cross-subsidy to the sick, the healthy consumer now pays an actuarially fair premium against the chance that *he* gets a long-term illness and, hence, a severance payment.

This simple implementation is not practical, since consumers cannot be forced to pay insurers *ex-post* if they do not get sick. This difficulty can be avoided if each consumer has a special account that can be used only to pay health insurance premiums and pay or receive severance payments. Every period, the consumer pays a constant amount into this account, and the account pays a premium to an insurer for one-period insurance. Competition requires that sick people pay higher premiums and healthy people pay lower premiums. If a person is diagnosed with a disease that raises his premiums, the insurer pays into the account a lump sum equal to the increase in the present value of premiums. If he gets healthier and his premiums decline, the account pays the insurer a lump sum equal to the decline in the present value of premiums. The arithmetic, presented below, shows that there is always enough in the account to make any required severance payment.

The account may be used only for health insurance payments, because as long as the sum paid *by* the insurer when a consumer got sick is located in the account, it is easy to require that the consumer pay the lump sum *back* to the insurer if he gets healthier. If the lump sum were paid directly to the consumer, it might be hard to get it back. The consumer might spend the money and declare bankruptcy. Finally, one hopes that courts will enforce an insurer's right to receive payments from an account that is explicitly set up for that purpose, while they may not enforce severance payments taken directly from consumers.

The time-consistent contract provides "premium insurance," insurance against rises in premiums, as well as "health insurance," insurance against the uncertain component of one-period health expenditures. Premium insurance does not have to be provided by the health insurer; financial services companies could offer insurance against the event that a person's health insurer raises his premiums. Therefore, time-consistent insurance can be offered by simply adding such premium insurance contracts to existing health insurance.

There are many additional ways to implement time-consistent contracts. If insurers are successfully forbidden from raising premiums or limiting coverage for the sick, severance payments could happen only when a consumer decides to change insurers. If the special accounts I described above are unworkable, the contract could state that the current insurer will pay a new insurer to take the consumer if he is sick, or the current insurer will have the right to receive a payment from a new insurer if the consumer is healthier than average. Contracting costs and the vagaries of court enforcement will determine which of these or other implementations of the time-consistent contract are chosen. The essence is just some enforceable mechanism for settling long-term debts.

By contrast, most policy proposals herd consumers into large pools, outlaw health-based premiums and pre-existing conditions clauses, and attempt to outlaw selection based on health. These proposals *require* a heavily regulated system that enforces a uniform product and eliminates competition, because economic incentives to select are not eliminated. Insurers must be effectively prevented from subtly and cleverly trying to improve their pool of customers or from discreetly providing lower levels of care for sick and expensive consumers. Worse, they must be prevented from competing for the healthy. If they just focus their marketing and advertising to healthier groups, the pooling solution will break down. Similarly, healthy *consumers* must be stopped from trying to join better groups.

The time-consistent contract described above most closely resembles proposals to allow medical savings accounts. But the accounts in current proposals do not provide *insurance*; each person's lifetime resources are still reduced one-for-one by his lifetime health expenses. Time-consistent contracts add insurance to medical savings accounts. Money is added to the accounts of people who get sick and is drawn from the accounts of those who stay well or get better.

Optimal Health Insurance Contracts

Figure 4.1 presents the timing of events. In the beginning of each period, wealth W_t is evaluated, premium payments p_t can be made, and the consumer earns income e. Then information about the consumer's health is revealed, including current health costs x_t, as well as information about future health costs. State-contingent payments y_t can be made, health costs x_t are paid, and finally the consumer consumes c_t. The consumer earns interest $1 + r$ between periods. The term E_t denotes the expectation conditional on time t information before x_t is revealed, and E_{t+1}, refers to time t information after x_t and any other news is revealed. Therefore, an expression such as $E_t x_t$ means the expected value of x_t in the first half of period t, before x_t is revealed.

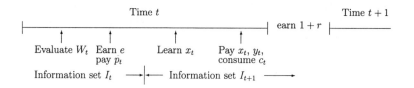

Fig. 4.1 Timing of events.

Consumers maximize a standard intertemporal utility function,

$$\max E_0 \sum_{t=0}^{\infty} \beta^t u(c_t). \tag{1}$$

For simplicity, the discount factor β equals $1/(1 + r)$. Different values or varying interest rates complicate the algebra without changing the basic point. I treat uncertain lifetimes below. Since budget constraints are linear, we can separately treat health insurance and insurance against other shocks. For this reason, I simplify the model to a constant labor income e.

I assume that insurers are risk neutral and competitive, and they can borrow or lend at the interest rate r. Risk neutrality follows when individual illness is a perfectly diversifiable risk. A later section argues that the results are not substantially altered with imperfect credit markets or nondiversifiable risks. For simplicity, I also focus on contracts with zero economic profits. Larger profits or administrative expenses are straightforward extensions.

Pareto-optimal allocations maximize the consumer's objective for each value of the insurer's objective. In this model, Pareto-optimal allocations give constant consumption streams: Given the present value of net payments to consumers, the insurer cares nothing about rearranging payments to provide a constant consumption stream. Given a constant consumption stream and concave utility, there is no way to increase the consumer's utility without raising the present value of the consumption stream.

We can most easily derive the Pareto-optimal allocation by finding the allocation that results from complete contingent claims markets. At time zero, the consumer sells claims to his income stream and buys contingent claims to cover health expenses and consumption. Since insurers are risk neutral (aggregate marginal utility is independent of an individual's health in the underlying general equilibrium), the time-zero value of contingent claims equals their discounted expected present value. Thus, the consumer's time-zero budget constraint in a contingent claim market is

$$E_0 \sum_{t=0}^{\infty} \beta^t c_t = W_0 + E_0 \sum_{t=0}^{\infty} \beta^t (e - x_t).$$

The first-order conditions to the consumer's optimization problem— maximize utility (1) subject to this constraint—specify a constant consumption level c at every date and in every state. Solving the budget constraint with constant consumption, we find

$$c = r\beta W_0 + r\beta E_0 \sum_{t=0}^{\infty} \beta^t (e - x_t).$$

Time-zero contingent claims contracts are (among other impracticalities) not *time consistent*; they do not satisfy a *participation constraint*. As soon as health status is revealed, healthy consumers and the insurers of sick consumers will withdraw. Since both parties are free to abandon the contract at the end of any period, a time-consistent contract must be equivalent to a series of one-period contracts. Therefore, we search for a market structure of one-period contracts that implements the Pareto-optimal or contingent claims allocation.

We need only two contracts or securities, one-period insurance, and riskless period-to-period saving (bank accounts). For insurance, the consumer pays a premium p_t in the first part of the period (see fig. 4.1). The insurer then pays this period's health expenses x_t, plus a potentially state-contingent severance payment y_t, whose value is determined below. This severance payment is the key to the chapter and the innovation that allows one-period contracts to insure lifetime health expenses.

Since insurers are risk neutral and competitive, the insurance premium must equal the expected value of payments,

$$p_t = E_t(x_t + y_t). \tag{2}$$

The insurer must expect to make zero profits from each consumer, period by period. Sick consumers must pay higher premiums or insurers will try to get rid of them; healthy consumers must pay lower premiums or other insurers can woo them away. Competitive insurers cannot cross-subsidize in the absence of two-sided commitment to long-term contracts.

Now we determine the severance payment y_t. After all payments are made, consumption equals the time t present value of resources:[1]

$$c_t = r\beta \left(W_t - p_t + y_t - E_{t+1} \sum_{j=1}^{\infty} \beta^j x_{t+j} \right) + e. \tag{3}$$

If consumption is to be constant, we must have $c_t = E_t c_t$. If we take expectations of equation (3), the unexpected severance payment must equal the innovation in the present value of health expenses:

$$y_t - E_t(y_t) = (E_{t+1} - E_t) \sum_{j=1}^{\infty} \beta^j x_{t+j}. \tag{4}$$

The market for one-period loans means that the consumer's intertemporal budget constraint is

$$W_{t+1} = (1 + r)(W_t + e + y_t - p_t - c_t). \tag{5}$$

One can verify that consumption is constant over time by combining this equation with the consumption decision rule, equation (3), and the value of severance payments y_t, equation (4).

The one-period, zero-profit condition, equation (2), and the full-insurance condition, equation (4), do not uniquely determine the optimal contract. If we add \$1 to the premium p_t, and \$1 to the payment y_t, neither condition is affected. Therefore, all Pareto-optimal (fully insuring), time-consistent, zero-profit contracts have the form

$$p_t = E_t(x_t) + b_t \tag{6}$$

and

$$y_t = (E_{t+1} - E_t) \sum_{j=1}^{\infty} \beta^j x_{t+j} + b_t, \tag{7}$$

where b_t is an arbitrary amount in the time t information set. The quantity b_t can be thought of as a bond. The consumer pays a premium equal to one-period expected health costs, $E_t(x_t)$, plus the bond; the bond is then returned along with the severance payment.

The choice $b_t = 0$ gives the simplest contract. Each period's premium equals expected health care costs in that period:

$$p_t = E_t(x_t). \tag{8}$$

The severance payment y_t is simply the revision in the present value of health expenses, by equation (7),

$$y_t = (E_{t+1} - E_t) \sum_{j=1}^{\infty} \beta^j x_{t+j} = (E_{t+1} - E_t) \sum_{j=1}^{\infty} \beta^j p_{t+j}. \tag{9}$$

Armed with this severance payment, a sick consumer can pay higher premiums with no change to his consumption stream. The second equality, derived from equation (8), shows that the severance payment is also the innovation in the present value of premiums. Therefore, we do not need to measure health expenses. The insurer's announced schedule of premiums provides all the information needed for the contract.

This contract requires that a consumer who gets unexpectedly *healthier* must make an ex-post severance payment *to* the insurer, equal to the unexpected *decline* in his health care expenses. Such payments may be hard to collect. Even one-period contracts may not be enforceable against consumers; we may wish to impose a participation constraint that the consumer can abandon the contract at any time, even in the middle of a period.

The health account described in the Introduction solves this problem. The consumer pays an amount q_t into the account in the first part of each period. The account pays health insurance premiums $p_t = E_t(x_t)$ and pays or receives severance payments y_t. Therefore, health account balances A_t evolve as

$$A_{t+1} = (1 + r) \, (A_t + q_t - p_t + y_t). \tag{10}$$

The consumer keeps the rest of his wealth in a savings account with balances K_t, so $W_t = K_t + A_t$. This component of wealth evolves as

$$K_{t+1} = (1 + r) \, (K_t + e - q_t - c_t).$$

Since income is constant, we might as well specify a constant out-of-pocket payment $q_t = q$. The account may be used only for health care or insurance payments, so the present value of out-of-pocket payments q_t must equal the present value of health expenses. Therefore, a constant payment q implies that q equals the time-zero flow present value of health expenses:

$$q = r\beta E_0 \sum_{j=0}^{\infty} \beta^j x_j. \tag{11}$$

In practice, income and health expenses typically rise through time, so it might make sense to specify a rising schedule of out-of-pocket expenses.

This system is still Pareto optimal and time consistent. Nothing has changed; we have just split the consumer's wealth into two accounts. Now, we check that the health account balance is always nonnegative. Then, the contract never requires ex-post out-of-pocket expenses; if the account is bonded to the contract, the consumer can leave at any time, including in the middle of a period.

Combining equations (11), (10), and (9), we find the health account balance:[2]

$$A_t = (1 + r)^t A_0 + E_t \sum_{j=0}^{\infty} \beta^j x_{t+j} - E_0 \sum_{j=0}^{\infty} \beta^j x_j. \tag{12}$$

Therefore, if the consumer enters the account healthy—if the present value of health expenses at the beginning of the contract is as low as it can be—then the amount A_t in the account will always be nonnegative, even if the consumer posts no initial bond $A_0 = 0$.

We have made no restriction on the time path of health expenses or expected health expenses. Therefore, the fact that health costs typically rise with age does not matter. If an old consumer reverts to perfect health, there is a large change in the present value of health expenses, but by then the account has built up a large balance.

A larger apparent difficulty results from the possibility of death. In our setup, death is a state of perfect health, since health expenditures will be zero forever after. As death approaches, the present value of health expenses declines. But at death, equation (12) seems to specify a large negative account balance.

However, consumption and income should also be zero after death, not constant as specified by the model so far. A generalized version of the model includes the possibility of death. (*Editor's note*: The details of the generalized model can be found in the appendix of J. H. Cochrane's article "Time-Consistent Health Insurance." 1995, *Journal of Political Economy* 103 (3):445–73). The consumer chooses consumption that is constant if he is alive and zero if he is dead. A time-consistent Pareto-optimal sequence of one-period contracts can again implement the optimum. The severance payment now includes the market value of an annuity as well as the market value of lifetime health expenses.

With the possibility of death, the health account balance of an alive consumer who starts with $A_0 = 0$ generalizes from equation (12) to

$$\frac{A_t}{E_t \Sigma_{j=0}^{\infty} \beta^j a_{t+j}} = \frac{E_t \Sigma_{j=0}^{\infty} \beta^j x_{t+j}}{E_t \Sigma_{j=0}^{\infty} \beta^j a_{t+j}} - \frac{E_0 \Sigma_{j=0}^{\infty} \beta^j x_j}{E_0 \Sigma_{j=0}^{\infty} \beta^j a_j} \tag{13}$$

where $a_t = 1$ if the consumer is alive at time t and $a_t = 0$ if he is dead at time t. The expression $E_t \Sigma_{j=0}^{\infty} \beta^j a_{t+j}$ is the value of a \$1 annuity and captures the changing probability of death.

This formula verifies that declining present values of health expenses due to higher probabilities of death do *not* trigger out-of-pocket payments or negative balances in the health account. For example, if health expenses are a constant x when alive, but their present value can change with changing probabilities of death, then equation (13) simplifies to

$$\frac{A_t}{E_t \Sigma_{j=0}^{\infty} \beta^j a_{t+j}} = \frac{x E_t \Sigma_{j=0}^{\infty} \beta^j a_{t+j}}{E_t \Sigma_{j=0}^{\infty} \beta^j a_{t+j}} - \frac{x E_0 \Sigma_{j=0}^{\infty} \beta^j a_j}{E_0 \Sigma_{j=0}^{\infty} \beta^j a_j} = 0.$$

The account has a constant balance for *any* probability of death.

The contract with an account amounts to a choice of a bond b_t in the setup of equations (6) and (7). If we drop the distinction between the consumer and the account, the consumer pays a premium equal to current wealth in the account plus q. This amount is equal to current expected health expenses plus a large bond b_t:

$$p_t = q + A_t = E_t(x_t) + b_t. \tag{14}$$

This bond is so large that the severance payment y_t always goes from insurer to consumer. If there is no change in health, the entire amount b_t is returned, to be posted as a bond again the next period. In practice, there is no point in having an actual payment move back and forth every period. *Rights* to the account are exchanged between insurer and consumer each period instead.

A time-consistent contract does not need to have severance payments every period. For example, the contract could specify a constant payment q per period, and the insurer pays health costs x_t. Both sides have the right to have the contract marked to market and an account created at any time, but they will typically do so only rarely.

Costs and Comparison with Other Contracts

One might think that time-consistent contracts are more expensive than other contracts. This turns out not to be true. Time-consistent contracts require no increase in payments relative to enforced standard contracts or the guaranteed renewable contracts described by Pauly, Kunreuther, and Hirth (1992).

Standard Contracts

The standard contract has no severance payment. There is a constant premium $\bar{p}$. For firms to make zero profits, the present value of premiums must equal the present value of health care expenditures. Hence,

$$\bar{p} = r\beta E_0 \sum_{j=0}^{\infty} \beta^j x_j.$$

A standard long-term contract, if enforced on both parties, *is* Pareto optimal (in the absence of product variety and competition considerations). Since the payments are constant, the consumption stream is constant. However, unless illness is entirely transitory—if $E_t\sum_{j=0}^{\infty}\beta^j x_{t+j}$ can differ from $E_0\sum_{j=0}^{\infty}\beta^j x_j$—the standard contract does not give time t zero expected profits and so is not time consistent.

The health account contract described above was set up so that the payment each period is $\bar{p}$. Thus, it obviously has the same cost as the standard contract. More generally, *every* time-consistent, Pareto-optimal contract has the same cost, ex-post, as the standard contract. It must. The essence of insurance is that ex-post wealth does not depend on losses. This statement can be verified as follows. Starting with equations (6) and (7), we have

$$\beta^j(p_j - y_j) = \beta^j E_j(x_j) - (E_{j+1} - E_j) \sum_{k=1}^{\infty} \beta^{j+k}x_{j+k} = E_j \sum_{k=j}^{\infty} \beta^k x_k - E_{j+1} \sum_{k=j+1}^{\infty} \beta^k x_k.$$

Summing over j, we obtain

$$\sum_{j=0}^{\infty} \beta^j(p_j - y_j) = E_0 \sum_{j=0}^{\infty} \beta^j x_j = \frac{\bar{p}}{r\beta}.$$

The left-most expression is the ex-post present value of payments in a time-consistent contract. It equals the time-zero expected present value of health expenses and the present value of standard contract premiums.

Of course, a fully insuring contract is more expensive than a zero-profit standard contract on which the insurer can default as soon as one suffers a long-term illness! Nonetheless, overall health care expenditures may or may not increase. Ex-post uninsured consumers currently find some alternative sources of financing—savings, charity, or the government—rather than forego all health care. Insured care is often thought to be cheaper than care for the uninsured, so overall expenses could decline.

Guaranteed Renewable Contracts

Pauly, Kunreuther, and Hirth (1992) advocate *guaranteed renewable* contracts to provide long-term insurance. In these contracts, the consumer always has the right to continued insurance at a prearranged premium. Guaranteed renewable contracts do not feature the severance payment, so all consumers of the same age must pay the same premium. To keep the healthy from defecting to a competing insurer, the premium charged to all must be the same as that charged to a healthy person. Therefore, consumers must prepay the expected value of the rise in premiums that will occur if they become sick.

Sick consumers must depend on and enforce the long-term commitment of their current insurers in a guaranteed renewable contract, whereas they are free to change in time-consistent contracts. And time-consistent contracts can be arranged to specify *exactly* the same payments as guaranteed renewable contracts. Again, the improvement is free.

Pooling

The majority of health insurance is currently provided through group plans or pools. Initially, group plans seem strange to an economist: What function do insurers serve except to *form* pools and diversify risk? But a system in which only pools, formed on a characteristic independent of health status, can be insured helps standard contracts to provide long-term insurance. Pools bind consumers to long-term contracts: If only a pool can be insured, ex-post healthy consumers cannot defect.[3]

However, pooling provides imperfect long-term insurance in a number of ways. Healthy individuals must be prevented from obtaining individual insurance at a lower, actuarially fair, rate. The tax deduction for employer-provided insurance may help to keep healthy individuals in employer-run pools from doing so. (At last, a reason for the much-disparaged deduction!) Labor contracts in which the employer contributes to a group plan, but will not contribute to a privately chosen plan or pay higher wages to consumers who choose such plans, have the same effect. These provisions have obvious distortionary consequences.

Furthermore, pool formation and movement into and out of a pool must be based on events that are independent of health status. They are not, and this is why employer-based groups are now losing long-term insurance. The ability to get or keep a job is obviously correlated with long-term illness. Since it is illegal to vary wages with health status, firms have an incentive to select healthier workers, and firms with healthy workforces can woo healthy workers away from competitors with less healthy workforces.

Most important, the stronger and larger the pool, the less product variety, competition, and resulting market discipline. It must be so: The *point* of the pool is to keep insurers from competing for healthy individuals or groups. Imagine the effect on the car market if everyone in a city or place of employment had to purchase exactly the same make and model of car!

Most current health regulation proposals seek to provide better long-term insurance by strengthening the pool mechanism, enlarging pools, and limiting freedom to change pools or insurers. The health alliances, community rating, employer mandate, limited options, and other features of the Clinton plan are devices to strengthen the pool mechanism. Strengthening and enlarging pools is also the essence of academics' plans, such as those of Enthoven and Kronick (1989) and Diamond (1992).

But the difficulties of providing long-term insurance and the resultant impetus to continue to expand the pools and limit competition will continue. Most plans propose location-based pools, but location is not uncorrelated with health status. Retired people move to Florida and Arizona, drug users live in inner cities, and people can move or change legal residence in order to pay lower premiums and receive better care. And many long-term illnesses may still not be covered in large regulated pools, since levels of treatment will depend on administrators' ideas of cost effectiveness or lobbying by patients with specific diseases, rather than individuals' preferences for health care versus other expenditures. Furthermore, as Weisbrod (1991) argues emphatically, further regulation of health care may dramatically reduce the rate of technical improvement in medicine.

In summary, the only pool that can provide complete long-term insurance is nationalized health insurance with mandated individual participation, because this is the only system that can really bind healthy consumers to a long-term contract and eliminate selection. This solution has zero competition, flexibility, and product variety. As pools are made smaller, competition and product variety increase, but the amount of long-term insurance decreases. Time-consistent contracts provide long-term insurance and allow competition at the individual level.

Extensions and a Few Objections

Measuring Health Expenses

Time-consistent contracts do not require a difficult and possibly contentious computation of expected health expenses. Changes in premiums can determine payments to the health account, since competition forces premiums to reveal expected health expenses. And if premiums do not change, the consumer does not need a severance payment to insure long-term illness, no matter what happens to expenses.

Calculating the change in the present value of future premiums is a little harder, but not impossible, since premium schedules are public information.[4] And even a rough accounting, say a severance payment equal to twenty times the change in premiums or an annuity that pays the higher premiums each period, can provide a workable approximation and a big improvement over no insurance. Similarly, home insurance is viable and useful, even though the exact value of a home and its contents is difficult to measure.

Imperfect Credit Markets

Time-consistent contracts can be implemented without credit markets. Diversified, competitive insurers earn zero profits each period, ex-post as well as ex-ante. Individual consumers save, but do not borrow, in premium accounts. The net amount in these accounts is constant, so a company that provides premium accounts does not need access to capital markets either.

Start-Up Problems

What about consumers who are *not* healthy when they first purchase insurance? They can sign on to the contract described above, paying the same amount per period $\bar{p}$ as everyone else, if they deposit in their account the amount that would be there if they had started the contract healthy. By equation (12), this is the current present value of their health expenses, less those of a healthy person, $E_\tau \sum_{j=0}^{\infty} \beta^j x_{\tau+j} - E_0 \sum_{j=0}^{\infty} \beta^j x_j$, where τ is the date on which the contract is signed.

It is likely that consumers can pay a much smaller deposit. Part of the account is a bond against the event that the consumer becomes healthier. If there is no chance that the consumer will revert to perfect health, there is no need for the corresponding portion of the bond. For example, if the consumer cannot get any healthier, he can pay each period the flow present value of his (higher) lifetime expenses, $\bar{p}_\tau = r\beta E_\tau \sum_{j=0}^{\infty} \beta^j x_{\tau+j}$, and deposit nothing in the account.

Alternatively, the contract can specify that the health account is simply not debited if the consumer becomes healthier than he is at the start of the contract. With this specification, the contract no longer provides perfect insurance. If the consumer becomes healthier than at the beginning of the contract, he will be able to consume more since his premiums decline and there is no offsetting severance payment. On the other hand, premium insurance will no longer be free. Consumers will have to be charged a higher premium to cover the missing severance payments. The contract is now an option and has positive value.

It is likely that this increase in premiums is small. In practice, most people with long-term illnesses are very unlikely to revert to perfect health, that is, become eligible for the low health insurance premiums of people with no history of disease. Therefore, the probability that they do so, times their lowered present value of health expenses, is quite small, and it would result in a small increase in premiums.

The government may wish to provide initial accounts or subsidize higher payments per period for consumers with genetic defects or poor family histories or those who are already sick when a time-consistent system starts. As with all insurance, there is a good argument that government policy should insure events that happened before contracts could be signed. Since the government is currently partially liable for the chronically ill, through Medicare, Medicaid, and other programs, the net cost may not be large. And subsidies based on long-term health status are less distorting than regulatory proposals to shore up long-term insurance.

Quality Variation

Individuals desire large variation in quality and other attributes of health care, as with all goods. Poor people generally choose lower quality care for lower premiums. Others vary in their trade-offs among cost, convenience, promptness of appointments, treatment by many specialists versus a single familiar general practitioner, desired level of treatment for specific conditions (e.g., professional athletes are willing to pay for much more extensive treatments of injuries than economists), willingness to suffer a restricted choice of physicians, and so forth.

Variations in quality and other attributes can be accommodated fairly easily in time-consistent contracts. The severance payment equals the change in present value of the *current* insurer's premiums. The consumer can change to a new insurer of the same quality at no out-of-pocket cost. However, if the consumer decides to change to a higher quality of insurer, he must pay the higher premiums out of pocket. Unobservable changes in preferences are not insurable.

Nondiversifiable Shocks and Technical Change

There are potentially important nondiversifiable shocks to health care expenses—events that do not average to zero over the insurer's customer base. Epidemics and natural disasters come quickly to mind, but regulatory surprises and unexpected improvements in technology are perhaps the most important nondiversifiable shocks in practice. Imperfectly diversifiable shocks do not rule out insurance. Insurance companies take risks, and large risks can be insured: hurricanes, oil spills, satellite launches, and so forth. Nondiversifiable shocks do raise some subtleties, and I examine three in turn.

Bankruptcy

Insurers may declare bankruptcy after a large negative shock. This problem can be addressed, as it is now, by requiring insurers to maintain loss reserves and capital requirements. Insurance contracts specifically exclude events so large that there is no hope of solvency, such as war. Year-to-year innovations in aggregate health expenses are not larger than other currently insured nondiversifiable risks or risks in other industries. There is nothing peculiar about long-term illness or health care in this limited liability problem.

Risk Premiums

With nondiversifiable shocks, insurers may require somewhat more than actuarially fair premiums. Faced with such premiums, sufficiently risk-neutral consumers may choose not to insure or to partially insure. But if risk premiums are small and consumers not too risk neutral, they may choose to buy essentially full insurance anyway.

Since insurers are public companies, risk premiums are determined in financial markets. Risks that are not diversifiable in the insurance sense may well be diversifiable in the finance sense: uncorrelated with the factors, such as market return, that drive expected returns in capital markets. If so, insurers will still act risk-neutrally. If not, the covariance of a risk with asset market factors determines its premium. Year-to-year variation in aggregate health expenses is small compared to other risks in the economy, and not highly correlated with those risks, so nondiversifiable health risk premiums are likely to be small, or at least not much larger than risk premiums in other, thriving insurance markets.

A quantitative example follows. Cutler (1992) analyses nondiversifiable technological risks in nursing home care. He estimates that profit rates in nursing home insurance are on the order of five percentage points larger than other, more diversifiable, insurance. Five percent is about as high a figure as one can hope to defend on the grounds of nondiversifiable risk in capital markets.[5] Now, in the simplest model,[6] the consumer buys insurance until

$$\frac{\text{wealth if sick}}{\text{wealth if well}} \simeq \left(\frac{\text{probability of loss}}{\text{premium per dollar coverage}}\right)^{1/\text{risk-aversion coefficient}}$$

With risk aversion of 1 (log utility) and a 5 percent risk premium, consumers will insure until sick wealth is only 5 percent below well wealth. If risk aversion is 10 or more, as suggested by the asset pricing literature, consumers will insure to the point at which sick wealth is only 0.5 percent less than well wealth: They will buy essentially full insurance. But nursing homes cost roughly $100 per day or $36,500 per year. Without insurance, sick wealth is likely to be 50 percent or less of well wealth. Thus, nondi-versifiable risks do not account for the unpopularity of nursing home insur-ance. (Good alternatives are that the contracts are not time consistent or that consumers plan to transfer or spend down assets and rely on Medic-aid.) Similar numbers are likely to apply for other long-term insurance.

On reflection, it is not surprising that risk premiums and risk aversion have small effects. Insurance policies already charge as much as 50 percent loadings for reasons unrelated to nondiversifiable risk premiums, and con-sumers buy them. An extra 5 percent loading is unlikely to have huge effects.

Technical Change

Expected improvements in technology, like any other expected event, do not trouble insurance contracts. *Unexpected* technical change is the only potential problem.

Technology does not automatically raise costs. Almost by definition, im-provements in technology imply declines in the *price* of treatment. When a cure for a previously untreatable disease is discovered, the *price* declines from infinity to some possibly large value. This decline in price, together with an elastic demand for medical care, can result in increased expendi-tures. Newhouse (1992) argues that this scenario explains the bulk of health care expenditure growth. When demand elasticities are low, improved technology lowers costs, such as when a drug treatment is discovered to replace surgery.

Technological innovations are basically events that trigger a changed de-sire for quality. Given that a heart transplant is possible, consumers are willing to pay for a policy that gives more generous payments to patients with heart disease.

Under current contracts, premiums are changed to accommodate in-creased use of new technology, and the consumer bears most of the risk. Time-consistent contracts can at least incorporate new technology in the same way. As with other changes in quality, the contract can state that individual customers who are reclassified in the current premium structure receive severance payments. After severance payments have been made, the insurer can announce an across-the-board premium change to accommo-date different treatments or expenditures, which does not trigger a sever-ance payment.

In fact, time-consistent contracts may smooth the adaptation to new technology. In a long-term contract, consumers are wary that the insurer that raises premiums is trying to avoid long-term debts to individuals or groups that have become sicker than average, rather than adapt to new tech-nology. With a time-consistent contract, consumers who do not like the new premiums and level of care, or who simply think that the insurer is trying to gouge them, can take their severance payment to another insurer that charges the original premiums and provides the original level of care.

However, we cannot insure against technological risks by keying sever-ance payments to any changes in premiums, including those that adapt to new technology. Consumers would claim that a new technology should be used for every ache, that expenses and premiums should skyrocket, and that a huge severance payment should be made so that they can pay for the much higher level of health expenses. Insurers would claim the opposite.

The problem with changes in technology is not time consistency or pri-vate information. The problem is contracting costs. If contracting costs were zero, the contract could specify in advance the level of expenses for every health state, in every possible state of technology. Then consumers would choose not to pay for contracts that provide too lavish treatment when new technology is introduced.

Contracting costs are obviously not zero, and contracts contingent on undreamed-of inventions are obviously impractical. The question is, To what extent can feasible contracts or institutions approximate this contin-gent claim result? Many other contracts are successfully written and en-forced even though every contingency cannot be spelled out. In this case, we just need some mechanism for deciding how much health expenses should adapt to unexpected changes in technology. The standard solution is appeal to a disinterested third party. Contracts could index the adoption of new technology to standards promulgated by the American Medical As-sociation, other private organizations, or independent bodies set up for the purpose, or government rules such as Medicaid reimbursement rules. Then severance payments keyed to any premium increases would provide at least some insurance against unexpected technical change.

Adverse Selection, Moral Hazard, and Participation

Private information is a standard objection to any insurance contract. Pri-vate information about health at the beginning of the contract can cause adverse selection. Private information about actions taken during the con-tract or about what state has actually occurred can cause moral hazard.

Selection is not "adverse selection." The stories of sick consumers who lose their insurance represent selection based on *public* information, and so they are not evidence for a private-information failure of the long-term health insurance market.

Adverse selection has not been documented to cause specific failures of health insurance contracts and the absence of long-term insurance in particular. Do individuals, armed with private information about their aches and pains, really know much more than a doctor, armed with a medi-cal history and simple tests? The answer is not obvious. If anything, the health economics literature stresses the opposite conclusion. Pauly (1986, 650–51) notes several aspects of current health insurance that are at odds with adverse-selection models. Among others, the fact that insurers do not now condition on easily observable indicators of health status argues against a market right up against an information constraint, and the fact that most people *are* insured argues against a lemons model in which only the sickest get insurance. Cutler (1992, 35–37) argues similarly that private information does not account for the failure of the nursing home insurance market.

Private information about lifestyle choices that affect long-term health is also a doubtful explanation for the lack of long-term insurance. Many lifestyle choices alleged to influence long-term health risks are in fact observable: eat too much, don't exercise, and you get fat; it's easy to tell who smokes, uses intravenous drugs, and so forth. And the influence of lifestyle choices on the incidence of disease is (alas) not that great. Many long-term illnesses, such as Alzheimer's disease, are not related to any known controllable and potentially unobservable actions by the individual, so moral hazard does not explain why they should not be insured.

Private information about ex-post health cannot account for the lack of long-term insurance. There is no question that someone with, say, cancer or AIDS actually has the disease and needs *some* treatment. While overuse of medical services resulting from the fact that doctors and patients know more than the insurer about the patient's health is an important issue, it should doom insurance according to the observability of an illness, not according to the persistence of an illness. Mental illness is poorly insured precisely because its severity is hard to measure. Many long-term illnesses have clear diagnoses and narrow ranges of treatment and yet are still not insured.

In summary, textbook private-information stories are not easy explanations for the absence of long-term health insurance, especially given that short-term health insurance does exist. At a minimum, the analysis of time-consistent contracts in a public-information setting is a good starting point for understanding how and what private information is really at the bottom of inadequate health insurance. At a maximum, private information, though the subject of an enormous and fascinating literature, may just not have much to do with this particular economic problem.

More recently, contract theory has found an explanation for imperfect insurance under perfectly symmetric information, in a participation constraint. In Kocherlakota's (1994) example, two people share a constant income that will be divided randomly and publicly between them. They can write contracts, but either side can always revert to autarky. Therefore, the optimal sharing rule must partially reward the lucky agent to keep his utility above what he could get by eating the lucky draw and withdrawing from the contract. The result is imperfect insurance despite complete information. I have argued above that it is exactly the consumer's inability to commit not to defect to a competing insurer if he turns out to be healthy—a state observed by both sides—that makes the standard contract unravel. Therefore, the branch of contract theory that studies imperfect commitment or participation constraints under symmetric information seems a much more useful parable for the failures of long-term health insurance. In these models, the Pareto optimum is again achievable if one side can be forced to honor state-contingent severance payments. This chapter presumes that insurers can be held to one-period contracts, and it shows how such payments can be arranged.

Why Don't We Observe Them Already?

If better contracts are available, why have they not already been instituted? Imperfect credit markets, measurement of health status, variation in quality, nondiversifiable shocks, technical change, risk aversion, and private information do not pose insurmountable obstacles to the implementation of time-consistent contracts, so none of these factors explains why we do not already see such contracts. In addition, time-consistent contracts do not seem outlandishly costly to write.

Contracts may simply have adapted imperfectly to changed medical and economic circumstances. A generation ago, health expenses were mostly temporary. Health care was largely devoted to treating injuries and some infectious diseases. Other illnesses, such as cancer, usually led to rapid and inexpensive death or to chronic but untreatable and, hence, inexpensive conditions. Only recently has technology changed to allow long-term, expensive treatment of persistent illnesses.

Furthermore, health insurance was less competitive a generation ago. Large insurers could cross-subsidize sick customers from the premiums of healthy customers. As competition increased, new entrants vigorously searched for healthy customers, leaving the older insurers with only the sick or old. Insurers were forced to respond by charging higher premiums for the sick. In the same way, telephone companies have been forced to stop cross-subsidizing local from long-distance telephone service following the breakup of AT&T.

Contracts did adapt. Group plans now predominate, whereas most people bought individual health insurance a generation ago. Since pooling is a partial solution to the time inconsistency of long-term contracts, we can read this transition as an evolutionary adaptation to the increasing need for and difficulty of providing time-consistent long-term insurance.

But contracts are now stuck at a local maximum. More pooling will hurt competition and product variety, whereas less pooling will imply less insurance of long-term illness. The *optimal* contract cannot be found by local variation about existing contracts. It requires the simultaneous institution of severance payments and publicly acknowledged risk rating.

In addition, health insurance is already a highly regulated market, and current regulations or the fear of future regulation may discourage the radical experimentation required to arrive at time-consistent contracts. An insurer that proposed the extreme experience rating of time-consistent contracts would certainly wake up insurance regulators! Epstein (1997) argues that regulatory and legal impediments account for many pathologies of insurance markets. In particular, he argues that courts often reinterpret insurance contracts ex-post, judge the merits of each clause separately rather than how the clauses fit together to form a reasonable contract, and will not enforce severance payments or bond forfeiture against consumers. He finds that the fear of court reinterpretation has eliminated innovation in product warranties of a much smaller scale than the change to time-consistent health insurance contracts.

In summary, it seems at least possible that time-consistent contracts can be implemented, even though they have not yet been implemented. A well-documented story for the absence of long-term and time-consistent insurance is an important topic, requiring a detailed study of the regulatory and competitive history of the health insurance market that is obviously beyond the scope of this chapter. The correct story for the absence of long-term health insurance will also have important policy implications. If the story is an unintended pathology of regulation, it will argue for a careful *de*regulation of insurance markets.

Concluding Remarks

I have described Pareto-optimal, time-consistent health insurance contracts. These contracts *fully* insure consumers against all health risks, even long-term, expensive risks that are not insured under current contracts. The contracts feature severance payments equal to the present value of premium changes or, equivalently, insurance against changes in premiums. Consumers are not tied to insurers, so the disasters that befall sick consumers who now lose their health insurance do not occur, and this freedom promotes competition and product variety in health care and insurance. Surprisingly, contracts with this feature don't require more payments than standard health insurance contracts, but merely require a rearrangement of the rights to which those payments give rise.

The Clinton plan, most congressional proposals, and most regulation plans advanced by academics take exactly the opposite approach. At a most basic level, the plans force insurers and consumers into long-term contracts, rather than specify a time-consistent structure. The plans herd people into large pools, whereas individuals can purchase time-consistent contracts. The plans try to stop insurers from using health information to set premiums, whereas time-consistent contracts allow extreme rating. The plans force healthy consumers into the system to pay for the sick, whereas everyone pays actuarially fair premiums in a time-consistent contract. To avoid competition for healthy consumers, the plans must mandate much uniformity of health care and severely limit competition, whereas time-consistent contracts allow any amount of competition and product variety. Most important, the plans all feature a large regulatory structure. They must, to keep people from responding to obvious economic incentives: to keep insurers and providers from trying to improve their pool or reduce levels of care and to keep individuals from trying to get better care at lower prices. Time-consistent contracts are a decentralized market solution, and it is likely that deregulation will be required to implement them.

Notes

I acknowledge financial support from the National Science Foundation and the University of Chicago Graduate School of Business. I thank Richard Epstein, Deborah Haas-Wilson, David Meltzer, Sherwin Rosen, Tom Sargent, José Scheinkman, Jonathan Skinner, anonymous referees, members of the Applications Workshop at the University of Chicago, and especially Elizabeth Fama for many helpful comments.

1. Precisely, equation (3) gives consumption if contingent claims markets are opened in the second half of period t. Since we are implementing a contingent claim outcome, this expression must also give consumption in our restricted market structure.

2. Equation (12) obviously holds at time zero. Supposing it holds at time t, I show that it holds at time $t + 1$. From equations (8), (9), and (10),

$$\beta A_{t+1} = A_t + q - x_t + (E_{t+1} - E_t) \sum_{j=0}^{\infty} \beta^j x_{t+j}$$

From equations (11) and (12),

$$\beta A_{t+1} = (1 + r)^t A_0 + E_t \sum_{j=0}^{\infty} \beta^j x_{t+j} - E_0 \sum_{j=0}^{\infty} \beta^j x_j + r\beta E_0 \sum_{j=0}^{\infty} \beta^j x_j + \beta E_{t+1} \sum_{j=0}^{\infty} \beta^j x_{t+1+j} - E_t \sum_{j=0}^{\infty} \beta^j x_{t+j}$$

$$= (1 + r)^t A_0 - \beta E_0 \sum_{j=0}^{\infty} \beta^j x_j + \beta E_{t+1} \sum_{j=0}^{\infty} \beta^j x_{t+1+j}.$$

Canceling β and rearranging, we get equation (12).

3. It is often claimed that the prevalence of group insurance reflects economies of scale—higher administrative costs for servicing individuals or greater bargaining power of pools (see, e.g., Diamond 1992, 1234). But if this is the reason for pools, why don't individuals or third companies form pools to buy health insurance? Or why don't competitive insurance companies form the pools, that is, sell individual insurance at the pool rate in the first place? The alternative story in the text gives an answer: Pools must be formed on characteristics unrelated to health status. If one could form the pools for the purpose of getting or providing health insurance, selection based on health status would start, and the system would no longer provide long-term insurance.

4. See Feenberg and Skinner (1992) for a good example of dynamic health cost calculations.

5. For example, the capital asset pricing model states that expected returns obey

$$E(R^i) - R^f = \beta_{im}[E(R^m) - R^f],$$

where R^i is the return on a given security or investment project, R^f is the risk-free rate, R^m is the market return, and β_{im} is the regression coefficient of R^i on R^m. The market risk premium $E(R^m) - R^f$ is about 7 percent, so a profit rate of 5 percent over the risk-free rate requires a regression coefficient of nursing home technology risk on the market return of about $5/7 = 0.7$. Cutler estimates the standard deviation of the present value of an insurance company's liability at 4–14 percent, and the standard deviation of the market return is about 17 percent. To generate a 0.7 regression coefficient, then, we need the highest standard deviation estimate and the unlikely assumption that nursing home technology risk is almost perfectly correlated with the market return ($\beta_{im} = \rho_{im}\sigma_i/\sigma_m$). If a 5 percent risk premium is taken over a normal rate of return that is higher than the Treasury bill rate, even more extreme assumptions are required.

6. There are two states, sick s, and well w. State s occurs with probability π. There are two dates, and consumption equals wealth at the second date. A premium p pays $1 in the s state. The consumer's first-order condition is

$$\frac{u'(c_s)}{u'(c_w)} = \frac{p/(1-p)}{\pi/(1-\pi)}.$$

With constant relative risk-aversion preferences, $u'(c) = c^{-\gamma}$, and for small p and π we can ignore the $(1-p)/(1-\pi)$ term, so this expression implies

$$\frac{c_s}{c_w} \approx \left(\frac{p}{\pi}\right)^{\frac{1}{\gamma}}.$$

References

Aaron, Henry J. (1994) "Issues Every Plan to Reform Health Care Financing Must Confront." *Journal of Economic Perspectives* 8, 31–44.

Cutler, David M. (1992) "Why Doesn't the Market Fully Insure Long-Term Care?" NBER Working Paper 4301.

———. (1994) "A Guide to Health Care Reform." *Journal of Economic Perspectives* 8, 13–31.

Diamond, Peter A. (1992) "Organizing the Health Insurance Market." *Econometrica* 60, 1233–54.

———. (1994) "Two Improvements on the Clinton Framework." *Journal of Economic Perspectives* 8, 61–66.

Enthoven, Alain C., and Richard Kronick (1989) "A Consumer Choice Health Plan for the 1990's." *New England Journal of Medicine* 320, 29–37 and 94–101.

Epstein, Richard (1997), Mortal Peril: Our Inalienable Right to Health Care? New York: Addison-Wesley.

Feenberg, Daniel, and Jonathan Skinner (1992) "The Risk and Duration of Catastrophic Health Care Expenditures." NBER Working Paper 4147.

Fudenberg, Drew, Bengt Holmstrom, and Paul Milgrom (1990) "Short-Term Contracts and Long-Term Agency Relationships." *Journal of Economic Theory* 51, 1–31.

Himmelstein, David U., et al. (1989) "A National Health Program for the United States: A Physician's Proposal," *New England Journal of Medicine* 320, 102–8.

Kocherlakota, Narayana R. (1994) "Efficient Bilateral Risk Sharing Without Commitment," unpublished manuscript, University of Iowa.

Malcomson, J., and F. Spinnewyn (1988) "The Multiperiod Principal-Agent Problem," *Review of Economic Studies* 55, 391–407.

Newhouse, Joseph P. (1992) "Medical Care Costs: How Much Welfare Loss?" *Journal of Economic Perspectives* 6, 3–21.

———. (1994) "Symposium on Health Care Reform," *Journal of Economic Perspectives* 8, 3–12.

Pauly, Mark V. (1986) "Taxation, Health Insurance, and Market Failure in the Medical Economy," *Journal of Economic Literature* 24:2, 629–75.

———. (1994) "Universal Health Insurance in the Clinton Plan: Coverage as a Tax-Financed Public Good," *Journal of Economic Perspectives* 8, 45–54.

Pauly, Mark V., Patricia Danzon, Paul Feldstein, and John Hoff (1991) "A Plan for Responsible National Health Insurance," *Health Affairs* 10, 5–25

Pauly, Mark V., Howard Kunreuther, and Richard Hirth (1992) "Guaranteed Renewability," unpublished manuscript, University of Pennsylvania.

Poterba, James M. (1994) "A Skeptic's View of Global Budget Caps," *Journal of Economic Perspectives* 8, 67–74.

Rey, Patrick, and Bernard Salanie (1990) "Long-Term, Short-Term and Renegotiation: On the Value of Commitment in Contracting," *Econometrica* 58, 597–619.

Weisbrod, Burton A. (1991) "The Health Care Quadrilemma: An Essay on Technological Change, Insurance, Quality of Care and Cost Containment," *Journal of Economic Literature* 29, 523–52.

Zeckhauser, Richard (1994) "Public Finance Principles and National Health Care Reform," *Journal of Economic Perspectives* 8, 55–60.

PART II

THE USE OF INFORMATION IN MARKETS

5

Decision Markets

ROBIN D. HANSON

The human part of any large intelligent system is by far the most intelligent part. As long as this remains true, the biggest system advancements will come from aids that fill big holes in human abilities, rather than from artifacts that stretch engineers' abilities. Consider Post-it Notes or, better yet, plain paper notepads. These probably seemed like trivial ideas, but they turned out to be terribly useful. Why? Because the marvel that is the human brain has a horrible short-term memory, which means that dumb-as-dirt memory aids can make people substantially smarter.

I mention all this because I want you to consider a simple, not very technically challenging idea—one that might nevertheless fill a gaping hole in our collective intelligence, similar to the way notepads fill a gaping hole in our individual memories. I am talking in general about speculative markets and in particular about decision markets. Decision markets might allow us to more accurately estimate the consequences of important decisions by helping us to better share relevant information.

Consider, for example, a clearly important policy question such as, How would crime rates change if more citizens could legally carry hidden guns? Many observers say hidden guns obviously increase crime, while many others strongly disagree (see Lott, 2000).

I suspect that the existence of such divergent opinions reflects the fact that we suffer from a serious failure to share information. The so-called Information Revolution has greatly improved our ability to find out what others have said. However, it has done much less to improve our ability to find out what other people know. We can now find a blizzard of words on a topic such as the interplay between guns and crime, but we know that most of those words are written by people with axes to grind. The real problem is not finding more words, but judging who really knows about the topic and whether these experts are saying what they know. We are in many ways bit-full, yet information-poor.

I suggest that speculative markets are a neglected way to help us find out what people know. Such markets pool the information that is known to diverse individuals into a common resource, and they have many advantages over standard institutions for information aggregation, such as news media, peer review, trials, and opinion polls. Speculative markets are decentralized and relatively egalitarian, and they can offer direct, concise, timely, and precise estimates in answer to questions we pose. These estimates are self-consistent across a wide range of issues and respond quickly to new information. They also seem to be cheap and relatively accurate. In particular, for questions concerning hidden guns and crime, I suggest we consider decision markets, which are speculative markets focusing on particular decisions.

How Decision Markets Work

Imagine that we created markets where people could bet on future crime rates, conditional on allowing or not allowing more hidden guns. That is, if the market prices predicted that murder rates would be 10 percent higher should a certain hidden-gun bill pass, then anyone who thought this estimate too high could easily identify a particular profitable trade. If you made this trade and the market estimate then fell to 5 percent, for example, you could undo this trade for a profit.

Imagine further that if market prices said that crime rates would be 10 percent higher given more hidden guns, most nonexperts would accept this estimate as our "best answer" or as a neutral "consensus." In particular, a state legislature might accept this estimate when considering whether or not to pass this hidden-gun bill.

I call such a set of markets a decision market. In this situation, advocates for each side of an issue would be forced to influence speculators if they wanted to influence general opinion. Speculators, in turn, would have a clear incentive to be careful and honest in contributing what they know and in judging what advocates know. This is because speculators must "put their money where their mouth is."

Six steps are required to create a decision market to help us better share information on a topic such as the effect of hidden guns on crime.

First, you must state your claim clearly. For example, you might focus on a particular bill B before your state legislature, which would allow more citizens to carry hidden guns. You might decide to focus on your state's murder rate, using some standard government statistic M as your official measure of it. You should choose a lowest and highest relevant murder rate, and scale M so that $M = 0$ at the lowest rate and $M = 1$ at the highest rate. (You might choose, for example, the lowest rate to be zero murders and the highest rate to be the population size, which is the highest conceivable murder rate.)

Next, you must choose some particular trusted third party who will finally declare a murder rate M within [0,1] and determine whether bill B passed. (This party might be a jury randomly drawn from some pool.) You must also pick a date by which these judges are to decide, tie the judging to some other event like the release of murder statistics, or grant the judges discretion to choose this date for themselves.

Third, you must choose what asset A you will bet. If the bet is going to last any substantial time, asset A ought to give a reasonable rate of return to induce speculators to invest in it. You might pick a safe government bond or a broad-index stock mutual fund.

Also, given M, B, and this asset A, you authorize some financial institution to make exchanges between units of A and the following set of four assets:

1. M units of A if B passes,
2. M units of A if B does not pass,
3. $1 - M$ units of A if B passes,
4. $1 - M$ units of A if B does not pass.

Note that because $M + (1 - M) = 1$, and because B either will or won't pass, this financial institution takes no risk from these exchanges; each set of four assets will be worth exactly one unit of A in the end.

Fifth, you create markets in which people can trade various combinations of these assets with each other. In particular, if people trade asset 1 for the bundle of assets 1 and 3, the market price (asset ratio in trades) is an estimate of the murder rate conditional on the bill passing. Similarly, the price in trades of asset 2 for the bundle of 2 and 4 is an estimate of the murder rate conditional on the bill not passing. Moreover, comparing these two estimates tells you whether, and by how much, speculators expect this bill to increase or decrease the murder rate.

Finally, you have to decide how much to subsidize this market. If interest in your topic is strong enough, simply creating these markets might induce people to trade in them. Failing that, sufficient interest might be induced if someone committed to make a policy choice based on the market estimate. A state legislature, for example, might commit to pass the bill or not depending on the market estimate of its effect on the murder rate.

You can also safely and directly subsidize a market to induce more participation. Doing this, in effect, creates an information prize offered to those who first make the market price better reflect relevant information. (In econo-speak, one way to do this is to create a market maker whose bid and ask prices are monotonic functions of its assets held.)

In addition to estimating the effect of hidden guns on crime, decision markets might give us estimates on

- Murder rates—with or without capital punishment?
- Average mortality rates—with or without national health insurance?
- Health-care spending—with expanded or curtailed use of health maintenance organizations?
- Employment change—raise minimum wage or rescind NAFTA?
- Global sea-level and temperature changes—impose or not impose a carbon dioxide tax?
- Military casualties—with a Republican or a Democratic president?
- Stock prices—with a Republican- or Democrat-controlled U.S. Congress?
- World per capita food consumption—raise or lower average tariffs?
- Student test scores—with or without school choice or voucher reform?
- Future national economic growth—raise or lower interest rates, or with or without an education subsidy?

Science fiction writers have posited even more ubiquitous betting markets (see John Brunner's *Shockwave Rider* and Marc Steigler's *Earthweb*). In general, decision markets can estimate the net effect of any policy choice of interest on any outcome of interest, as long as there is a decent chance that, after the fact, we can reasonably verify what outcome happened and what policy was chosen.

How Well Do Markets Work?

By its nature, a betting-market estimate is decentralized, direct, concise, timely, precise, self-consistent, and responds quickly to new information. It is also egalitarian if everyone is allowed to participate. But how clear, cheap, and accurate are such market estimates?

On accuracy, decades of research on the efficiency of financial markets have found little price-relevant information that is not reflected in market prices. Any inefficiencies seem to be weak and to go away with publicity, because they represent a profit opportunity. If you think the current price is too low, you expect to profit by buying now and selling later, and buying now will raise the price, partially correcting the error you perceived.

Speculative markets have done well in direct tests against standard information-aggregation (IA) institutions. For example, orange juice futures prices have been shown to improve on government weather forecasts (Roll 1984). Also, markets where traders can bet on election results predict vote totals better than opinion polls (Forsythe et al. 1992).

How do markets do so well? After all, aren't they made of the same fallible humans as other institutions? A study of those election markets found that while most traders tended to suffer from cognitive biases such as expecting others to agree with them, the most active traders were not biased this way—and active traders set the prices. Speculative markets thus seem to induce the real experts to self-select and participate more. Lab experiments also indicate that speculative markets tend to aggregate information when traders are experienced with their roles and know the payoffs for other roles (Forsythe and Lundholm 1990).

Older economics writings sometimes give the impression that speculative markets will not function unless you have thousands of traders frequently trading millions of dollars worth of goods. Recent Web markets, however, clearly show that markets can be much smaller and slower than this. Furthermore, a subsidized market can function over any time period with only one trader. If an information prize is offered, and only one person is induced to learn enough to only once correct the initial market price to something else, the market has still served a valuable information role.

With subsidies, the key question is not whether we can create speculative markets or whether such markets can induce people to learn and reveal information. The key questions are whether the information gained is worth the costs paid and whether a similar benefit could have come cheaper via some other institution.

What's the Holdup?

If speculative markets are so great at IA, why don't we already use them to form consensus on topics such as the correlation between hidden guns and crime? Until the last few centuries, the cost of simply handling trades was enough to sharply limit the number of speculative markets that could be made widely available. Yet today, ebay.com routinely sells $10 items by having a handful of people bid a few times each over a period of a week. Moreover, play-money Web betting games have shown that just a handful of people, each making a few small trades over several years, can create reasonable estimates to a wide variety of questions. (See http://www.hsx. com, http://myhand.com, and especially http://www.ideosphere.com.)

More important, most speculative markets are now illegal. The short history of financial market regulation is that everything was once illegal until limited exemptions were granted for specific purposes. Betting on cards was a foolish waste of money, only fools would invest in a business they did not closely monitor, and it was the height of folly to let people bet on the death of others. So casinos, stocks, and insurance were all banned (Rose 1986).

Gradually, exceptions were granted for what came to be seen as worthy purposes, such as teaching people about horses (horseracing) or raising state revenue (lotteries). Stocks were allowed for the purpose of capitalizing firms, and insurance was allowed to let individuals hedge risks. More recently, commodity futures and financial derivatives were allowed to let firms hedge more risks. All these areas are highly regulated, however, in part to prevent limited exemptions from devolving into general gambling.

Accepted functions of markets now include entertainment, capitalization, and hedging, but not IA. Thus, while it is widely recognized that markets created for other purposes accomplish IA, we're prevented from creating a market whose primary function is IA. So we cannot create a market whose legal price would inform raging policy debates, such as the interplay between crime rates and hidden guns.

Okay, betting markets are mainly illegal. But if economists have data suggesting that speculative markets do well at IA, why aren't lots of economists pushing the idea of better IA via more markets?

Actually, it's worse than you think; economists also have sophisticated theory that suggests that IA should not be that hard on factual topics like the effect of hidden guns on crime (Hanson 1997). Thus, economic theory really does suggest that we humans have a gaping hole in our social intelligence.

So why aren't economists pushing IA markets? One answer is that economists are just spread too thin. Economic theory suggests many policy improvements over the status quo, and there are few economists that anyone else will listen to. These few economists thus have to choose their battles carefully.

The relevant theory for IA is also recent, and most economists don't yet know about it. Worse, the IA functions of markets seem too complex to model in much generality. When systems become too complex to model in detail, engineers usually resort to building and testing theory-inspired prototypes. However, economic-theorist types who understand this area are reluctant to move that far away from theory. (Capitalization and hedging functions of markets are easier to model, and economists do use theory to design market prototypes for these functions.)

Therefore, it seems to fall to a few economics-savvy and engineering-minded folks to think of using prototypes to explore the idea of using more speculative markets for IA. On the types of topics to which they have been applied so far, IA markets have looked promising. There remain, however, many legitimate concerns. For example, does the existence of speculative markets discourage communication via other channels, and is this a net benefit or loss?

Tests of prototypes might help us answer such questions. But how can we test prototypes if IA markets are generally illegal? Well, there is one plausible loophole (besides offshore gambling), which I have saved for those of you who are still reading this far: internal corporate markets. Corporations have great leeway in what they make employee bonuses depend on, and a contingent bonus is pretty close to a bet. So several companies, including Hewlett-Packard and Siemens, have begun experimenting with real-money internal speculative markets for estimating things such as future sales.

Corporations also need to make decisions, and they often have problems inducing relevant parties to reveal information about the consequences of those decisions. Furthermore, companies have a good rough-and-ready measure of "good for the company"—the stock price. Thus, you could create decision markets that estimate whether any particular decision, such as introducing a new product, is better or worse than some alternative for the stock price. Alternatively, you might predict the sales of some product contingent on some important product-design decision.

Just as notepads fill a gaping hole in our individual cognitive abilities, speculative markets might fill a gaping hole in our collective ability to share information. Economic theory suggests that IA should not be that hard, at least for factual policy questions like the effect of hidden guns on crime rates. Speculative markets seem to work well at such tasks. Let us develop prototypes to explore this potential, in the hopes of someday lifting current legal barriers to widespread use of more effective institutions for IA.[1]

Note

1. For more information on this topic, see http://hanson.gmu.edu/ideafutures.html.

References

Forsythe, R., and R. Lundholm, "Information Aggregation in an Experimental Market," *Econometrica*, Vol. 58, No. 2, Mar. 1990, pp. 309–47.

Forsythe, R., F. Nelson, G. R. Neumann, and J. Wright, "Anatomy of an Experimental Political Stock Market," *American Economic Review*, Vol. 82, No. 5, Dec. 1992, pp. 1142–61.

Hanson, R. Four Puzzles in Information & Politics, PhD thesis, California Inst. of Technology, Pasadena, Calif., 1997.

Lott, J. *More Guns, Less Crime*, University of Chicago Press, Chicago, 2000.

Roll, R. "Orange Juice and Weather," *American Economic Review*, Vol. 74, No. 5, Dec. 1984, pp. 861–80.

Rose, I. N. *Gambling and the Law*, Gambling Times Inc., Hollywood, Calif., 1986.

PART III

THE SHORTAGE OF HUMAN ORGANS

6

A Market for Organs

ANDY H. BARNETT, ROGER D. BLAIR,
AND DAVID L. KASERMAN

Public awareness of the critical shortage of cadaveric human organs made available for transplantation was recently heightened by the unfortunate case of Mickey Mantle. Mr. Mantle's need for and relatively rapid receipt of a liver transplant brought widespread attention to the plight of thousands of other sufferers of heart, liver, lung, and kidney failure whose lives depend upon timely receipt of a suitable organ for transplantation. It also brought considerable suspicion and outright scorn regarding the integrity of the current system used to allocate these scarce organs among the growing pool of patients who need them. Disputes about allocation issues, however, tend to have the undesirable effect of diverting attention away from the more serious topic of devising public policies that will ultimately resolve the organ shortage. If the shortage problem is eliminated, allocation issues become moot.

Consequently, the principal message that should emerge from Mr. Mantle's case is not one involving the fairness of the system used to allocate those organs that are procured. Rather, it is that our current public policy has miserably failed to address the organ shortage. And that failure, in turn, has caused needless suffering and death. Rather than begrudging Mr. Mantle his transplant, we should seek out new public policies that will deliver the gift of life to others as well.

In this essay, we propose an alternative public policy that, we believe, is capable of fully resolving the organ shortage. This policy relies upon the powerful incentives provided by free-market forces to bring forth the additional supply of organs required to meet demand. We compare this policy—organ markets—to the major policy alternatives currently under discussion and find that, in every case, the performance properties of the market system dominate. We also consider both the economic and ethical arguments that have been raised in opposition to organ markets and find each of them to be demonstrably specious. As a result, we conclude that the current legal restriction on the purchase and sale of cadaveric organs should be lifted. This relatively simple alteration of our public policy would eliminate the organ shortage and, thereby, save thousands of lives each year.

The Cause of the Shortage

Thousands of critically ill patients presently wait for cadaveric organs that are desperately needed for transplantations, and many of these patients will die before a suitable organ becomes available. Numerous others will experience declining health, reduced quality of life, job loss, lower incomes, and depression while waiting, sometimes years, for the needed organs. And still other patients will never be placed on official waiting lists under the existing shortage conditions, because physical or behavioral traits make them relatively poor candidates for transplantation. Were it not for the shortage, however, many of these patients would be considered acceptable candidates for transplantation.

At the same time, however, many more organs are buried each year than the number of patients needing them. The sad fact is that only 15–25 percent of the cadaveric organs that could be donated are recovered. Thus, the current organ shortage and its associated costs are not mandated by nature but are the result of a failed public policy that refuses to recognize the intrinsic economic and human value of cadaveric organs.

The policy that yields this unfortunate result has been in place since kidney transplants first became feasible in the mid-1950s. It was eventually codified into law with the passage of the National Organ Transplant Act of 1984, sponsored by then-U.S. Senator Albert Gore. This act makes the purchase or sale of human organs, even cadaveric organs, a felony. The official price of transplantable organs, then, is legally fixed at zero regardless of the relationship between demand and supply or the suffering and deaths that result. With the price fixed at zero, altruism is the sole motivating force for generating a supply of cadaveric organs under this policy. Importantly, this myopic policy has *never* yielded enough organs to satisfy demand, nor is there any reason to expect that it ever will.

The chronic failure to meet the annual demand for cadaveric organs has created a large and growing backlog of patients in need of transplantable organs. In 1987, there were 11,872 persons waiting for kidneys, 450 for livers, and 646 for hearts; by 1995 those numbers had grown to 29,238, 4,817, and 3,241, respectively, and there were 1,796 persons waiting for lungs. Moreover, this backlog (or waiting list) has recently begun to expand at an increasing rate as organ demand has continued to grow at an accelerated pace and organ supply has remained approximately constant. The resulting shortage is a tragedy.

Anyone who has studied basic economics could readily explain that the zero-price policy is the obvious cause of the current organ shortage: There are virtually no products, including cars, oranges, or other medical services, for which such a policy would not create a shortage. Consequently, responsibility for the unnecessary deaths and human suffering that are caused by this policy-created shortage falls squarely on the sponsors and supporters of the ill-conceived law that proscribes voluntary market exchange at a positive price. Similarly, any student of economics could suggest a straightforward policy to eliminate the shortage of transplantable organs: Allow the market price to rise to its equilibrium value. In other words, legalize the purchase and sale of cadaveric organs. Such a policy would vastly increase the number of organs made available for transplantation, thereby saving numerous lives. Both organ recipients and organ donors (or suppliers) would benefit from such free-market exchange.

Proposals to adopt a market system of cadaveric organ procurement, however, have met strong opposition, particularly from physician and hospital groups. These groups have made both economic and ethical arguments in support of the current altruistic system and in opposition to a market system. In this essay, we critically evaluate these arguments and find that each is specious on either theoretical or empirical grounds or both.

The question then arises: If the current organ procurement policy is so obviously flawed and the arguments against a market system are clearly mistaken, then why was the current system adopted and, more important, why has it persisted so long? The rather cynical but, we believe, correct answer lies in the policy's impact on profits to physicians and hospitals. The economic truth is that reliance on altruism at one stage of production can serve the purpose of greed at another. The supply restriction that accompanies a zero-price policy increases physicians' and hospitals' profits in much the same way that the politically motivated crude oil "shortage" of the early 1970s increased petroleum companies' profits to so-called obscene levels. A legal restriction on the purchase and sale of transplantable organs is economically equivalent to the formation and maintenance of a cartel in the provision of transplant services. The supply of transplant operations cannot expand if additional organs are not made available. Therefore, the current policy and the shortage it creates enhance the overall profitability of transplant providers. Such profitability, in turn, ensures continuing political support for that policy.

Costs of the Current System

Many of the costs created by the organ shortage are obvious to the most casual observer of the present system. These costs include the more than two thousand deaths that result each year from the inability to obtain needed organs, plus the myriad social costs associated with the waiting process itself (declining health, reduced quality of life, unemployment, reduced earnings, and the medical costs of trying to keep patients alive while waiting for an organ). Other costs are perhaps less obvious but are equally substantial.

First, a clear symptom of the chronic organ shortage is the use of living donors for those organs for which such donation is possible (primarily kidneys). The number and percentage of kidneys transplanted from living donors in the United States have increased noticeably in recent years, from 1,811, 20 percent of the total number of kidneys transplanted, in 1988, to 2,663, 24.1 percent of the total, in 1994. Currently, approximately 25 percent of U.S. kidney transplants use living donors.

The marginal improvement in results obtained from using living donors instead of cadaveric organs is rapidly declining as new immunosuppressive drugs are discovered. Today, that margin is arguably not worth the added costs associated with subjecting a young, healthy individual to even a slight risk of subsequent renal problems or death. In addition to these risks for living donors, the operation required to remove the donated kidney (the nephrectomy) is painful, and the long recovery period is costly. Thus, the suffering and lost time from work experienced by living donors add to the social costs of the current cadaveric organ procurement system. If the supply of cadaveric organs could be expanded, reliance on living donors could be reduced substantially.

We are not arguing that these costs fail to yield substantial social benefits in terms of recipients' health and productivity, but, rather, that they are unnecessary given the more-than-adequate supply of cadaveric kidneys that would result under a market system of procurement. Such a system would largely obviate the need for living donors.

Dialysis of patients awaiting kidney transplants is a second source of costs that could be substantially reduced by a more rational organ procurement system. In 1993, there were 158,214 patients undergoing dialysis each year. Of these, as many as half were potential candidates for transplantation. Moreover, transplantation is a significantly more cost-effective treatment than dialysis. Researchers have estimated that five years on dialysis costs approximately $60,000 more than a successful kidney transplant. Because both dialysis and transplant costs are paid by the Health Care Financing Administration, a substantial increase in the number of kidney transplants performed each year would help reduce the federal budget deficit by lowering the costs of this program by several million dollars annually.

Moreover, these cost savings reflect only the direct financial costs of the two alternative treatment modalities. They fail to account for the additional social benefits associated with the more active and productive lifestyles that transplantation provides. Dialysis treatments are extremely time consuming. They generally require three to five hours per treatment, with three such treatments per week. Setting up and disconnecting the patient from the dialysis machine adds at least another hour to each treatment. In addition, the dialysis process tends to be debilitating. Most patients are unable to perform even sedentary work for several hours following treatment. As a result, most dialysis patients are unemployed and experience an overall quality of life that is significantly below that of a successful transplant patient.

A third source of unnecessary costs is the inefficient market structure that the current policy fosters in the organ transplant industry. Specifically, the public policy that outlaws sales of cadaveric organs encourages hospitals to start their own transplant programs, because that is the only way they can capture the economic rents (or true market value) contained in the organs they collect for free. The artificial shortage created by the zero-price policy pushes the value of the relatively few organs that are collected far above the market-clearing level. This rise in value is especially large given the highly price-inelastic demand for organs. Such value is referred to as economic rent. Because the agent (currently the hospital) that collects these organs cannot legally sell them to a transplant center or to a patient, it can only capture the economic rent by also performing the transplant operation. That is, the economic rents that go uncollected by the altruistic donor do not disappear but are, instead, captured by the transplant surgeon and the hospital at a subsequent stage of production—the transplant operation.

As a result of this economic incentive, we have witnessed a surge in the number of transplant centers in the United States over the past decade, even as the number of transplants performed annually has remained virtually constant. Many of these new centers perform fewer than five transplants per year. In economic terms, the transplant industry is experiencing substantial entry by inefficiently small firms. Entry occurs when profits rise above normal levels in an industry. Normally, such entry then drives the market price back down to the competitive level by increasing supply, therefore eliminating excess profits.

In the transplant industry, however, entry does not increase supply; it merely redistributes the available organs among a larger number of transplant centers. Consequently, entry reduces profitability by pushing costs up rather than pushing prices down. The result is a highly inefficient industry structure with more than the cost-minimizing number of transplant centers.

Alternative Procurement Schemes

Of course, we are not the first to recognize that the current organ procurement system is woefully inadequate and that the social cost of failure to reform the system is high. In addition to popular press accounts, academic studies of organ procurement span a wide range of disciplines and are published in a variety of medical, legal, economic, political science, and public policy journals. This literature contains several specific proposals for reforming organ procurement.

Before we turn to a description of these proposals for reform, it is useful to identify two reasons that current organ procurement efforts are unsuccessful. First, some of those charged with collection fail to ask potential donors for permission to collect organs. Second, when asked, some potential donors fail to give permission for organ collection. All proposals for procurement reform attempt to address one or both of these fundamental reasons for failure to collect available organs.

Variations of six alternative organ procurement proposals have appeared in the extensive literature on the subject. The proposed alternatives include: (1) express donation (the current system), (2) presumed consent, (3) conscription (also termed an "organ draft"), (4) routine request, (5) compensation, and (6) a market for cadaveric organs. We describe briefly each policy in turn.

Express Donation

In general, a cadaver suitable for organ removal is one of an individual who was relatively young and healthy at the time of brain death. Such patients typically die as a result of a head injury that leaves the remainder of the body intact. Express donation requires that someone on the medical team treating the deceased patient, or a designated organ procurement officer, approach the patient's family at or near the time that brain death is declared to request permission to remove organs for transplantation.

Current law prohibits any offer of tangible compensation for permission to collect the organs. The system depends entirely on altruism on the part of the family of the deceased. Furthermore, physicians and other health care personnel attending the potential donor at the time of death are also motivated by altruism, because no explicit payment is made for their services in obtaining the necessary permission for the organ collection process to proceed.

Although altruism may be an admirable trait, it has consistently failed to generate an adequate number of organs to meet the needs of potential transplant recipients. Despite efforts to increase supply through increased advertising, expanded education of potential donors and their families, and training of physicians in more effective methods of asking for donation, for each of the last twenty years, the number of organs donated annually has fallen short of the number of patients added to the transplant waiting list. Thus, there is absolutely no question that the current policy has failed and that continuing attempts to somehow make it work will be futile.

Presumed Consent

Because the current system has failed so resoundingly to provide an adequate number of organs for transplantation, some analysts have advocated a policy that removes the necessity of asking potential organ donors, or their families, for permission to remove organs. Instead, they propose that unless a patient has made an affirmative statement to the contrary, the presumption is that there is no objection to organ collection. Such a presumption relieves medical personnel of the necessity of asking for permission to remove organs of the deceased. Instead, it requires that those who object to organ donation make a premortem declaration of their preferences.

The impact of presumed consent on organ collection rates could vary considerably depending upon the requirements set for "opting out" of the organ donation process. For example, refusal of rights to collect could require that individuals register their opposition with a central registry. As an alternative, withholding collection could be accomplished simply by carrying a signed "organ nondonor card." Surviving family members may, or may not, be given a right to object to organ collection under this policy. Obviously, the more difficult it is to object and the fewer the number of parties allowed to object, the larger the collection rate will be under presumed consent.

The logic behind this proposal is that most people do not object to having their organs removed for transplantation and that most would give permission if given the opportunity. The shortage of organs, then, is seen as largely attributable to the failure of medical personnel to ask for permission to remove organs. In other words, this policy addresses the "failure-to-ask" problem associated with the current policy.

This proposal, however, raises two serious concerns. The first is a practical matter of political feasibility. Any strategy for organ procurement is likely to meet with only limited success if most of the public object to its enactment. In a recent survey of U.S. citizens, the United Network for Organ Sharing found that most individuals objected to a policy that would allow physicians to remove organs without the donor's express permission. Fifty-two percent of respondents answered no when asked if physicians should be allowed to act on presumed consent, 39 percent said yes, and 8 percent were undecided.

The second issue is one of abstract ethics. In evaluating medical policies and procedures, ethicists typically subject those policies and procedures to some set of basic criteria in judging their ethical acceptability. While the criteria differ somewhat among ethicists, most would include a requirement that the policy respect the autonomy of individuals, including their autonomous choices. A policy that presumes that an individual agrees to donate their organs without an affirmative statement to that effect fails this basic ethical test.

Thus, a policy of presumed consent faces obstacles of both a political and ethical nature. Moreover, presumed consent policies have been adopted in several European countries. While organ collection rates appear to improve under this policy, they have failed to rise sufficiently to eliminate the organ shortage.

Conscription ("Organ Draft")

Conscription addresses the problems of failure to ask and of failure to give permission for organ collection. It does so by largely or entirely removing the necessity for acquiring donors' permission before organs are removed for transplantation.

In its strongest form, conscription would allow physicians to collect the organs of any deceased patient, without regard for the wishes of the patient or the patient's family. In a somewhat weaker form, the patient may have a right to prevent collection by registering a formal objection prior to death. But the surviving family members would have no rights in the matter. Thus, conscription is merely a strong form of presumed consent, and as such, it is subject to the same criticisms.

Because conscription either completely denies the patient any right to object to organ collection or, at the least, makes refusal to donate relatively burdensome, it is likely that this policy, if adopted, would substantially increase the number of organs collected. But this increase comes at a cost. The ethical and political feasibility issues that arise with presumed consent are amplified with conscription. Indeed, conscription fails the basic ethical test of respect for the autonomy of individuals to such an extent that it is difficult to imagine how such a policy could ever be acceptable in a democratic society.

Routine Request

This policy is designed to insure that those who would be willing to donate organs if asked have an opportunity to express their preferences. It does little, however, to provide any incentive for potential donors to grant permission when they are asked.

With routine request, everyone would be required, at some convenient point of contact, to express their preference for or against allowing their organs to be removed in the event that they die under conditions that would make organ collection feasible. For example, an expression of preferences could be required on income tax returns or at the time that driver's licenses are issued or renewed. These stated preferences would then be recorded in a way that would make them easily accessible to hospitals. Hence, when an individual who may be a candidate for organ collection dies or is near death, attending health care personnel could consult the source in which organ donation preferences are recorded.

Such a scheme for organ procurement could potentially increase the number of organs collected. This increase is most likely if the preferences expressed by potential donors are considered binding, that is, if surviving family members are not allowed to revoke permission to collect organs. On the other hand, if surviving family members are consulted and allowed to revoke permission, the increase in donations becomes speculative and is likely to be modest at best. It is worth noting that several states have tried routine request in driver's license renewals without substantial increases in the number of organs collected.

Compensation

Growing disillusionment with the ability of current organ procurement practices to provide an adequate number of transplantable organs, along with discontent over apparent inequities in transplantation, has prompted a small but increasingly vocal group of individuals to advocate compensation for donors or their families as an added inducement to consent to organ collection. While appeals to altruism and human kindness could still be made when potential donors are approached, advocates of compensation propose some form of payment as added inducement to grant permission for organ collection.

Such payments could be made either to donors who make premortem commitments to have their organs removed at death or to family members when permission to remove organs is given postmortem. For example, Dr. Thomas G. Peters has proposed a $1,000 payment to donor families, and Dr. Stephen Jensik has proposed paying burial expenses for donors. Other proposals include waiving driver's license renewal fees or providing income tax credits for those who are willing to sign binding organ donor agreements.

Although compensation focuses on the problem of providing an incentive to allow organ collection when asked (that is, it does not address the failure-to-ask problem), as it becomes well known that donors can receive payment, donor families may take the initiative in inquiring about opportunities to donate. Hence, over time, compensation may also increase the number of organs collected, because it may reduce problems associated with failure to ask. Nonetheless, it is apparent that compensating donors does nothing to directly provide an incentive for medical personnel to ask permission to collect organs. Therefore, this policy option falls short on that front.

The principal drawback of the compensation proposal, however, is that under this policy there is no assurance that the monetary (or other) incentive provided will be sufficient to bring forth the additional supply required to eliminate the organ shortage. If the amount chosen is inadequate, the shortage will continue. And in the unlikely event that it is excessive, there will be an excess supply and waste. Because the system contains no equilibrating mechanism, the number of organs supplied is unlikely to ever be in line with the number demanded.

Organ Markets

Because the issue of markets for human organs is so emotionally charged and often misunderstood, let us be clear about what advocates of markets do, and do not, propose. They do not propose barkers hawking human organs on street corners. They do not envision transplant patients, or their agents, dickering for a heart or liver with families of the recently departed. They do not advocate a market for organs from living donors. Indeed, markets are seen as a device that could reduce the need for living donors by increasing the number of cadaveric organs collected. Proponents of markets do not advocate an auction in which desperate recipients bid against each other for life-sustaining organs. And most market advocates propose using the price system only for organ collection, not for distributing collected organs among potential recipients.

What *is* proposed is a system in which agents of for-profit firms offer a market-determined price for either premortem or postmortem agreements to allow the firm to collect organs for resale to transplant centers. For example, insurance companies could enter the organ procurement market by merging with existing organ procurement organizations. Then, organ procurement officers who presently negotiate with families of recently deceased individuals could offer payment in cash or burial expenses for the right to remove the needed organs. Such a system would be equivalent to providing the deceased with an ex-post term life insurance policy with no premium. Alternatively, individuals may be offered a reduction in medical insurance rates in return for a premortem annually renewable agreement that allows their insurance company to collect and sell their organs in the event that they die during the policy year in a way that makes organ collection feasible. Firms that collect organs would then sell them to transplant centers that place orders for needed organs.

Compared to the current policy, markets for organ procurement dramatically change both the incentive of organ procurement personnel to ask permission to remove organs and the incentive of potential donors to grant that permission when asked. Markets provide tangible rewards, that is, profits, to those who are successful at organ collection. Hence, organ procurement firms have incentive to seek out potential donors and to structure requests and payment packages that are most likely to induce a positive response to the request for permission to collect the organs. Further, payment to organ donors provides a direct incentive, in addition to any altruistic inclination they may have, to grant permission.

Compensation versus Organ Markets

Like markets, compensation for organ suppliers provides payment to those who make a premortem commitment to have their organs collected at death or payment to family members when permission to remove organs is given postmortem. Nonetheless, markets for cadaveric organs and compensation for organ suppliers differ in several important respects. Because these differences are often not well understood, a brief discussion of them is in order.

The most important distinctions between markets and compensation concern the way in which prices (compensation) are determined and the types of incentives generated by these prices. Market prices are determined by demand and supply. In organ markets, the prices in question are those paid to organ suppliers (donors) by buyers (organ procurement firms) who, in turn, sell the acquired organs to transplant centers, who may then allocate those organs on the basis of medical need or some other medical criterion. An important goal of the procurement firm operating in such a market is to make a profit on organ transactions. The opportunity to enhance income by procuring organs provides an incentive for those engaged in procurement to develop strategies (including offering cash, in-kind payments, or a package of both) that are most effective in inducing organ suppliers to agree to have organs removed. Further, since reducing costs can increase profits, organ procurement firms, operating in a market regime, have an incentive to acquire organs in a cost-efficient manner.

With market procurement, when shortages arise, prices increase. Such increases in price cause the potential profitability from organ procurement to grow. As a result, organ procurement firms offer increased inducements (including higher prices) to organ suppliers. Other things being equal, we would expect these higher prices to induce more organ suppliers to agree to have organs removed, thereby increasing the number of organs supplied. As a consequence, market forces ensure that prices will adjust toward equilibrium (market-clearing) levels, thereby reducing and eventually eliminating shortages. That is precisely how these forces operate in other markets, and there is no reason to expect any different performance in organ markets.

The amount paid to organ donors under a compensation policy, however, is not determined by market forces. As noted above, Peters has proposed a $1,000 payment and Jensik has proposed compensation equal to burial expenses for the donor. Other proposals are similar in that the proposed compensation is set more or less arbitrarily. Further, compensation proposals contain no mechanism that would allow prices to adjust as demand and supply change. This means that prices would not move toward equilibrium levels and, consequently, shortages or surpluses may persist indefinitely.

In addition, with compensation, those who procure organs do not acquire a property right in the organ; therefore, they are not the claimants of any profits that might be generated from the efforts required to obtain organs. Compensation, unlike markets, offers little opportunity for those who are in a position to procure organs to directly increase their personal wealth by more effective and efficient procurement efforts. Consequently, those charged with organ procurement simply have less incentive in a compensation system than in a market system to acquire additional organs and to do so in a way that is cost efficient. Therefore, to the extent that the existing organ shortage is due to a failure to ask potential donors for permission to remove organs at death, compensation does very little to resolve the problem.

In short, organ markets and compensation differ in two important ways. First, with compensation, the form and amount of payment to organ suppliers are largely arbitrary, whereas market prices change with supply and demand so as to eliminate shortages. Second, markets provide greater incentives to individuals involved in the procurement process both to acquire more organs and to acquire them in a cost-efficient manner.

Opposition to an Organ Market

Arguments opposing market-based organ procurement are most often based either upon impassioned claims regarding the moral or ethical superiority of altruism over market forces or upon mistaken impressions about how such a market would actually function. In addition, several economic arguments against the use of markets have been offered. Both sets of arguments demand critical evaluation.

Economic Arguments

Several commentators have argued that payment to organ donors may reduce some individuals' desire to supply organs freely. That is, although some people who will not donate at a zero price might be willing to supply organs if they receive payment, others who might freely donate without compensation will refuse to supply organs if offered payment. If the number discouraged by compensation exceeds the number for whom payment is a positive inducement, then the total number of organs available for transplantation could conceivably fall when payment is offered.

Whether the introduction of positive prices will actually reduce organ supply by driving out altruistic donors is essentially an empirical issue. Unless one actually tries our proposed solution, the data will not be available to resolve the issue. We do know, however, that our current reliance upon altruism is misplaced because the quantities donated are consistently less than the quantities needed. In any event, we do not believe that the net effect will be a reduction in the number of organs available for transplant.

Two observations that appear beyond dispute suggest that the number of organs available under a market-based procurement system will not fall but will, instead, increase substantially. First, the number of organs demanded for transplantation is more a biological necessity than a decision based on price; hence, the number of organs demanded is unlikely to fall substantially when organ prices rise above zero.

Second, in general, there is some price at which the quantity of transplantable organs demanded and the quantity supplied will be equal: the market equilibrium price. As we noted above, quantity supplied is substantially less than quantity demanded at the current zero price (i.e., there is a large shortage). Because the demand for organs is insensitive to price movements, the quantity of organs demanded is unlikely to be substantially less at this equilibrium price than at the current zero price. If quantity demanded changes little with price and if there is a shortage at the current price of zero, then the number of organs supplied must be greater at the equilibrium price than at a zero price. In short, simple economic reasoning strongly suggests that the number of organs supplied with market-based procurement will be greater than the number supplied under the altruistic system.

Will market procurement affect the quality of organs harvested? Substituting payment for altruism may reduce the share of organs obtained from comparatively higher income individuals and increase the share obtained from lower income individuals. If the quality of harvested organs is influenced by the general health of donors and if income and health are positively correlated, then average organ quality may be adversely affected by market-based procurement. But if market-based procurement makes more organs available, as we believe it will, a decline in the quality of organs *collected* need not mean a decline in the average quality of organs *transplanted*. The current shortage forces surgeons to use substandard organs or to perform transplants despite a poor tissue match. For example, a recent policy change increases the maximum age of potential organ donors in order to increase the available supply. And many kidney transplant centers have also increased the number of transplants performed using living, unrelated donors. When more organs are available, higher standards can be set for transplantable organs. The average quality of transplanted organs, then, will be higher, not lower, with organ markets.

Ethical Arguments

Although opponents' ethical concerns about organ markets are seldom clearly stated, the primary issues are ensuring accessibility to organs by the poor, maintaining incentives to provide adequate care for critically ill patients, and promoting altruism in society. These ethical concerns, however, stem entirely from misinformation and faulty reasoning.

First, misperceptions about accessibility to organs are based on the premise that recipients will pay donors for organs and on the conjecture that organ prices will be high. At present, most of the costs of an organ transplant are borne by insurance companies and Medicare; otherwise, low-income patients would simply be unable to have transplants. In other words, under the current system, transplants are paid for by someone other than the organ recipient. This system of subsidizing transplant costs for relatively poor patients could easily be extended to cover the costs of organ procurement.

On a more technical note, the alleged inability of the poor to purchase organs is based on the unlikely premise that only a high price can induce an adequate supply of organs. This argument confuses anecdotal evidence regarding the current value, which is greatly inflated by the shortage, with a market equilibrium price. Because there is now a severe shortage, potential organ recipients may be willing to pay a very high price for a suitable organ to avoid extended waiting times. But if a relatively modest payment is all that is required to induce potential donors to contribute an adequate supply of organs, the market equilibrium price of organs will be low. Given this low price, the likelihood of third-party payment, and the expected increase in the number of organs collected, moving to a market-based organ procurement system will, in fact, increase the availability of organ transplants to the poor.

Moreover, there is some evidence that the current altruistic system discriminates against the poor. Claims of list jumping by wealthy or influential recipients are widespread. The Mickey Mantle incident is a case in point. The 1984 National Organ Transplant Act, which created a nationwide computerized network for matching donors and recipients, has reduced opportunities for abuse, but some argue that a well-placed contribution to a medical facility can still influence the distribution of scarce organs. Where legalized trade of a valuable asset is prohibited, black-market activity is likely, if not inevitable. A market-based policy that makes organs plentiful and relatively inexpensive will reduce such abuses and benefit poor patients.

How will the presence of organ markets affect the care of critically ill patients from whom organs could be harvested? Some market opponents have argued that when cadaveric organs can be sold, physicians may have an incentive to withdraw care prematurely from critically ill potential organ donors. This concern is totally misplaced. First, it is based on the presumption that the market price of organs will be high enough to make premature termination of care tempting for attending physicians. As we explained above, however, market prices of organs will likely be low. When the procurement system produces an adequate supply at a comparatively low price, there is little incentive to allow patients to die so that their organs can be sold.

Second, and more important, the attending physician for a critically ill patient is not the seller of organs harvested from that patient. Indeed, in the market system we envision, participation in organ transplantation by medical personnel attending the donor could be and probably should be prohibited. In this event, attending physicians gain nothing from the donor's death. The market value of the organs of critically ill patients is assigned much like a bequest in a will. Someone will receive compensation from the patient's death, but not the attending physician. Thus, concerns about premature termination of care under a market system are founded upon blatant misconceptions about how the system would operate in practice.

Finally, some commentators advocate maintaining the current system in order to promote altruism in society. At the risk of oversimplifying, the argument appears to be that promoting altruistic organ donations is a step in the direction of promoting a kinder, gentler genuine concern for each other. It is a laudable goal, but should medical practitioners expect those who desperately need organs to delay transplantation or to die for a lack of a suitable organ so that others can indulge their penchant for altruism? If we pursued a similar policy for providing food, people would starve. More to the point, if, in a spirit of altruism, we prohibited surgeons or transplant centers from being paid for transplant procedures, we might find a shortage of both surgeons and transplant centers. We might also find a change in the views of medical associations toward the social virtues of altruism.

Organ Shortages and Economic Profits

The preceding discussion reveals that the predominant arguments supporting the current system over market-based organ procurement systems are seriously flawed. As a result, one must ask why the altruistic system has persisted for so long. The answer lies in the economic interest of physicians and hospitals in maintaining an organ procurement policy that effectively restricts supply. For example, those parties involved in the treatment of end-stage renal disease stand to profit from a kidney shortage. Dialysis is both a substitute for transplantation and a means of survival until a suitable organ can be found. A shortage of kidneys for transplantation, therefore, increases the market demand for dialysis, which in turn increases the profits of dialysis centers. Recent increases in the rate of entry into the dialysis business by new, for-profit dialysis centers suggests not only that these profits exist but also that they are quite large. The number of for-profit providers of dialysis has increased by more than 150 percent since 1980.

In addition, economic reasoning suggests that transplant centers and surgeons also profit from an organ shortage. Because transplants cannot be performed without transplantable organs, restricting the supply of organs effectively restricts the number of transplant procedures performed. Just as restricting the supply of crude oil increases the price at which it can be sold, restricting the number of transplants performed increases the price that can be charged for transplant operations. In effect, reliance upon altruism in the supply of cadaveric organs becomes a mechanism through which a cartel-like restriction on transplant output can be enforced.

Evidence that transplant centers and surgeons profit from the organ shortage is found in the rate at which new transplant centers have been opening. A 1989 *Wall Street Journal* article by Ron Winslow chronicled the "rush to transplant organs," noting that "health experts fear an explosion in the number of transplant facilities." Apparently, many health care facilities want their share of the lucrative and prestigious transplant business.

Obviously, medical professionals and their societies do not base their public opposition to organ markets on an overt observation that such markets would reduce profits or incomes. Moreover, we do not doubt that physicians' expressed concern for the well-being of patients is sincere. Nonetheless, the fact remains that the current system, which these parties continue to support, serves the economic self-interest of physicians and medical institutions. A market for cadaveric organs, on the other hand, would serve the interests of patients and organ suppliers at the expense of suppliers of medical services. While self-interest may not directly dictate physicians' policy positions, it tempers their receptiveness to the arguments they confront.

Prospects for Real Reform

The adage "If it ain't broke, don't fix it" clearly does not apply to our current cadaveric organ procurement policy. By any objective standard, it is a failed policy costing thousands of lives each year in addition to unnecessary suffering and financial loss. As long-time students of public policy issues, we have witnessed many other ill-conceived policies, yet we can safely say that we have never encountered a policy more at odds with the public interest than our current organ procurement system. In short, the present policy has two pronounced effects: It increases costs and it kills patients.

The issue of organ procurement is an emotional one, and discussing solutions objectively and analytically is difficult. But emotional issues do not require illogical solutions. Until the interested parties—physicians, hospitals, patients, and policymakers—can rationally consider alternative cadaveric organ procurement policies that rely on the powerful forces of the free market, the existing shortage will only worsen. Although Mickey Mantle suffered scorn because he received an organ, thousands of other patients will suffer death because they will not receive an organ. It is these latter patients that deserve our attention.

Suggested Further Reading

A. H. Barnett and David L. Kaserman, "The Shortage of Organs for Transplantation: Exploring the Alternatives," *Issues in Law & Medicine*, Fall 1993, pp. 117–37.

———, "The 'Rush to Transplant' and Organ Shortages," *Economic Inquiry*, July 1995, pp. 506–15.

A. H. Barnett, T. Randolph Beard, and David L. Kaserman, "The Medical Community's Opposition to Organ Markets: Ethics or Economics?" *The Review of Industrial Organization*, December 1993, pp. 669–78.

A. H. Barnett, Roger D. Blair, and David L. Kaserman, "Improving Organ Donation: Compensation versus Markets," *Inquiry*, Fall 1992, pp. 372–78.

Roger D. Blair and David L. Kaserman, "The Economics and Ethics of Alternative Cadaveric Organ Procurement Policies," *Yale Journal on Regulation*, Summer 1991, pp. 403–52.

L. R. Cohen, "Increasing the Supply of Transplant Organs: The Virtues of a Futures Market," *George Washington Law Review*, 1989, pp. 1–51.

Henry Hansmann, "The Economics and Ethics of Markets for Human Organs," *Journal of Health, Politics, Policy, and Law*, Spring 1989, pp. 57–85.

Ron Winslow, "Hospitals Rush to Transplant Organs," *Wall Street Journal*, 29 August 1989, p. B1.

7

The Organ Shortage

A Tragedy of the Commons?

ALEXANDER TABARROK

The current system for motivating the supply of human organs has failed to end the shortage. Thousands of people die every year while they wait helplessly for an organ transplant and thousands more will die in the next few years. These deaths could be avoided if more people signed their organ donor cards. Yet, every year, the organ shortage tends to become worse as medical technology increases the number of potential beneficiaries while social apathy and fear keep the number of donors relatively constant. Today, roughly 60,000 people are waiting for organ transplants, although less than 10,000 will become donors. Despite a prominent advertising campaign with Michael Jordan as spokesperson and a national campaign of pastors, rabbis, and other clergy supporting donation, the number of donors remains far below what is necessary to save everyone on the waiting list.

For many years, a number of economists and economics-minded lawyers have offered their solution to the crisis: remove the legal restrictions on the purchase and sale of human organs (Becker 1997; Epstein 1993, 1997; Cohen 1989; Pindyck and Rubinfeld 1998; Barnett, Blair & Kaserman (1996, this volume).[1] The economic argument is familiar. Just as rent controls create a shortage of rental apartments, government rules that outlaw the buying or selling of organs on the open market hold the price of organs at zero and make an organ shortage inevitable. Lift the restrictions, Becker and others say, and the shortage will end.

Despite the strong support of a number of economists and the publicity given to the organ market idea through newspaper opinion-editorial pieces, television segments (*60 Minutes* ran an excellent segment on the idea that featured Lloyd Cohen), and other media outlets, many people remain uncomfortable with the thought of providing compensation for the donation of or "selling" of human organs. Discomfort with organ sales is so strong that even some people who are desperately waiting for an organ are against allowing monetary compensation for donation. Many people feel that organ sales violate a moral intuition about the inalienability of the body (the same argument is often raised against legalizing prostitution).[2]

Others believe that opening a market for human organs would lead to an unfair distribution of organs. At present, most people believe that organs are allocated solely according to medical criteria (matching donors to recipients to prevent rejection), need, and length of time on the waiting list. This is not entirely correct because current rules favor local donations, thereby creating gross discrepancies in waiting lists across arbitrary U.S. regions (Institute of Medicine 1999). Nevertheless, most people believe the current system is fair.[3]

Allocating organs, at least in part, by ability to pay is often perceived as unfair. Perceptions of unfairness are so pervasive that markets in organs may be precluded politically, even if they would increase organ donation rates and result in fewer overall deaths. Monetary compensation to the donor could be arranged without the necessity of payment from the recipient, thereby avoiding this issue. But the counterargument of those who think that markets are unfair is that monetary compensation is the "thin edge of the wedge" that would eventually usher in monetary purchase.

For these reasons, it appears unlikely that markets in human organs will be created at any time in the foreseeable future. For better or worse, few politicians are willing to take up the banner of laissez-faire in organ procurement and donation. If the organ shortage is to be alleviated, it must be done through a method consistent with moral intuitions.

Economists typically analyze current government policy toward organ donation as a price control set at zero. Eliminating the price control is the natural policy prescription given this perspective. It is possible, however, to analyze the issue quite differently but still through an economic lens. The current government policy toward organ donation creates a commons—and thus a tragedy of the commons. Enclosing the commons is the natural policy prescription from this perspective.

At present, the policy of the United Network for Organ Sharing (UNOS) is that organs are a "national resource." Any citizen who meets certain conditions is allowed access to this national resource regardless of whether he or she contributed to the upkeep. Organs are treated like fish in a lake owned in common. Anyone is allowed to fish in the lake, but the decision to restock is private and voluntary. Since the benefits of restocking flow to everyone whether or not they bear any of the costs of restocking, we can expect that the lake will become overfished and understocked. The same thing has occurred with the supply of organs. Anyone is allowed access to the supply, but contributing imposes private costs on signers of the organ donor card.[4]

The costs of signing an organ donor card are in part psychological—perhaps the potential donor does not want to think about his own mortality or suspects that donation will interfere with proper enjoyment of the afterlife.[5] More concretely, some potential donors fear that if they sign their cards and are involved in a life-threatening accident, they are less likely to be revived than nondonors.[6] The costs of signing an organ donor card, whatever their source, are significant enough so that most people *do not* sign their organ donor cards. Further, and most important, nonsigners have just as much access to the organ pool as signers. Since the "national resource" of transplantable organs is owned in common, and since those who refuse to contribute to the resource lose no tangible benefits from their refusal, it's not surprising that relatively few people agree to be potential organ donors.

The traditional solution to a tragedy of the commons problem is to enclose or "privatize" the commons. In the case of transplantable human organs, this can be done by restricting organ transplants to those who previously agreed to be organ donors; in short, a "no-give, no-take" rule. I suggest that we think of signing the organ donor card not as an altruistic gift but as the necessary price to be paid for entry into a club, the club of potential organ recipients. Under this policy, transplantable organs are the resource of potential organ donors, and signing an organ donor card is equivalent to buying insurance. Being willing to give up an organ, should it no longer be of use to you, is the premium to be paid for the right to receive someone else's organ if one of yours fails.

At present, nonsigners face no costs to not signing their donor cards. The no-give, no-take rule raises the costs of not signing or, equivalently, increases the benefits of signing, and thus it will increase the number of organ donors. Moreover, the increase in the number of potential donors will be efficient because all those whose expected benefits exceed their expected costs will sign, and none will sign otherwise.

How would the no-give, no-take rule work in practice? Anyone could sign an organ donor card at any time and be registered as a potential donor. Most people would sign their cards when they receive their driver's license, as occurs today. Children would be automatically eligible to receive organs until the age of sixteen, when they would have the option to sign their cards. To prevent people from signing after learning they were in need, there would be a mandatory waiting period of at least one year after the age of, say, 18 before the right to receive an organ took effect.

The no-give, no-take rule may result in the deaths of some people who would have lived under the current rules. Thousands of people are dying today, however. If the no-give, no-take rule increases the number of potential donors, then fewer people will die on net. If enough people sign their donor cards, this plan could even produce a surplus of organs.

The no-give, no-take rule does not mean abandoning the use of medical criteria for allocating organs. The point system in which medical need, the probability that the transplant would be effective, and the length of time already spent on the waiting list all play a role would still be used to allocate organs within the group of people who had previously signed their organ donor cards. Any remaining organs could then be allocated on the same basis to nonsigners.[7] A more modest version of the no-give, no-take rule could be implemented by stating that, henceforth, points should also be awarded for previously having signed one's organ donor card.[8] It would then be allowable, for example, to give an organ to a nonsigner before giving it to a signer if the nonsigner had been on the waiting list for a long time.

A considerable advantage of the no-give, no-take rule over organ markets is that far fewer moral qualms are raised. In informal surveys of hundreds of students over the years, I have found very little disagreement about the moral principle that those who are willing to give should be the first to receive. Nor have I found qualms about the application of this rule to the organ shortage. Although it is understandable that some people may have misgivings about becoming donors for personal or religious reasons, why should someone who was not willing to give an organ be allowed to take an organ? This reasoning resonates with most people. Moreover, unlike organ markets, the no-give, no-take rule does not raise issues of distributional concern. Anyone, from the poorest orphan to the richest software magnate, can opt to be a potential organ donor and thus satisfy the requirement to receive an organ. The no-give, no-take rule is fundamentally egalitarian and fair.

What is needed to end the shortage of human organs, and to save the thousands of individuals who die because of the shortage, is a rethinking of the basis of organ collection and donation. If we wish to end the current tragedy, then organs should no longer be owned in common but, rather, by you and me and every other person who has agreed to be a potential organ donor.

Notes

1. Some of the authors suggest a simple payment for organ donation (perhaps in the form of funeral expenses); others go further and suggest opening up a futures market for organs.

2. For an argument along these lines, see Radin (1996).

3. Questions have arisen about the fairness of organ transplantation across races. Although no explicit biases are present, discrepancies between donation rates and need combined with the fact that cross-race donations tend to work less well than intra-race donations cause some to question the fairness of the eventual distribution. See Epstein (1997) for a discussion of these issues.

4. Signing an organ donor card "restocks" the organ supply probabilistically rather than as a certainty. With a large population, as the number of people who sign their organ donor cards increases the stock of organs increases, with near certainty.

5. Although all the major religions support donation, I suspect that atavistic fears about loss of limb in the afterlife may motivate many nonsigners, if perhaps only subconsciously.

6. In my experience discussing this issue with students, I have found that this fear is especially prevalent among African Americans. Given the history of medical treatment of African Americans in the United States, such a fear is not unwarranted and may explain why donation rates among African Americans are lower than those among whites (Arnason 1991).

7. This is what economists refer to as a lexicographic ordering, because everyone in category A (signers) is served before anyone in category B (nonsigners).

8. A little-known provision gives kidney transplant patients points for previously having donated a kidney or part of another vital organ, that is, live donors are given some assurance that, all else being equal, they will be served first should they ever need a kidney. Oddly, previous donation helps you get a kidney but not, say, a liver or lung (an indication of the arbitrariness of the UNOS point-allocation scheme). This provision has probably increased live donation rates and should be extended along the lines indicated in the text in order to increase cadaveric donation rates.

References

Arnason, W. B. 1991. Directed Donation—The Relevance of Race. *Hastings Center Report* (Nov.–Dec.).

Barnett, A. H., R. D. Blair, and D. L. Kaserman. 1996. A Market for Cadaveric Organs. *Society* 33:8.

Becker, G. 1997. How Uncle Sam Could Ease the Organ Shortage. *Business Week* 3510 (20 Jan.):18.

Cohen, L. R. 1989. Increasing the Supply of Transplant Organs: The Virtues of a Free Market. *George Washington Law Review* 58 (1):1–51.

Epstein, R. A. 1993. Organ Transplants: Is Relying on Altruism Costing Lives? *The American Enterprise* Oct./Nov.: 50.

———. 1997. *Mortal Peril.* New York: Addison-Wesley Publishing Co.

Institute of Medicine, Committee on Organ Procurement and Transplantation Policy. 1999. *Organ Procurement and Transplantation: Assessing Current Policies and the Potential Impact of the HHS Final Rule.* Washington, D. C.: National Academy of Science, Institute of Medicine.

Pindyck, R. S., and D. L. Rubinfeld. 1998. *Microeconomics.* 4th ed. Upper Saddle River, N.J.: Prentice-Hall.

Radin, M. J. 1996. *Contested Commodities.* Cambridge, Mass.: Harvard University Press.

PART IV

EFFICIENT JUSTICE

8

A Modest Proposal to Improve Judicial Incentives

STEVEN LANDSBURG

It is a recurring American nightmare: The accused criminal out on bail commits a grisly murder while awaiting trial. The judge who signed the release order is second-guessed in the press and sometimes at the voting booth. Politicians decry the leniency of the justice system and call for stricter standards in the granting of bail.

There are two separate problems here. The first is to decide where we stand regarding the trade-off between public safety and rights of the accused. How much certainty about a prisoner's character do we require before we are willing to accept the risk of freeing him prior to trial? Reasonable people will disagree about their answers to this question. Ordinarily, in our system, we consider such difficult trade-offs to be properly in the domain of the legislature.

The second problem, once the legislature has agreed on a standard, is to induce judges to abide by it. We can appoint watchdog agencies, but the watchdogs are likely to have far less information than the judge about the character of various defendants. They can therefore never be certain that the judge is really using all of his information to the best of his ability.

Economic theory tells us that when we cannot monitor a decision maker, we should at least endeavor to present him with the right incentives. Judges will begin to have the right incentives when we make them personally liable for criminal damage done by the defendants they release.

Personal liability would at least give the right incentive in one direction: Judges would be loath to release those defendants whom they believe to be the most dangerous. Unfortunately, they would be loath to release *any* defendants. So I propose a simultaneous countervailing incentive in the form of a cash bounty to the judge for each defendant he releases.

Whether judges would release more or fewer defendants than they do today would depend on the size of the cash bounty, which could be adjusted to reflect the wishes of the legislature. The advantage of my proposal is not its effect on the number of defendants who are granted bail but its effect on which defendants are granted bail. Whether we favor releasing 1 percent or 99 percent, we can agree that those 1 percent or 99 percent should not be chosen randomly. We want judges to focus their full attention on the potential costs of their decisions, and personal liability has a way of concentrating the mind.

I make no plea for greater strictness or for greater leniency. I plead only that we recognize the nature of the trade-off. My proposal's second advantage is that it would encourage clarity. Through ongoing debate about adjustments to the cash bounty, legislators would be forced to take unambiguous stands on fundamental issues of safety versus freedom. Rather than being able to hide their views in complex and mutually contradictory legislation, they would have to face the voters and defend an unambiguous position, which the voters could then accept or reject.

You might object that we should not trivialize a complex issue by asking legislators to commit themselves to a single number. I respond that they commit themselves to a single number already. The current network of laws does select some specific point on the scale between strictness and leniency. We just aren't told exactly what it is. Why should the complexity of an issue be an excuse for being coy about the choices that have been made?

My proposal would force judges to be more diligent and legislators to be more straightforward. Those are its two advantages. I see no offsetting disadvantages, and therefore I move that it be adopted forthwith.

9

Privatizing Probation and Parole

MORGAN REYNOLDS

At the end of 1998, 3.4 million people in the United States were on probation and 705,000 were on parole.[1] That's one in fifty adult U.S. residents
"under the supervision of the criminal justice system" yet free on the
streets. A majority (57 percent) of those convicted and released to straight
probation (nonincarceration) were convicted of a felony crime (crimes pun-
ishable by one year or more in prison), 40 percent were guilty of misde-
meanors, and the remaining 3 percent were guilty of other infractions. With
regard to parole, over four in five prisoners are released short of serving
their full sentences in favor of some form of "community supervision." Currently, a large public bureaucracy of probation and parole officers (there are
50,000 probation officers alone, many of them members of the American
Probation and Parole Association [APPA]) is responsible for supervising
these 4.1 million offenders.

There are problems with the performance of the current probation and
parole systems, to put it mildly. For example, people on probation or parole
commit new crimes and some are brutal and highly publicized:

- Kenneth McDuff, a rapist and multiple killer from Texas whose
  death sentence was commuted to life imprisonment, was paroled
  and shortly thereafter raped and murdered another woman.
- A California parolee abducted and murdered twelve-year-old Polly
  Klass in a case that drew national attention.
- A Florida parolee, Louis Brooks, served six years of a fifteen-year
  sentence for rape, and he returned to rape the same elderly woman
  in her home.
- One killer of former basketball star Michael Jordan's father was a
  parolee, and his accomplice was under indictment and on release.

- Probationer Buford Furrow wounded five when he opened fire on a Jewish day-care center in Los Angeles and murdered a Filipino letter carrier.

In Furrow's case, a judge in Washington state had ordered Furrow to give up his guns, but the probation officer never checked to make sure he had done so. Nor did the officer ever make any of the recommended visits to Furrow's home.[2]

This is par for the course according to a recent comprehensive study by the Manhattan Institute, a product of two years' work by fourteen experienced practitioners in the field, including leaders of the two industry associations.[3] In nearly 70 percent of cases, probation officers do not make "collateral contact" to verify such things as employment or attendance in drug treatment programs.[4] Indeed, at any moment in time, one in ten adult probationers cannot be located because they have "absconded."[5] In a probation bureaucracy of 50,000, only an estimated 11,500 directly supervise adult probationers, according to the *National Institute for Justice Journal*, producing an average caseload of 258 adult offenders versus an "ideal caseload" of 30.[6] Another study calculates that only 4,420 of these officers supervise felons, an average caseload of 337 persons.[7]

Other data tell a similar tale of defective performance by the criminal justice system. Thirty-six percent of persons arrested for felony crimes are already "supervised" at the time of their arrest—either on probation, parole or pretrial release.[8] While 10 percent of adult probationers abscond, 17 percent are "returned to incarceration," and another 9 percent are deemed "other unsuccessful." Only 59 percent are deemed successful in completing probation.[9] A summary of seventeen follow-up studies of adult felony probationers found that felony rearrest rates ranged from 12 to 65 percent.[10] More than 10 percent of the persons convicted of murder in Virginia from 1990 to 1993, for example, were on probation at the time they killed. Probationers convicted in 1991 were responsible for at least 6,400 murders, 7,400 rapes, 10,400 assaults, and 17,000 robberies.[11]

Other data tell much the same story. Parole and conditional release violators made up 206,000 of the 565,000 admissions to state prisons in 1998.[12] Even those who complete parole and conditional release supervision ("discharge") return to prison or jail at the rate of 42 percent.[13] As *World Net Daily* Editor Joseph Farah points out, criminals under government "supervision" commit fifteen murders a day.[14]

Clearly, probation officers have more cases than they can effectively handle and relatively few incentives to perform efficiently and energetically. Similar problems affect the parole system. Not only are there too few officers to monitor parolees, but parole boards are often forced to parole criminals to alleviate shortages of prison beds rather than decide which criminals are truly ready for a return to community life. In 2000, nearly 600,000 state and federal prisoners will be released, a 38 percent boost over 1990, and four of five will be on parole or other conditional release.[15]

We can put the competitive market mechanism to work on this problem by privatizing the probation and parole systems. Privatization is not a radical concept—it would involve little more than transferring the principles of the commercial bail bonding system, used successfully for criminal defendants, to those found guilty of crimes but eligible for early release on probation or parole.[16]

The Bail Principle for Defendants

In accordance with our precious civil liberties, the American criminal justice system allows most people who are arrested and charged with a crime to be released on bail pending trial.[17] Bail operates on the principle that a criminally accused person will be freed from jail once he guarantees his presence in court on a certain date by posting a significant sum of money. If he shows up, he gets his money back; if he doesn't, he suffers a major financial loss. Because most criminal defendants do not have enough money to post the full amount, the market provides the professional bail bondsman. If the bail agent is willing, he posts the entire bond in exchange for a fee, customarily 10 percent of the total bond. The bail agent loses all of the bond and usually his 10 percent commission if the defendant fails to show up in court.

The private bail agent can stay in business only if the vast majority of his clients show up in court—95 percent is the break-even industry rule of thumb. Uncounted numbers of agents have gone broke for failure to run their bonding business as a business. Surviving private bail agents are thus very efficient at ensuring the appearance of their clients—at no cost to the taxpayers. Frank Callahan, a bail agent in New Jersey, says, "I lose 100 percent of my profit if the guy jumps bail. That's a real incentive for me to monitor my people."[18] Bail bondsmen expend a great deal of energy and ingenuity in getting their defendants to court. Usually, bondsmen require a cosigner for the defendant's bond, typically a family member. Callahan says, "I try to get Mom and Dad on the hook." With family members' property at risk, the odds improve that the defendant will come to court. If he is a no-show, his family, as well as the bondsman, loses a lot of money.

Another significant reason that private bail works is the use of bounty hunters, or "bail enforcement agents," to recover fugitives. Most work part-time because their primary business is as bail bondsman or private investigator. Every state requires that they be licensed and regulated. In a majority of cases, bounty hunters directly apprehend the fugitives. In the remaining cases, they locate and identify the fugitive and let the police make the arrest. They are driven by a powerful incentive—they receive no compensation unless the fugitive is returned to the court. Bounty hunters generally earn between $20,000 and $30,000 per year (at $1,000 to $2,000 per fugitive recovered) for their part-time efforts.

On the whole, the private bail bonding system seems to work well, especially compared with public pretrial release programs:

- Only 15 percent of felony defendants released on surety bonds initially failed to appear in court versus failure rates of 26 percent for those released on their own recognizance and 42 percent released on unsecured bonds, according to a 1992 Department of Justice study of the seventy-five largest counties.[19]
- Only 3 percent of defendants released on surety bonds are fugitives at the end of one year compared to 9 percent for recognizance releases and 19 percent for unsecured bond releases.[20] An Alexander Grant study claimed that private bail agents have a 0.8 percent fugitive rate versus 8.0 percent for unsecured public releases.[21]
- Felony defendants released on surety bonds had a 9 percent rearrest rate during their release compared to 15 percent for recognizance releases and 16 percent for unsecured bonds.[22]

The difference in privately secured release versus public release persists despite the considerable advantage that pretrial service agencies have because they get first crack at recommending the release of the most eligible defendants ("cream skimming"), while bail bondsmen must deal with the remainder, yet they do a better job. A 1995 analysis of the Bureau of Justice Statistics pretrial release data for Los Angeles, San Diego, and San Francisco counties found that, by a factor of almost three to one, defendants released on surety bonds are accused of more violent offenses than those on nonfinancial releases.[23] These "undesirable" bailees were almost twice as likely to have multiple prior violent convictions and by almost any measure were a more violent and criminal population. Presumably, they would be less likely to treat their court-appearance obligations seriously, especially since they have more to lose by going through the entire process.

Yet, the private bail system did much better at ensuring that defendants appear at required times than the nonfinancial release system. Defendants on nonfinancial releases were twice as likely to fail to appear as those released through a private surety company. Defendants on nonfinancial releases also were 50 percent more likely to remain fugitives for a year or more. For those without a prior record of arrest, nonfinancial releasees were almost five times more likely to fail to appear than surety releasees.[24]

Harris County (Houston, Texas) has experimented with a blended system in which some defendants have been released on a combination of cash or surety bail bond and supervision by the county's pretrial service agency. These conditional, pretrial financial releases form a blended system that seems to have sharply reduced failures to appear in court. From January 1994 to June 1997, the failure-to-appear rate, as indicated by warrants issued, was 8.5 percent for surety bond releases (8,246 warrants out of 97,176 straight surety bond defendants) but only 2.2 percent for the surety bond combined with pretrial supervision under judicial order (55 warrants issued out of 2,538 defendants).[25]

The Bail Principle for Probation and Parole

Those convicted of crimes but eligible for probation or early release from prison (parole) can be required to post a financial bond against specified violations of the terms of their probation or parole (reporting regularly to their bondsman, submitting to drug tests, and so on).[26] The amount should be set by the courts or parole boards based on the criminal's history, the amount necessary to be a significant inducement to good behavior (which will depend on the criminal's wealth), and the criminal's prospects for a productive, noncriminal life. A typical bond might be $10,000.[27]

As with the current system of bail bonds, many criminals would have to seek the help of family and friends in order to acquire the cosigners and the initial wherewithal to pay the bondsman's fee and receive probation or parole. Another source of funds for parolees could be wages earned while in prison, under a liberalized prison labor system, or they could pay by installment from wages earned in the free world.[28]

If no intimate of the criminal nor any private bondsman cared enough to risk his own money on the candidate for probation or parole, why should the general public risk that person on the streets? Privatizing the probation and parole systems provides a market mechanism for deciding whom to release on probation or parole and whom to continue incarcerating.

There would be no cost to taxpayers under complete privatization. A flat fee of, say, $500 per year per probationer or parolee for supervision and processing by private bondsmen might be paid privately by the probationer or parolee. Alternatively, the fee may be a percentage of the bond, say, 10 percent. Market competition can help to set and adjust these fees over time. There is ample precedent for payment of such fees since a majority of the states already allow local probation departments to collect fees from probationers.[29] Persons violating the terms of their probation or parole would forfeit their bond, generating revenues for the criminal justice system, victim restitution, and other uses.

Advantages of Private Bonding

Such a voluntary, privately financed market would be a tremendous help to parole boards and courts in selecting promising parolees over the unpromising. A private bonding system would reduce, though probably not eliminate, the need for probation and parole officers on the public payroll. With their own money at risk, relatives and bondsmen would have a serious financial incentive to supervise their charges with care and assure that the fugitive rate would be low.[30] Dropping the "absconding" or failure-to-appear rates would reduce crime, save the taxpayers' money, and help restore confidence in the justice system and the rule of law.

Pursuit of those who violate probation or parole would be more effective because, unlike police, bounty hunters have strong incentives to recover fugitives because they only get paid if they get their man.[31] In addition, they can freely go to any jurisdiction and use any lawful means to apprehend a fugitive.[32] The Supreme Court, in an 1872 decision that is still good law, stated that these powers include the right to pursue a fugitive into another state, arrest him at any time, and enter a fugitive's house without a warrant. These powers have been granted to the bail bondsman who guaranteed a defendant's courtroom appearance, but the bondsman can transfer his power to an agent of his choosing.

Although some states explicitly prohibit private supervision of probationers, there is a trend toward contracting out "some aspects of probation supervision" to the private sector.[33] In at least ten states, private agencies are currently responsible for providing primary probation supervision services for misdemeanor or lower risk felony cases. Since 1987, the APPA has endorsed "private sector services to enhance or supplement supervision and casework services."[34] This open-mindedness to private sector involvement in administering probation contrasts sharply with the hostility of the pretrial service agencies (more below).

The exact details of financial bonding for probationers and parolees would remain open to experimentation. Private surety agents could simply perform financial functions and aid in the apprehension of absconders and fugitives. Under this partial privatization arrangement, public agencies would continue to administer the drug testing, electronic monitoring (usually contracted to private companies anyway), and other conditions of probation and parole, presumably under a reformed system with increased efficiency, similar to the blended pretrial release system operating in Harris County. Alternatively, and more radically, surety agents and other private contractors would be responsible for performing all or most release and supervisory functions in a privatized parole and probation system.

Turf Wars and Resistance to Privatization

Bureaucracies are famously territorial about potential interlopers who might perform a core function presently monopolized by the bureaucracy. As Robert J. Bosco, director of the Connecticut Office of Adult Probation, says of the trend toward transferring government functions to the private sector, "[T]he field of community corrections generally resists the trend. It is seen as a threat to our jobs and our security . . . an intrusion . . . a false promise to reduce crime effectively and efficiently, while also reducing taxpayer cost."[35]

Although the political battle to privatize probation and parole is in its early stages, we might learn from the similar, ongoing battle between so-called pretrial release agencies and the private bail bond industry. A government bail system administered by pretrial release bureaus operates alongside and in competition with the commercial bail bonding system, usually funded by county governments, traditionally subdivisions of state government but with significant local autonomy. Pretrial release staff members are government employees who interview defendants and recommend to judges whether they should be released. In this public system, defendants rarely post any kind of monetary bond and are usually released on their own recognizance. Under these "free bonds," the defendant simply promises the judge that he will appear in court. As a result, the accused has little or nothing to lose if he fails to appear. Therefore, no-show and fugitive rates are far higher than under surety bonds or under the commercial bail system.[36] An uncounted number of bench warrants for the rearrest of fugitives clogs the justice system.[37] Like many public bureaucracies, the National Association of Pretrial Service Agencies (NAPSA) vigorously resists any public accounting for the results of its release recommendations, claiming it would be too expensive to gather the data and that no funding has been provided.[38] Thirty years of bureaucratic funding and we still have no systematic evidence on the results of the bureaucratic activities in question.

Not surprisingly, NAPSA doesn't like competition and states in its "performance standards and goals for pretrial release" that "the use of financial conditions of release should be eliminated."[39] NAPSA also insists that "a presumption in favor of pretrial release on a simple promise to appear should apply to all persons arrested and charged with a crime," and agencies should "provide direct services to pretrial releasees" and coordinate services with other agencies "for the benefit of pretrial releasees."[40] Charles E. Noble, the retired executive director of the Harris County Pretrial Services Agency and a past vice president of NAPSA, calls NAPSA an organization of "zealots" who refuse to entertain any but their own ideology.[41]

It's unfortunate that NAPSA focuses all its efforts on releasing criminal suspects without bail and not on the innocent, who are all too often the victims of crimes perpetuated by those on release. NAPSA has been aided in its efforts to eliminate commercial bail systems by a substantial number of judges, criminal lawyers, and legislators. An article by U.S. Judge James G. Carr of the Northern District of Ohio urges all federal courts to eliminate the use of corporate surety bonds, contending that they "fulfill no function and provide no service that cannot otherwise be accomplished within the framework of the [1984] Bail Reform Act."[42] Another bail critic in 1965 asserted that "the bondsman's few legitimate functions can be filled better by other agencies," a 1976 study concluded that financial bail "does not perform any useful system function," and in 1980 the American Bar Association called for abolition of surety bonds. Four states, including Illinois, have eliminated commercial bail bonds and, thus, have removed an option for the accused.[43]

Yet, the bail system has proven itself superior to pretrial release ("free bond" or "RR"—released on own recognizance) in ensuring that the accused are properly tried in a court of law. The commercial bail system thus plays a critical role in seeing that justice is done, at no expense to taxpayers.

Do the political difficulties of the surety industry in a well-established market spell doom for expanding surety bonding into parole and probation? No. First, because corrections tops all other major categories in rate of spending growth, legislatures are pressing for ways to improve performance and yet restrain the growth of public spending. Second, the American Legislative Exchange Council, a nationwide bipartisan group of conservative legislators, has drafted model legislation, "Conditional Post Conviction Release Act," and promoted the idea of privatizing probation and parole to legislatures.[44] Third, the surety industry has worked for a decade to persuade legislators that secured release works and that such legislation should pass. The market is potentially huge. With over 4 million people on probation and parole, and a typical post-conviction release bond of $5,000 or more, the potential bond market exceeds $20 billion. Therefore, direct revenues to bail agents would be over $2 billion.

Legislation to permit such secured, post-conviction release may be closest in California. Key legislators are receptive to the industry, partly because it has formed an alliance with the sheriffs' association, judges' association, prosecutors' association, and police and victim groups.[45] "Legislators are starting to get it. They are upset with failures to appear and they realize the impact it has on the criminal justice system," says Terry Fowler, a surety bonding consultant.[46] "They're fed up, especially with the disrespect for the system, and they understand that secured release works." Such releases produce fewer crimes and more personal accountability. Superior performance at lower taxpayer cost does have its political appeal, eventually.

The opposition consists of active resistance by the parole and probation departments, combined with the power of the status quo. The bureaucracy is often unionized and its members belong to the APPA and sometimes the National Association of Probation Executives. Political clout, combined with "expertise" and high motivation in protecting turf, make such bureaucratic opposition formidable. But, in the long run, ideas win, not vested interests, especially bureaucratic interests with little or no public support.

Conclusion

No bond for probation or parole has yet been written. But it's a good idea whose time seems near. If individual accountability is the answer to crime, then it must include the most powerful kind of accountability: financial responsibility.

Notes

1. Bureau of Justice Statistics (BJS), Probation and Parole Statistics, http://www.ojp.usdoj.gov/bjs/pandp.htm; or BJS, Probation and Parole in the United States, 1998, August 1999, NCJ-178234.

2. "Reinventing Probation," *The Wall Street Journal*, August 19, 1999, p. A18.

3. "Broken Windows" Probation: The Next Step in Fighting Crime, Civic Report No. 7, August 1999, http://www.Manhattan-Institute.org/html/cr_7.htm. The report has few statistical facts but recommends "reinventing probation," which "requires leadership committed to enforcing violation warrants, supervising offenders primarily in the community rather than in probation offices, and not directing probation officers to avoid dangerous areas."

4. Michael Hotra, "Missing Persons: Most Probation Officers Aren't Watching Criminals," American Legislative Exchange Council, F.Y.I., May 22, 1998, as summarized by National Center for Policy Analysis, Daily Policy Digest, May 1998; Joan Petersilia, "Probation in the United States," *National Institute of Justice Journal*, September 1997, pp. 2–8.

5. BJS, Probation and Parole, n. 1 above.

6. Petersilia, n. 4, p. 3.

7. Hotra, n. 4.

8. BJS, Felony Defendants in Large Urban Counties, 1996, October 1999, NCJ-176981, p. 8. In thirty states, both adult probation and parole functions are administered by the same state agency or local agencies. See U.S. Department of Justice, National Institute of Corrections, *State Organizational Structures for Delivering Adult Probation Services*, report prepared by LIS, Inc., NIC contractor, June 1999, p. 7. In sixteen states, both adult and juvenile probation are administered together.

9. BJS, Probation and Parole, n. 1.

10. Michael Geerken and Hennessey D. Hayes, "Probation and Parole: Public Risk and the Future of Incarceration Alternatives," *Criminology*, 1993, Vol. 31, No. 4, pp. 549–64, as cited by Joan Petersilia, n. 4, p. 4.

11. Almost certainly the number of probationers convicted of a crime understates the number who actually commits crimes. On the last two figures, see "Broken Windows" Probation, n. 3.

12. Allen J. Beck, Chief, Bureau of Justice Corrections Statistics, "State and Federal prisoners returning to the community: Findings from the Bureau of Justice Statistics," presented at the First Reentry Courts Initiative Cluster Meeting, Washington, D.C., April 13, 2000.

13. Beck, n. 12.

14. Joseph Farah, "Crime and Punishment," March 30, 2000, or http://www.worldnetdaily.com/bluesky_btl/20000330_xcbtl_crime_and_.shtml.

15. Beck, n. 12.

16. On the success of the commercial bail bond system and the failure of public pretrial service/release agencies, see Morgan O. Reynolds, "Using the Private Sector to Deter Crime," National Center for Policy Analysis, Policy Report No. 181, March 1994, http://www.ncpa.org/studies/s181.

17. Only 6 percent of defendants are denied bail; BJS, Felony Defendants, n. 8.

18. John Carlisle, "Criminal Welfare: A Jail Reduction Failure," Policy Insights, April 1992, No. 406, Free Congress Research and Education Foundation, Washington, D.C., pp. 1–2.

19. BJS, Pretrial Release of Felony Defendants, 1992, November 1994, NCJ-148818, p. 10.

20. Ibid.

21. Jane Marino Reed and Rhonda Sue Stallings, "Bounty Hunting: The Alternative Justice System," publication of the Professional Bail Agents of the United States, Houston, Texas, August 1992, p. 5.

22. Note 19, p. 11. These are the most recent published data available. See note 38 below for an explanation of the failure to publish more recent data on failure-to-appear and fugitive rates.

23. Michael K. Block and Steven J. Twist, "Evidence of a Failed System: A Study of the Performance of Pretrial Release Agencies in California," American Legislative Exchange Council, Washington, D.C., April 1995.

24. Ibid., p. 22.

25. Harris County Criminal Courts at Law, Office of Court Management, memorandum from Dennis Potts, Research Analyst, to Charles E. Noble, Director, Harris County Pretrial Services Agency, November 11, 1998. In a telephone interview with the author on December 10, 1999, Noble, director of Harris County Pretrial Services from 1984 to 1998, said that Harris County was unique in that at least three-fourths of defendants released were out on financial bail, especially the blended, conditional releases that included drug testing and electronic monitoring. No other county has administered these on a mass basis. Private bondsman cannot administer mandatory drug tests and electronic monitoring, but pretrial service agencies can (usually contracted out to private enterprises).

26. It was the late bail bondsman, Gerald Monks of Houston, Texas, former executive director of the professional Bail Agents of the United States, who originally brought this idea to my attention.

27. The Eighth Amendment to the Constitution says, "Excessive bail shall not be required, nor excessive fines imposed, nor cruel and unusual punishments inflicted." About half of those with bail amounts in 1996 had them set at $10,000 or higher, including one in four at $25,000 or higher. The median bail was $10,000 and the mean $31,000, with the mean for murder defendants with bail set at $133,000. See BJS, Felony Defendants, n. 8, p. 18.

28. Morgan O. Reynolds, Factories Behind Bars, National Center for Policy Analysis, September 1996, Policy Report No. 206, http://www.ncpa.org/studies/s206/s206.html; The Economic Impact of Prison Labor, Brief Analysis No. 245, November 17, 1997, http://www.ncpa.org/ba/ba245.html; Mark Tatge, "Prison Labor: With Unemployment Low, a New Group Is In Demand: Ex-Cons," The Wall Street Journal, April 24, 2000, p. A1.

29. Making the Offender Foot the Bill: A Texas Program, National Institute of Justice, U.S. Department of Justice, October 1992, NCJ-136839.

30. All recovery programs recommend support groups to help prevent relapses. Unsecured release separates the criminal from the support group that matters most—his family.

31. About 35,000 defendants jump commercial bail every year (one in seven) and bounty hunters return four out of five to justice; see The Economist, June

19, 1999, p. 18. Bounty hunters, an estimated network of 7,000, are paid approximately 10 percent of the bond value for recovery within a predetermined amount of time.

32. Charles A. Donelan, "The Bondsman's Right to Arrest," *FBI Law Enforcement Bulletin*, December 1972 and January 1973, reprint; John A Chamberlin, "Bounty Hunters: Can the Criminal Justice System Live Without Them?" *University of Illinois Law Review*, Vol. 1998, No. 4, pp. 1175–205; Holly J. Joiner, "Private Police: Defending the Power of Professional Bail Bondsmen," *Indiana University School of Law*, 1999, Vol. 32, pp. 1413–35.

33. U.S. Department of Justice, National Institute of Corrections, *Topics in Community Corrections, Annual Issue 1998: Privatizing Community Supervision*, American Probation and Parole Association, Position Statement: Privatization, appendix.

34. Ibid.

35. Robert J. Bosco, "Connecticut Probation's Partnership with the Private Sector," in U.S. Department of Justice, National Institute of Corrections, *Topics in Community Corrections*, Annual Issue 1998: Privatizing Community Supervision, pp. 8–12.

36. Reynolds, n. 16, and BJS, Pretrial Release of Felony Defendants, 1992, November 1994, NCJ-148818.

37. "Tide of outstanding warrants sweeps over police, resources," *Houston Chronicle*, AP dispatch, July 6, 1999, p. 10A.

38. Telephone conversation with Brian Nairin, President, National Association of Bail Insurance Companies, November 12, 1999. After being deposed in a lawsuit by the National Association of Bail Insurance Companies, BJS statistician Brian Reaves decided to drop the relevant tables in the 1996 report on felony defendants that previously had allowed interested parties to compare postrelease failure-to-appear and fugitive rates between nonfinancial and financial pretrial releases. Unpublished tabulations provided by Reaves, however, show a continuing advantage in financial releases.

39. http://www.napsa.org/docs/Standards.

40. Ibid.

41. See n. 25. NAPSA, stimulated by Noble's initiative (unbeknownst to your author at the time), invited your humble author to participate in a panel on privatization at its annual conference in October 1995, in Cincinnati, Ohio, where he was met by a surprisingly emotional series of attacks by other panelists. Help came from an unexpected quarter, however, when the first comment from the floor in a packed room asserted that if the session had been televised on ABC's *Nightline*, "The typical viewer would have believed that Dr. Reynolds had won the debate"!

42. James G. Carr, "Bail Bondsmen and the Federal Courts," *Federal Probation*, March 1993, p. 9.

43. *The Economist*, June 19, 1999, p. 18. The bail conditions in Illinois are so onerous and restrictive that bail was effectively eliminated. The other states are Oregon, Kentucky, and Wisconsin. Bail was reintroduced in the city of Philadelphia, however, recently. The elimination of bail reduces defendants' options and such systems experience higher failure-to-appear rates, larger jail populations, and reduced respect for the justice system, as Illinois is busy demonstrat-

ing, because those released have little or no financial accountability for subsequent court appearances.

44. See the model legislation at http://www.alec.org/viewpage.cfm?id=250& xsectioinid=11.

45. Telephone conversation with Terry Fowler, surety bonding consultant and past president of the California Bail Agents Association, November 15, 1999.

46. Ibid.

10

More Justice for Less Money

A Step beyond *Cimino*

DAVID FRIEDMAN

> It is apparent from the effort and time required
> to try these 160 cases, that unless this plan or
> some other procedure that permits damages to
> be adjudicated in the aggregate is approved,
> these cases cannot be tried. Defendants
> complain about the 1% likelihood that the
> result would be significantly different. However,
> plaintiffs are facing a 100% confidence level of
> being denied access to the courts. The Court
> will leave it to the academicians and legal
> scholars to debate whether our notion of due
> process has room for balancing these
> competing interests.
> —Judge Robert Parker, *Cimino v. Raymark*

In *Cimino v. Raymark*,[1] Judge Parker of the Eastern District of Texas implemented a radical solution to the problem of litigating mass torts. Instead of
conducting individual trials for several thousand plaintiffs, he selected a
random sample of 160 of them, tried their cases, and based the awards
given to the remaining plaintiffs on the outcome of those trials. In defending the procedure against the charge that it deprived the parties of due
process, he argued that if he had instead required individual trials, most of
the cases would never have been resolved.

The procedure of *Cimino* was explained and defended in a 1992 article
by Michael J. Saks and Peter David Blanck.[2] The purpose of this essay is
not to dispute either their views or those of Judge Parker but, rather, to
suggest a further step along the same path. The procedure of aggregation

and sampling implemented in *Cimino* does a reasonably good job of estimating the total damages that the defendants would have paid if every case had been tried separately[3] and does so at a cost much lower than that of individual trials. It does a much poorer job of allocating that total among the plaintiffs. My proposal is intended to solve that problem.

In part I of this chapter I explain the procedure used by Judge Parker in *Cimino*, the improvements suggested by Saks and Blanck, and the limitations of the procedure, even with such improvements. Part II describes my proposal for generating an estimate of the relative claims of the plaintiffs and incorporating that estimate into the procedure. Part III considers the legal status of the modified procedure, arguing that it is in some ways more defensible than the version implemented in *Cimino*. Part IV discusses potential problems, both those implicit in the original idea of aggregation and sampling and additional ones created by my proposed modifications. Part V suggests ways in which the procedure I suggest could be extended beyond the context of class actions. Part VI describes the results of the application of the procedure to an explicit formal model; the mathematics are presented in appendix B of Friedman (1996). Part VII summarizes my conclusions.

I. Aggregation and Sampling: Judge Parker's Solution to Mass Tort Litigation

> If the Court could somehow close thirty cases a month, it would take six and one-half years to try these cases and there would be pending over 5,000 untouched cases at the present rate of filing.
> —Judge Parker in *Cimino*

Cimino v. Raymark went to trial as a class action with 2,298 plaintiffs and five defendants. The trial consisted of three phases. In phase 1, a set of issues common to all plaintiffs and defendants was resolved.[4] Phase 2 apportioned causation among the defendants and determined which plaintiffs had had sufficient exposure to asbestos, based on each plaintiff's workplace and craft, for such exposure to be a producing cause of an asbestos-related injury or disease.[5]

The purpose of phase 3 was to determine damages. Instead of trying all cases, the court divided the plaintiffs into five categories according to which asbestos-related disease each suffered from. A random sample was drawn from each category; the sample was larger for categories with more plaintiffs.[6] The sample cases were tried. Plaintiffs in the sample received the damages that they were awarded. Plaintiffs not in the sample received the average of the damages awarded to the tried cases in their category.

Judge Parker argued that the result was fair to the defendants since the total amount awarded was an accurate estimate of the total that would have been awarded if all cases had been tried. He cited confidence levels ranging from 95 to 99 percent, but he did not explain what those numbers meant or what assumptions were used to calculate them.

The situation is not quite so clear as Judge Parker apparently believed. The statistical conclusions reported, if correct, depend on assumptions about the distribution of the awards that would be produced by jury trial. It is possible to describe distributions consistent with the observed data for which the result of even as large a sample as was used in *Cimino* would be a very imprecise measure of the total damages that would be awarded.[7] With such a distribution, the expected result of the *Cimino* procedure would still be correct: If the procedure were repeated a large enough number of times, the average outcome would be very close to the result of trying every case separately. But the probability that the result produced by the *Cimino* procedure would be substantially different from the result of trying all cases might be much larger than implied by the confidence levels cited by the judge.[8] This suggests that it might be worth looking for a procedure superior to random sampling.

Even if, as Judge Parker argues, the procedure is fair to the defendants, there remains the question of whether it properly allocates the damage payment among the individual plaintiffs. The procedure used in *Cimino* does not do so, as Judge Parker himself conceded.[9] He dealt with that problem by obtaining the plaintiffs' assent in advance. In future litigation involving such procedures, however, the question will be important for at least five reasons.

1. Many people regard justice as part of what litigation is supposed to produce. If a procedure collects the right amount of damages but gives them to the wrong people, or to the right people but in the wrong amounts, it is not just.
2. One purpose of some of the legal rules that determine damages, such as contributory negligence, is to affect the incentives of potential plaintiffs. In *Cimino*, some plaintiffs whose cases were tried received no damages, possibly because their decision to smoke was regarded by the jury as contributory negligence.[10] The effect of such verdicts was to reduce the award given to all plaintiffs in the same disease category whose cases were not tried, smokers and nonsmokers alike. So the use of the procedure undercuts the effectiveness of such a legal rule.
3. In order for a class to be certified, the judge must find that the representative parties will fairly and adequately protect the interests of the class.[11] A procedure that predictably awards some plaintiffs more and others less than they would get from trying their case themselves may not meet the requirement.
4. Even if the class is certified, individual members are free to withdraw. A procedure that predictably awards some plaintiffs less than they would receive at trial gives such plaintiffs an incentive to withdraw from the class, which reduces the benefit both of the class action and of the procedure.[12]

5. In awarding the right amount of damages to the wrong people, the *Cimino* procedure resembles fluid recovery. Under fluid recovery, where it is difficult to identify the members of the plaintiff class and determine how much of the award each is entitled to, money awarded to the plaintiffs is instead used to benefit a group of people similar to those who were injured. That approach has been seriously questioned by the courts.[13]

For all of these reasons, it is desirable to construct procedures that approximate the correct result among plaintiffs, as well as between plaintiffs and defendants. In *Cimino*, Judge Parker attempted to do so in two ways. Phase 2 of the trial was designed to eliminate from the case plaintiffs whose exposure to asbestos was not a producing cause of an asbestos-related injury or disease. In phase 3, plaintiffs were grouped according to the particular sort of injury or disease they had suffered, presumably because individuals suffering from the same disease would have some tendency to be owed the same damages.

Both of these are very imprecise ways of allocating damage payments to individual plaintiffs. Saks and Blanck offer two additional possibilities. One is to use statistical analysis to define groups with common characteristics. The other is to construct a linear model relating damages to characteristics, use trial results to estimate the parameters of the model, and then use the estimated parameters to calculate damage awards for the untried cases.[14]

Although these procedures can improve on the simple approach of giving every plaintiff the same amount or the slightly more complicated approach implemented in *Cimino*, they suffer from a common problem. It is neither obvious in advance nor uncontroversial what characteristics are relevant to the damage award or how they are related. Even if we knew the characteristics, there is no reason to assume the relation is linear.[15] As statisticians are aware, the same data can be fit with a multitude of different specifications. If, after trying a few thousand, the court finds one that happens to fit the tried cases fairly well, that should not give us much confidence that it will also fit the untried cases.

What we need is not a procedure for dividing the damage award among the plaintiffs—the best way of doing that will almost certainly vary from case to case. What we need is a procedure that makes it in the interest of someone to figure out, for any particular case, what the correct division among the plaintiffs in that case is. Part II describes one such procedure.

II. Plaintiffs Cut, Defendant Chooses: An Incentive-Compatible Procedure for Litigating Mass Torts

I define the strength of a plaintiff's case as the average of what would be awarded if it were tried many times by many separate juries; I call this average verdict (for plaintiff i) d_i.[16] The objective of the procedure is to produce a damage award of about d_i for each plaintiff i, at a cost much lower than the cost of trying every case many times or even trying every case once.

By examining the facts relevant to an individual plaintiff i, an investigator can estimate the value of d_i. The more resources spent on the investigation, the more accurate the estimate will be. This is true both for an individual investigator and for a judge or jury calculating an award in the course of a trial. I assume the cost to a competent individual investigator of estimating d_i is much lower than the cost of a trial that produces an estimate, in the form of a verdict, with the same accuracy, since the investigator is a specialist in such investigations, is an individual rather than a committee, and is not limited by the elaborate procedural rules that control court trials.[17] We start with a group of N plaintiffs represented by an attorney. The procedure is as follows:

> Step 1: The plaintiffs' attorney produces, for each plaintiff i, a claim C_i, which is the amount the attorney claims that plaintiff i ought to receive in damages. For reasons that will become clear below, it will be in the attorney's interest to make C_i proportional to his estimate of d_i.

> Step 2: The plaintiffs' attorney gives his list of claims to the defendant's attorney.

> Step 3: The defendant's attorney selects from the list a small number of cases to be tried. For simplicity in exposition, assume that ten cases are to be selected and that the cases selected turn out to be those of plaintiffs one through ten.

> Step 4: These cases are tried. The court awards damages D_i to each of the ten plaintiffs.

> Step 5: The court calculates $R = (D_1/C_1 + D_2/C_2 + \ldots + D_{10}/C_{10})/10$ and awards damages of $R \times C_i$ to each of the N plaintiffs.

Under this procedure, it should be possible to resolve the N cases much more cheaply than with N separate trials. Only ten cases actually have to be litigated. All plaintiffs have their damages estimated, but the estimate is made for everyone else by the plaintiffs' attorney.

Why does the procedure generate actual damages for plaintiff i close to d_i? Consider the situation first from the standpoint of the defense attorney at step 3. He wants to select plaintiffs whose claims are large relative to d_i, the amount a court would, on average, award them. By selecting plaintiffs who have overclaimed, he produces a low value of R and thus reduces the total amount $(R \Sigma_i C_i)$ his client must pay in damages.

Next, consider the situation from the standpoint of the plaintiffs' attorney at step 1. Because he knows that the defense attorney will try to select for trial plaintiffs with a high ratio of C_i to d_i, he maximizes the total payments his clients receive by trying to make the ratio the same for all clients. The simplest way of doing so is to set C_i equal to his estimate of d_i for each client.[18] So the amount claimed for each plaintiff will be equal to his attorney's estimate of what he can expect to get at trial.[19]

The award received by a particular plaintiff may deviate from what he ought to receive for two reasons: The court may give the wrong verdicts for the cases tried, or the plaintiffs' attorney may claim the wrong amount for a particular plaintiff. Since ten cases are tried separately and their results are averaged, the first source of error should be much smaller than if each plaintiff's case had been tried by itself.[20] Since the attorney can estimate d_i much less expensively than a court, the second source of error can be made smaller than it would be with an actual trial, while still keeping litigation expenses (including the expense of making such estimates) well below those of individual trials. So it should be possible to produce a more accurate verdict at lower cost with this procedure than with individual trials. The cost is higher than with the *Cimino* procedure since additional costs are borne by the plaintiffs' attorney in making claims and the defendant's attorney in choosing cases to litigate. But this procedure, unlike that one, generates separate results for each plaintiff proportioned to the strength of each plaintiff's case.

The procedure as I have described it makes sense for a hundred plaintiffs, for a thousand, or perhaps for more. In *Cimino*, the information actually collected included medical evaluations for about 1,400 of the 2,298 plaintiffs who eventually went to trial, so much of the research required by my suggested procedure had actually been done. But it makes less sense for the sort of class action that involves a very large number of plaintiffs, most with very small claims. In such a case, evaluating each plaintiff's case in order to decide how much to claim for him might cost more than the total damages awarded.

One approach to such a situation would be to allow the plaintiffs' attorney to state C_i for classes of plaintiffs rather than for individual plaintiffs. Thus, he might claim that each heavy smoker born before 1960 was entitled to $10, each light smoker born between 1960 and 1970 to $2, and so on. The defendant's attorney would select classes for trial; individual cases would be selected from those classes at random. Such a variant on the procedure might be appropriate in situations where individual claims are low and separate estimates for each case are thus unreasonably expensive.

A more sophisticated approach would combine the procedure described here with an idea suggested by Saks and Blanck.[21] Instead of producing a claim for each plaintiff, the plaintiffs' attorney produces a statistical model showing how he believes that the amount each plaintiff is entitled to should depend on the characteristics of each plaintiff. The defendant's attorney specifies a sampling protocol, describing how plaintiffs are to be selected for trial based on their characteristics. The court then selects plaintiffs for trial at random, subject to the constraints of the sampling protocol. The verdicts for those plaintiffs are used to estimate the parameters of the model, and awards for all plaintiffs are calculated accordingly.

In the simplest version of this, the plaintiffs' attorney would specify the entire model save for one multiplicative parameter A. If, for example, he believed that the amount awarded ought to depend linearly on the age of the plaintiff and the number of years he had worked at a site using asbestos, he might offer the model

$$\text{Damages} = A(\$100{,}000 - \$1{,}000 \times \text{Age in Years} + \$10{,}000 \times \text{Years Worked on Site}).$$

The defense would then specify the range of ages and work histories that were to be sampled, and the court would choose plaintiffs within that range at random. Their cases would be tried, and the results would be used to calculate A.

In a more elaborate version, the plaintiffs' attorney would specify only the form of the model. An example might be

$$\text{Damages} = A - B \times \text{Age in Years} + C \times \text{Years Worked on Site} + D \times (\text{Years Worked on Site})^2.$$

The defense would again specify the characteristics of plaintiffs to be selected for trial, and the court would choose at random plaintiffs with those characteristics. While both variants of this approach may sound complicated, especially to nonstatisticians, their logic is the same as that of the simpler version described earlier. The difference is that the plaintiffs' attorney is providing a description of how damages relate to characteristics rather than a claim for each plaintiff. The same logic as before makes it in his interest to get the description right. If, for example, he erroneously claims that the amount plaintiffs are entitled to does not depend on their age when a jury would actually award more to younger plaintiffs, the defense can specify a sample heavily weighted toward older plaintiffs, and the result will be to push down the total amount awarded.

The same logic applies to more subtle errors. Suppose the plaintiffs' attorney specifies a linear relation of the form

$$\text{Damages} = A + BL,$$

where L is, say, length of exposure to asbestos. Further suppose that the real relation, the one that correctly predicts jury verdicts, is a quadratic of the form

$$\text{Damages} = A + BL^2.$$

The defense, if it recognizes the error, can specify a sample containing only small values of L. Again, the result will be to push down the total verdict.

In each of these situations, just as with the simpler version of my proposed procedure discussed earlier, an inaccurate specification by the plaintiffs' attorney of the relative claims of different plaintiffs gives the defense an opportunity to reduce the total amount awarded, which in turn gives the plaintiffs' attorney an incentive to do an accurate job of specifying the relative claims.

So far, I have assumed that the cases we are considering are ones where the plaintiffs seek money damages. The procedure can be generalized to any case with a quantitative award—one describable by some cardinal measure. An example would be a suit where the plaintiffs were employees claiming seniority. Another assumption I have been making is that tort litigation under my procedure is always resolved by trial. What is the effect on the analysis if we include the possibility of settlement?

Even if there is some possibility of settlement, the plaintiffs' attorney still has an incentive to estimate the relative claims of the plaintiffs accurately. If the case goes to trial, inaccurate estimates will result in lower total damages, because the defense will select the overclaimed cases for trial. A case will settle on less generous terms if the defense believes that the estimates are inaccurate, and the plaintiffs would likely do badly at trial.

So even when litigation leads to settlement, the procedure still provides a mechanism for allocating damage payments to plaintiffs that reflects the relative strength of their cases. By doing so, it should reduce the conflict among plaintiffs over settlement terms and so make settlement easier.

III. The Legal Status of the Proposed Procedure

Suppose a judge wished to implement the procedure described in part II above. What legal problems would he face?

To begin with, he would face the same problem faced in *Cimino*: the argument that due process required that each plaintiff have an opportunity to make his case in court, and that the defendant should have the opportunity to rebut each plaintiff's case. If, as in *Cimino*, the plaintiffs assented in advance to the procedure,[22] that argument should be no stronger here than there. If anything, the defendant's grounds for objection are even weaker under the procedure I have proposed. Insofar as the defense believes that some plaintiffs have weak cases—weaker cases, relative to other plaintiffs, than their claims indicate—the defense is free to select those cases for trial.[23]

If the plaintiffs, instead of or in addition to the defendant, object, the situation is somewhat more difficult. While the procedure saves the plaintiffs the cost of litigating every case separately, it also, for reasons I will discuss in part IV, has some built-in bias against the plaintiffs. The plaintiffs might reasonably demand either that the procedure be modified to eliminate that bias (a possibility discussed below) or that they be compensated for accepting a biased procedure. Supposing that such objections were met, the plaintiffs under my procedure seem to be in the same situation as the defendants in *Cimino*; although their cases are not all being tried, they are being given an opportunity to get approximately the same awards they would get if they were tried and at a much lower cost of litigation.

There is one respect in which the procedure is more defensible than that employed in *Cimino*—or, arguably, more defensible than the ordinary procedure for a class action. Rule 23(a)(4) of the Federal Rules of Civil Procedure requires that the representative parties in a class action fairly and adequately protect the interests of the class. Under the procedure I have proposed, the representative parties have a clear interest in doing so. If they attempt to benefit themselves at the expense of other members of the class by arranging for their attorney to overclaim on their behalf, the defense will select their cases for trial.[24] The representative parties will gain nothing, and their attorney will have a lower total award out of which to compensate himself.

IV. Problems with the Procedure

There are two fundamental problems with the procedure I have described. The first is that while it could produce a more accurate result at a much lower cost than would individual trials, it is not entirely clear that it will; it might instead produce a much more accurate result at a higher cost. The second is that the procedure, as so far described, has a built-in bias in favor of the defense.

Does It Save Money?

> The method incorporated into phase III produces a level of
> economy in terms of both judicial resources and transaction
> cost that needs no elaboration.
> —Judge Parker in *Cimino*

At first glance, it seems obvious that trying 160 cases costs a great deal less than trying 2,298 cases, but this is not quite so clear as it seems. Under the procedure employed in *Cimino*, the verdicts in the tried cases determined the outcome for all of the other cases. The result is that the amount at stake in each tried case was about fourteen times as much as it would have been if each case had only determined the outcome for that plaintiff. With more at stake, we would expect both parties to spend more on trying to win.

Whether this eliminates the cost savings of fewer trials depends on how litigation expenditure varies with the amount at stake.[25] If the increase is proportional, the total cost of trials under either *Cimino* or the procedure I have suggested will be the same as if every case were tried separately. The only advantage of the procedure would then be the increased accuracy, due both to trying cases much more carefully and to using the average of the tried cases, rather than the result of one case, in calculating the amount to be awarded to each plaintiff.[26]

Suppose, however, that expenditure rises less than proportionally with the amount at stake, and everything else is held constant.[27] Under that assumption, expenditure on the tried cases becomes less important as the number of plaintiffs increases, because the larger the number of plaintiffs, the smaller the fraction necessary to provide an adequate sample. In the limit of a very large number of plaintiffs, expenditure on trying the sample of cases is negligible compared to the cost of trying the cases individually. That is consistent with what actually happened in *Cimino*.

So far, I have been considering a problem raised by both the *Cimino* procedure and the procedure I have proposed. There is an additional cost problem that applies only to the latter. Under that procedure, the plaintiffs' attorney spends resources estimating the relative claims of each plaintiff[28] and the defendant's attorney then spends resources examining plaintiffs in order to decide which cases to select for trial.

Under our assumptions, the plaintiffs' attorney can produce his estimates of claims more accurately and less expensively than verdicts would be produced by individual trials. The same should be true for the defense attorney. In addition, if the number of cases is large, the defense need only examine a random sample of cases in order to do a reasonably good job of locating overclaimed cases to select for trial. It follows that the attorneys can act in a way that, under the proposed procedure, produces more justice at a considerably lower cost than would individual trials.

It is not, however, clear that it is in their interest to do so. Each attorney's objective, at least in part, is to benefit his clients at the expense of the other party. By making a more accurate set of estimates, the plaintiffs' attorney not only produces a more just distribution among his clients, he also makes it harder for the defense to locate overclaimed plaintiffs for trial. The more he spends on improving the accuracy of his claims, the larger the amount his side will receive. He must balance that benefit against the associated cost. The defense attorney faces a similar situation.

Here, as elsewhere in the economics of litigation, there is no reason to assume that the level of expenditure that is privately optimal for one party to a legal dispute is also socially optimal. The amount spent on estimating claims and detecting overclaimed plaintiffs will depend on detailed assumptions about information costs and distributions of claims, as discussed in part VI.

It follows from these arguments that we cannot be sure that the procedure as described will cost less than ordinary trial without aggregation and sampling. This suggests two further queries. The first is whether we can say anything interesting about the relation between the costs of alternative approaches and the number of plaintiffs. The second is whether, if experience suggests that expenditures associated with the procedure are undesirably large, there may be ways of modifying it to reduce such expenditures.

An increase in the number of plaintiffs reduces the percentage of cases that must be tried. If expenditure per case increases less than proportionately with the amount at stake, the result is that trial costs for my suggested procedure (or the *Cimino* procedure) decrease, relative to the cost of trying all cases, as the number of plaintiffs increases. The same is probably true for the cost to the defense of selecting cases for trial. The larger the number of plaintiffs, the smaller the fraction that must be sampled in order to find ten cases from, say, the most overclaimed 5 percent. We would expect defense expenditures to increase less than proportionally with the number of plaintiffs and so become smaller and smaller, relative to the total amount at stake, as the number of plaintiffs increases. This result is demonstrated in appendix B of Friedman (1996) for the particular distributions assumed there.

The opposite result can be expected for the cost to the plaintiffs' attorney of calculating claims. The more plaintiffs there are, the easier it is for the defense to locate those who have overclaimed. The more accurately the defense can locate overclaimed plaintiffs, the greater the incentive for the plaintiffs' attorney to make accurate claims. So, an increase in the number of plaintiffs will tend to increase the amount spent per plaintiff by the plaintiffs' attorney. That is one reason why it might be desirable to shift from individual claims to statistical models when the number of plaintiffs becomes sufficiently large. The cost per plaintiff of estimating the parameters of a model to a given accuracy will fall as the number of plaintiffs increases.

The size of the expenditures by the attorneys will depend on details of the distribution of claims and on functions relating expenditure on investigating a claim to information produced. We cannot predict a priori how large it will be any more than we can predict a priori, in the case of ordinary litigation, how much of the damages awarded will be eaten up in litigation costs. But, if experience indicates that the attorneys are spending more than the improved accuracy their expenditure generates is worth, we can lower the amount they spend by a minor change in the procedure.

The incentive for the expenditures we, hypothetically, wish to reduce comes from their influence on the damages that will be awarded.[29] A court that wishes to reduce those expenditures can do so by selecting some cases for trial in the fashion I have described and some at random. The smaller the proportion of cases selected for trial by the defense, the lower the incentive that both attorneys have to spend more money estimating claims more accurately. Thus, courts have a mechanism by which they can adjust the procedure to move its outcome closer to an optimal level of cost and accuracy. An alternative approach would be to try to impose limits on the amount each party was permitted to spend on evaluating claims.[30]

Bias in the Procedure: Who Cuts, Who Lies, and Other Fine Points

In the procedure as I have described it, the plaintiffs' attorney calculates claims and the defendant's attorney selects which will be tried: The former cuts and the latter chooses, to take the obvious analogy from the incentive-compatible procedure for dividing a piece of cake. Is there any good reason to do it this way instead of requiring the defendant's attorney to list the amount he believes each plaintiff should receive and letting the plaintiffs' attorney choose which cases will be tried?

One reason is that the attorney who is calculating claims will need information from the plaintiffs that they might be reluctant to provide to the defense attorney for fear that it would be used against them in trial. The procedure I have described does not eliminate this problem—the defense attorney still needs enough information to decide which cases to select for trial. But, if the group is large, he can do an adequate job by examining only a small subset of the plaintiffs, and he can thus afford to spend much more per case examined than the plaintiffs' attorney. That should make it possible for him to produce a reasonably accurate estimate even with less cooperation from the individual plaintiffs.[31]

The defense attorney is not the only one who must worry about being misled by individual plaintiffs. Plaintiff i gains by increases in C_i above d_i, even though the plaintiffs as a group lose; so each plaintiff has an incentive, in dealing with his own attorney, to inflate his claim. The plaintiffs' attorney would presumably specify in his contract with the plaintiffs, whether representative plaintiffs in a class action or joint plaintiffs in an ordinary joint action, their obligations to furnish information that he requires in estimating their claims. Thus, the procedure yields a contractual equivalent of discovery rules between the plaintiffs and their attorney. Although each plaintiff gains by his own ability to mislead his attorney, he loses by the ability of all other plaintiffs to do the same; so plaintiffs and their attorney have a common interest in agreeing to rules that will allow the attorney to make an accurate estimate of the strength of each plaintiff's case.

One consequence of having the plaintiffs' attorney cut and the defendant's attorney choose is to give the latter a cost advantage, at least in situations where the number of plaintiffs is large. As discussed earlier, the party who chooses can use random sampling to identify overclaimed cases at a relatively low total cost. This advantage may or may not outweigh the advantage that the plaintiffs' attorney has due to the fact that the plaintiffs, who possess private information relevant to the strength of their cases, are his clients and have agreed to make such information available to him.

A second consequence is to give the defense an advantage in the final verdict. As I show in the appendix, the defense can produce an expected total damage payment equal to the expected payment under a system of individual trials by simply selecting cases for trial at random, with probabilities proportional to C_i. By examining cases and selecting those that appear to be overclaimed, the defense should be able to improve on that result.

How significant these advantages are will depend on the details of the underlying fact-finding technology—how accurately and at what cost each attorney can estimate d_i. If the net advantage to the defense turns out to be large,[32] and if we wish neither to change the tort system in a way that advantages defendants in mass torts nor to give plaintiffs an incentive to avoid the procedure in favor of individual litigation, we could compensate by altering other legal rules applicable to the procedure in ways that aid plaintiffs.

An alternative approach would be to eliminate the bias by allowing both parties to cut and both to choose. Under such a system, the plaintiffs' attorney produces a set of claims C_i^p, and the defense produces a set of claims C_i^d. Each attorney selects a set of cases to be tried. The court calculates two values of R: R_p is calculated using the plaintiffs' claims and the verdicts of the cases selected by the defense; R_d is calculated using the defense claims and the verdicts of the cases selected by the plaintiffs' attorney. Each plaintiff i receives the average of R_p C_i^p and R_d C_i^d. This version of the procedure will cost more to produce a given level of accuracy in the relative claims because each is being calculated twice. But it eliminates the bias in the outcome.[33] It may or may not increase the total cost of the procedure. Since each set of calculations plays only half the role it did before in determining the amount actually awarded, the parties have an incentive to spend less than before on increased accuracy. That may or may not balance the increased cost of having each claim calculated twice and having each party try to identify cases that the other has overclaimed.[34]

V. Applications outside of Class Actions

My analysis so far has assumed that the procedure I am describing will be used, as the *Cimino* procedure was, in a class action. It might also be applied to an ordinary joint action with a large number of plaintiffs. The use of the procedure ought to make such a joint action easier to organize because it provides a mechanism for solving the problem of allocating damages among the joint plaintiffs. After a putative mass tort had occurred, a lawyer would announce that he was forming a group of plaintiffs to litigate under the procedure; his announcement would include the formula by which he would be reimbursed. Plaintiffs would be free to join his group, to join another group, or to litigate individually.

My discussion has focused on mass torts because the procedure requires a single agent representing the defense and a single agent representing the plaintiffs. A lawyer who assembles a group of plaintiffs for a joint action satisfies the second requirement; the fact that all of the plaintiffs are suing the same defendant satisfies the first. This raises the question of whether other ways of satisfying these requirements might make it possible to use the procedure to reduce litigation costs outside of the context of mass torts. Consider the following radical proposal.

A court bundles the cases before it into large groups defined by common characteristics—a thousand intellectual property cases, a thousand personal injury cases, a thousand defamation cases. Each group is then auctioned off twice, with attorneys bidding for the right to represent all plaintiffs and for the right to represent all defendants. In the former auction, the attorney is offering to pay a sum in exchange for the right to represent the plaintiffs and collect all damages awarded to them; the high bid wins. In the latter, the attorney is stating for what sum he will agree to represent the defendants and pay all damages awarded against them; the low bid wins.

The two winning attorneys then go through the procedure I have described. When it is over, the defense attorney pays the plaintiffs' attorney the total damages awarded: $R \times \Sigma_i C_i$. Each defendant pays the defense attorney $(C_i/\Sigma_i C_i) \times B_d$, where B_d is the attorney's bid: the amount for which he agreed to be responsible for all costs and damages. Thus, the defendants are dividing their total costs in proportion to the amounts owed to their respective plaintiffs. Similarly, the plaintiffs' attorney pays each plaintiff i an amount $(C_i/\Sigma_i C_i) \times B_p$, where B_p is the plaintiffs' attorney's bid: the amount he offered to pay for the right to collect all damage payments.

There are obvious problems to implementing this radical version of my proposal within our legal system because it deprives both plaintiffs and defendants of the right to choose their own attorneys. One solution would be to treat it as a form of alternate dispute resolution: Cases go into groups subject to the procedure only if both plaintiff and defendant agree.

The general procedure would also be used in situations other than class actions where a single agent already controls what are really multiple cases. One example would be disputes between insurance companies, each of which controls a large number of legal claims for accidents involving its customers. In that context, the procedure would be a way of guaranteeing to each customer that the insurance company was fairly representing his interests in the litigation.

The procedure would be inappropriate if the agent who controlled multiple cases also fully owned them. Such an agent would care about the total awarded to all of the cases he owns, not the distribution among them. The *Cimino* procedure would give the correct total at a lower cost than the procedure discussed here. Such a situation could occur in the insurance context. It might also arise if, as some writers have suggested, tort claims were made fully marketable, allowing legal entrepreneurs to buy up large numbers of related claims and litigate them en masse.[35] Under such institutions, the damage award would reach the victim in the form of the price for which he sold his claim, so the distribution among victims would be determined by the market rather than directly by the court. In this context, the radical version of the procedure described above can be seen as an alternative way of selling claims designed to eliminate the cost of separately bargaining over each transaction.

VI. Results of the Formal Model

Appendix B in Friedman (1996) presents a formal model based on an error distribution that is bounded and uniform. I demonstrate that, as the number of cases goes to infinity, the defense is able to perfectly identify over-claimed cases at a cost that is vanishingly small relative to the amount at stake. The plaintiffs maximize their net return by spending the same amount in investigating each case and claiming an amount equal to their estimate of the expected return at trial.

The result becomes more complicated if we assume that some cases are more difficult to evaluate than others. The optimal strategy is then to esti-mate those cases less accurately, insuring against the risk that the resulting estimate may be too high by deliberately claiming less than their estimated value.

Several further points are worth noting about this situation. The first is that cases that are difficult for the plaintiffs' attorney will also be difficult for the defense attorney, so the defense has an incentive not to examine those cases. The lower the probability that a certain sort of case will be examined, the less the risk of overclaiming for such cases, so this effect will work in the opposite direction from that demonstrated in the model.[36]

A second point arises if plaintiffs are risk averse. Cases that are difficult for the attorneys are also difficult for the court, so plaintiffs with hard cases face a bigger gamble if they go to court individually; Thus, they gain more by replacing that gamble with the more certain outcome generated by the procedure I have proposed. In addition, hard cases are likely to be more expensive to litigate, again making the procedure particularly attractive as a substitute to individual trials for plaintiffs with hard cases. So, even if the procedure gives plaintiffs with hard cases somewhat less than their ex-pected return at trial, that may not make them less willing to join the class than plaintiffs with easy cases. If, despite these considerations, the incen-tive to underclaim hard cases turns out to be a serious problem, it can be dealt with in the same way suggested earlier for dealing with the proce-dure's pro-defense bias. The analysis of strategies with regard to hard cases is symmetrical; if the defense cuts and the plaintiffs' attorney chooses, the defense has an incentive to overclaim hard cases. So, if both parties cut and both choose, the biases will tend to cancel.

One important limitation of the formal model is that its error distributions are bounded. The result is that, as the number of cases increases, the additional gain to the defense of more and more accurately identifying the overclaimed cases becomes less and less; there are no cases to be found that are overclaimed by more than a factor of $1 + \varepsilon_p$. If the error distribution for the plaintiffs' estimates is unbounded, and if the defense can make the error of its estimate as small as it likes by spending enough money examining enough cases, it is in the interest of the defense to push R further and further down the larger the number of cases, so that in the limit of an infinite number of cases, damages awarded would go to zero.

How serious a problem this is likely to be with plausible numbers of cases and error distributions is an empirical issue. If it does turn out to be a problem, it might be controlled by any of several modifications to the procedure suggested earlier.

VII. Conclusions

I have proposed a procedure that has the potential to settle mass torts at a cost much less than individually litigating each claim. Like the *Cimino* procedure, it produces about the same outcome for the defense as would individual trials. Unlike the *Cimino* procedure, it provides outcomes for the individual plaintiffs tailored to the strength of their individual cases; indeed, it may well produce a more accurate allocation of damage payments to plaintiffs than would individual trials.

One can imagine applying the procedure in a variety of different contexts. In a case such as *Cimino v. Raymark*, where there are a large number of plaintiffs, each with a substantial claim, individual attorneys might compete to form groups to litigate under the procedure, thus avoiding some of the usual problems with class actions. Where individual claims were smaller, the class could be formed in the usual way; the procedure[37] would then provide a way of allocating damages among plaintiffs. By reducing the risk that the plaintiffs' attorney would sacrifice the interests of the absent plaintiffs to his own interest and that of the representative plaintiffs, the procedure makes it more likely that a class would, and should, be certified in such situations.

The procedure is not perfect; it provides no guarantee of an optimal expenditure on evaluating cases in order to allocate damages. This is equally true of alternatives, including the alternative of litigating each case separately. Also, although the plaintiffs' attorney will find it in his interest to make his claims roughly proportional to the strength of the individual cases, the relation will not be exact; differences in the difficulty of evaluating cases may, as demonstrated in the formal model, make it in his interest to deliberately underclaim some cases relative to others.[38] Finally, the simpler versions of the procedure are to some degree biased in favor of the defense, since the plaintiffs cut and the defense chooses. If such problems prove serious, there are ways in which the procedure can be modified to reduce them.

Appendix

A Simple Strategy for the Second Mover

Suppose we are dividing a cake under the conventional rule of "I cut, you choose." Further suppose that we have identical tastes; each of us prefers the larger slice. It seems obvious that, if there is any inaccuracy in cutting cakes, the party who moves second has the advantage. One way of seeing this is to note that if he selects his slice at random, he will, on average, get half the cake; if he has any ability at all to recognize the larger piece, he will do better than that. An analogous argument implies that, under the procedure described in this article, the defense can always do at least as well as it would with individual trials, and it may be able to do better. The analysis goes as follows: Suppose that, instead of examining cases and trying to select the ones that are overclaimed, the defense simply selects cases by a random process, with a probability

$$p_i = \frac{C_i}{\Sigma_i C_i}$$

of selecting case i. We then have

Expected Total Damage Payment = $<R> \times$ Total Claims

$$= \left[\sum_i p_i \frac{\langle d_i \rangle}{C_i} \right] \sum_i C_i = \left[\sum_i \frac{C_i}{\Sigma_j C_j} \frac{\langle d_i \rangle}{C_i} \right] \sum_i C_i = \sum_i \langle d_i \rangle,$$

which is expected total damage payment with individual trials.

So, a random procedure, with no examination at all, produces as good a result for the defense as individual trials. By selecting cases that are overclaimed, the defense can get a better result than that—a lower expected total damage payment—at some cost. If the cost is less than the gain, the defense does better with this procedure than with individual trials. If the cost is greater than the gain for all levels of expenditure on examining cases, the defense follows the strategy described above and does as well as it would with individual trials.

Notes

I would like to thank an anonymous referee and my colleagues at the University of Chicago and Cornell Law Schools, especially Jonathan Macey, Geoffrey Miller, and Richard Posner, for many helpful suggestions.

1. Claude Cimino, et al. v. Raymark Industries, Inc., et al., 751 F. Supp. 649.

2. Michael J. Saks & Peter David Blanck, Justice Improved: The Unrecognized Benefits of Aggregation and Sampling in the Trial of Mass Torts, 44 Stan. L. Rev. 815 (1992).

3. This assumes, of course, that the cases would have been tried. As Judge Parker pointed out in his opinion, the defendants "assert a right to individual trials in each case and assert the right to repeatedly contest in each case every contestable issue involving the same products, the same warnings, and the same conduct. The strategy is a sound one; the defendants know that if the procedure in *Cimino* is not affirmed, these cases will never be tried." (Cimino v. Raymark *651–52).

4. The issues were whether each asbestos-containing insulation product manufactured by each defendant, settling and nonsettling, was defective and unreasonably dangerous, the adequacy of warnings, the state-of-the-art defense, and the fiber type defense. The question of punitive damages in the entire case of the 2,298 class representatives was also submitted for jury determination.

5. Phase 2 was resolved by stipulation by the parties.

6. The increase in sample size was less than proportional, as one would expect if the objective was to get equally reliable results for each category. The opinion states that "[w]hen setting the sample size for each disease category, the Court sought a confidence level of 95%, in other words ±2.00 standard deviations" (Cimino v. Raymark *664). The numbers (samples of 50 each for two categories with 1,050 and 972 plaintiffs) suggest that the court did not apply any very precise statistical rule.

7. One example is a distribution in which a very small number of plaintiffs have cases that, if tried, will generate enormous damage awards. If there is only one such plaintiff, and 10 percent of the cases selected at random are tried, there is a 90 percent chance that his case will not be selected and will thus have no influence on the observed results. But if the damage award he would get is large enough, his case may have a very large effect on what the total award to all plaintiffs would be if all cases were tried.

8. Judge Parker's statement that "[d]efendants complain about the 1% likelihood that the result would be significantly different" (Cimino v. Raymark *666) suggests that he interprets a 99 percent confidence level as a probability of 99 percent that the procedure will yield a result within some (unspecified) significant error—where "significant" means "important," not "statistically significant." Whatever error he did use, what ought he to have used? One possibility would be to compare the procedure to the result of individual trials, taking account of the difference in litigation costs. Suppose, for example, that aggregation saves the defense $1 million in legal expenses. One might then ask how likely it is that the award is more than $1 million greater than what would have been awarded if all cases were tried. If the answer is .01, there is then only one chance in a hundred that the procedure has made the defendants worse off.

While that approach solves the problem of picking an appropriate error, it still leaves the problem that statistics cannot generate such probabilities without making assumptions about the characteristics of the sample.

9. "Individual members of a disease category who will receive an award that might be different from one they would have received had their individual case been decided by a jury have waived any objections" (Cimino v. Raymark *665).

10. The opinion discusses under what circumstances smoking would constitute contributory negligence and notes that some plaintiffs received no awards, but it does not say whether any received no awards for that reason.

11. Federal Rules of Civil Procedure 23a(4).

12. Suppose the court uses an aggregation process that awards every plaintiff the average of what all plaintiffs in the class are entitled to. Plaintiffs who can expect an above-average return withdraw from the class. That lowers the average that the remainder can expect to get, causing more plaintiffs to withdraw. Under some circumstances, the entire class may come apart in this way. This is a form of adverse selection, more familiar in the context of insurance. See George Akerlof, The Market for "Lemons": Quality Uncertainty and the Market Mechanism, 336 Q. J. Econ. 488 (1970).

13. It was permitted in *David Daar v. Yellow Cab Co.* (67 Cal. 2d 695, 433 P.2d 732, 63 Cal. Rptr. 724), rejected by the Second Circuit in *Eisen v. Carlisle and Jacquelin* (479 F.2d 1005), and has not been ruled upon by the Supreme Court.

14. Saks & Blanck, *supra* note 2, at 851. Glen O. Robinson & Kenneth S. Abraham, Collective Justice in Tort Law, 78 Va. L. Rev. 1481 (1992), suggests and discusses several other statistical approaches to dealing with mass torts, using information from the outcomes of similar cases to determine, or at least affect, awards.

15. As Saks and Blanck point out, average jury awards seem to increase less than linearly with the amount of injury suffered by the plaintiff (Saks & Blanck, *supra* note 2, at 840).

16. In explaining my proposed procedure, I assume that it is being applied to a case with many plaintiffs and one defendant; the application to the less common case of one plaintiff and many defendants should be straightforward.

17. One reason such rules are necessary is that the decision maker in a trial has only weak incentives to reach the correct decision and can therefore not be trusted to do so unless severely constrained. Under the proposed procedures, it is in the private interest of the decision maker (the plaintiffs' attorney) to estimate the strength of claims accurately, making such constraints less necessary.

18. The plaintiffs' attorney can achieve the same objective by attempting to set C_i proportional to d_i: $C_i = Kd_i$, where K is some constant. The value of K has no effect on the outcome; R, on average, will be $1/K$, so plaintiffs will receive $R \times C_i = \langle d_i \rangle$, independent of K where $\langle x \rangle$ indicates the expected value of x. I therefore assume $K = 1$ for simplicity in exposition.

19. As we will see later, this statement is only approximately true. If some cases are harder to evaluate than others, the optimal strategy for the plaintiffs' attorney may deviate somewhat from that described here.

20. This is one of the central points made by Saks and Blanck in defending the *Cimino* procedure. Saks & Blanck, *supra* note 2, at 833–36.

21. *Id.* at 851.

22. Since the class was certified before the procedure was proposed, the assent was presumably by the representative plaintiffs controlling the litigation rather than by the unanimous decision of all plaintiffs. But the procedure created a conflict of interest among members of the class, which arguably called into question the ability of the representative plaintiffs to represent the interests of the remaining plaintiffs.

23. For an extensive discussion of legal issues associated with aggregation, see Robinson & Abraham, *supra* note 14.

24. If it is not obvious that they are overclaiming, the defense may miss some of their cases and some of the overclaimed representative defendants will get more than they should. On the other hand, given that possibility, one would expect the defense to take special care in examining the claims made for the representative plaintiffs. I am assuming here that plaintiffs whose cases are actually tried get the amount awarded to them, rather than having their award calculated from their claim in the same fashion as plaintiffs whose cases are not tried. Without that assumption, representative plaintiffs gain by overclaiming even if they are sure their cases will be among those tried, although the attorney for the class of plaintiffs loses if his recompense is an increasing function of the total amount awarded.

25. I do not know of any definitive analysis of this question. One possible approach would be to assume Nash equilibrium. The amount at stake is S. The probability P that the plaintiff will win the case depends on expenditures L_p (by the plaintiff) and L_d (by the defendant): $P(L_p, L_d)$. The parties increase their expenditures until they reach the point where a \$1 increase in expenditure by the plaintiff increases his expected return $(P(L_p, L_d)S)$ by \$1, and a \$1 increase in expenditure by the defendant increases his expected return $(-P(L_p, L_d)S)$ by \$1:

$$\frac{\partial P(L_p, L_d)}{\partial L_p}S = 1; \; \frac{\partial P(L_p, L_d)}{\partial L_d}S = -1.$$

Under these assumptions, the question of how expenditure increases with amount at stake becomes the question of how rapidly

$$\frac{\partial P(L_p, L_d)}{\partial L_{p,d}}$$

decreases as L_p and L_d increase. If, for example,

$$\frac{\partial P(\alpha L_p, \alpha L_d)}{\partial L_{p,d}} = \frac{1}{\alpha^\beta}\frac{\partial P(L_p, L_d)}{\partial L_{p,d}},$$

then expenditure increases more (less) than in proportion to the amount at stake if $\beta < 1(\beta > 1)$. One objection to this approach is that Nash equilibrium is not very plausible in a game involving only two parties, and it is still less plausible in a situation where the two parties can and do bargain with each other.

26. In the case of the *Cimino* procedure, that must be balanced against the decreased accuracy from awarding plaintiffs whose cases are not selected for trial average verdicts, even though the particular plaintiff may not have average characteristics.

27. The comparison is between two cases whose only difference is the amount at stake. Each of my ten cases is simply one of the thousands of cases that might be tried individually. I am not assuming that the ratio of litigation cost to the amount at stake for the typical large case is smaller than for the typical small case; presumably, the typical large case not only has more at stake but also has a more complicated set of legal and factual issues than the typical small case.

28. Or the plaintiffs' attorney spends resources determining how the amount a plaintiff is entitled to is related to the plaintiffs' characteristics under the alternative version that I proposed for cases with very large numbers of plaintiffs and small average claims.

29. It is possible that the plaintiffs' attorney may have additional incentives due to concerns with either justice or risk among his clients. They might prefer that claims be proportional to the actual injury each client has suffered, even if claims did not affect the total amount paid out.

30. In a class action, a judge could limit expenditure by one side simply by limiting the expenses he was willing to permit the class attorney to claim. Limiting expenditure by the other party, or by both parties if the procedure was being used outside of a class action, would be more difficult.

31. Presumably, there would be legal rules requiring some cooperation from the plaintiffs. "(M)ost courts have taken the view that reasonably necessary discovery against individual class members should be allowed as a matter of judicial discretion, but that discovery is not available of right as it would be against a party to a nonclass suit. (e.g., Brennan v. Midwestern United Life Ins. Co., 450 F.2d 999 (7th Cir. 1971)"; Fleming James, Jr., and Geoffrey C. Hazard, Jr., Civil Procedure 579 (Little, Brown, 3d ed. 1985)).

32. This does not require the defense attorney to be better at estimating $<d_i>$ than the plaintiffs' attorney, as should be clear from the analysis above. If, for example, accurate estimates are very expensive and the number of plaintiffs is large, the plaintiffs' attorney will produce very inaccurate estimates and the defendant's attorney, spending much more per case on a small fraction of the cases, will be able to find cases that are greatly overclaimed, thus greatly reducing the total amount paid out in damages.

33. That conclusion depends on assuming that both sides are equally able to generate the relevant information. If, as suggested earlier, the plaintiffs' attorney has better access to information about plaintiffs, the version of the procedure described here is biased in favor of the plaintiffs. If one knew how great the informational advantage was, one could compensate for it by using an appropriately weighted average of the awards calculated from the two different sets of claims.

34. If we assumed that each party aimed at the same level of accuracy as under the earlier version of the procedure, expenditure would be increased but not doubled by requiring each party to both cut and choose. The information generated in cutting could also be used in choosing. The defense attorney's first step in identifying overclaimed cases would be to compare the plaintiffs' attorney's claims with his own.

35. For discussions of the idea of marketable claims, see Marc J. Shukaitis, A Market in Personal Injury Tort Claims, 16 J. Legal Stud. 329–49 (1987); David Friedman, Private Creation and Enforcement of Law: A Historical Case, 8 J. Le-

gal Stud. 399 (1979); David Friedman, What is Fair Compensation for Death or Injury? 2 Int'l Rev. L. & Econ. 81 (1982); Jonathan R. Macey & Geoffrey P. Miller, The Plaintiffs' Attorney's Role in Class Action and Derivative Litigation: Economic Analysis and Recommendations for Reform, 58 U. Chi. L. Rev. 1 (1991).

36. That is not true for the formal model of appendix B in Friedman (1996) in the limit of large N because, in that situation, the defense is able to perfectly identify overclaimed cases at negligible cost.

37. Possibly the statistical version discussed above.

38. I have presented this as a fault of the procedure, but it could be viewed as a desirable consequence. It may be desirable, on grounds of either efficiency or justice, for parties who insist on litigating difficult cases to bear part or all of the cost of doing so. Underclaiming difficult cases costs plaintiffs less than estimating the strength of their cases as accurately as easy cases are estimated. Thus, this feature of the procedure has consequences similar to those of the usual (American) rule that each party must bear his own litigation costs: Plaintiffs with cases that are expensive to litigate take home less, net of litigation costs, than parties who have suffered similar damage but have easy cases.

References

Akerlof, George A. "The Market for 'Lemons': Quality, Uncertainty, and the Market Mechanism." *Quarterly Journal of Economics* 84 (1970): 488–500.

Friedman, David. "More Justice for Less Money." *Journal of Law and Economics* 39 (1996): 211–40.

―――. "Private Creation and Enforcement of Law: A Historical Case." *Journal of Legal Studies* 8 (1979): 399–415.

―――. "What Is 'Fair Compensation' for Death or Injury?" *International Review of Law and Economics* 2 (1982): 81–93.

James, Fleming, Jr., and Hazard, Geoffrey C., Jr. *Civil Procedure*. 3d ed. Boston: Little, Brown. 1985.

Macey, Jonathan R., and Miller, Geoffrey P. "The Plaintiffs' Attorney's Role in Class Action and Derivative Litigation: Economic Analysis and Recommendations for Reform." *University of Chicago Law Review* 58 (1991): 1–118.

Robinson, Glen O., and Abraham, Kenneth S. "Collective Justice in Tort Law." *Virginia Law Review* 78 (1992): 1481–519.

Saks, Michael J., and Blanck, Peter David. "Justice Improved: The Unrecognized Benefits of Aggregation and Sampling in the Trial of Mass Torts." *Stanford Law Review* 44 (1992): 815–51.

Shukaitis, Marc J. "A Market in Personal Injury Tort Claims." *Journal of Legal Studies* 16 (1987): 329–49.

PART V

BANKRUPTCY AND
SECURITIES REGULATION

11

Improving Bankruptcy Procedure

PHILIPPE AGHION, OLIVER HART, AND JOHN MOORE

There is a widespread dissatisfaction with bankruptcy procedures throughout the world. Bankruptcy reform is being actively considered in the United Kingdom and France and is in the air in the United States. East European countries that must select a bankruptcy law for their new capitalistic economies have had a hard time making the choice and, in some cases, dissatisfied with their original decisions, they are already making changes.[1] Russia has recently implemented a bankruptcy law that seems complex and apparently suffers from many of the disadvantages of Western procedures.[2]

We believe the reason for this unsettled state of affairs is that bankruptcy law has developed in a fairly haphazard manner, as a series of attempts to solve perceived immediate problems. There has been relatively little effort to step back and ask what the goals of bankruptcy procedure should be or to consider how one would set up an optimal bankruptcy procedure if one were starting from scratch. To put it another way, economic analysis— which has been applied with such great success to other aspects of law in the last thirty years—has, with a few notable exceptions, not been used to shed light on optimal bankruptcy procedure.[3]

This chapter attempts to provide an economic perspective on bankruptcy procedure. In parts I and II, we discuss the rationale for, and goals of, bankruptcy procedure. Part III describes how existing procedures fall short of these goals. Our main point is that reorganization procedures like Chapter 11 are flawed because they mix the decision of who should get what with the decision of what should happen to the bankruptcy company. In part IV, we turn to a procedure that we have proposed elsewhere, which we believe would improve on existing procedures[4] In our scheme, debt claims are converted into equity, and the decision about whether to reorganize or liquidate is then put to a vote. The merit of the scheme is that all claimants, once they are shareholders, have a common interest in voting for the efficient outcome. In part V, we discuss some practical difficulties concerning our proposal and how they might be resolved. Part VI contains concluding remarks.

I. Background

Companies take on debt for many reasons. To mention just a few, they may wish to reduce taxes, they may wish to commit themselves to reduce slack, or they may wish to signal that future prospects are good. Whatever the reason, there will be circumstances, arising perhaps from an unexpected shock, in which the company will be unable to pay its debts. Bankruptcy law is concerned with what should happen in such situations.

The analysis of optimal bankruptcy law is complicated by the following observation. In an ideal world, debtors and creditors would anticipate the possibility of default and specify as part of their initial contracts what should happen in a default state: in particular, whether the company should be reorganized or liquidated and how its value should be divided up among the various creditors. In other words, the parties would provide their own bankruptcy procedure; there would be no need for a state-provided bankruptcy procedure.

In practice, transaction costs are likely to be too large for debtors and creditors to craft their own bankruptcy procedures, particularly in situations where debtors acquire new assets and new creditors as time passes. Instead, parties may prefer to rely on a "standard form" bankruptcy procedure provided by the state. It is a long way from this observation, however, to any conclusions about the *nature* of such a standard-form procedure. The problem is that the theory of optimal contracting in the presence of transaction costs (the "theory of incomplete contracts") is in its infancy. In particular, we are aware of no formal analysis that *both* explains why it is rational for parties to leave out of their contract what should happen in a default state and shows how a state-provided procedure can improve matters.[5]

Thus, in what follows, we do not derive an optimal bankruptcy procedure from first principles. Instead, our approach is to use economic theory to guide us as to the nature of a "good" bankruptcy procedure. In the next section, we suggest some goals that an efficient bankruptcy procedure should satisfy. Later (in part IV), we describe a procedure that we believe meets these goals. Although we do not claim that our procedure is optimal, we think that it is practical and avoids some of the pitfalls of existing procedures. Also, the procedure is sufficiently simple and natural that future work may show it to be optimal within a reasonable class of procedures.[6]

It is also worth pointing out that, while we propose our procedure for use by the state, it could, in principle, also be adopted by companies of their own accord. In other words, to the extent that a company can opt out of existing bankruptcy procedures, it may wish to select our procedure—as a mechanism for resolving financial distress—as part of its initial contracts with its creditors.

II. Goals of Bankruptcy Procedure

As noted, we do not proceed from first principles. However, on the basis of economic theory, we believe that the following are desirable goals for a bankruptcy procedure. As we shall see, some of these goals may conflict.

First (goal 1), a good bankruptcy procedure should try to achieve an ex-post efficient outcome (i.e., an outcome that maximizes the total value of the proceeds—measured in money terms—received by existing claimants). The efficient outcome may be to close the company down and sell off the assets for cash, to sell the company as a going concern for cash, or to reorganize the company.[7] Second (goal 2), a good bankruptcy procedure should give managers the right ex-ante incentives to avoid bankruptcy. In particular, a good procedure should not favor incumbent managers, although it should not preclude them from retaining their jobs if the bankruptcy was due to bad luck rather than bad management.

Third (goal 3), a good bankruptcy procedure should preserve absolute priority. That is, the most senior creditors should be paid off before anything is given to the next most senior creditors, and so on down the ladder (with ordinary shareholders at the bottom). Finally, as a fourth goal (goal 4), a good bankruptcy procedure should, whenever possible, put ultimate decision-making power in the hands of the claimants rather than in the hands of the judiciary or experts.

Let us briefly discuss the rationale for goals 1–4. Goal 1 simply reflects the idea that, other things being equal, more is preferred to less; in particular, if a procedure can be modified to deliver higher total ex-post value, then, given that absolute priority is preserved (i.e., goal 3), everybody will be better off. Goal 2 reflects the idea that debt may have an important role in constraining or bonding managers to act in the interest of claimholders. Managers may have taken on debt at an earlier stage as a way of committing themselves to reduce slack.[8] A bankruptcy procedure that lets managers off too lightly if they fail to pay their debts—for example, by favoring them in the reorganization process—will interfere with the ex-ante bonding role of debt.

Absolute priority (i.e., goal 3) is desirable for several reasons. First, it corresponds to what the parties contracted for outside of bankruptcy; that is, if the company were sold outside bankruptcy and there were not enough cash to pay creditors off, senior creditors would be paid off, followed by junior creditors, and so on. If contracts are not upheld within bankruptcy, creditors, particularly senior ones, may be less willing to lend to the company in the first place. In addition, as Thomas Jackson has argued, any discrepancy between what a class of claimants receives inside bankruptcy and what it receives outside bankruptcy could lead to inefficient rent seeking—some people bribing management into deliberately precipitating bankruptcy, and other people attempting to forestall bankruptcy.[9]

Second, the priority of a company's capital structure provides an important instrument for constraining management's ability to raise fresh capital. Under certain circumstances, for example, management may issue senior debt—which mops up earnings from assets in place—in order to restrain itself from raising further capital in the future to fund unprofitable, but empire-enhancing, projects. This ability to commit to profitable projects will be weakened to the extent that the seniority of initial claims is not respected, that is, to the extent that new claims issued at a later date are not treated as junior to existing claims in a bankruptcy procedure.[10]

Goal 4 simply captures the idea that it is better to put decisions in the hands of claimants who suffer the consequences of these decisions than in the hands of outsiders (e.g., judges, insolvency practitioners) who do not. This does not mean, of course, that the *advice* of experts may not be very useful to claimants when they make their decisions—in fact, they may simply follow this advice (for more on this, see part IV).

Although we believe that goals 1–4 have great appeal, they are not beyond question. Bankruptcy scholars have raised doubts about goal 3 in particular. Critics argue that if equityholders get little or nothing in a bankruptcy proceeding, then management—acting on the equityholders' behalf—will engage in highly risky, but inefficient, behavior when a company is close to bankruptcy, because while the shareholders gain if things go well, it is the creditors who lose if things go badly.[11]

We are skeptical about this argument. It supposes that management acts on behalf of shareholders, an assumption that may be plausible for small, owner-managed companies, but that is questionable for large, public companies. The recent theoretical literature on agency costs and capital structure argues that it is more reasonable to suppose that management is self-interested.[12] Under these conditions, there is a case for making bankruptcy procedure less harsh for managers—to prevent them from engaging in highly risky behavior to save their jobs—but this is already covered under goal 2.[13] Even in the case of small, owner-managed companies, it is far from clear that departures from absolute priority are the best way to soften the blow of a golden parachute in the form of senior debt.

Given the above, we shall assume that goals 1–4 *are* desirable, ceteris paribus. It is worth noting, however, that the procedure we propose in part IV could easily be modified to allow for departures from absolute priority if this was found to be a desirable goal.

A final important point to make is that some of the four goals may be in conflict. For example, suppose incumbent management has special skills. In that situation, ex-post efficiency (goal 1) might call for the incumbent management of a bankrupt company to be retained. However, knowing this, management might have little incentive to avoid bankruptcy, that is, goal 2 would not be served.[14]

In view of this, it is unlikely that any bankruptcy procedure can achieve all of the four goals. The best we can probably hope for is a reasonable balance between these goals—particularly goals 1 and 2. The procedure discussed in part IV is constructed with this in mind. Although we feel that it does a satisfactory job in this respect, the procedure could quite easily be fine-tuned if the balance was felt to be wrong; we return to this point in the conclusion.

III. Existing Procedures

Although there are many different bankruptcy procedures used around the world, these procedures fall into two main categories: cash auctions and structured bargaining. We discuss these in turn, paying particular attention to their application in the United States and the United Kingdom.

Cash Auctions (e.g., Chapter 7 in the United States or Liquidation in the United Kingdom)

In a cash auction, the company is put on the block and sold to the highest bidder. Often, the company's assets are sold piecemeal, that is, the company is liquidated. Sometimes, however, the company is sold as a going concern. Whichever occurs, the receipts from the sale are distributed among former claimants according to absolute priority.

In a world of perfect capital markets, a cash auction would (presumably) be the ideal bankruptcy procedure.[15] Anybody who could make the company profitable would be able to raise cash from some source (e.g., a commercial bank, an investment bank, the stock market) and make a bid for the company. Perfect competition among bidders would ensure that the company was sold for its true value.

In practice, there is widespread skepticism about the efficacy of cash auctions. The feeling is that a combination of transaction costs, asymmetric information, and moral hazard makes it difficult for bidders to raise sufficient cash to maintain a company as a going concern (i.e., capital markets are not perfect). As a consequence, there may be a lack of competition in the auction and few bids to keep the company whole. The result will be that some companies are liquidated piecemeal and/or sold at a low price.

It is worth spelling out a transaction-cost reason for imperfect capital markets. Suppose a large, public company is put on the block. Someone making a cash bid for the company is, in effect, taking the company private (unless the bidder represents a public company). The bidder's intention may well be to take the company public again later. The problem is that, in the interim period, the bidder is bearing the risk of changes in the company's value. The bidder will, of course, "charge" for this risk bearing by offering a lower price in the original auction. The consequence of this is twofold. First, the going-concern bid may lose to a collection of piecemeal bids for the company's assets, since the latter achieve risk sharing by spreading risk over a large number of bidders. Second, regardless of who wins the auction, the amount of cash raised will tend to be lower.[16]

The above transaction cost arises because of the difficulty of assembling a suitable group of investors to be risk bearers for the new company.[17] Note, however, that there is a natural group of risk bearers at hand: the former claimants (who were, after all, the previous risk bearers). Transaction costs would be reduced if bidders could reach this group directly by offering them securities in the postbankruptcy company. This is not allowed for in a cash-only auction like Chapter 7, but it is a key feature of the procedure we propose in part IV (and also of Chapter 11).

Neither the above theoretical argument nor the empirical evidence described in note 17 provides much indication of the magnitude of this imperfection in capital markets. Given this, any bankruptcy procedure adopted should work well both in the case where capital markets are perfect and in the case where they are not. The procedure described in part IV has this flexibility. As we shall see, it consists of an auction in which both cash and noncash bids for the company are allowed. If capital markets are perfect, the company will go to the bidder with the highest willingness to pay—moreover, this bidder can do no better than to offer cash—and thus the outcome will be exactly the same as in a cash-only auction. On the other hand, if the capital markets are imperfect, the procedure can deliver an outcome that is superior to that achievable by a cash auction.

Structured Bargaining (e.g., United States Chapter 11 or United Kingdom Administration)

Because of the concern about the effectiveness of cash auctions, a number of countries have developed alternative procedures based on the idea of structured bargaining. The basic idea behind these procedures is that the company's claimants are encouraged to bargain about the future of the company—in particular, whether it should be liquidated or reorganized and how its value should be divided up—according to predetermined rules. The leading example of a structured bargaining procedure in the West is Chapter 11 of the U.S. Bankruptcy Code; however, U.K. Administration is based on similar ideas, as are procedures in France, Germany, and Japan.

The details of Chapter 11 are complicated, but the basic elements are as follows: Creditors' claims are stayed, claimholders are grouped into classes according to the type of claim they have, committees or trustees are appointed to represent each class, and a judge supervises a process of bargaining among the committees to determine a plan of action and a division of value for the company. During the process, incumbent management usually runs the company. An important part of the procedure is that a plan can be implemented if it receives approval by a suitable majority of each claimant class; unanimity is not required.

We remark that U.K. Administration was introduced in the 1986 Insolvency Act as "the British version of Chapter 11."[18] An important difference between U.K. Administration and Chapter 11 is that the administrator (who is an insolvency practitioner), rather than incumbent management, runs the company during bankruptcy. There are also a number of differences in the voting rules between the two procedures. To date, the costs of Administration are such that it has rarely been used.

Chapter 11 has been subject to a great deal of criticism in the last few years. Among other things, practitioners and commentators have claimed that it is time consuming, that it involves significant legal and administrative costs, that it causes considerable loss in the bankrupt company's value, that it is (relatively) soft on management, and that the judges who run it sometimes abuse their powers.[19]

It would undoubtedly be possible to modify Chapter 11—and procedures like it—to improve matters, and a number of suggestions along these lines have been made. However, we believe there are two fundamental problems inherent in any structured bargaining procedure that no amount of tinkering can solve. These problems are associated with the fact that a structured bargaining procedure like Chapter 11 attempts to make two decisions at once: what to do with the company, and who should get what in the event of a restructuring of claims.

Problem 1

Restructured companies do not have an objective value. Consequently, it is hard to know what fraction of the postbankruptcy company's securities each group of creditors is entitled to receive. This is true even if there is no dispute about the amount and seniority of each creditor's claim. As a result, there can be a great deal of haggling.

Problem 2

Perhaps even more serious, there is a danger that the wrong decision will be made concerning the company's future. The voting mechanism is fixed in advance, which means that those people whose payoff ought not to be affected by the outcome (either because they are fully protected anyway, or because they are not entitled to anything) may end up controlling the pivotal votes.

Problem 1 is well understood, having been discussed at some length in the literature.[20] Problem 2 has also been noted but has been subject to less analysis. An example may help to illustrate it.

> *Example A.* Suppose senior creditors are owed $100, and the liquidation value of the company is $90. Assume that if the company were maintained as a going concern for six months, then it would be worth on average $110 (suppose the discount rate is zero). However, there is uncertainty: If things go well, it will be worth $180; if things go badly, it will be worth only $40. (The average of $180 and $40 is $110.) Clearly, the value-maximizing choice is to keep the company going, since $110 exceeds the liquidation value of $90. However, it is not in the senior creditors' interest to do this. If things go well, the company is worth $180, and the senior creditors get only the $100 they are owed. But if things go badly, they get just $40. The average of these amounts is $70, which is less than the $90 the senior creditors receive from immediate liquidation.

In this example, senior creditors may vote to liquidate the company immediately rather than enter into a lengthy negotiation that might lead to the company's being saved. This is in spite of the fact that there is enough value in the efficient outcome for the senior creditors to be paid off in full: $110 exceeds the $100 senior debt. Had the senior creditors been paid off, and the vote left in the hands of the junior creditors and the shareholders (whose money is at stake), then the junior creditors would have made the efficient decision about the company's future.

Things may go the other way, though. Consider a variant on Example A:

> *Example B.* Assume the same facts set forth in Example A, except that the upside value from continuation is lower—only $120 rather than $180. Thus, the average value from continuation is $80 (the average of $120 and $40).

In Example B, the junior creditors and shareholders are not entitled to anything, since the best that can happen to the company is that it is liquidated for $90, which is less than the senior debt. So, the junior creditors and shareholders ought not to be party to the decision over the company's future. And yet, the rules of Chapter 11 dictate that they do have votes, and as a result, they may be in a position to press for continuation (since they can see the upside potential of $120).[21] If the junior creditors and shareholders have enough votes to veto a liquidation plan, then at best the senior creditors may have to bribe them to accept it—which would lead to a violation of absolute priority—and at worst the company may be inefficiently kept going. Notice that, had the vote been left in the hands of senior creditors, they would have made the correct decision about the company's future.[22]

At this point, it is worth standing back and asking why the various claimants cannot bargain around the inefficiencies described in Examples A and B, that is, why the Coase Theorem does not solve Problems 1 and 2. Probably the most important reason is that, in the case of large companies, there are often numerous claimants (e.g., bondholders, trade creditors, and shareholders), which can make negotiation around a given (inefficient) procedure very difficult and lengthy (due to free rider and holdout problems, combined with asymmetries of information among claimants).

Consider Example A where senior creditors might vote to liquidate the company. This outcome could be avoided if junior creditors and shareholders could bribe the senior creditors not to liquidate—for example, they could buy out the senior creditors at a price between $90 and $100. However, the more numerous and heterogeneous the junior creditors and shareholders are, the more difficult it is—and the longer it will take—to coordinate such an offer (each junior claimant will want the other junior claimant to bribe the senior creditors). As a result, either an agreement will not be reached or it will require lengthy negotiation (there may be a war of attrition).[23]

Similar problems arise in Example B, where senior creditors must collectively decide to make concessions to junior claimants to compensate them for not pursuing reorganization. It may be easier to achieve agreement in Example B, however, to the extent that the number of senior creditors is relatively small and the creditors find it easier to coordinate their actions.

A structure procedure like Chapter 11 reduces the severity of the above bargaining problems by making the majority's will binding on the minority (this mitigates free riding and holdout behavior). However, even in this case, an efficient outcome may not be reached, for example, because of asymmetries of information. Suppose, in Example A, junior claimants are unsure whether the company's liquidation value is really $90 as opposed to some lower figure, while senior creditors know the true value. Then junior creditors may quite rationally "lowball" the senior creditors by offering them less than $90 to compensate them for not liquidating. In this case, the senior creditors will turn them down if the true liquidation value is $90, and a valuable going-concern opportunity will be lost.[24]

IV. An Alternative Procedure

We can summarize the previous discussion as follows. We believe existing bankruptcy procedures are flawed for two reasons: either they assume perfect capital markets (as in Chapter 7) or they mix the decision of what should happen to the company with the decision of who gets what (as in Chapter 11). We now describe a procedure that does not suffer from these defects. The key lies in transforming a group of people with different claims (and therefore different objectives) into a homogeneous class of shareholders and then putting the company's future to a simple vote. Our proposal also avoids bargaining over the division of the pie, because it uses a mechanical procedure for distributing shares that preserves absolute priority.[25]

The philosophy underlying the procedure—and the procedure itself—can be most easily understood in the case of a company with a single class of creditors, who are owed D by the company. Suppose the company defaults on its debt and for some other reason enters bankruptcy. The presumption is that the company is worth less than D, because otherwise it should have been able to avoid bankruptcy by borrowing or issuing new equity to pay off existing creditors. Given this, the following bankruptcy procedure seems natural: cancel the company's debts, give all the equity to the former creditors, and let these creditors—as the new owners—decide what to do with the company, that is, whether it should be sold off for cash or reorganized as a going concern. To this end, let the judge supervising the procedure solicit bids for the company, but permit noncash bids as well as cash bids. In a noncash bid, someone offers securities in the postbankruptcy company instead of cash; thus, a noncash bid embraces the possibility of reorganization and/or recapitalization of the company as a going concern. The following are some examples of a noncash bid.

- The old managers propose to keep their jobs and offer claimants a share in the postbankruptcy company.
- The same financial arrangement might be offered by a new management team.
- The managers of another company might propose to buy the bankrupt company, offering shares in *their* company as payment.
- Management (old or new) might induce some debt in the company's capital structure. One way to do this would be to arrange for a bank to lend money to the postbankruptcy company (the loan is conditional on the bid succeeding) and offer claimants a combination of cash and equity in the (levered) company. Another way would be to offer claimants a combination of shares and bonds in the postbankruptcy company.

Three months are allowed for bids to be made.[26] Finally, after the bids are in, let the new owners—the former creditors—decide by a single majority vote which bid to select. The company then exits from bankruptcy. (At this point, it may be helpful to consult the time line in figure 11.1; some aspects of this time line will be explained later.)

Note that, for the bidding process to work well, it is important that potential bidders have reasonably accurate information about the company's prospects. Part of the bankruptcy judge's job, therefore, would be to ensure that bidders have access to the company's books during the three-month bid solicitation period. Another part of the judge's job might be to evaluate, and make recommendations about, the bids, possibly with the help of appointed outside experts (e.g., an investment bank). These evaluations and

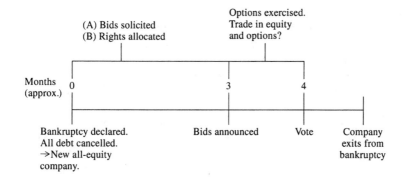

Fig. 11.1 Time line of proposed new bankruptcy procedure.

recommendations would not be binding, however, and the creditors would be free to ignore them.

The above is the bare-bones description of the Aghion-Hart-Moore (AHM) procedure. Let us now discuss two elaborations. First, it is possible that the company really is worth more than D. This could be the case if the company was being run inefficiently by incumbent management prior to bankruptcy but will be run efficiently postbankruptcy. Under these conditions, the above scheme overpays creditors—they get equity worth more than D—and initial shareholders are shortchanged. In order to deal with this possibility, the AHM procedure incorporates an idea attributable to Lucian Bebchuk.[27] Each shareholder is given the option to buy out the creditor for the pro rata value of his debts. (That is, a shareholder who held 1 percent of the equity is given the right to buy back up to 1 percent of the equity for a price of D per 100 percent. Note that creditors who are bought out must relinquish their equity—they cannot hold on.)[28] These options are exercised once the bids are in—so that an assessment of the company's value can be made—but *before* the vote. An extra month is allowed for this purpose (refer again to the time line in figure 11.1 above). In addition, options can be bought and sold (unexercised options expire at month four and are thus worthless). The point of these options is simple. Any shareholder who thinks former creditors are being overpaid can do something about it; he can, on a pro rata basis, pay the former creditors what they are owed and get their equity in return.

Second, companies often have several classes of creditors. The AHM procedure can be extended to this case quite easily, again using Bebchuk options. Suppose, for instance, there are two classes of creditors: senior creditors owed D_1 and junior creditors owed D_2. Initially, all the equity is given to senior creditors. However, junior creditors are given options to buy equity back from the senior creditors for a price of D_1 per 100 percent, while shareholders are given options to buy equity back from senior and junior creditors for a price of $D_1 + D_2$ per 100 percent. (The scheme generalizes in a natural way to the case of n classes of creditors.) Again, these options are exercised after the bids are announced but before the vote.

To see how this process works, suppose first that the best bid is perceived to value the company at less than D_1. Then no one will want to exercise their options (the junior creditors will not want to spend D_1 to get something worth less; and, a fortiori, the former shareholders will not want to spend $D_1 + D_2$), and the creditors will end up with all the equity. Suppose next that the best bid is perceived to be worth more than D_1 but less than $D_1 + D_2$. Then the junior creditors will choose to buy out the senior creditors, but the former shareholders will not want to exercise their options. Finally, if the best bid is perceived to be worth more than $D_1 + D_2$, then the shareholders will buy out both classes of creditors. It should be clear that these options preserve the absolute priority of claims even though there is no objective valuation of the company.

The other important point is that, at the time of the vote, all claimholders' interests are aligned. Whether those voting are former creditors or former shareholders (who have bought out the creditors), they are now all shareholders and so have an incentive to vote for the highest value bid.

Of course, there may be a divergence of opinion about the value of the best bid (or, indeed, about which bid will win). No matter, because the scheme is decentralized—everyone can act as they wish. The more bullish people will buy out the creditors above them, and the others will not. For larger companies, markets may develop (during the fourth month) in which shares and options could be traded.[29]

Let us take a look at how our scheme operates in Examples A and B. In Example A, there are two alternatives: liquidate for $90 or keep the company going for an average value of $110. The big difference between our scheme and structured bargaining is that if the former creditors *as shareholders* get to vote, they will choose to keep the company going because they enjoy all of the potential upside gains for continuation. Of course, in this instance, the former shareholders will be eager to exercise their options, since by spending $1.00 they obtain a share worth $1.10 (we are ignoring junior creditors). That is, the former creditors will get paid their $100 in full by the former shareholders, and the former shareholders—as residual claimants—will vote to maintain the company as a going concern. A good company has been saved.

In Example B, the alternatives are to liquidate for $90 or to keep the company going for an average value of $80. Here, the former shareholders will not exercise their options, and the former creditors—as the new shareholders—will vote to liquidate and receive $90. A bad company has been shut down.

Notice that Problems 1 and 2 have been resolved without eliminating the possibility of reorganization. In Example A, incumbent managers are able to retain their jobs even though they may not have the cash in hand, and any incentive on the part of the creditors to liquidate the company prematurely is avoided. In Example B, managers are rightly unable to keep their jobs. In neither example is there room for haggling. And in both examples, the people who end up voting over the future of the company are the residual claimants (i.e., those who bear the consequences of their actions); as a result, the final outcome is the value-maximizing choice.

V. Further Considerations

In this part, we briefly raise some additional issues and discuss a number of practical problems that might arise under our scheme.

Treatment of Junior Creditors and Former Shareholders

In our scheme, junior creditors are required, before they receive anything, to buy out senior creditors. A concern may be that junior creditors do not have the cash on hand to exercise their options and, therefore, will be unduly disadvantaged by the need to raise cash.

We have a modification of our scheme that ameliorates this problem. Once the bids are in, the bankruptcy judge will be able to place a lower bound on the value of the company, equal to the size of the best *cash* bid, V^c (an objective amount). Given this, he could proceed *as if* the firm were worth V^c and distribute shares accordingly. If V^c exceeds the amount owed to senior creditors, the junior creditors will receive a fraction of the shares in the initial distribution. For example, if the senior creditors are owed $100, and the best cash bid that comes in is for $150, then the senior creditors would be issued two-thirds of the shares and the junior creditors would be issued one-third. Of course, there may be a noncash bid that the junior creditors perceive to be worth more than $150, in which case the senior creditors would still be getting too much; but, in that case the junior creditors could exercise their options to buy out the senior creditors.

Of course, even with this modification, junior creditors might still be shortchanged. The worst case would be if there were *no* cash bid; here, V^c = 0, and all the equity is initially allocated to senior creditors. How bad are things for the junior creditors in such a case? We think they are not too bad for at least three reasons.

First, junior creditors do not collectively have to raise the cash to buy out the senior creditors. Each junior creditor can act as an individual. The pro rata cash injection may be quite small (indeed, an individual need not exercise his options in full; he may choose to exercise only a fraction). Second, a market for options may well develop during the bankruptcy process—especially for large firms. (Indeed, the bankruptcy judge might be obliged to establish such a market.) In this case, junior creditors need not come up with cash—they could simply sell their options. Third, even if some junior creditors are unable to raise the cash and so are left empty-handed, they will probably fare no worse than they do under current arrangements.[30]

Finally, it is important to realize that the problem facing junior creditors who wish to raise cash in order to exercise their options is quite different from that of a bidder who wishes to make a cash bid for the whole company. Because junior creditors act individually, no junior creditor who exercises her option bears much risk, nor does someone who buys the option and exercises it on her behalf. In contrast, someone who makes a cash bid for the whole company may bear a great deal of risk.[31] Hence, there is no contradiction between supposing on the one hand that capital markets are sufficiently imperfect that noncash bids have a role to play, and supposing on the other hand that junior claimants will be able to obtain a reasonable fraction of the postbankruptcy pie in exercising or selling their options.

Claims Disputes

We have so far paid little attention to the question of how the amounts and seniorities of creditors' claims are established. The adjudication process is complex and forms an important part of any bankruptcy procedure, including our own. It may be argued that our time scale of three months is too short for the purpose of allocating shares and options.

There is a way of dealing with awkward claims disputes without jeopardizing our scheme, as long as a reasonable proportion of the claims can be established within the three months: Take the claims that can be established, allocate shares and options on the basis of these claims alone, carry out the vote, and emerge from bankruptcy with the contentious claims still outstanding. Once these claims have been decided, there could be an appropriate ex-post settling up—with the claimants being given securities in the postbankruptcy company.[32] Notice that the people with contentious claims do not participate in the vote, but this is not too serious, since one may presume that they too would have voted for the value-maximizing bid.[33]

In other words, we do not agree with those commentators who have argued that the complexity of the adjudication process favors a liquidation procedure like Chapter 7 over a reorganization procedure like Chapter 11 or like ours.[34] Their point is that if a company is liquidated for cash, then the cash can be held in an interest-bearing escrow account and disbursed when the claims are resolved. We would argue that something similar can be done in the case of a reorganization plan. If a noncash bid is voted in, any subsequent dividends or debt repayments can be placed in an escrow account and distributed, along with fresh equity, once the claims are resolved.

To put it another way, we think that a bankrupt company is not so different from a solvent company that has uncertain claims against it. If there is a threat of a tort claim, a solvent company carries on operating until the tort claim is resolved and ex-post settling up occurs. The company is not liquidated just because a tort claim *may* be established in the future.

Urgent Cases

For some kinds of businesses, the worry may be that three to four months is too long a period rather than too short. This is particularly true of companies with customers and suppliers that, unless the uncertainty is resolved quickly, will shift elsewhere.

There may be a case for granting the bankruptcy judge discretion to speed up the process—that is, to hold the vote sooner. The drawback is that there may be less information available at the time of the vote, and a number of claims may still be outstanding. But, as we have explained above in "Claims Disputes," this need not be fatal to the efficacy of our procedure. To safeguard against abuse, it would probably be desirable to limit the bankruptcy judge's discretionary powers to cases in which he had clear evidence that the normal timetable would severely jeopardize creditors' claims and the future of the business.

Treatment of Secured Creditors

We propose that a secured creditor's collateral be appraised. If the appraisal value is greater than the debt, the creditor should simply be treated as if all his debt was senior—that is, he should be allocated shares, not options. If his debt is less than fully secured, then he is given an appropriate mix of shares and options. We do not believe that secured creditors should have the right to seize collateralized property (unless it can be shown to be unnecessary to the company's reorganization), since this could lead to an inefficient dismantlement of the company's assets through a "me-first" grab. Note that this is also the position taken by the current U.S. bankruptcy law.[35]

Of course, we realize that there is tension between the view that a secured creditor's rights to seize assets should be restricted and the view, which we hold, that private contracts should be upheld (the secured creditor's contract may have included the right to seize assets). In some cases, there may be efficiency gains from letting an outside party *exercise* its rights to seize a specific asset. Note that the parties may be able to achieve something like this arrangement—even under our scheme—by making the outside party the owner of the asset and having the company rent the asset from him. In this case, if the company goes bankrupt, the outside party might be in a stronger position to repossess its property (a bidder for the company could, of course, negotiate with the outside party for the continued use of the asset if this is desirable).[36]

Who Runs the Company during Bankruptcy?

In Chapter 11, incumbent management typically runs the company during bankruptcy. An alternative is for a trustee to run the company, as in old Chapter X of the U.S. Bankruptcy Code. Clearly, this is an important issue for *any* bankruptcy procedure. Notice that our procedure can be applied regardless of how this issue is resolved.

Debtor-in-Possession Financing

The viability of certain kinds of bankrupt companies (such as retail stores) can depend to a great extent on management being granted debtor-in-possession financing, whereby suppliers' credit is placed ahead of existing (unsecured) senior debt. (Ensuring this financing is often mentioned as an important role played in Chapter 11.) There is no reason why a comparable arrangement could not be used during the four months of our proposed bankruptcy process, with the judge's approval.

Partial Bids

We have implicitly assumed that the bids received are for the entire company. In fact, bids may be for parts of the company. The problem then arises as to how to deal with overlapping or inconsistent bids. Before a vote can be taken, a menu of coherent options has to be assembled.

We think that it makes the most sense to leave the matter of assembling "whole" bids in the hands of the judge and his appointed agents. It may well be necessary to solicit supplementary bids for parts of the company in order to package a whole bid.[37] Although this seems messy, it should be noted that a similar difficulty—how to bundle or unbundle the assets of the company so as to maximize cash receipts—is faced in a Chapter 7 proceeding.

Voting Procedures

Another issue concerns the voting procedure per se. If there are only two bids, it seems natural to have a simple vote between them. However, with more than two bids, there are many possibilities. Shareholders could cast their votes for their most preferred plan, with the plan that receives the most votes being the winner; shareholders could rank the plans, with the plan that receives the highest total ranking being chosen; or there could be two rounds in which shareholders rank the plans in the first round and have a subsequent runoff between the two highest ranked plans in the second round. One point to note is that thorny issues in voting theory (such as the Condorcet Paradox) are less likely to arise in the present context, given that shareholders have a common objective: value maximization.

Small Companies

Our scheme is likely to be most valuable in the case of medium to large companies with multiple creditors, for which bankruptcy raises the thorniest problems. However, most bankruptcies relate to small companies, for which a bank is typically the single main creditor. Under our scheme, the bank would get all the equity (presuming that it is not bought out) and could "vote" on whether to liquidate or reorganize the company. In addition, our scheme allows junior creditors (e.g., trade creditors) to buy out the bank; trade creditors might have an incentive to vote to keep the company going because they anticipate profitable trade with the company in the future. In short, our scheme may also have a role to play in the case of small companies.

Workouts

Many of the problems of bankruptcy plague company workouts. There is no reason why a company could not, of its own accord, choose our scheme as a vehicle for facilitating such workouts.

VI. Concluding Remarks

First, it is worth repeating what we see as the main point of this chapter. Current reorganization procedures are flawed because they mix the decision of who should get what with the decision of what should happen to a bankrupt company. We have proposed a procedure that separates these two issues.

Second, it may help to say a few more words about the philosophy underlying our procedure. Our view is that a bankrupt company is not fundamentally different from a solvent company that is performing badly. In the case of a solvent company, shareholders elect a board of directors who are entrusted with deciding, on a day-to-day basis, whether to keep the company going, sell it, or close it down. We believe that the same menu of options should be available to the claimants of a bankrupt company. In other words, we do not see why bankruptcy should automatically trigger the termination of a company via a cash sale (either as a going concern or in pieces). We see bankruptcy as an indication that something is wrong with *management* rather than with the company itself. The appropriate response is to allow new management teams the opportunity to replace existing management. Our scheme does this through the device of a noncash bid. Noncash bids allow for Chapter 11–type reorganization plans. However, in our scheme, unlike in Chapter 11, the company's future is decided by a simple vote—a procedure that is standard for solvent companies— rather than by a complex bargaining procedure that is never seen outside bankruptcy.

An interesting insight into how our scheme might work is provided by the recent takeover battle for Paramount. There were two bidders for Paramount—Viacom and QVC—and each put in a bid with a noncash component and a cash component. Paramount shareholders chose between the bids—and the option of keeping Paramount independent—by what was, in effect, a vote. (Viacom won the vote.) Thus, the choice Paramount shareholders were asked to make is analogous to the choice claimants would make in our scheme in the presence of noncash bids.

We noted in part III that a good bankruptcy procedure should balance two goals: to achieve an ex-post efficient outcome and to be neither too hard nor too soft on incumbent management (so as to encourage the appropriate behavior prior to bankruptcy). We believe that our procedure does a reasonable job of balancing these objectives. Note, however, that the procedure can be modified to be softer or harder on incumbent management (at some probable cost in terms of ex-post inefficiency) if that is thought to be desirable. For example, incumbent management could be *favored* by handicapping other bidders in the auction—for example, the auction rules could state that an outside bidder has to win more than two-thirds of the votes. (Another way to soften the blow of bankruptcy is to give managers a golden parachute in the form of senior debt in their company.) Conversely, management could be disfavored by a requirement that *they* must win more than two-thirds of the votes to retain their jobs.

Finally, it is worth repeating a point we made in part III. A good bankruptcy procedure should work well both when capital markets are imperfect and when they are perfect. Our procedure has this feature. If capital markets are perfect, the company will go to the bidder willing to pay the highest amount—moreover, this bidder can do no better than offer cash— and, thus, the outcome will be exactly the same as in Chapter 7. For this reason, while believers in perfect capital markets may not see the merit of our scheme relative to Chapter 7, they should not be strongly opposed to it. In contrast, those with doubts about the adequacy of capital markets should, we feel, find value in the scheme.

Notes

We would like to thank Rabindran Abraham, Barry Adler, Donald Franklin, Lynn LoPucki, Paul Sheard, Andrei Shleifer, and Geoff Stewart for helpful comments on earlier versions of this article.

1. An example is the case of Hungary. In the original Hungarian bankruptcy law, the debtor was obliged to announce a reorganization or bankruptcy proce-

dure after ninety days of failure to pay any of its debt. This triggered a huge wave of bankruptcies, and in mid-1993, an amendment to the bankruptcy law abolished the mandatory announcement of bankruptcy. *See* Institute for East-West Studies, Enterprise Bankruptcy in Russia: Critical Recommendations for Microeconomic Restructuring (1993).

2. *See id.*

3. The notable exceptions include Douglas G. Baird, *The Uneasy Case for Corporate Reorganizations,* 15 J. Legal Stud. 127 (1986); Lucian A. Bebchuk, *A New Approach to Corporate Reorganizations,* 101 Harv. L. Rev. 775 (1988); Thomas H. Jackson, The Logic and Limits of Bankruptcy Law (Harvard University Press: 1986); and Mark J. Roe, *Bankruptcy and Debt: A New Model for Corporate Reorganizations,* 83 Colum. L. Rev. 527 (1983).

4. *See* Philippe Aghion et al., The Economics of Bankruptcy Reform, 8 J. L. Econ. & Organization 523 (1992). This procedure is currently under consideration in the United Kingdom. It appears as Appendix E in The Insolvency Service, the Insolvency Act 1986: Company Voluntary Arrangements and Administration Orders, a Consultative Document (1993).

5. The fundamental importance of transaction costs has been stressed by Ronald H. Coase, *The Nature of the Firm,* 4 Economica 386 (1937) and Oliver E. Williamson, The Economic Institutions of Capitalism: Firms, Markets, Relational Contracting (Free Press: 1985). For a recent discussion of the difficulties of analyzing the state's role in filling in the gaps of contracts, see Oliver Hart, *Is "Bounded Rationality" an Important Element of a Theory of Institutions?* 146 J. Institutional & Theoretical Econ. 696 (1990).

6. We do not believe that our procedure should be mandatory. Anybody who wishes to deviate from it and craft his own procedure should be allowed to do so.

7. Note that we exclude "external" considerations from our definition of efficiency: that is, we assume that the important benefits and costs have been incorporated into the valuation of the firm. For example, we do not include such items as the external benefit from maintaining employment in the local area. Our view is that if there are external considerations, government action may indeed be warranted, but bankruptcy law is the wrong instrument for dealing with such considerations. It would be better to have a general employment subsidy to save jobs than to distort bankruptcy procedures in order to save bad firms.

8. The use of debt as a bonding device presumably arises because other devices to keep management in check—incentive schemes, proxy fights, and takeovers—cannot always be relied upon. The stimulus for the increase in debt might have been a hostile takeover bid that management was trying to resist; or, management might have been trying to raise funds from capital market and found it necessary to issue debt in order to convince the market that it would use the funds wisely. For more on this issue, see Aghion et al., *supra* note 4.

9. *See* Jackson, *supra* note 3, at 21.

10. For further details, see Oliver Hart & John Moore, *Debt and Seniority: An Analysis of the Role of Hard Claims in Constraining Management,* 85 Am. Econ. Rev. 3, 567–85 (1995).

11. *See* Michelle J. White, *The Corporate Bankruptcy Decision,* J. Econ. Persp., Spring 1989, at 129, 149 (1989) ("As long as streamlining the bankruptcy

procedure involves compensating creditors according to the [absolute priority rule], then managers will have an incentive to gamble with creditors' assets as they try desperately to avoid bankruptcy's draconian treatment of equity under the [absolute priority rule].")

12. For a recent survey of this literature, see Oliver Hart, *Theories of Optimal Capital Structure: A Managerial Discretion Perspective,* in The Deal Decade: What Takeovers and Leveraged Buyouts Mean for Corporate Governance, Margaret M. Blair, ed. (Brookings Institution: 1993).

13. In addition, in order to prevent managers from delaying a bankruptcy filing for too long, it may be desirable to give creditors greater powers to push a company into involuntary bankruptcy.

14. The conflict between goals 1 and 2 is analyzed in Elazer Berkovitch et al., The Design of Bankruptcy Law: A Case for Management Bias in Bankruptcy Reorganizations (University of Michigan, School of Business and Finance, Mimeograph) (1993) (on file with the *Washington University Law Quarterly*).

15. We put in the qualification "presumably" because we are aware of no formal derivation of this result.

16. The problems of financing a cash bid will be exacerbated to the extent that other companies in the industry, which may be the natural purchasers of the bankrupt company, are also suffering from financial distress, because the shock hitting the bankrupt company is industrywide. *See* Andrei Shleifer & Robert Vishny, *Liquidation Values and Debt Capacity: A Market Equilibrium Approach,* 47 J. Fin. 4 (1992).

17. There is some empirical support for the idea that it is costly to find investors to put up the cash to buy a public company. One piece of evidence comes from the work on initial public offerings. This work finds significant costs of going public, at least some of which are attributable to the premium charged by investment banks for bearing the risk that the offer will not be fully subscribed. (Other costs are attributable to direct expenses and various forms of asymmetric information.) *See* Jay R. Ritter, *The Costs of Going Public,* 19 J. Fin. Econ. 269 (1987).

A second, more casual piece of evidence concerns workouts. When a company is financially distressed, it often tries to persuade its creditors to renegotiate their claims by lengthening the maturity of their debt or by swapping their debt for equity. The question is, why do creditors often go along with this, rather than pushing for bankruptcy and liquidation? It would seem that the latter strategy would be rational if a cash auction could be relied upon to generate maximum value, that is, if bidders could easily raise cash to buy the company. (Part of the desire for renegotiation can be possibly traced to the fact that most bankruptcies in the United States are filed under Chapter 11, rather than Chapter 7, and creditors may prefer to avoid Chapter 11. However, this does not explain workouts in other countries where Chapter 11 does not exist.)

A third piece of evidence comes from another area of corporate finance: takeovers. Companies taking over other companies sometimes offer shareholders a mixture of cash and securities for their existing shares. In fact, in 1993, 66 percent of all mergers and acquisitions with value between $100 million and $1 billion had a noncash component. *See* Merrill Lynch Business Advisory Services, Mergerstat Review (1994). Noncash bids are harder to evaluate than cash bids, so one might expect that—particularly in a contested situation—bidding companies would prefer to offer straight cash. The fact that they do not suggests that it is difficult for them to raise cash. (There may, however, be other reasons why companies make noncash bids, such as the presence of taxes and asymmetric information.)

18. S.I. 1986, No. 1925, as amended by the Insolvency (Amendment) Rules 1987, S.I. 1987, No. 1919, and S.I. 1989, No. 397.

19. For some of the literature on these issues, see David M. Cutler & Lawrence H. Summers, *The Costs of Conflict Resolution and Financial Distress: Evidence from the Texaco-Pennzoil Litigation,* 19 Rand J. Econ. 157 (1988); Stuart C. Gilson, *Bankruptcy, Boards, Banks, and Blockholders: Evidence on Changes in Corporate Ownership and Control When Firms Default,,* 27 J. Fin. Econ. 355 (1990); Stuart C. Gilson, *Management Turnover and Financial Distress,* 25 J. Fin. Econ. 241 (1989); Lynn M. LoPucki & William C. Whitford, *Corporate Governance in the Bankruptcy Reorganization of Large Publicly Held Companies,* 141 U. Pa. L. Rev. 669, 758–59 (1993); Lawrence A. Weiss, *Bankruptcy Resolution: Direct Costs and Violation of Priority of Claims,* 27 J. Fin. Econ. 285 (1990); and Lawrence A. Weiss, Restructuring Complications in Bankruptcy: The Eastern Airlines Bankruptcy Case (Tulane University, Mimeograph) (1991).

20. *See, e.g.,* Roe, *supra* note 3; Bebchuk, *supra* note 3. The recent bankruptcy of Macy's provides a clear example of Problem 1. Senior creditors claimed that the reorganized company was worth little (implying that they should receive a large fraction of it). Junior creditors and shareholders claimed the opposite. *See, e.g.,* Patrick M. Reilly & Laura Jereski, *Macy Strategy Seems to Sway Senior Creditors,* Wall St. J., May 2, 1994, at A4; Laura Jereski & Patrick M. Reilly, *Laurence Tish Leads Dissent on Macy Board,* Wall St. J., Mar. 29, 1994, at B1.

21. This is unless the cram-down procedure is adopted. See Douglas G. Baird & Thomas H. Jackson, Cases, Problems, and Materials on Bankruptcy 676 (Little, Brown: 1st ed. 1985). Under cram-down, junior claimants' voting rights are removed on the grounds that they would receive nothing in liquidation. Id. (describing the procedure of 11 U.S.C. § 1129(b) (1988)). The cram-down procedure cannot be relied upon, however; among other things, it requires an accurate judicial evaluation of the company's liquidation value.

22. The empirical work on departures from absolute priority suggests that junior claimants do indeed have enough power to force concessions from senior creditors, that is, the problem described in Example B is relevant in practice. *See* Julian R. Franks & Walter N. Torous, *An Empirical Investigation of U.S. Firms in Reorganization,* 44 J. Fin. 747 (1989). There is less formal empirical evidence on the problem described in Example A. However, practitioners frequently mention (and write about) this problem, so it would seem to be a mistake not to take it seriously. Also, the conflict between the desire of senior creditors to terminate a bankruptcy proceeding quickly and that of junior creditors to drag it out on the off chance that there will be something of value for them seems to have been a factor in the recent Macy's bankruptcy. *See, e.g.,* Patrick M. Reilly & Laura Jereski, *Media & Marketing: Macy May Seek Shorter Period for Extension,* Wall St. J., Feb. 18, 1994, at B2.

23. For a discussion of the bargaining problems faced by companies in financial distress, see Rajesh Aggarwal, The Capital Structure Holdout Problem:

Why Firms in Financial Distress Remain Overleveraged (Harvard University, Mimeograph) (1993) (on file with authors).

24. There is a vast literature on bargaining under asymmetric information. A representative article is Drew Fudenberg & Jean Tirole, *Sequential Bargaining with Incomplete Information,* 50 Rev. Econ. Stud. 221 (1983).

25. However, our procedure does *not* avoid disputes over the amounts and seniorities of claims. Judges and the courts would undoubtedly have a very important role in resolving these disputes under our procedure, just as they currently do.

26. The scheme does not depend on this particular time horizon, and adjustments might be desirable. *See, e.g.,* discussion in the "Further Considerations" section, this chapter.

27. *See* Bebchuk, *supra* note 3.

28. *See* Bebchuk, *supra* note 3, at 800.

29. At the same time that our proposal was being developed, two other proposals for bankruptcy reform appeared in literature. *See* Barry E. Adler, *Financial and Political Theories of American Corporate Bankruptcy,* 45 Stan. L. Rev. 311 (1993); Michael Bradley & Michael Rosenzweig, *The Untenable Case for Chapter 11,* 101 Yale, L. J. 1043 (1992); *see also* Barry E. Adler, *A World Without Debt,* 72 Wash. U. L. Q. 811 (1994). These proposals, like ours, envisage that when a company goes bankrupt, the company's equity is transferred to creditors. Adler's proposal removes the right of individual creditors to foreclose on a bankrupt company's assets, while Bradley and Rosenzweig's does not. In both proposals, the company's debt is not accelerated and no bids are solicited. Also, while both proposals envisage that the transfer of control to creditors will bring about improved management, neither is very explicit about how this will happen.

30. LoPucki and Whitford examined 43 firms that filed for bankruptcy in the United States after October 1, 1979, had declared assets in excess of $100 million, and had a plan confirmed by March 21, 1988. They found that the mean return to unsecured creditors was 49.5 ¢ per $1 and that the median return was 38.7 ¢ per $1. *See* Lynn M. LoPucki & William C. Whitford, *Bargaining Over Equity's Share in the Bankruptcy Reorganization of Large, Publicly Held Companies,* 139 U. Pa. L. Rev. 125, 142 (1990).

Fisher and Martel studied 236 incorporated firms that filed for reorganization in Canada during the period 1978–87. They divided the sample into 16 "large" firms (with liabilities in excess of Can$5 million) and 220 "small" firms (with liabilities below Can$5 million). For large firms, the mean return to unsecured creditors was 57.7 ¢ per $1 and the median return was 30 ¢ per $1. *See* Timothy C. G. Fisher & Jocelyn Martel, Facts About Financial Reorganization in Canada (University of Montreal, Mimeograph) (1994) (on file with the *Washington University Law Quarterly*).

31. See the discussion in part IV, *supra,* about the transaction cost of making a cash bid.

32. There are several ways of doing this; one is to give new claimants the same securities that equivalent creditors elected to hold as a result of the bankruptcy process.

33. We are oversimplifying a little here. Those shareholders who think a senior claim may materialize later have an incentive to choose a risky reorgani-

zation plan since they gain if things turn out well and do not suffer if they turn out badly. See Example B *supra* for a similar phenomenon.

34. *See, e.g.*, Michael C. Jensen, *Corporate Control and the Politics of Finance*, J. Applied Corp. Fin., Summer 1991, at 13, 32 (advocating auction-oriented bankruptcy reform).

35. *See* Douglas G. Baird, the Elements of Bankruptcy § 8 (Foundation Press: 1992).

36. In practice, however, U.S. bankruptcy law puts restrictions on the rights of owners to repossess property from a bankrupt company. *See* 11 U.S.C. § 365 (1988).

37. Another possibility is to put the onus of assembling whole bids on the bidders themselves, that is, a bidder for part of the company would have to find someone else to bid for the complementary part.

12

Empowering Investors

A Market Approach to Securities Regulation

ROBERTA ROMANO

The U.S. securities laws have repeatedly been assailed as burdensome or ineffective. Reform efforts have conversely been attacked for undermining an effective mechanism by which shareholders can discipline management. Moreover, even reformers have been dissatisfied with the effectiveness of their product. For example, after enacting the Private Securities Litigation Reform Act of 1995,[1] members of Congress became concerned that their efforts to rein in frivolous private lawsuits under the federal securities laws were being circumvented by state court filings and introduced legislation to preempt such action.[2] There is some validity to their concern: In a report to President Clinton on the impact of the 1995 act, the Securities and Exchange Commission (SEC) cited preliminary studies indicating a decrease in federal court filings and an increase in state court filings.[3]

This chapter contends that the current legislative approach to securities regulation is mistaken and that preemption is not the solution to frivolous lawsuits. It advocates instead a market-oriented approach of competitive federalism that would expand, not reduce, the role of the states in securities regulation. It thereby would fundamentally reconceptualize our regulatory approach and is at odds with both sides of the debate over the 1995 act, each of which has sought to use national laws as a weapon to beat down its opponent's position by monopolizing the regulatory field.

The market approach to securities regulation advocated in this chapter takes as its paradigm the successful experience of the U.S. states in corporate law, in which the fifty states and the District of Columbia compete for the business of corporate charters. There is substantial literature on this particular manifestation of U.S. federalism indicating that shareholders have benefited from the federal system of corporate law by its production of corporate codes that, for the most part, maximize share value.[4] This chapter proposes extending the competition among states for corporate charters to two of the three principal components of federal securities regulation: the registration of securities and the related continuous disclosure regime for issuers, and the antifraud provisions that police that system. The third component, the regulation of market professionals, is not included in the proposed reform. The proposed market approach can be implemented by modifying the federal securities laws in favor of a menu approach to securities regulation under which firms elect whether to be covered by federal law or by the securities law of a specified state, such as their state of incorporation.

Under a system of competitive federalism for securities regulation, only one sovereign would have jurisdiction over all transactions in the securities of a corporation that involve the issuer or its agents and investors. The aim is to replicate for the securities setting the benefits produced by state competition for corporate charters—a responsive legal regime that has tended to maximize share value—and thereby eliminate the frustration experienced at efforts to reform the national regime. As a competitive legal market supplants a monopolist federal agency in the fashioning of regulation, it would produce rules more aligned with the preferences of investors, whose decisions drive the capital market.

Competitive federalism for U.S. securities regulation also has important implications for international securities regulation. The jurisdictional principle applicable to domestic securities transactions is equally applicable to international securities transactions: Foreign issuers selling shares in the United States could opt out of the federal securities laws and choose those of another nation, such as their country of incorporation, or those of a U.S. state, to govern transactions in their securities in the United States. The federal securities laws would also, of course, not apply to transactions by U.S. investors abroad in the shares of firms that opt for a non-U.S. securities domicile. Under this approach, U.S. law would apply only to corporations affirmatively opting to be covered by U.S. law, whether they be U.S.- or non-U.S.-based firms. It therefore would put an end to the ever-expanding extraterritorial reach of U.S. securities regulation, which currently extends to transactions abroad involving foreign firms with any U.S. shareholders or U.S. effects.[5]

Stemming the trend of extraterritorial application of U.S. law will not harm U.S. investors because they have, in fact, often been disadvantaged by the expansion of U.S. securities jurisdiction. For example, to avoid the application of U.S. law, foreign firms have frequently explicitly excluded U.S. investors from takeover offers, and such investors have thus missed out on bid premiums.[6] In addition, adoption of the market approach would facilitate foreign firms' access to capital, as they would be able to issue securities in the United States without complying with U.S. disclosure and accounting rules that differ substantially from their home rules, a requirement that has been a significant deterrent to listings.[7] This consequence of the proposed modification of U.S. law would also benefit U.S. investors, who would no longer incur the higher transaction costs of purchasing shares abroad in order to make direct investments in foreign firms.

The market approach to securities regulation[8] is a natural extension of the literature on state competition for corporate charters, and commentators, recognizing the possibility of this extension, have occasionally mentioned it as an alternative to the current system of securities regulation. Advancing those earlier suggestions, this chapter makes a systematic case for competitive federalism by articulating the rationales for the approach and by crafting the mechanics of its implementation. The position advocated in this chapter—elimination of the exclusive mandatory character of most of the federal securities laws—may seem on first impression to many readers surprising, if not unrealistic or worse. In my judgment, a compelling case can be made on the substantive merits of the proposal.

There may be an understandable desire to discount the need for the proposal because of the vibrancy of U.S. capital markets and the calls for piecemeal reform rather than comprehensive revamping of the current regime by issuers and investors. This would be a mistake. While U.S. capital markets are the largest and most liquid in the world, it is incorrect to attribute this fact to the federal regime. United States capital markets were the largest and most liquid global markets at the turn of the century,[9] before the federal regime was established, and their share of global capitalization has declined markedly over the past two decades,[10] facts at odds with the contention that the current federal regime is the reason for the depth of U.S. capital markets. The absence of calls for comprehensive reform is a function of a lack of imagination, rather than evidence that the current regulatory apparatus does not produce deadweight losses.[11] Blind adherence to the securities regulation status quo imposes real costs on investors and firms, and there is a better solution.

Some may conclude that the proposal does not go far enough and that all government interference in capital markets, whether federal or state, should be abolished. I believe that the intermediate position advocated in this chapter is a more sensible public policy than eliminating all government involvement. This is because state competition does not foreclose the possibility of deregulation should that be desired by investors: A state could adopt a securities regime that delegates regulatory authority over issuers to stock exchanges, just as the current federal regime delegates regulatory authority for market professionals to the stock exchanges and National Association of Securities Dealers (NASD). State competition permits experimentation with purely private regulatory arrangements, while retaining a mechanism to reverse course easily—migration to states that do not adopt such an approach—which is not present in a purely private regime. On a more pragmatic level, there is a more immediate point to the chapter: to caution against the current impetus to extend the federal government's monopoly over securities regulation. Instead of supplanting state securities regulation, Congress should rationalize it by legislatively altering the multi-jurisdictional, transactional basis of state regulatory authority to an issuer-domicile basis.

The argument proceeds as follows. In part I, a market-based approach to U.S. securities regulation is outlined, and the mandatory federal system is critiqued. Comparisons with alternative market-oriented reforms, such as regulation by exchanges, are also provided. Part II discusses the details for implementing the proposal, including changing the current choice-of-law rule for securities transactions from one that focuses on the site of the transaction to an issuer-based approach analogous to the internal affairs rule applied in corporate law, and conditioning opting out of the federal regime upon compliance with two procedural requirements. The requirements, which seek to ensure the integrity of the investor decisions that drive the regulatory competition, are the disclosure of the issuer's securities domicile at the time of a security purchase and a shareholder vote to effectuate a change in securities domicile. Finally, part III extends the proposal to international securities regulation.

I. Competitive Federalism: A Market Approach to Securities Regulation

Although both the states and the federal government regulate securities transactions, the current regulatory arrangements are a far cry from competitive federalism. The federal securities regime, consisting of the Securities Act of 1933[12] and the Securities Exchange Act of 1934,[13] applies to all publicly traded firms and is a mandatory system of disclosure regulation, bolstered by antifraud provisions. While the federal laws do not preempt all state regulation,[14] states cannot lower the regulatory standards applicable to firms covered by the federal regime because its requirements are mandatory. They have also been prevented from raising regulatory standards on some occasions.[15] As a consequence, the states have essentially abandoned the regulation of public firms to the SEC. In the proposed system of competitive federalism, state and federal regulators would stand on an equal regulatory footing, and firms would be able to choose the applicable regulatory regime.

The Essence of Competitive Federalism

A market approach to U.S. securities regulation requires two significant departures from current law. First, a public corporation's coverage under the national securities laws must be optional rather than mandatory. Second, the securities transactions of a corporation that elects not to be covered by the federal securities laws are to be regulated by the corporation's selected domicile for securities regulation. This approach is premised on the idea that competition among sovereigns—here the fifty states, the District of Columbia, and the federal government (represented primarily by the SEC)—in the production of securities laws would benefit investors in public corporations by facilitating the adoption of regulation aligned with investors' preferences, as has been true of the competitive production of corporation codes. The motivation for the proposal is that no government entity can know better than market participants what regulations are in their interest, particularly as firms' requirements are continually changing with shifting financial market conditions. Competing regulators would make fewer policy mistakes than a monopolistic regulator as competition harnesses the incentives of the market to regulatory institutions.

Regulatory competition is desirable because when the choice of investments includes variation in legal regimes, promoters of firms will find that they can obtain a lower cost of capital by choosing the regime that investors prefer. For example, as long as investors are informed of the governing legal regime, if promoters choose a regime that exculpates them from fraud, investors will either not invest in the firm at all or will require a higher return on the investment (i.e., pay less for the security), just as bondholders charge higher interest rates to firms bearing greater risk of principal nonrepayment.[16] Investors set the price because financial capital is highly mobile and financial markets are highly competitive; the set of investment opportunities is extensive and, with the use of derivatives, virtually limitless. It is plausible to assume that investors are informed about liability rules given the sophistication of the institutional investors who comprise the majority of stock market investors and whose actions determine market prices on which uninformed investors can rely.[17] Promoters will thus bear the cost of operating under a legal regime inimical to investor interests, and they will therefore select the regime that maximizes the joint welfare of promoters and investors.

The analytical point concerning the ability of capital markets to assess legal regimes and consequently the beneficial effect of competition is confirmed by empirical research in the bond indenture and corporate law contexts: Creditor protection provisions in bond indentures are positively priced,[18] and firms experience statistically significant positive changes in stock prices upon changing their incorporation state.[19] The entrepreneurial motivation to reduce capital costs that operates in a competitive legal system mitigates the otherwise core problem for a government regulator of identifying what regulation will benefit investors in capital markets.

Federal intervention in capital markets in the 1930s was justified by a contention that securities markets operate poorly on two dimensions: First, they fail to protect investors from stock price manipulation and fraud; and second, they produce an inadequate level of corporate disclosure because the benefits of information concerning a firm cannot be appropriated solely by the firm that bears the cost of the information's production (i.e., corporate information is a public good).[20] Analytically, a demonstration that there are information externalities necessitating government intervention depends on the mix of informed and uninformed investors.[21] But a theoretical need for government regulation to prevent a market failure is not equivalent to a need for a monopolist regulator. The premise of competitive federalism is that if, for example, corporate information would be underproduced to investors' detriment in an unregulated market, then there would be a demand for, matched by a supply of, mandated disclosure regulation in a regime of state competition for securities regulation, just as in the monopolist SEC system.

A third rationale more recently offered for federal intervention is a refinement of the public good rationale. This rationale identifies the information problem as involving information that would benefit an issuer's competitors, as well as investors.[22] According to this theory, because competitors can use such information to compete more effectively with the issuer and thereby diminish the issuer's profitability, investors, as well as firms, would not wish to reveal such information, even though it would improve investors' ability to evaluate firms. Such an externality would render mandatory disclosure rules necessary. It can be shown analytically, however, that even in the case of such third-party externalities, mandatory disclosure is not always optimal compared to voluntary disclosure, and it would in all likelihood be extremely difficult for a regulator to determine when mandatory disclosure is optimal.[23] But, putting aside the theoretical uncertainty of the need for a mandatory regime, even this third-party externality argument does not require an exclusive federal regulator. The majority of investors hold portfolios, not single shares of stock, and therefore, unlike the issuer, they will internalize the externality if they make the disclosure decision. That is, they will desire a regime requiring the information's disclosure because, by definition of a positive externality, the expected gain on their shares in competitors will offset the loss on their shares in the issuer.

Because the antifraud rationale does not depend on the presence of an externality for government action, it presents even less of an objection to a system of competitive federalism than the mandatory disclosure rationale: It is silly to contend that investors will choose regimes that encourage fraud. Joel Seligman states that a federal antifraud law was needed in the 1930s because state securities laws did not reach out-of-state sellers.[24] Whatever the merit of the argument at that time, it is not applicable to modern jurisdictional doctrines and is therefore not relevant to today's policy discussions.[25]

Moreover, if there was concern in the 1930s over the states' capacities to handle securities fraud cases, this is no longer a serious issue. Given the overlapping nature of the current antifraud regime, the states have developed active securities law enforcement divisions and coordinating capacities to deal with interstate fraud.[26]

Is Abandoning a Mandatory Federal
Securities Law Justified?

This section first reviews the empirical literature that has sought to measure the impact of the federal securities regime on investors. The analysis rests on contemporary empirical studies because the historical "evidence" of market abuses, whose revelation congressional investigators orchestrated during the hearings preceding the creation of the federal regime as part of the New Deal agenda, has been shown to be inaccurate.[27] The hearings were held for the purpose of furthering a political end (federal regulation of the stock market), and the statistical techniques used by modern researchers were not available to researchers in the 1930s to develop the case for or against regulation. Even today, little empirical evidence suggests that the federal regime has affirmatively benefited investors. To develop an educated prediction of what the counterfactual (a competitive securities regime) would produce, this section reviews the empirical evidence on investor welfare of the next best thing—state competition for corporate charters. It compares favorably.

The difficulty of discerning an affirmative impact on investors from the federal regime detailed in this section supports abandoning its exclusivity. While it does not prove the counterfactual—that state competition would be better—the near total absence of measurable benefits from the federal regulatory apparatus surely undermines blind adherence to the status quo. Under regulatory competition, lawmakers have incentives to replace regimes that do not measurably support their objectives with those that do. In a competitive regulatory system, undesirable mandatory policies cannot be maintained over time because they are not enforceable: Firms will migrate to the regulatory regime that does not impose such mandates.

The competitively produced state corporation codes, in contrast to the federal securities laws, consist primarily of enabling provisions that reduce the cost of business by providing firms and investors with a standardized contractual form to govern their relationships. Thus, to the extent the empirical literature suggests that federal securities laws have been fashioned from a set of misguided premises, adoption of the market approach to securities regulation will weed out inefficiencies in the federal regime by permitting capital market participants to establish a new regulatory equilibrium with a mix of enabling and mandatory provisions, if that is what investors prefer.

Empirical Evidence on the Rationales for
Federal Securities Regulation

Mandatory Disclosure   There is little tangible proof of the claims that corporate information is "underproduced" in the absence of mandatory disclosure or that the benefits to investors from information that firms would not produce in the absence of mandatory disclosure actually outweigh their costs. For instance, before the enactment of the federal securities laws in the 1930s, public corporations voluntarily disclosed financial statements, typically under a stock exchange listing requirement, that contained substantially all of the information subsequently required under the federal laws. In an important and still underappreciated study, George Benston found that the only major mandated item that was not reported by a significant set of firms prior to the 1934 legislation was sales. Comparing the pre- and postlegislation stock returns of the firms for which the legislation was relevant (firms that had not previously reported their sales, which were 38 percent of New York Stock Exchange (NYSE)–listed corporations) with those for which it was not (the remaining 62 percent of NYSE corporations that had disclosed sales information), he found no significant price effect from the new mandated disclosure.[28]

Benston's finding, upon reflection, should not be surprising: Because firms need capital and investors need information, firms have powerful incentives to disclose information if they are to compete successfully for funds against alternative investment opportunities. Consistent with this explanation, studies have found that the quantity and quality of publicly traded firms' voluntary disclosures (such as earnings forecasts) are positively correlated with the issuance of securities[29] and with information asymmetry in the market for the firms' stock (i.e., managers release information voluntarily when there is greater information asymmetry, as measured by the stock price's bid-ask spread)[30] and negatively related to the cost of capital (i.e., increased voluntary disclosure reduces firms' cost of capital).[31] In addition, European firms listing in London typically comply with the higher U.K. disclosure requirements rather than with the lower ones of their home countries, although they need not comply with U.K. rules under the European Community disclosure directives.[32] A further datum relevant to the issue of information production is the fact that European stock markets are no less efficient than U.S. stock markets even though the European accounting and disclosure regimes require the revelation of considerably less information than does the SEC.[33]

There is, accordingly, ample evidence that firms voluntarily disclose significant amounts of information beyond that mandated by securities regulators. It is difficult to prove what, if any, item among required disclosures is of less value to investors than items voluntarily disclosed, but the great variety in content across disclosure regimes—a recent study identified 100 SEC disclosure items deemed excessive compared to international standards[34]—suggests that a number of mandates are not cost effective. Although the estimates are extremely crude and conservative, Susan M. Phillips and J. Richard Zecher calculated in 1975 that the termination of the SEC's mandatory periodic disclosure programs would reduce corporate disclosure costs by at least $213 million.[35] These data make it plain that regulators do not have superior knowledge concerning what information investors need (otherwise firms would not on occasion disclose more than required), which bolsters the desirability of regulatory competition, as it will reduce regulatory mistakes.

In a detailed defense of federal legislation, Seligman challenges Benston's findings with data compiled by the SEC during the 1940s and 1950s in order to expand its jurisdiction, data which indicate that small firms not subject to the federal securities laws disclosed less information than the SEC required of its larger sized registrants:[36] In particular, Seligman notes that the SEC reported that most of the small firms did not disclose management compensation or insider transactions in proxy statements and that some firms did not furnish income statements or provided inadequate accounting information, compared to SEC requirements, in their balance sheets.[37] But these data do not provide proof of the efficacy of the federal securities regime. The failure to provide voluntarily the information that the SEC mandates does not demonstrate that such disclosure enhances investor welfare. It does so only with an additional assumption—that the SEC, and not the firms, has made the correct cost-benefit calculation.

To address the issue of the adequacy of the differential level of disclosure by nonregistrants, we need to know the answers to the following questions: Were financial analysts and shareholders unable to value firms accurately under the more limited voluntary disclosures? If so, did they underpay or overpay for the shares (i.e., did promoters and insiders bear the cost of the allegedly inadequate disclosure, or did the outside investors)? It would be difficult to make such judgments directly, although a finding of significant changes in stock prices upon firms' increased disclosures under SEC requirements would be probative on the issue.

There is no study of which I am aware that examines the effect of the 1965 extension of the continuing disclosure requirements to small firms. But there was no significant increase in stock prices after enactment of the 1933 act for new issue registration,[38] a finding that strongly suggests that the new federal regime had, at best, no effect on investor welfare. If the 1933 act did not increase stock prices of covered firms, it is unlikely that the 1965 extension of the act did so, for the absence of a price increase after 1933 suggests that the market elicited the right level of disclosure. A similar conclusion can be drawn from studies of a more specific instance of SEC-mandated disclosure—the requirement that large corporations disclose the current replacement cost of inventories, plant, and equipment. Researchers found no stock price effect when firms disclosed the newly mandated replacement cost information, suggesting that investors did not find the SEC's mandated disclosure useful for valuing firms.[39]

The variance of stock returns, however, decreased after the enactment of the 1933 act.[40] A plausible interpretation is that the legislation simply forced riskier investments off the market.[41] Consistent with this explanation, after the 1933 act, there was a decrease in the proportion of outstanding new issues of common stock compared to debt, and there was a dramatic increase in private placements of debt concentrated among bonds of higher risk.[42] Such a result—reduction in the investment opportunity set—does not obviously benefit investors, who merely require higher compensation for riskier securities, while in all likelihood it reduces social welfare by restricting the availability of financing for the riskiest ventures.

The finding of a decrease in return variance has also been interpreted as indicating that the disclosure mandated by the act enabled investors to form more accurate price predictions.[43] Even this alternative explanation does not, however, demonstrate that the act benefited investors. A core tenet of modern finance theory is that investors are compensated for bearing market risk, and it was firm-specific risk and not market risk that was measured to have decreased with the 1933 act. In this regard, it is not surprising that there is no stock price effect: A reduction in own-return variance (i.e., more accurate stock prices) is of no value to diversified investors. Consequently, commentators who point to the return variance reduction as evidence affirming the efficacy of the 1933 act are mistaken; investors benefit only from reductions in risk that is priced.

Seligman provides a further datum in support of the contention that the SEC's mandatory disclosure program benefits investors: From 1955 to 1971, "approximately two percent of the registration statements filed with the SEC were withdrawn after receipt of an SEC letter of comment [seeking additional disclosures] or . . . [an SEC] stop order."[44] This datum does not, however, indicate that the SEC's program aided investors. The key datum, which is not knowable, is whether, had those withdrawn issues been marketed as planned, investors would have overpaid for the issue or otherwise been defrauded concerning the firms' value. Emphasis on registration withdrawal data presupposes gross investor stupidity by assuming that an investor reading a prospectus that SEC staff thought deficient would not similarly recognize the deficiency and discount the share price. Why assume that the analytical ability of the SEC staff is superior to that of financial analysts or investors? Such an assumption simply does not square with what we know.

One reason for the surreal character of the arguments based on historical data that are raised in support of the federal regime is that capital markets have changed dramatically since the securities laws were adopted. The institutional investors who dominate today's markets have far greater ability, as well as financial incentives, to process information and price securities than does the SEC staff.[45] Institutional investors' pricing determinations better protect unsophisticated investors than any of the SEC's mandated disclosure requirements because, given the efficiency of U.S. capital markets in information aggregation and the fact that securities sell for one price, institutional investors cannot use their superior information-processing ability to extract wealth systematically from uninformed investors, particularly those long-term investors who follow a buy-and-hold strategy.[46] The federal regime has not adapted well to this changed context. The interests of sophisticated and unsophisticated investors in the choice of securities regime will not diverge for the issuer-investor relations that come under the regime of competitive federalism proposed by this chapter. They will, in fact, be better served by the new regulatory arrangement.

One particularly egregious example of the SEC's problematic disclosure policies will serve to underscore the point that it would be a profound mistake to presume that the SEC gets things right. The SEC prohibited for decades the disclosure of projected earnings. Such information, however, is far more valuable to investors than the accounting information the SEC required, because stock value is a function of future cash flows, not historical data.[47] The SEC modified its position in 1979 to permit the disclosure of projections within a safe harbor rule,[48] but even today the agency's approach is still quite guarded when it comes to such disclosures. For instance, when Congress recently legislated a safe harbor from civil liability for forecasts, the SEC was responsible for the extended list of transactions excluded from the safe harbor provision.[49]

The SEC's historic concern was that projections were more susceptible to abuse than accounting data. This concern was premised on a bizarre view of investor decision making—that investors believe all figures are "written on stone," they do not discount managers' optimism, and they therefore have to be protected from all but "verifiable" information (namely, historical cost).[50] This approach has made SEC disclosure documents of limited value for investment decision making and was the subject of sustained criticisms throughout the 1970s. Ironically, the SEC's approach particularly disadvantaged public investors by closing off their ability to obtain information on projected earnings, as firms would not make public earnings forecasts for fear of liability, although they would provide them to analysts and other professionals.[51]

The 1979 modification did not substantially increase public forecasts, given firms' liability concerns,[52] and was clearly outmoded for modern markets populated by institutional investors. Congress, therefore, sought to increase the disclosure of forecasts in the 1995 securities reform legislation by explicitly creating a safe harbor from civil liability for the release of forecasts.[53] Whether the legislation will have the intended effect is not yet ascertainable, but some early indications suggest that the new law is having minimal impact on the disclosure of projections.[54] The restrictions on the applicability of the safe harbor so vigorously advanced by the SEC surely enhance the likelihood that the statute's impact will be limited, and they serve as a useful reminder of how difficult it is for a monopolist government agency to alter course and implement significant policy changes.

This illustration of utterly misguided SEC disclosure mandates makes plain that an SEC disclosure initiative does not itself provide evidence that the market is inadequately producing relevant information and, consequently, should not be privileged by assuming that the agency is always (or even more often than not) right. It indicates quite the opposite, that the SEC may not possess even a rudimentary understanding of, much less a superior capacity over anyone else to identify, what information investors require for decision making. Such regulatory mistakes would be far less likely with competition: Investors would be able to reveal their preference for particular information by bidding up the price of firms subject to a regime in which they could make forecasts, compared to firms subject to one that prohibits such disclosures.

Antifraud Provisions   The federal antifraud laws have not been a focus of as much empirical research as the federal disclosure regime.[55] But, even here, there is little evidence indicating that federal, as opposed to state, securities laws are necessary to protect investors from fraud and manipulation. In truth, the data that would be probative of the efficacy of the federal antifraud regime have not been compiled. Because all states had antifraud statutes prior to the adoption of the federal securities laws, and only Nevada did not have an administrative entity to investigate securities fraud at that time,[56] an investigation of whether reported instances of investor fraud decreased after the enactment of federal securities laws would be a useful step in determining the efficacy of the federal regime. The difficulty, however, of establishing a preenactment baseline rate (given differences in enforcement regimes across states, for example) probably would make the task infeasible. Other probative research would examine whether securities issued outside of the SEC's jurisdiction (intrastate issues of small firms, state and local government securities, or foreign issues) have higher frequencies of fraud and price manipulation than SEC-registered securities, although, again, developing good estimates of comparative base-rate frequencies would be quite difficult.

The evidence supporting the contention that rampant fraud necessitated the federal laws is itself quite thin. After reviewing the legislative record and other sources, Benston concludes, in contrast to Seligman, that there is scant evidence of fraudulent financial statements prior to the 1934 act.[57] Harold Bierman has also reviewed the evidence concerning stock market fraud and manipulation prior to the 1929 crash, scrutinizing in particular the sensational charges raised against several prominent financiers in the Pecora hearings that led to the federal securities legislation. He concludes that the hearings and the attempted prosecutions in their aftermath did not uncover fraudulent or dishonest behavior on Wall Street and that the amount of manipulation in the 1920s was "surprisingly small."[58] More important, a recent empirical study of the operation of stock pools that were a principal focus of the congressional investigation leading to the enactment of the federal securities laws found no evidence that the pools manipulated stock prices.[59]

In short, a fair reading of the empirical literature on the effects of the federal securities laws points to an expansive regulatory apparatus with no empirical validation for its most fundamental objectives. The SEC appears to be a regulatory edifice without foundation. A competitive regulatory system would put such a characterization to the test, as firms would be able to seek out the securities regime that investors prefer.

Empirical Evidence on Corporate
Charter Competition

The most prudent approach to the considerable data reviewed in the previous subsection, which cast doubt on the efficacy of the federal securities regime, is to replace the monopolist federal regulator with regulatory competition. This is, of course, the gist of the market approach embedded in a system of competitive federalism. To find fault with a market approach, one must maintain that a competitive regulatory setting will do a worse job than the federal monopolist in achieving the investor-protection goals of securities regulation. For such a contention to be correct, a further assumption is required—that the states will engage in a "race for the bottom" and enact rules that favor promoter-issuers over investors.[60] This assumption cannot be directly tested because there is at present no competitive regime for securities laws; besides the national mandates, the governing regime is fixed by the investor's residence or place of sale. But there is a competitive regime for corporate charters. The most important data bearing on the question of whether the federal securities regime should be eliminated are, consequently, the research on the impact on shareholder welfare of state competition for charters. This research indicates convincingly, in my judgment, that investors are at a minimum not harmed from the competition and, in all likelihood, benefit from changes in corporate domicile to states such as Delaware, the leading incorporation state.

There have been six event studies of the effect of state competition on shareholder wealth. The wealth effect is measured by the stock price reaction to a domicile change. Measured over a variety of time periods and sample firms, these studies find either a significant positive stock price effect or no significant price effect upon reincorporation.[61] No study observes a negative stock price effect. The empirical research on state competition undermines the race-for-the-bottom argument against eliminating the federal securities monopoly by demonstrating that choice of jurisdiction does not leave investors defenseless against unscrupulous promoters.[62]

The race-for-the-bottom view of state competition is no longer the consensus view of scholars in the debate over the efficacy of state competition for corporate charters precisely because its advocates cannot provide tangible proof that competition is, in general, harmful to investors. There is no reason to expect state competition to operate differently for securities law than it does for corporate law. The informational efficiency of capital markets and the dominant presence of institutional investors in such markets ensure that the content of legal regimes will be impounded in the cost of capital, whether they concern only corporate governance or include securities transactions. Accordingly, if mandatory securities rules benefit shareholders, notwithstanding the absence of empirical support in their favor, then competitive federalism will produce mandatory rules as well.

This is not to say that state competition is perfect. In the 1980s, when hostile takeovers emerged as a mechanism for changing control and, correlatively, for replacing incumbent management, the vast majority of states enacted laws that attempted to lower the probability of a hostile takeover. Because shareholders receive substantial premiums in hostile takeovers, most commentators hypothesized that the objective of these statutes was not to enhance shareholder welfare, but to entrench management.[63] Indeed, some antitakeover statutes made explicit their non-shareholder-wealth-maximization objectives. Such laws, referred to as "other constituency statutes," permit management to consider interests other than those of shareholders (i.e., factors besides the offered price) in deciding whether to oppose a bid.[64]

Consistent with the view that restricting hostile takeovers is not beneficial to shareholders, the enactment of antitakeover laws produced negative or statistically insignificant stock price reactions.[65] Delaware, with the largest stake in the chartering business, stands out, however, as an anomaly in the takeover statute legislative process. In contrast to its position as an innovator in corporation code provisions, in the takeover context, Delaware was a laggard behind other states, and its regulation is considerably less restrictive of bids.[66] More important, charter competition limits the extent to which states can restrict takeovers: When Pennsylvania enacted what was considered to be a draconian statute, a majority of firms opted out of its coverage because of demands made by their investors, who raised the prospect of selling their shares and reinvesting in firms incorporated in states with no statutes or less restrictive statutes, such as California and Delaware.[67] Consequently, other states did not adopt the Pennsylvania statute.[68]

There is also no evidence that a monopolist-regulator enforcing one national corporation law would produce better takeover regulation than the states. Quite to the contrary, in all likelihood, a monopolist regulator would make the situation worse. The political dynamics of takeover regulation at the state level would be unchanged at the national level. The groups that are influential in state politics outside of Delaware—local firm managers—are as influential in Washington. They provide, for instance, the bulk of the witnesses testifying for takeover regulation.[69] In addition, members of Congress whose districts included hostile takeover targets were the principal advocates for antitakeover legislation,[70] just as states with hostile targets were the enactors of similar protective legislation.[71] Moreover, the congressional legislation on takeovers enacted under the securities laws, the Williams Act,[72] paralleling the state statutes, favors incumbent managers over bidders by delaying bids, and the overwhelming majority of bills introduced concerning federal takeover regulation since the Williams Act have sought to make hostile bids more difficult.[73]

With only a national law, there would be no safety valve offered by a competing jurisdiction (such as California and Delaware in the current federal system of corporate law) to constrain takeover legislation, and a legislative or judicial mistake would be more difficult to reverse, as Congress moves considerably more slowly than state legislatures.[74] As the experience with state takeover laws indicates, although in the short run there will be deviations from the optimum in a federal system, in the longer run competitive pressure is exerted when states make mistakes, as in the example of firms opting out of Pennsylvania's takeover statute. Such pressure is absent in an exclusive one-regulator system.

The empirical literature concerning the efficacy of state competition for corporate charters has been my focus of analysis, not only because an assessment of the efficacy of charter competition underlies the arguments for and against the market approach to securities regulation, but also because economic theory provides limited guidance concerning whether a monopolist will provide the optimal degree of product quality, variety, or innovation, issues of importance in the regulatory context. Whether a monopolist's choice of quality is socially optimal depends on the difference between the marginal and average consumers' willingness to pay for quality, as is true of price-taking competitors; whether the monopolist will undersupply quality compared to the competitive market depends on the elasticity of demand.[75] There is a similar ambiguity concerning whether a monopolist will produce too few or too many products; the answer again depends on the elasticities of demand and whether the goods in question are substitutes.[76]

Extending the theory of monopolistic firms to regulators, William P. Albrecht et al. present a model in which competing regulators, in contrast to a monopolist (or to collusive regulators), provide efficient regulation when the goods regulated are substitutes.[77] Although it is most plausible to conceptualize the products in the securities regulation context as substitutes, as all states' securities codes are available to all firms, if different states' laws are appropriate for specific types of firms and diversified investors desire to hold such firms in fixed proportions, the products could be conceptualized as complements. Lacking information on demand elasticities for securities laws, Albrecht et al.'s model is only suggestive of the benefits of the policy advocated in this chapter, and we must rely instead on the best available empirical evidence, the evidence from state competition for corporate charters. Charter competition has not resulted in product differentiation across states (i.e., corporate law regimes are substitutes),[78] and investors have benefited from the competition. These data are consistent with the existence of substantial benefits for investors from opening securities regulation up to competition as well.

How Would State Competition for Securities Regulation Work?

For states to compete in the production of specific laws, a state must receive some benefit from the activity. In the corporate law setting, the benefit is financial: States collect franchise tax revenues from locally incorporated firms. Over the past thirty years, the franchise tax revenue collected by Delaware, which is the leading incorporation state despite having few local corporations, averaged 16.7 percent of its total tax revenue. This revenue greatly exceeds what Delaware spends on its corporate law system.[79] If the regulation of securities transactions depended on the incorporation state as well, the incentive to obtain franchise tax revenues would increase, as there would be more dimensions on which a state could serve its corporate clientele. That is, a state could increase the number of incorporations, and hence its franchise tax revenues, by offering a desirable securities regime, as well as a desirable corporation code.

An additional potential revenue source for states competing over securities regulation is filing fees, which accompany the registration of a public offering of securities. These fees can be substantial.[80] Since 1983, the SEC's fee collections have been more than 100 percent, often more than 200 percent, of its gross outlays.[81] As a monopolist, the SEC has been able to charge a higher fee for registration than could competitive states, but competition need not drive such fees to zero. Delaware, for instance, charges higher incorporation fees than other states and is still the leading incorporation state—a phenomenon indicating that firms are willing to pay a premium for a superior legal product.[82]

Securities transaction taxes could be a further source of revenue, as they would accrue to the securities-regulating state, but the competitiveness of capital markets has constrained states from imposing substantial taxes on share transfers. The trend in European countries, for example, has been to reduce or eliminate securities transaction taxes because of competition for stock exchange business.[83] Annual securities domicile franchise fees, analogous to incorporation franchise fees, would be preferable to securities transaction taxes as a revenue source, however, because they are assessed per firm, rather than according to individual trades, and will thus not adversely affect liquidity by deterring particular transactions.

The financial incentives generating state charter competition have resulted in a race that has tended to the top in corporate law. This result suggests that it would be beneficial for investors to create similar financial incentives for states in the securities law context. Presently, however, states have little of value to offer firms in return for the payment of securities "franchise" taxes. State securities case law is not as extensive as that for corporate law because, until recently, the national securities laws have occupied the field, given expansive interpretations of the federal antifraud provisions by the SEC and courts and the desirability of using federal courts.[84] State securities law is not a complete void, however, because some litigants began turning to state actions in the aftermath of the Supreme Court's restrictive interpretations, beginning in the 1970s, of the federal antifraud provisions.[85] This trend is expected to increase given Congress's recent tightening of procedural requirements for federal securities actions,[86] unless Congress enacts the proposed preemption bills.[87]

The relative dearth of a developed body of securities case law places states at a distinct disadvantage in competing for corporations with the federal government in terms of substantive securities regulation. In choosing their statutory domicile, corporations place a premium on the presence of comprehensive case law because a stock of precedents facilitates business planning: Firms can structure transactions to minimize the possibility of liability.[88] States can, however, compensate for the problem of meager judicial precedents by formally incorporating federal court decisions interpreting the national laws, through either legislation or judicial action, to the extent that the state's statutory language tracks the national laws. This approach is not novel and has, in fact, been adopted in the corporate law context: It facilitated the replacement of New Jersey as the leading incorporation state by Delaware when corporations sought an alternative statutory domicile after a lame-duck Governor Woodrow Wilson and the Progressive Party majority in the New Jersey legislature drastically revised the corporation code. Delaware's judiciary had incorporated New Jersey precedents in interpreting its code, which was modeled on the former New Jersey statute.[89] Moreover, a state such as Delaware, with a specialized corporate law court, can compensate for the dearth of precedents by offering litigants the prospect of far greater judicial expertise than the federal courts.

The limited experience of states with securities regulation is one important reason for maintaining a federal government option—at a minimum as a transitional mechanism—in the context of creating competitive federalism for securities law in contrast to corporate law, for which there is no analogous federal code in the United States. It is, however, probable that opening securities regulation up to state competition would enhance Delaware's dominant position as an incorporation state. This is because, to the extent that the national securities laws have been accurately taken to task for requiring costly and excessive disclosure and fostering frivolous antifraud litigation, Delaware, in all likelihood, would offer a securities regime that mitigates these problems.

Delaware's fiscal prosperity depends to a significant extent upon providing rules that reduce firms' costs of doing business. As a small state, it would not have indigenous income sources to replace the substantial revenue it derives from the franchise tax were it to lose incorporations to a state more responsive to business needs. This motivation is a key to Delaware's chartering market success: Delaware's reliance on franchise tax revenues serves as a commitment device to ensure firms that it will continue to enact legislation that firms desire (statutes that maintain share values as new business conditions warrant code revision).[90] Such a commitment device is critical to the production of corporate charters because a corporate charter is a relational contract, extending over many years during which unforeseen contingencies are likely to arise. Such uncertainty makes it difficult for contracting parties to specify in advance their obligations, and, as performance is not simultaneous, the possibility of opportunistic breach is increased. In particular, firms select their domicile and pay franchise taxes based on the extant legal regime and run the risk that as business conditions change thereafter, the state will not adapt its code (or will repeal key provisions to firms' disadvantage). The opportunism problem of relational contracting is exacerbated when one of the contracting parties is the state, given its role as the enforcer of contracts through the court system.

Delaware has surmounted the commitment problem by investing in assets that have no value outside of the chartering market, thereby guaranteeing to firms that it will continue to be responsive in its code after they incorporate. These assets include its specialized corporate court system and a reputation for responsiveness dependent on its high ratio of franchise taxes to total tax revenues. To the extent that Delaware can gain further franchise revenues from crafting a responsive securities regime, the same factors will operate in the securities, as in the chartering, context, and Delaware will have stronger incentives than the SEC to find the desirable regulatory balance.

Alternative Market-Oriented Proposals

There are two alternatives to the competitive federalism approach to securities regulation advocated in this article that are also market oriented: eliminating the mandatory features of the federal regime by converting the federal securities laws into default provisions from which firms could opt out analogous to the enabling form of corporation codes, and replacing the government regulatory apparatus with a private, exchange-based regulatory regime.[91] Both of these alternatives harness market-based incentives to the regulatory system. Neither is precluded by this article's multiple-regulator approach.

A Federal Default Regime

In a federal default regime, firms that did not wish to be governed by particular SEC rules or statutory provisions could specify alternative provisions in their corporate charters or bylaws (or in the indenture contracts for debt securities). Congress would either specify itself, or delegate to the SEC to determine, which securities regulations, if any, a firm must opt out of by a charter, as opposed to a bylaw, amendment.[92] A default system would clearly be more desirable than the present one-size-fits-all regime, which is difficult to change because consensus must be developed among all participants regarding a new rule, even if their needs are quite different. For example, the SEC has been surveying registrants with a view to updating its rules regulating shareholder proxy proposals, and on the question of whether to retain the current voting thresholds for a proposal's resubmission, ten corporate respondents produced eight different threshold proposals.[93] A lack of consensus among firms on such a matter is of far lesser import under a default system because firms can obtain the threshold level most appropriate for their shareholder configuration by provision in their charter or bylaws.

Under an enabling approach, if a default rule is suboptimal (i.e., the rule's compliance costs outweigh benefits to investors), the majority of firms will elect not to be subject to the rule. Assuming the SEC became informed of firms' choices, perhaps by a requirement that firms file securities "charters" with the agency so that it could track deviations from the defaults, this market response would feed back into the SEC's decision-making process, leading it to readjust its beliefs concerning what regulation was most appropriate and, ultimately, to alter the default rule to one more compatible with investors' needs, just as would occur with state competition. There would also be a potential benefit compared to state competition for securities regulation: Transaction costs would be reduced because investors would not have to determine which regime governs their transactions. But if the SEC is not attentive in updating its defaults, there would be little savings in transaction costs, because investors could have to identify whether a firm was operating under particular outdated SEC defaults or its own alternatives.

An enabling national regime would be preferable to the current mandatory one, but, in my judgment, a competitive system of securities regulation is even more preferable. State competition would not preclude a national enabling regime, as the federal government could adopt an enabling regime in competition with the states, as may any or all states. But state competition would provide an additional benefit over a federal enabling regime: There would be a straightforward mechanism by which regulators learn of firms' adoption of statutory defaults. Under regulatory competition, there would be some variety in defaults across states, even if key innovations diffuse over time across the states, as has occurred in the corporate law context. This phenomenon would accelerate regulators' identification of the rules most desired by investors, as more firms would register in the states with the more desirable default rules. This would also reduce investors' transaction costs of learning whether a firm has customized an outdated default.

A further benefit of state competition compared to a federal enabling regime would be a more rapid updating of undesirable defaults because of financial incentives. A state such as Delaware would be considerably more attentive to the need to reduce the transaction costs generated by obsolete defaults than the SEC because of the state's financial dependence on the relevant franchise taxes. Because firms have no alternative regulator in the monopolist enabling regime, the SEC is not exposed to the same code-updating incentives as would be experienced by states—declining revenues due to declining registrations.[94] The pressure experienced by the SEC from global competition, whether under an enabling statute or the mandatory regime currently in effect, is quite weak because resort solely to foreign capital markets for financing is not a viable option for publicly traded U.S. firms. The best evidence that global competition is not as effective a motivator for the SEC as direct domestic regulatory competition comes from the regulation of derivative securities. In the derivatives regulatory context, where the SEC has exclusive jurisdiction over the derivatives disclosures of publicly traded domestic companies, it has been minimally responsive to issuers' concerns about regulatory costs and competitiveness.[95] Where the SEC competes with the Commodity Futures Trading Commission (CFTC) for jurisdiction, however, it has shifted from an initial position of opposing equity derivative products to one encouraging and promoting innovation by its regulatees, stock exchanges, to facilitate their competition against the futures exchanges regulated by the CFTC.[96]

A final potential benefit of state competition compared to an enabling national regime turns on whether any mandatory rules are desirable in the securities context, for instance, to facilitate a firm's credible commitment to investors that it will not engage in opportunistic behavior by altering a securities default to one offering less protection after the investments are made.[97] Mandatory rules could not be effectuated satisfactorily under a national enabling approach. For if the national enabling regime consisted of a mix of defaults and mandatory provisions, then we would be left with the problem endemic in the current monopolist-regulator setup: There would be no mechanism to check whether the mandatory provisions were, in fact, the ones that investors would voluntarily choose. Multiple regulators would permit mandatory provisions without the consequent costs, as such provisions could vary across jurisdictions, and information would therefore be provided concerning which provisions were desirable through the registration decisions of firms.

Regulation by Exchanges

A more decidedly deregulatory approach would be to leave securities regulation to the stock exchanges on which firms list.[98] In such a regime, exchange-listing conditions would include the substantive content of securities laws, such as periodic disclosure requirements. Exchanges can solve free rider problems concerning information production encountered by individual firms, as well as coordination problems presented by investors' need for standardized disclosure. Thus, exchanges could replace the government as the solution to a securities market failure. Indeed, much of the disclosure predating the 1934 act discussed by Benston was an NYSE listing requirement.[99] Moreover, multiple exchanges compete for listings. To the extent that maximizing trading volume is a function of listings, exchanges would be subject to the same incentives as states competing for charters, leading them to adopt listing requirements preferred by investors (or to shares discounted accordingly).[100]

As with a national default regime, an exchange-based regime would be likely to save transaction costs compared to state competition, because investors are directly informed of which regime applies when they trade shares.[101] But there could still be a regulatory role for the states in an exchange-regulated system. Although the over-the-counter market for the largest stocks, NASD's Automated Quotation System (NASDAQ), is a sufficiently developed regulatory organization capable of offering its own securities regime, if the NASDAQ regime were poorly suited for the smallest firms traded over-the-counter ("bulletin board" and "pink sheet" issues), it might be more cost effective for a state, rather than for the firms' market makers, to organize and operate a separate securities regime.

State regulation would, however, offer some decided benefits over stock exchange regulation: a more effective mechanism of private dispute resolution for securities suits against issuers, and a public enforcement system, should the deterrent effect of criminal prosecution for securities law violations be a necessary complement to civil liability. Class-action litigation is not well suited[102] for private arbitration, and it is not surprising that arbitration programs currently administered by exchanges resolve individual complaints against brokers, not class complaints against issuers. As a consequence, even when courts have permitted classwide arbitration, they have retained substantial judicial involvement, including the initial determination of the certifiability of the class and review of the settlement.[103] Thus, state or federal courts would be required to enforce the exchanges' regulatory regime. This creates two difficulties. First, the use of tribunals not operated by exchanges externalizes the cost of their legal proceedings, which is a disadvantage from a social welfare, as opposed to investor, perspective. With state securities regulation, the fees the states earn in the registration process would defray the costs of administering securities cases.

Second, regulatory competition is most effective when the sovereign's jurisdiction includes both the court and the legislature. Canada, for instance, has not developed a vigorous charter competition across the provinces in large part because the provincial governments do not control the adjudication of corporate law disputes; securities administrators (of any province) and the national supreme court share that authority with the incorporation province.[104] This renders it impossible for a province to guarantee a responsive legal regime to prospective incorporators, because a securities administrator can impose obligations on firms countermanding provincial laws. A similar difficulty would be experienced by exchanges that were unable to adjudicate all of the disputes arising under their securities regimes. This problem is, in fact, raised in a weaker form even under the competitive federalism proposal advocated in this article, for unless firms adopt forum clauses specifying that all securities claims are to be adjudicated in courts of their securities domicile, investors would be able to file in nondomicile courts. Although these courts would apply the law of the domicile, they might lack the expertise to adjudicate disputes as effectively as the domicile.[105] In sum, regulation by exchanges will at best be a dual regulatory system, with much of the enforcement of exchange rules performed by the government.[106]

It is important to note that state competition for securities regulation would not preclude exchange-based regulation. A state could, for instance, adopt a securities regime only for nonexchange-traded corporations or enact no mandatory disclosure requirements at all, thereby leaving the determination of such requirements to exchanges. Because such an outcome would be within the realm of possible outcomes under competitive federalism, the prudent approach to regulatory policy reform would be to implement incremental experimentation: replace the current monopolist-regulator with state competition and permit the competitive process to reach the judgment that an exchange-based securities regime provides a set of rules as good as or more optimal than those provided by the states.

II. Implementing the Market Approach to Securities Regulation

Operationalizing a market approach to securities regulation for issuers requires two legislative reforms. The first and more straightforward reform is to make the federal securities laws optional. This could be achieved by an act of Congress. Alternatively, the SEC could cede its exclusive authority over public corporations under its newly granted exemptive power.[107] This solution is, however, akin to asking the agency to put itself out of business, behavior that would be decidedly out of character for an agency that has historically sought to increase, not to decrease, its jurisdictional scope.[108] In addition, an act of Congress expressly eliminating the SEC's exclusive regulatory authority over publicly traded firms is the preferable course of action because the statute creating the SEC's exemptive authority also preempted the states from applying registration requirements to nationally traded securities.[109] The facial inconsistency between using the exemption to increase state authority when Congress was otherwise reducing state authority would provide opponents of the market approach to securities regulation reform the opportunity to use litigation to delay, if not defeat, its implementation.

The second major policy reform, adapting the choice-of-law rule governing securities transactions (site of sale) to one compatible with competition (issuer domicile), could be more complicated to accomplish because it would entail coordination by the states to adopt a new rule. It would therefore be more expedient for the congressional legislation making the federal regime optional also to institute the requisite change in choice of law, and this article advocates such an approach. But because Congress has not typically legislated choice-of-law rules, this part of the article not only explains the requisite change but also justifies its adoption and critiques the reigning conflict's approach.

Two additional requirements for the successful implementation of the proposal are also discussed in this part: disclosure of the securities domicile to the purchaser of a security at the time of the purchase and a shareholder vote to accomplish a change in securities domicile. These refinements would ensure that the new market-oriented regime meets the stated goal of the federal securities laws: investor protection.

An Internal Affairs Approach to the Choice-of-Law Rule for Securities Transactions

With a market approach to securities regulation, only one sovereign's law can apply to an issuer's securities transactions. This means that only one state's securities law would govern securities transactions when the SEC option is not invoked. Similarly, when the SEC regulatory option is selected, it would preempt all state securities regulation, including antifraud provisions. The state with legislative jurisdiction[110] must be connected to the issuer to ensure that state competition operates properly—that one state's law governs and that it is the state chosen by the issuer. This would necessitate recrafting the reigning choice-of-law approach, which follows the site of the securities transaction and not the issuer's domicile.

Applicability of the Internal Affairs Approach to Securities Transactions

The prevailing choice-of-law approach to securities transactions is codified in provisions of the Uniform Securities Act: The applicable law is that of the site of the transaction, which is the state in which either the offer or the acceptance to buy the security takes place.[111] More than one state can claim legislative jurisdiction over a transaction under this approach, and the state whose law governs is not connected to the issuer.

The present choice-of-law rule, under which the securities law varies across a firm's stockholders based on where they purchased their shares, has a number of undesirable consequences for a legal system. These include lack of uniform treatment across similarly situated individuals and unpredictable standards of conduct for issuers, given the possible application of fifty-one (state and D.C.) statutes. These difficulties are, in fact, on occasion presented as the reason for the federal securities laws in cases involving the states' overlapping jurisdiction with the federal regime, such as the regulation of broker-dealers.[112] In the corporation code setting, the operational problems created by an absence of uniformity and predictability due to multistate shareholders are eliminated because the choice-of-law rule recognized by all of the states fixes one state's law, that of the incorporation state, as governing all shareholders' claims. This choice-of-law rule is referred to as the "internal affairs doctrine," because the subject matter of corporate law is characterized as the internal affairs of the corporation.[113]

The rationale for application of the internal affairs rule to corporate law disputes is equally applicable to the choice of law for securities transactions. In particular, choice-of-law commentators justify the internal affairs doctrine by the need for uniform treatment of shareholders. For example, "It would be intolerable for different holders of the same issue of stock to have different sets of rights and duties by reason of their stockholdings, perhaps according to the laws of the various places at which they acquired their stock. Unity of treatment is desirable, and the only single law by which it can be achieved is that of the corporation's domicile."[114] The *Restatement (Second) of Conflicts of Law* similarly stresses as the rationale for preserving the internal affairs rule the need for "[u]niform treatment of directors, officers and shareholders . . . which can only be attained by having [their] rights and liabilities . . . governed by a single law."[115] The Supreme Court has also followed this approach in considering whether state takeover laws violate the Commerce Clause. The Court's validation of such statutes depends critically on a state's exclusive legislative jurisdiction as the incorporation state (i.e., on the internal affairs rule), which avoids the impermissible risk of a corporation's encountering "inconsistent regulation by different States."[116]

Application of the internal affairs rule to securities transactions should go further than covering litigation arising from initial public offerings under state registration requirements and should include secondary market trading. Fraud claims against an issuer should be uniformly adjudicated across investors. It is even more troubling to differentiate fraud claims from corporate internal affairs than to differentiate securities registration requirements from corporate law. There is no plausible rationale for distinguishing a fiduciary standard of conduct to govern an officer's or director's judgment concerning a corporate transaction, such as payment of a dividend or undertaking a merger, from that officer's or director's judgment concerning disclosure about the firm's performance in a public document. Nor is there a rationale for permitting the differentiation of such standards across shareholders. Yet, choice-of-law rules establish the application of one state's (the incorporation state's) standard to fiduciary duties in corporate law, but leave the latter decision on disclosure to vary with the investor's domicile, even though a duty of full and fair disclosure is at the heart of the fiduciary duties of state corporate law. Such intellectual incoherence concerning fiduciary conduct is the fallout of current choice-of-law doctrine.

The bizarre possibility of fiduciary standards differing across shareholders according to their residence (or other location of their stock purchase or sale) has not yet been the focus of legislators' or commentators' attention because there have not been many cases involving conflicting fiduciary standards: The vast majority of securities claims are brought in federal court and settled.[117] In particular, the problem of certifying a class when the standard of liability depends on the shareholder's domicile or investment contract situs has not been raised with any frequency in the securities context, in contrast to the mass tort product liability context.[118] So, if securities cases are filed increasingly in state, rather than federal, courts, whether in response to the 1995 securities litigation reform[119] or for other reasons, such as a more amenable settlement process,[120] then the class certification issue will take on a pressing importance. Beyond accomplishing this article's immediate aim of empowering investors by creating a competitive regulatory regime, extending the internal affairs rule to state securities fraud claims would have the salutary effect of disposing of a thorny substantive law problem of varying liability standards, thereby ensuring that a class could be certified.

An additional salutary effect of following an internal affairs approach to securities regulation would be eliminating the potential problem of under-enforcement with multiple potential regulators. Without such an approach, ambiguity in regulatory responsibility can lead to regulatory free riding, as each regulator expects another regulator to be responsible. This is an increasing possibility with the expansion of Internet trading.[121] The internal affairs rule specifies precisely one regulator, the issuer's securities domicile, thereby removing the free riding problem.

Flaws in the Reigning Choice-of-Law Approach to Securities Transactions

Conflict-of-law scholars typically rationalize the disparate choice-of-law approach to securities law that insulates state regulation of transactions in foreign corporations' shares from application of the internal affairs rule by contending that individual securities transactions do not implicate concerns about uniformity.[122] The explanation advanced for the distinction has two prongs: (1) In stock transactions, the individual purchasers are not yet shareholders (i.e., not members of the "corporate community") and therefore the transaction can be characterized as having purely local effect, which is said to give the buyer's domicile state an interest in regulation more significant than that of the issuer's state; and (2) a corporation can avoid a state's regulation by not selling its shares in that state, and thus it need not be subject to inconsistent regulations.[123] The choice-of-law distinction between corporate and securities law is a legerdemain, but it has a certain practicality: It is more feasible for a corporation to issue fifty different disclosure statements to accompany the registration of securities than it is to operate with fifty different policies on dividend payouts and voting rights.

The flaw in the choice-of-law analysis that distinguishes corporate and securities laws is, however, easy enough to identify. The common shares of a corporation are the same in whatever state they are sold, and it is arbitrary to apply different criteria to transactions in the same securities simply because of differences in purchasers' residences. Indeed, securities litigation between investors and issuers is not individualized litigation: Management's defective disclosures are not differentially or personally directed at particular investors in the anonymity of modern capital markets, and the composition of the class of affected shareholders (those who entered into transactions in the relevant interval) is therefore fortuitous. In short, neither the prospective feature of the shareholder relation for a buyer of new securities nor the voluntary choice of selling securities in particular states can be characterized as individualizing the multiparty context of the corporate contract sufficiently to overcome the desirability of regulatory uniformity across security transactions for the issuer, as well as for investors, as they bear the increased cost of compliance with a panoply of regimes.

The demand for uniform and consistent treatment across investors is, in fact, recognized by the states' voluntary refusal to exercise regulatory authority over the securities of interstate (exchange-traded) corporations. The shift in legal regime from mandatory to optional federal coverage would not alter the desirability of this approach. Just as the federal law has trumped securities choice-of-law analysis under the exemptive policy of the state statutes, where a public corporation has chosen a specific state over the SEC as its securities regulator, registration requirements should be governed by that state's law.

Moreover, the limitation of a court's exercise of local legislative jurisdiction by a contract's choice-of-law clause's selection of a foreign state is well established.[124] Although there are specific circumstances when courts refuse to enforce such provisions—when there are defects in contract clause formation, such as when the contracts are unconscionable adhesion contracts or when the contracts contravene the public policy of the state that would otherwise exert legislative jurisdiction[125]—they are not relevant for securities law transactions. First, given the multiplicity of investment choices, securities transactions are not adhesion contracts. In addition, the proposed notice requirement concerning which state's law applies[126] would render highly improbable the possibility that an investor's agreement to a choice-of-law clause was fraudulently obtained. Second, securities transactions specifying the governing law of a state other than the buyer's state are also not contracts in contravention of public policy, the enforcement of which would deprive the plaintiff of an adequate remedy. Even in the remote possibility that the chosen securities domicile had no securities regulation at all, the absence of an appropriate remedy would not be an issue because a defrauded purchaser could still pursue a complaint under that state's common law fraud and fiduciary doctrines.[127]

The conventional conflicts-of-law objection to application of an internal-affairs-type doctrine to securities transactions, which is captured by the public policy exception to choice-of-law clause enforcement and to requirements that the chosen state have a reasonable connection to the transaction or the parties, is that the investor's domiciliary state has a more important "interest" in a securities dispute than the issuer's domicile.[128] The policy concern that is confusedly asserted as a state's "interest" in this instance is that the issuer's state will not provide an adequately protective regulatory regime against fraudulent sales practices because the buyers (or a majority of them) are not its citizens. This concern is founded, however, on a mistaken premise: The research on state competition for charters indicates that states that compete successfully for corporate charters do not enact regimes that diminish investors' wealth.[129] Investors would benefit from an internal affairs rule for securities regulation as well because, as occurs in the chartering market, investors' preferences drive the regulatory competition. In addition, the proposed requirement that disclosure of securities domicile must be provided upon stock purchase[130] would eliminate the concern of the buyer's state that its citizens were inadequately protected: Domicile notice would ensure that buyers were informed of which state's regime is applicable. If the regime of the issuer's state were less favorable to investors than that of the buyer's state, the investor would pay less for the shares or not purchase them in the first place. Consequently, a requirement of physical connection to the state to make contracting parties' choice of law effective makes absolutely no sense in the securities context.[131]

Which State Should Be the Securities Domicile?

There are three plausible candidates for the single state whose rules govern a firm's securities transactions in place of the SEC: (1) a state chosen specifically for securities regulation by the issuer, (2) the issuer's incorporation state, and (3) the issuer's principal place of business. The first approach would be implemented through a choice-of-law clause in the corporation's charter (and noticed on the security). It would create, in effect, a statutory domicile for securities law. Under a choice-of-law clause approach, the choice of securities domicile could vary across a firm's financial instruments, as well as differ from the firm's statutory domicile (its incorporation state). The other two approaches operate automatically by the firm's choice of statutory domicile or headquarters site and hence would not require independent action by the corporation to effect a securities domicile choice, unless that choice were the SEC.

The least desirable securities domicile approach is to choose the state of principal place of business. This is because a physical presence requirement introduces friction into state competition. When physical and human capital must be relocated in order to effect a change in legal regime, a firm's decision to move to a more preferable securities domicile is considerably, if not prohibitively, more expensive than when such a relocation can be accomplished by means of a paper filing. Few firms would change domicile to take advantage of incremental legal improvements under such a domicile approach compared to the other two approaches and, correspondingly, the incentives of states to provide securities codes responsive to investor preferences would be sharply diminished. The difference between the domicile choice of incorporation state (statutory domicile) and state of physical presence (referred to as the *siège réel*, the corporation's real or effective seat, in some European nations) in corporate law is, in fact, a principal reason for the absence of charter competition across the nations of the European Union compared to U.S. states[132]

Whether the most desirable approach for fostering competition over securities regulation is the choice-of-law clause or the incorporation state approach depends, in large part, on whether there are synergies from one state's administering both the corporate and securities law regimes. This is because the incorporation state approach harnesses the in-place apparatus of charter competition to the securities context. In general, such synergies should be substantial because corporate law expertise readily transfers to securities law. For instance, with one state's law adjudicating both corporate and securities issues, the standard for directors' and officers' fiduciary duties, including disclosure obligations, would be harmonized.[133] More specifically, all litigation relating to conduct during hostile takeovers would be governed by one state's law. In addition, all legal issues concerning shareholder meetings would be subject to the same legal regime, eliminating the considerable confusion surrounding the SEC's rules regulating shareholder proxy proposals, which simultaneously look to state corporate law's allocation of authority between shareholders and managers and effectively ignore it[134] Where the synergies of an incorporation state securities domicile include the expertise of the judiciary, a firm could adopt a forum clause to ensure that securities claims are filed in the incorporation state.[135]

But even if the substantive law synergies were limited in number, there is a further benefit associated with the incorporation state approach. Litigation costs would be reduced because the significance of line drawing over whether a dispute implicates securities or corporate law is reduced, as the same sovereign's rules would apply in either scenario.

Although the arguments supporting the choice of incorporation state as the securities domicile appear to be compelling, there are countervailing considerations that militate against mandating such an approach rather than leaving the choice of domicile up to the issuer (the choice-of-law clause approach). First and most important, the choice-of-law clause approach obviates the need to guess whether the potential synergies of one regime for corporate and securities law are substantial—market participants' domicile choices would provide the information. It is therefore most consistent with the market approach to securities regulation. Second, given the variety of securities issued by firms, it is possible that states would specialize in different securities and, consequently, that firms could benefit from being able to select different domiciles for different issues. This is particularly relevant for debt securities, where there are no regulatory synergies with the incorporation state because corporate law deals solely with manager-shareholder relations.[136] Third, permitting a self-standing securities domicile might enhance state competition, as a state could decide to compete more vigorously for securities issues than for corporate charters and thus prevent Delaware from being able to slouch on the securities regime it offers because of its success in obtaining incorporations.

Adapting the Securities Law Choice-of-Law Regime to the Market Approach

Choice-of-law rules are generally creatures of judicial, rather than legislative, determination. But, statutes may codify choice-of-law rules. For instance, some states have enacted the Uniform Securities Act's choice-of-law provisions, which select the most common judge-made choice, the state where the securities are offered for sale.[137] In addition, some states have adopted choice-of-law clause statutes, which guarantee enforcement of contractual choice-of-law provisions regardless of standard conflicts rules, such as whether the contracting parties have any relationship to the state.[138] Coordinated statutory action by the states altering the site-of-sale rule to an issuer securities domicile rule, such as by amendment to the Uniform Securities Act, would be a more expeditious route than reliance on judicial action for implementing the new domicile choice-of-law approach.

An even more efficacious alternative than coordinated state statutory action would be for Congress to legislate the mandatory application of the issuer domicile approach as the securities transactions choice-of-law rule in the statute rendering the federal securities regime optional. Although Congress has not mandated choice-of-law rules, it could do so under its Commerce Clause and Article IV powers.[139] Congressional action is the preferred mechanism for implementing the securities domicile choice-of-law rule, whether the incorporation state or choice-of-law clause approach is chosen, because it is the most expeditious method for achieving that end, as it does not require coordination by fifty state courts or legislatures.

Coordination can occur—the universal recognition of the internal affairs approach to corporate law is a prime example—but it takes time. For instance, most states enforce forum selection clauses; this sea change from an earlier era when such clauses were considered presumptively invalid has occurred by a mix of state legislative and judicial action, exemplifying a policy of reciprocity (i.e., the states recognize residents' contracts to litigate in another state) rather than conscious coordination through adoption of a uniform act.[140] But, while the gradual shift to acceptance has been led by Supreme Court decisions upholding such clauses in federal cases over the past two decades,[141] there are still some states that do not enforce them.[142] If there is a similar pattern in the securities context as in the recognition of forum selection clauses—increasing acceptance of the concept of securities domicile with an outstanding small number of holdouts after many years— making the federal securities regime optional would not engender successful competition in securities regulation, at a minimum in the short run, because the incentives of issuers, investors, and regulators are not aligned when the law of the issuer's selected domicile does not govern all securities transactions.

Congressional enactment of a securities domicile conflicts rule would shortcut such an evolutionary process by immediately implementing all states' adherence to the securities domicile choice-of-law approach, and it would thereby preserve the advantages of the market approach. It is, perhaps, ironic that the by-product of federal intervention in the states' securities choice-of-law rulemaking would be a greatly invigorated competitive federalism.[143]

Refinements to the Implementation of the Market Approach

To ensure that the investor-protection goal of the federal securities laws functions smoothly under the market approach, the congressional legislation that would render the federal regime optional and would fix an issuer domicile approach to the states' securities choice-of-law rule should contain two additional statutory mandates. These statutory requirements would establish investor safeguards at two critical transactional junctures, one occurring at the individual investor level and the other at the aggregate firm level. The first requirement is disclosure of the applicable legal regime (the firm's securities domicile) at the time an investor acquires a security; the second is a vote of the affected securityholders in order to accomplish a change in securities domicile.[144]

Disclosure of the Applicable Securities Regime

For state competition to function properly, investors must know what regime will apply to a particular security.[145] The domicile disclosure requirement would ensure that this condition holds. To accomplish this notice function, the securities domicile should be indicated on the instrument (stock certificate or note), just as corporate law requires that restrictions on share transferability, to be effective, must be noticed on the stock certificate.[146] But, because investors rarely receive a financial instrument even after purchase (most stock investments transfer electronically and remain physically held by the clearinghouse depositary), a further mode of notice is essential. The most plausible additional means of domicile disclosure would entail a two-pronged approach, directed at both brokers and firms. First, brokers should be required to inform prospective buyers of the securities domicile at the time of purchase (or short sale). Because federal broker regulation would not be transferred from the SEC under the proposed approach, such a requirement could easily be implemented by agency regulation.

Second, and more important, issuers should be required to disclose their securities domicile at the time of initial public offerings as a condition of opting out of the federal regime. The required disclosure should be permitted to take a variety of forms. Where the issuer's domicile requires use of a prospectus to sell securities, the federal requirement should be satisfied by indicating the domicile in that offering document. Where there is no prospectus or other offering document requirement, the issuer should have to inform the prospective buyer of the securities domicile in writing, an obligation that could be satisfied by the issuer's contracting with the underwriting syndicate to provide the information in writing to prospective purchasers. In addition, for public offerings of a firm whose securities are already traded and whose securities domicile imposes periodic reporting requirements, disclosing securities domicile in the required documents should satisfy the issuer's federal notice requirement as long as such reports are matters of public record (i.e., filed with a state office) and thus available to prospective purchasers. Where a domicile imposes no periodic reporting requirements, voluntary disclosure of securities domicile in a public document available on a continuing periodic basis (such as in an annual financial report or proxy statement sent to shareholders for the annual meeting to elect directors, in the corporate charter on file with the Secretary of State, or in a publicly available record kept by the stock exchange on which the shares trade) should also satisfy the federal disclosure requirement. These latter forms of disclosure would also suffice for any issuer responsibility regarding domicile notice to investors who acquire securities in secondary trading markets.

Domicile disclosure would not be a costly requirement for issuers under any of the possible mechanisms that have been outlined. It would also not be costly for brokers to identify an issuer's securities domicile to prospective purchasers. But mandating disclosure of securities domicile at the time of a securities purchase is not clearly necessary to protect investors: Markets would price significant differences in securities regimes as sophisticated investors obtain domicile information prior to their purchases, even if domicile disclosure were not mandated. But, given the historical application of the federal regime to all securities, mandated domicile disclosure would go a considerable distance toward mitigating the relatively remote possibility of less sophisticated investors' not knowing that the federal regime might no longer apply. Because such confusion is most likely to occur in the initial years following the adoption of the market approach, the domicile disclosure requirement could be enacted as a sunset provision, expiring, for example, three years after the statute's effective date. For securities trading in markets where unsophisticated investors are predominant, such as penny stocks, the domicile disclosure requirement could be retained beyond such a transition period as a protective measure for such investors.

The domicile disclosure requirement would not mandate disclosure of the substantive content of the relevant regime. Firms could, of course, provide such information to investors in their domicile disclosure, but the statutory requirement would leave acquisition of such details to investors. To the extent there might be concern that unsophisticated investors might mistakenly assume that all state regimes contain similar protections and could thereby be duped into buying penny stocks registered under a regime that institutional investors shun, a written disclaimer could be required at the time of such securities' acquisition, in addition to the domicile disclosure, that would inform investors, in large print, that "their rights under the securities laws may differ significantly across the states." Alternatively, a requirement could be fashioned to disclose the details of a regime's significant differences. I am reluctant to advocate such an approach given the costly line-drawing questions it is likely to entail. It would, at minimum, require careful drafting to specify the norm against which differences are to be measured, such as the rules of a majority of the states, the old federal regime, and so forth. The prospect of litigation over the fulfillment of the domicile disclosure requirement under such an alternative leads me to opt for the more generic disclaimer approach, should any disclosure beyond the domicile be required.

Securityholder Approval of Securities Domicile Changes

A different set of concerns regarding the securities domicile choice is implicated when an issuer determines to change its securities domicile midstream than is implicated when a shareholder purchases a security with a given domicile. Namely, the price the investor paid for its shares will not reflect the value of the new domicile (unless the change was anticipated at the time of purchase). This is of concern if corporate insiders can behave opportunistically and move to a securities domicile that requires less disclosure or has a lower securities fraud standard than the original regime. Such a move could shift value away from the public to insiders' shares, assuming, of course, that outside investors did not anticipate such opportunistic behavior and paid less for the more protective domicile in the first place.

Insider opportunism regarding domicile choice could be mitigated by requiring the voting approval of the affected securityholders before a domicile change can be effected.[147] As in the corporate law context, the federal statute would create a minimum default for the required vote of a simple majority. Firms wishing to operate under a higher, supermajority voting requirement would therefore be able to do so. The most practical means of implementing a supermajority voting requirement would be for the corporation to include such a rule in its corporate charter (and, if commitment to such a voting rule was of concern, to subject its repeal to an analogous supermajority vote). States could also establish higher voting minimum defaults in their securities codes. A supermajority voting default to accomplish changes in securities domicile, however, would not be desirable from the global perspective of competitive federalism: When exit from a regime is too difficult, the signals from migration patterns concerning firms' preferred provisions are weakened, and the beneficial effects of competition stymied.

A majority voting requirement for securities domicile changes could ultimately aid insiders. In the absence of a voting requirement, it is possible that investors would expect value-diminishing moves to occur and pay less for their shares initially. The presence of a voting requirement would commit insiders to proposing a domicile change only when the new regime increases firm value, rather than when the regime disproportionately benefits their own shares, and, as a consequence, investors would not discount shares for opportunistic midstream domicile changes. To the extent that promoters value such a precommitment device, a federal voting requirement may well be unnecessary because competitive state codes would include such a requirement. Nevertheless, placing the requirement in the federal statute would create a more robust commitment device because, as an integral part of the regulatory regime, it would be difficult to rescind. It is, for example, more difficult to change congressional than state legislation.

Some commentators contend that shareholder voting is not an effective safeguard against insider opportunism because it is irrational for shareholders to vote—that is, an individual shareholder's cost of becoming informed in order to vote his interest outweighs the pro rata benefit he will receive from a correct outcome.[148] This contention, in my judgment, is vastly overblown.[149] In a capital market dominated by institutional investors holding portfolios of stock, issues are repeatedly raised across portfolio firms, reducing information costs significantly on any one vote. Moreover, the preferences of these informed voters—institutional investors—regarding securities regimes would not conflict with those of uninformed individual investors. This is because the vast majority of institutional investors, whose choices would determine the regime, do not possess private information or great skill at obtaining such information, and they would accordingly not benefit from a regime that minimizes firms' public disclosures.[150] It is possible that some institutional investors possess a superior ability to process public information; such investors would support a high level of disclosure, as that furthers their competitive advantage.

A probative example of this congruence in interest between institutional and individual investors regarding disclosure policy concerns the issues sold to institutional investors under Rule 144A, which exempts such issues from federal registration and hence the prospectus disclosure requirements of the 1933 act.[151] These issues have come to include disclosures equivalent to those required in the prospectuses of registered public offerings.[152] Although the reason for this phenomenon could be underwriter concern over liability (the 1934 antifraud provisions still apply to such offerings[153]), it suggests that institutional investors find issuer disclosure more cost effective than reliance on private information collection.

Voting rights in corporate law are often accompanied by appraisal (dissenters') rights—the right of dissenters to be cashed out of the firm at a price set by a court under statutory guidance.[154] Appraisal rights mitigate adverse outcomes from uninformed voting: Informed shareholders can dissent and, under the statutory standard, obtain the cash value of their shares equal to the value "exclusive" of the transaction that was the subject of the vote.[155] Thus, for a value-diminishing transaction such as an unfavorable domicile shift, the share's appraisal value would be the stock price before any adverse effect from the market's assessment of the value in the new domicile (the outcome of the vote). Such rights could be mandated for dissenters to a domicile change. Appraisal rights, however, come with costs, such as the potential for an unwanted cash drain if many shareholders exercise their rights, the holdup power that comes from shareholders' exercising such rights against a non-value-decreasing proposal, and imprecise valuation of the dissenters' shares that may over- or undercompensate them.

There has not been empirical research examining cross-sectionally the functioning of appraisal rights for charter amendments. Such research could provide information concerning how frequently such rights are used, what the stock price reaction is to amendments when the rights are used, and whether charter amendment proposals and voting outcomes differ systematically across firms when such rights are present. In states where appraisal rights are not statutorily provided for dissenters to charter amendments, firms do not appear to include such rights in their charters.[156] A plausible inference from such behavior is that appraisal costs outweigh the benefits; either they are an inadequate remedy for opportunistic amendments or insiders rarely propose opportunistic charter amendments. Indeed, if midstream opportunism were rampant, institutional investors would become aware of the practice, and promoters would have incentives—higher share prices—to bind themselves against engaging in opportunistic charter amendments by providing appraisal rights for such votes or otherwise locking in initial charter provisions. Accordingly, rather than have Congress mandate dissenters' rights in the securities domicile context, their presence should be left to the decisions of securities domiciles, which can legislate such rights, and issuers, which can place such rights in their charters or bylaws if domiciles do not mandate them.

III. The Regulation of Foreign (Non-U.S.) Issuers

The desirability of regulatory competition does not stop at national borders, for the same incentives are at work in a global setting: Financial capital is as mobile across nations as it is across U.S. states, and capital providers will require higher returns from investments governed by regimes less protective of their interests, prodding firms to seek out the securities regime preferred by investors in order to reduce their cost of capital.[157] The market approach to securities regulation advocated in this article should, accordingly, apply equally to U.S. and non-U.S. issuers of securities.

Applying the Market Approach to Non-U.S. Issuers

The Market Approach

Under the market approach to securities regulation, the issuer's securities domicile controls for all securities sold in the United States, whether that domicile is a U.S. state or a foreign nation. This would be a dramatic turnabout from the SEC's current practice, which assumes jurisdiction over all transactions occurring in the United States and, until recently, asserted jurisdiction over foreign transactions involving U.S. citizens,[158] analogous to the states' choice-of-law rule for securities transactions that looks to the sale location or purchaser domicile.

The SEC's territorial approach to jurisdiction prevents foreign issuers who are in compliance with their home states' disclosure requirements (which are less extensive than the SEC's) from listing on U.S. stock exchanges. The principal reason that the vast majority of non-U.S. firms that could qualify for exchange trading do not list in the United States is that their disclosure costs would significantly increase, particularly with respect to accounting data, as they would have to comply with the SEC's regime.[159] Although the precise cost of reconciliation with U.S. generally accepted accounting principles (GAAP) is not publicly available, James Fanto and Roberta Karmel report that given compliance costs, companies find a U.S. listing worthwhile only if large amounts of equity capital (over $300 million) are required.[160] Other data suggestive of the costliness of reconciliation are that the London Stock Exchange lists five times the number of foreign firms that the NYSE lists[161] and that, after the SEC extended its reporting requirements to foreign firms trading on the NASDAQ, the number of such listings declined by almost 30 percent over the following seven years (after having tripled over the seven years prior to the change).[162]

The market approach would open up U.S. markets to non-U.S. issuers. This is a policy shift that would not only make U.S. securities regulation more respectful of other nations' policy decisions by reaffirming a norm of international comity, but would also benefit U.S. investors. They would no longer have to incur the substantial costs of purchasing shares on foreign exchanges, as they have been doing in increasing numbers to invest directly in non-U.S. corporations.[163]

Under the market approach, foreign firms (firms not incorporated in the United States) would be able to choose their securities domicile for U.S. trading purposes, and therefore they would not need to comply with SEC disclosure requirements in order to trade in the United States. This result has some precedent: The Multijurisdictional Disclosure System (MDS) adopted by the SEC and the Ontario and Quebec Securities Commissions in 1991 enables Canadian firms to trade in the United States by complying with Canadian disclosure requirements, although they must reconcile their financial data with GAAP.[164] Canada is the only nation with which the SEC has entered into such an agreement, however, because its disclosure requirements are similar to U.S. requirements.[165] In addition, the SEC has itself relaxed its disclosure requirements for non-U.S. firms, including eliminating certain nonfinancial items such as management compensation and related party transactions.[166] The market approach expands the SEC's MDS without requiring that disclosure regimes be harmonized with the SEC rules or GAAP reconciliation. But it goes still further than these precedents: It would render inapplicable to such issuers the antifraud provisions of the federal securities laws (unless they opt for SEC regulation), in contrast to the MDS, which retains U.S. antifraud liability for Canadian firms. If all nations adopt the market approach, then all of a firm's shareholders would be subject to the same securities regime, wherever they purchased their shares, and there would be uniform treatment of investors, as occurs in the corporate law context. Rather than harmonization of national securities regimes, the universal application of the market approach should be the goal of international securities regulation.

The SEC was unwilling to extend the multijurisdictional accord globally to nations with lower levels of disclosure than it requires because, in its view, investors in U.S. markets would not be adequately protected if firms traded without releasing all of the information that SEC and U.S. accounting standards mandate. There is, however, an absence of evidence that the lower levels of disclosure in other nations adversely affect investors. Studies of price reactions to foreign issuers' release of information reconciling their financial reports with GAAP do not consistently find any effects, leading a number of economists to conclude that the SEC's requirement that foreign firms' disclosures conform to GAAP is of no benefit to investors.[167] In addition, despite the lower level of disclosure required, foreign markets are not less efficient than U.S. markets.[168] Finally, differences in accounting systems do not appear to provide less information about firms' financial situations of importance to investors; for instance, although German accounting is considerably less rigorous than GAAP, the information it discloses provides as good a probability estimate of a German firm's bankruptcy as GAAP information does for U.S. firms.[169]

If the lower level of disclosure of other nations were, in fact, of concern to U.S. investors or adversely affected investments, investors would discount the shares of foreign firms or not invest in them in the first place. Because of such a reaction, many firms would voluntarily reveal more information than required by their home state, albeit less than the SEC would have required, under the market approach.[170] An increase in U.S. listings of non-U.S. issuers that were covered by less extensive disclosure regimes than the SEC requires would not, therefore, be harmful to investors and would instead lower the transaction costs entailed in direct foreign investment. To the extent that foreign firms chose to list in the United States—to come under the more stringent SEC disclosure requirements or to subject themselves to the more extensive U.S. liability regime—as a credible commitment to signal their quality to investors and thereby to reduce their cost of capital,[171] they could, of course, continue to do so under the market approach. The credibility of such firms' commitment to the U.S. regime could be sustained further by their placing a supermajority voting rule in their corporate charter in order to change their securities domicile.[172]

The securities domicile choice of foreign firms available under the market approach might be limited in practice to a firm's home country (assuming it does not choose the SEC), in contrast to U.S. firms' choices, because their home countries' choice-of-law rules might not recognize the legislative jurisdiction of a nation that is not the site of the securities transaction. For example, regarding corporate law domicile, many nations do not recognize a statutory domicile and follow instead a physical presence or "seat" rule.[173] If those nations were to follow this principle for securities domicile as well, then non-U.S. firms would have no securities domicile choice but their home country (or the United States as the site of the transaction). But, even if the domicile choice were circumscribed because of home country practices, the number of foreign firms listed on U.S. exchanges would markedly increase under the market approach because it would eliminate the need for such firms to undertake costly expenditures to comply with the SEC's disclosure regime, such as the GAAP reconciliation.

Securities Litigation Involving Non-U.S. Issuers

There is a potential problem for U.S. investors who invest in firms subject to a non-U.S. securities regime should they need to seek redress for a securities law violation. Namely, the collective action problem inherent in any type of shareholder litigation—the cost of pursuing a lawsuit exceeds a shareholder's pro rata share of any recovery but not the aggregate award[174]—would be exacerbated by requiring prosecution of a claim in a foreign forum, both because of the expense and because of the absence of mechanisms for aggregating claims in many countries.

U.S. investors would, of course, discount the shares of foreign firms against which they could never exercise their rights under foreign securities laws or would avoid such securities entirely. Foreign firms might therefore find it in their self-interest to ensure that U.S. investors could prosecute securities claims in U.S. courts. The institutional mechanism for obtaining a foreign corporation's consent to a U.S. court's jurisdiction would not be difficult to construct: The issuer could provide such a written consent in the documentation accompanying the sale of stock to a U.S. investor. In addition, U.S. stock exchanges competing for business could require issuers' consent to jurisdiction in the United States as a listing requirement, if they thought that such a rule would enhance the value of listed shares and thereby increase trading interest.

There is, however, a question of whether U.S. courts would accept jurisdiction as a forum state over a securities dispute between investors and an issuer that is subject to foreign (non-U.S.) securities law. Traditionally, in international litigation, securities law has been treated as a species of public law, over which local courts have either declined to exercise jurisdiction or accepted jurisdiction but applied their own substantive law. The distinction between public and private law is arcane, and it has largely been undone by the Supreme Court in the securities context through its validation of arbitration clauses to resolve securities law disputes, reversing the prior convention that considered arbitration inappropriate for public, as opposed to private, law subjects.[175] Accordingly, in keeping with the contemporary trend merging the jurisdictional approach in public and private law areas, it would be appropriate for U.S. courts to apply private law jurisdictional principles to international securities transactions.[176] In the private law setting, forum selection clauses are presumptively enforceable,[177] and the exceptions to this presumption—defects in contract formation, unreasonableness, and public policy,[178] as well as the *forum non conveniens* doctrine—have no relevance for our context: The foreign defendant will have consented to a U.S. forum, federal policy will have expressly authorized foreign legislative jurisdiction, and the plaintiff-investor's local domicile and purchase would provide sufficient "contact" with a U.S. forum to render the local forum's retention of jurisdiction both feasible and desirable.

While U.S. jurisdiction would be readily attainable, a more important question is whether a U.S. court should exercise jurisdiction at all, or, to put it another way, is it desirable from the perspective of regulatory competition for foreign firms to choose a U.S. forum for securities suits? The adjudication of securities disputes by nondomicile courts could undermine the effectiveness of competition, as the legislating state does not control the interpretation of its laws. The problem would not be as severe as it is for Canadian provinces competing for corporate charters because the U.S. courts would be attempting in good faith to apply the domicile's law, whereas Canadian securities administrators intentionally apply their own governance standards rather than the law of the domicile province.[179] But the difficulty here is not solely a matter of substantive law interpretation.[180] The U.S. approach that adopts the procedural rules of the forum can have a significant impact on substantive outcomes because, in addition to class-action mechanisms to aggregate individual claims not prevalent in other countries, U.S. procedures—including rules on discovery, pleading requirements, contingent fees, and the absence of a "loser pays" cost rule—are far more favorable to plaintiffs than those of foreign countries.[181]

A powerful competing consideration in favor of a U.S. forum and against the substantive concerns raised by a nondomicile adjudicator is the significant inconvenience for a U.S. investor to prosecute a securities claim abroad. The balancing of the factors regarding the appropriateness of a U.S. forum is a calculation that is best undertaken by the foreign issuer, rather than by Congress or regulators. As long as investors were informed of the issuer's choice-of-law and choice-of-forum selections, they would be able to price their ability to obtain relief for securities violations, and issuers would respond accordingly, trading off U.S. forum protections that facilitate securities litigation and affect the cost of capital with the substantive advantages of a foreign forum.

Comparison with Other Reform Proposals

The outcome of applying the market approach to non-U.S. issuers—that their shares will be able to trade in U.S. markets under a non-U.S. securities regime—is certainly not a novel idea. Several commentators have advocated reform of the SEC's approach to foreign issuers to enable such issuers' shares to trade in U.S. markets without coming under the SEC's regulatory regime (or its more onerous components, such as GAAP reconciliation).[182] Some commentators have simply called for an end to the extraterritorial application of U.S. securities laws. Depending on the particular concern of the commentator, the solutions have been to permit foreign firms to list on U.S. exchanges or, more narrowly, to permit U.S. investors to participate in foreign firms' takeovers, without having U.S. law apply,[183] or to advocate a strict territorial (site-of-sale) approach, regardless of the shareholders' ultimate residence or firms' domicile.[184] While these proposals resolve the most egregious problems in the extraterritorial application of U.S. law, to the extent that they are more restrictive than the domicile approach advocated in this article—by limiting their reach to the takeover context or by choosing the site of sale, which issuers cannot control as easily as domicile—they are suboptimal when international issues are considered within the broader context of fostering competitive securities regulation.

In a more comprehensive effort to rationalize international securities regulation, Merritt Fox contends that an issuer nationality rule (physical presence domicile) is the rule that maximizes social welfare.[185] Although the substantive policy outcomes of Fox's proposal and of this article may not be significantly different—that is, non-U.S. issuers trading on a U.S. exchange are likely to choose their home countries' securities regimes under the market approach—the rationales are fundamentally at odds. This is because Fox assumes that international regulatory competition would lead to a "race for the bottom" regarding disclosure requirements. Fox provides two reasons for this projected outcome: Firms would not voluntarily produce the desirable level of financial information because of third-party externality concerns; and U.S. stock exchanges' interest in increased listings would dominate the regulatory process, resulting in a lowering of disclosure requirements to enable them to compete for listings against foreign markets.[186] Fox therefore advocates a physical presence rule to stymie such regulatory competition. Not only would firms have to change their nationality in order to change regulators, which is a costly undertaking, but also exchanges would no longer have an incentive to lobby for lower local securities standards in order to increase foreign listings, as listing decisions would be independent of the regulatory regime of the stock exchange's location.

This chapter's proposal for shifting to an issuer-domicile-based rule is premised on an assessment of competition that is the precise opposite of Fox's. As discussed earlier,[187] neither of Fox's rationales depicting destructive competition holds up to scrutiny. The need to internalize third-party externalities is a tenuous rationale for securities regulation, and such externalities are not, in any event, likely to account for the items of mandatory disclosure pursued by the SEC or the differences across national regimes. More important, there is no reason to assume that firms would list on the exchange with the lowest level of disclosure requirements. Rather, they would choose the one whose requirements lower their cost of capital, which will not be the exchange operating under the least amount of disclosure because investors place affirmative value on information. The supporting evidence against the race-for-the-bottom thesis, as already noted, is that firms the world over voluntarily release more information than their securities regulators require in order to raise capital, with the best example being the European firms listing in London that voluntarily choose to meet higher local disclosure requirements.[188]

Finally, it should also be noted that Fox's concern regarding the political process in a competitive regulatory setting—the incentives of stock exchanges to lobby for lowered disclosure—is not relevant under the market approach. Whether the securities domicile is statutory, contractual, or Fox's proposed domicile of physical presence, the location of the stock exchange would not determine the issuer's securities regime; the issuer's securities domicile would. Accordingly, while Fox's proposed regulatory reform is compatible with the approach in this article, the rationales could not be much further apart.

IV. Conclusion

This chapter has advocated fundamental reform of the current strategy toward securities regulation by implementing a regulatory approach of competitive federalism, under which firms select their securities regulator from among the fifty states and the District of Columbia, the SEC, and other nations. Competitive federalism harnesses the high-powered incentives of markets to the regulatory state in order to produce regulatory arrangements compatible with investors' preferences. This is because firms will locate in the domicile whose regime investors prefer in order to reduce their cost of capital, and states have financial incentives (such as incorporation and registration fees) to adapt their securities regimes to firms' locational decisions. This prediction of securities market participants' and regulators' responses to competition is well grounded: There is substantial literature examining the workings of competitive federalism in the corporate charter setting that indicates that such regulatory competition does not harm, and in all likelihood benefits, investors.

To establish competitive federalism in the securities law context, the current choice-of-law rule for securities transactions must be altered to follow the issuer's securities domicile rather than the securities' site of sale. In addition, two procedural safeguards would be required of firms opting out of federal regulation: domicile disclosure upon securities purchases and a securityholder vote to effectuate a domicile change. These requirements ensure that informed investor preferences drive the regulatory competition. When competition is introduced, SEC rules and regulations that are not cost effective or are otherwise detrimental to investors will be replaced by competing regulators with rules investors prefer, as the domicile choices of capital market participants establish a new regulatory equilibrium.

The mandatory federal securities regime has been in place for over sixty years, but the theoretical support for it is thin, and there is no empirical evidence indicating that it is effective in achieving its stated objectives. In fact, there is developing literature pointing in the opposite direction. At a minimum, this literature suggests that the securities status quo should no longer be privileged and that it should instead be opened up to market forces by means of competitive federalism. Corporation codes have benefited from precisely such competition. Although the current legislative trend in Congress, supported by both the proponents and the opponents of the existing regulatory regime, is to seek to monopolize even further securities regulation at the federal level, this chapter maintains that it would be far better public policy to expand, not restrain, state regulatory involvement. As long as only one state's law, chosen by the issuer, controls the regulation of a firm's securities transactions, regulatory competition will emerge, and there are compelling reasons to prefer such a regulatory arrangement to the mandatory federal regime.

Notes

1. Pub. L. No. 104-67, 109 Stat. 737 (codified at 15 U.S.C.A. § 77 (West 1997)).

2. *See* Securities Litigation Improvement Act of 1997, HR. 1653, 105th Cong.; Securities Litigation Uniform Standards Act, H.R. 1689, 105th Cong. (1997).

3. *See* U.S. Sec. & Exch. Comm'n, Report to the President and the Congress on the First Year of Practice under the Private Securities Litigation Reform Act of 1995, pt. IV, at 22, pt. VII, at 72 (1997) (summarizing a study by National Economic Research Associates of securities litigation filings after the Act). Joseph Grundfest and Michael Perino also document a shift to state court filings. *See* Joseph A. Grundfest & Michael A. Perino, Securities Litigation Reform: The First Year's Experience (Stanford Law School, John M. Olin Program in Law & Econ. Working Paper No. 140, 1997). More recent data, however, suggest a rever-

sal of this trend, with state filings declining and federal filings increasing in the first half of 1997. *See 1995 Private Securities Litigation Reform Act: Federal Securities Class Action Filings Rise as State Filings Fall, NERA Finds,* 29 Sec. Reg. & L. Rep. (BNA) 1001 (July 18, 1997).

4. *See generally* Roberta Romano, The Genius of American Corporate Law (AEI Press: 1993).

5. For a discussion of SEC and court efforts at extraterritorial coverage in the context of securities regulations of takeover bids, see Arthur R. Pinto, *The Internationalization of the Hostile Takeover Market: Its Implications for Choice of Law in Corporate and Securities Law,* 16 Brook. J. Int'l L. 55 (1990).

6. *See id.* at 66–76.

7. *See* Franklin R. Edwards, *SEC Requirements for Trading of Foreign Securities on U.S. Exchanges, in* Modernizing U.S. Securities Regulation: Economic and Legal Perspectives 57–58, Kenneth Lehn & Robert W. Kamphuis, Jr., eds. (Irwin: 1992) [hereinafter Modernizing U.S. Securities Regulation].

8. *See, e.g.,* Romano, *supra* note 4, at 99–100, 107–8; Jonathan R. Macey, *Administrative Agency Obsolescence and Interest Group Formation: A Case Study of the SEC at Sixty,* 15 Cardozo L. Rev. 909, 935–36 (1994); Jeffrey G. Macintosh, International Securities Regulation: On Competition, Cooperation, Convergence, and Cartelization 31–32 (University of Toronto Faculty of Law, Law & Econ. Working Paper WPS-48, 1996).

9. *See* R. C. Michie, The London and New York Stock Exchanges 1850–1914, at 34 (Allen & Unwin: 1987) (arguing that the New York exchange gained preeminence among the world's security markets from World War I).

10. *See* Bruno Solnik, International Investments 168 exh. 6.1 (3d ed. 1996) (reporting that the U.S. share of global capitalization dropped from 57 percent to 36 percent between 1974 and 1994). With the recent market boom, the U.S. share rose to 41 percent in 1996. *See* Ibbotson Assocs., Al/RI Global Portfolio Intensive Classroom Program 1997, at Day 1–16 (1997) (citing *Developed Markets,* Morgan Stanley Capital Int'l EAFE and World Perspective (Morgan Stanley Capital Int'l, New York, N.Y.), Jan. 1996, at 5; IFC Emerging Market Data Base Monthly Review of Emerging Stock Markets 8 (n.d.)).

11. Issuers have focused their efforts on removing regulatory authority from the states to the federal level because they have not recognized the possibility of removing the source of the state-level problems of plaintiff forum shopping and burdensome registration requirements. Such problems could be solved by altering the state jurisdictional rule of investor domicile to that proposed in this article, under which only one state, chosen by the issuer as its securities domicile, would have jurisdiction over all transactions in the firm's securities.

12. 15 U.S.C.A. *§ 77a 10 -bbbb (West 1997).

13. *Id.* §§ 78a to -mm.

14. Although both statutes originally expressly reserved the rights of states to regulate securities, the 1933 act was amended in 1996 to preempt state regulation of the registration of publicly traded securities. *See* National Securities Markets Improvement Act of 1996, Pub. L. No. 104-290, § 102, 110 Stat. 3416, 3417–20 (codified at 15 U.S.C.A. § 77r).

15. *See, e.g.,* Edgar v. MITE Corp., 457 U.S. 624, 640–46 (1982) (invalidating a state takeover regulation that was more extensive than the federal regulation

as a burden on interstate commerce). Only a plurality of the court in *MITE* held that the takeover statute was preempted by the federal act. *See id.* at 634–40.

16. *See* Frank H. Easterbrook & Daniel R. Fischel, The Economic Structure of Corporate Law 17–21 (Harvard University Press: 1991) (discussing how entrepreneurs choose terms that enhance investors' expected returns in order to increase securities prices); Ralph K. Winter, Jr., *State Law, Shareholder Protection, and the Theory of the Corporation,* 6 J. Legal Stud. 251, 275–76 (1977) (arguing that securities of firms incorporated in states with codes unfavorable to shareholders will be unattractive investments).

17. In 1995, for example, institutional investors—pension funds, insurance companies, mutual funds, and bank-managed investment funds—held 50 percent of total equity in the United States, including 57.2 percent of the largest 1000 firms (*see* Carolyn K. Brancato, Institutional Investors and Corporate Governance 19–20 (Irwin Professional Pub.: 1997)), compared to less than 10 percent of total equity in 1950 (*see* New York Stock Exch., Fact Book 1995 Data 57 (1996)), and 46.6 percent of the top 1000 firms in 1987 (*see* Brancato, *supra,* at 20). Although there are formal models of informationally inefficient capital markets (markets with, for instance, speculative bubbles) that depend on the existence of irrational, uninformed traders termed "noise traders," these models provide no theory that can predict when irrational pricing will occur and are simply unrealistic with regard to market behavior. Namely, informed investors and arbitrageurs will trade against the irrational individuals, preserving market efficiency, as the noise traders experience significant losses and stop trading. For the development of this critique, see Milton Friedman, *The Case for Flexible Exchange Rates, in* Essays in Positive Economics 157 (University of Chicago Press: 1953); Eugene F Fama, *The Behavior of Stock-Market Prices,* 38 J. Bus. 34, 37–39 (1965); and Paul A. Samuelson, *The "Fallacy" of Maximizing the Geometric Mean in Long Sequences of Investing or Gambling,* 68 Proc. Nat'l Acad. Sci. 2493 (1971). Modelers of inefficient markets have been unable to amend the models to respond to these criticisms. For example, in models where noise traders affect price, they cannot be shown to survive over time (and thus to affect prices in the long run) (*see* J. Bradford De Long et al., *Noise Trader Risk in Financial Markets,* 98 J. Pol. Econ. 703, 713, 717 (1990)), but in the models in which noise traders can "survive" over time (i.e., they do not go bankrupt from their irrational trading), their misperceptions do not affect prices (i.e., the model is unsolvable if they are allowed to affect prices) (*see* J. Bradford De Long et al., *The Survival of Noise Traders in Financial Markets,* 64 J. Bus. 1, 2 (1991)). In addition, more generalized versions of models in which noise traders can affect prices have multiple equilibria, including the classical (efficient pricing) equilibrium. In such models, the noisy (inefficient pricing) equilibria require very strong and unrealistic assumptions concerning noise traders, such as their ability to hold infinite positions. *See* Ravi Bhushan et al., *Do Noise Traders "Create Their Own Space?"* 32 J. Fin. & Quantitative Analysis 25, 28 (1997). There is, however, one context in which unsophisticated investors are not protected by the actions of institutional investors (i.e., they cannot rely on prices set by informed investors): their relations with brokers. This provides another reason for excluding the regulation of brokers from the proposal.

18. *See, e.g.,* Robert E. Chatfield & R. Charles Moyer, *"Putting" Away Bond Risk: An Empirical Examination of the Value of the Put Option on Bonds,* Fin.

Mgmt., Summer 1986, at 26, 31–32; Leland Crabbe, *Event Risk: An Analysis of Losses to Bondholders and "Super Poison Put" Bond Covenants,* 46 J. Fin. 689, 690 (1991); Richard J. Kish & Miles Livingston, *Estimating the Value of Call Options on Corporate Bonds,* J. Applied Corp. Fin., Fall 1993, at 95, 97.

19. *See* Roberta Romano, *Law as a Product: Some Pieces of the Incorporation Puzzle,* 1 J. L. Econ. & Org. 225, 271 (1985); Jianghong Wang, Performance of Reincorporated Firms 14–18, 21 (Nov. 17, 1995) (unpublished manuscript, on file with the *Yale Law Journal*).

20. *See* Easterbrook & Fischel, *supra* note 16, at 277 (explaining the anti-fraud rationale); Joel Seligman, *The Historical Need for a Mandatory Corporate Disclosure System,* 9 J. Corp. L. 1, 9 (1983) (discussing the optimal disclosure level rationale). The economic theory underlying the argument concerning information production is ambiguous, however: Capital markets can overproduce information, as well as underproduce it. The informational efficiency of capital markets implies that only the first investor to obtain private information about a firm is likely to realize the value of the information through trading, and this creates an incentive for investors to engage in costly duplicative efforts at information production (i.e., overproduction) in a race to be first. *See* Jack Hirshleifer, *The Private and Social Value of Information and the Reward to Inventive Activity,* 61 Am. Econ. Rev. 561, 565–66 (1971). From this perspective, mandatory disclosure could be beneficial by reducing the amount of privately produced information.

21. The formal models indicate that information will not be underproduced if the proportion of investors who are informed (i.e., capable of understanding the significance of nondisclosure) is not too low. *See* Michael J. Fishman & Kathleen M. Hagerty, Mandatory vs. Voluntary Disclosure in Markets with Informed and Uninformed Customers 17 (Department of Fin., Kellogg Graduate Sch. of Management, Northwestern Univ. Paper No. 233, 1997); Ronald A. Dye, Investor Sophistication and Voluntary Disclosures 18 (1997) (unpublished manuscript, on file with the *Yale Law Journal*). As these essays show, if all investors are informed, no information externality exists—investors draw negative inferences from nondisclosure, forcing firms to reveal both good and bad information. *See* Fishman & Hagerty, *supra,* at 1–2; Dye, *supra,* at 1.

22. *See* Easterbrook & Fischel, *supra* note 16, at 290–91.

23. *See* Ronald A. Dye, *Mandatory versus Voluntary Disclosures: The Cases of Financial and Real Externalities,* 65 Acct. Rev. 1, 15–16, 18–19 (1990) (providing a formal model indicating that divergence between voluntary and mandatory disclosure depends on information—specifically, detailed a priori knowledge of the covariances of firms' returns—that regulators are unlikely to obtain).

24. *See* Seligman, *supra* note 20, at 21.

25. Frank Easterbrook and Daniel Fischel suggest an analogous reason for a federal law: the efficiency of enforcing all claims involving a particular transaction in one case. *See* Easterbrook & Fischel, *supra* note 16, at 285. The choice-of-law reform discussed in Part II, which adopts the issuer-based jurisdictional approach of corporate law for state securities regulation, can resolve this concern: As is true of shareholder class-action claims for fiduciary breach, all securities claims can be consolidated into one court action, with one law applying, that of the issuer's securities domicile. This reform also resolves Easterbrook and Fischel's other explanation for why state competition would not work in

the securities context: The potential to exploit out-of-state shareholders, with rules favoring in-state shareholders, given the multistate jurisdictional rules based on shareholder residence (*see id.* at 300–301), would disappear because the reform would result in only one state's law governing all shareholders' transactions, regardless of the shareholder's residence.

26. *See, e.g.,* Mark A. Sargent, *A Future for Blue Sky Law,* 62 U. Cin. L. Rev. 471, 504–5 (1993). A recent example illustrates the vigor of state enforcement activity. The New York state prosecutor's criminal enforcement action against an insider trading on material information was undercut by the federal government: The U.S. attorney seized the case and struck a plea bargain with the defendant after the state prosecutor had developed the case and obtained an indictment. *See Morgenthau v. White,* N.Y. Times, Dec. 6, 1997, at A18. The states have also agreed to coordinate regulation of electronic offerings on the Internet. *See* John C. Coffee, Jr., *Brave New World? The Impact(s) of the Internet on Modern Securities Regulation,* 52 Bus. Law. 1195, 1231–32 (1997). Indeed, the Internet is likely to facilitate state enforcement efforts, as it has for the SEC, as state securities regulator websites will offer a ready means for communication of complaints by nonresident investors. *See Microcap Fraud, Staffing Issues Top Enforcement Agenda,* 29 Sec. Reg. & L. Rep. (BNA) 1773 (Dec. 19, 1997) (reporting the statement of SEC Enforcement Division Director William McLucas that the Internet has made it easier for people to get in touch with the SEC concerning complaints, as well as for the agency to "run down" people engaged in misconduct because their electronic interactions with investors leave identifying trails).

27. *See* Harold Bierman, Jr., The Great Myths of 1929 and the Lessons to Be Learned 133–46 (Greenwood Press: 1991); *see also infra* text accompanying notes 57–59.

28. *See* George J. Benston, *Required Disclosure and the Stock Market: An Evaluation of the Securities Exchange Act of 1934,* 63 Am. Econ. Rev. 132, 144–45 (1973) [hereinafter Benston, *Evaluation*]; *see also* George Benston, *An Appraisal of the Costs and Benefits of Government-Required Disclosure: SEC and FTC Requirements,* Law & Contemp. Probs., Summer 1977, at 30, 51–52. Joel Seligman criticizes the significance of this finding (*see* Seligman, *supra* note 20, at 16–17), but his objections, which follow those of Irwin Friend and Randolph Westerfield (*see* Irwin Friend & Randolph Westerfield, *Required Disclosure and the Stock Market: Comment,* 65 Am. Econ. Rev. 467 (1975)), actually reinforce Benston's conclusions. For example, in criticism of Benston's finding of no stock price effect of the SEC's disclosure requirements, Seligman cites more recent studies showing that the data in SEC filings affect stock prices in an effort to prove that the SEC's mandated disclosure program is of value to investors. *See* Seligman, *supra* note 20, at 16. But it is not the SEC's disclosure requirements that are affecting stock value in these studies, because they have not added any new items into the information mix already disclosed: The information examined in the studies Seligman cites, earnings, was disclosed, as Benston demonstrates, even prior to the creation of the SEC and would continue to be disclosed if there were no SEC. *See* Benston, *Evaluation, supra,* at 135–36. Seligman acknowledges this point by adding that the issue is whether the SEC compels information that otherwise would not have been voluntarily disclosed, rather than where the item is disclosed (SEC report or otherwise). *See* Seligman,

supra note 20, at 16. But the studies he cites (*see id.* at 16 n.48), do not bear upon this issue. Seligman also objects to Benston's test because it did not adequately distinguish between disclosure and nondisclosure firms, as all the firms in his sample disclosed earnings. But this is precisely Benston's point: The SEC's mandated disclosure added only one item—sales—that had not been disclosed by NYSE firms, and release of the new information under its requirement had no effect on the stock prices of those firms that previously had not been disclosing sales. *See* Benston, *Evaluation, supra,* at 141–42.

29. *See, e.g.,* Richard Frankel et al., *Discretionary Disclosure and External Financing,* 70 Acct. Rev. 135, 141 (1995) (finding that firms are significantly more likely to forecast earnings if they access capital markets over the sample period); Mark Lang & Russell Lundholm, *Cross-Sectional Determinants of Analyst Ratings of Corporate Disclosures,* 31 J. Acct. Res. 246, 265–69 (1993) (finding that a firm's Financial Analyst Federation disclosure quality rating increases with security issuance); William Ruland et al., *Factors Associated with the Disclosure of Managers' Forecasts,* 65 Acct. Rev. 710, 720 (1990) (finding that firms reporting forecasts are more likely to issue new capital); *cf.* Frederick D. S. Choi, *Financial Disclosure and Entry to the European Capital Market,* 11 J. Accr. Res. 159, 168–70 (1973) (finding that firms entering the Eurobond market increase disclosure).

30. *See* Carol A. Marquardt & Christine I. Wiedman, Voluntary Disclosure, Information Asymmetry, and Insider Selling through Secondary Equity Offerings 16, 19–20, 22 (John M. Olin School of Business, Washington Univ. Working Paper No. 97-05, 1997) (finding that, in secondary offerings, managers act as if reduced information asymmetry is correlated with reduced cost of capital, such that their participation in an offering explains the frequency of voluntary disclosure); Maribeth Caller & Ten Lombardi Yohn, *Management Forecasts and Information Asymmetry: An Examination of Bid-Ask Spreads,* 35 J. Acct. Res. 181 (1997) (finding that firms with increasing bid-ask spreads release forecasts to reduce spread).

31. *See* Christine A. Botosan, *Disclosure Level and the Cost of Equity Capital,* 72 Acct. Rev. 323, 344, 346 (1997) (showing that voluntary disclosure in the annual report significantly explains the cost of capital of firms with small analyst followings).

32. *See* Hal S. Scott & Philip A. Wellons, International Finance: Transactions, Policy, and Regulation 314 (Foundation Press: 3d ed. 1996) (citing references concerning Danish and French firms' compliance with U.K. standards); G. K. Meek & S. J. Gray, *Globalization of Stock Markets and Foreign Listing Requirements: Voluntary Disclosures by Continental European Companies Listed on the London Stock Exchange,* 20 J. Int'l Bus. Stud. 315 (1989) (reviewing a sample of European companies trading in London).

33. *See* Gabriel Hawawini, European Equity Markets: Price, Behavior and Efficiency (Salomon Brothers Center for the Study of Financial Institutions: 1984); William J. Baumol & Burton G. Malkiel, *Redundant Regulation of Foreign Security Trading and U.S. Competitiveness, in* Modernizing U.S. Securities Regulation, *supra* note 7, at 39, 46–50; Edwards, *supra* note 7, at 64–66.

34. See Frederick D. S. Choi, *Financial Reporting Requirements for Non-U.S. Registrants: International Market Perspectives,* 6 Fin. Markets Institutions & Instruments 23, 29 (1997). There are also significant differences in the securities

disclosure regimes of emerging markets, where we might expect a need for substantial disclosure to encourage foreign investment. *See* Shahrokh M. Saudagaran & Joselito G. Diga, *Financial Reporting in Emerging Capital Markets: Characteristics and Policy Issues,* Acct. Horizons, June 1997, at 41.

35. *See* Susan M. Phillips and J. Richard Zecher, The SEC and the Public Interest (MIT Press: 1981), at 49–51. Their estimate of the extra costs imposed in the 1975 new issue market was $193 million. *See id.* at 51.

36. *See* Seligman, *supra* note 20, at 36–39.

37. *See id.* at 36.

38. *See* George J. Stigler, *Public Regulation of Securities Markets,* 37 J. Bus. 117, 120–21 (1964) (finding that SEC registration requirements had no effect on returns); *see also* Gregg A. Jarrell, *The Economic Effects of Federal Regulation of the Market for New Securities Issues,* 24 J. L. & Econ. 613, 645, 666 (1981) (reaching the same conclusion by examining returns over five years from issuance); Carol J. Simon, *The Effect of the 1933 Securities Act on Investor Information and the Performance of New Issues,* 79 Am. Econ. Rev. 295, 305 (1989) (finding no effect on returns of NYSE and seasoned regional exchange issues). Simon did find that one subsample of firms, unseasoned issues traded on regional exchanges, had greater returns after the enactment of the act (they were overpriced before the act) (*see* Simon, *supra,* at 305–6), but this subsample performed significantly worse in all periods than the other new issues in the study (*see id.* at 308). Irwin Friend and Edward S. Herman, in a study on which Seligman relies heavily, criticized Stigler's interpretation of his data because, although not statistically significant, postact issues had higher returns than preact issues and because there was a significant positive return after four years. *See* Irwin Friend & Edward S. Herman, *The S.E.C. through a Glass Darkly,* 37 J. Bus. 382, 391 (1964). These criticisms do not, however, impeach Stigler's findings. The length of the interval over which they find a stock price effect—four years—is so long that it is impossible to attribute the price change to the legislation. Friend and Herman also do not provide a theory explaining why the 1933 act should improve a new issue's returns only four years after its issuance. Not only is such a result inconsistent with a relatively efficient stock market, but we would also expect mandated disclosure to have the greatest impact over the shorter interval of Stigler's study, as short-term performance would be more predictable than long-term performance from financial disclosures. Nor do Friend and Herman explain why statistically insignificant findings should be given any evidentiary weight, counter to conventional social scientific practice. Further damaging to Friend and Herman's critique is the confirmation of Stigler's basic results by the more recent studies of Jarrell and Simon. A study of existing stocks, rather than new issues, finds that the 1933 act had a negative price impact, which the author attributes to the act's restrictions on accounting procedures, which may have adversely affected the firms' ability to comply with debt covenants that were based on accounting numbers. *See* Chee W. Chow, *The Impacts of Accounting Regulation on Bondholder and Shareholder Wealth: The Case of the Securities Acts,* 58 Acct. Rev. 485, 489, 502, 507 (1983). Chow expected to find a wealth transfer from shareholders to bondholders given the accounting covenants hypothesis, but he was unable to identify such an effect. Because the sample stocks were not new issues (to which the 1933 act applied), it is difficult to interpret the study's results without knowing whether these

firms planned to issue new securities in the future. A further difference, which is a serious shortcoming, between this study and the others is that, in contrast to the other studies, this one did not adjust stock returns for market movements, which may account for the results. *See id.* at 503.

39. *See* Ross L. Watts & Jerold L. Zimmerman, Positive Accounting Theory 174 & n.9 (Prentice-Hall: 1986) (citing studies).

40. *See* Jarrell, *supra* note 38, at 646; Simon, *supra* note 38, at 309; Stigler, *supra* note 38, at 122.

41. *See* Jarrell, *supra* note 38, at 648–49, 668; Stigler, *supra* note 38, at 122. Seha Tinic offers a further gloss on this explanation, finding that the kind of securities that underwriters were willing to offer changed to larger, less risky issues after enactment of the 1933 act because the underwriters were fearful of their legal liability under the act. *See* Seha M. Tinic, *Anatomy of Initial Public Offerings of Common Stock,* 43 J. Fin. 789, 813 (1988).

42. *See* Jarrell, *supra* note 38, at 661, 664, 667, 669.

43. *See* Seligman, *supra* note 20, at 10; Simon, *supra* note 38, at 313.

44. Seligman, *supra* note 20, at 43.

45. This discrepancy in expertise is evident in recent rulemaking activity by the SEC. By abandoning its usual approach of standardized disclosure requirements in its new rule requiring disclosure of the market risk of derivative securities, the SEC implicitly acknowledged that it is, and will always be, woefully behind market participants in understanding and developing the most accurate valuation techniques for these complex instruments. *See* Disclosure of Accounting Policies for Derivative Financial Instruments and Derivative Commodity Instruments and Disclosure of Quantitative and Qualitative Information about Market Risk Inherent in Derivative Financial Instruments, Other Financial Instruments, and Derivative Commodity Instruments, Exchange Act Release No. 33-7386, 62 Fed. Reg. 6044, 6048 n.45, 6057 (1997) (to be codified at 17 C.F.R. pts. 210, 228, 229, 239, 240, 249) [hereinafter SEC Derivatives Disclosure] (explaining why the rule permits choice of quantitative disclosure methods, including model parameters).

46. For a recent review of the research on market efficiency, see Eugene F. Fama, *Efficient Capital Markets: II,* 46 J. Fin. 1575, 1600–1602 (1991).

47. *See, e.g.,* Homer Kripke, *Can the SEC Make Disclosure Policy Meaningful?* J. Portfolio Mgmt., Summer 1976, at 32, 35–37.

48. *See* 17 C.F.R. § 240.3b-6 (1997), *originally promulgated in* Safe Harbor Rule for Projections, Exchange Act Release No. 33-6084 (June 25, 1979), *available in* 1979 WL 16388; 17 C.F.R. § 230.175 (1997).

49. *See, e.g.,* Noelle Matteson, Comment, *Private Securities Litigation Reform Act of 1995: Do Issuers Still Get Soaked in the Safe Harbor?* 27 Golden Gate U. L. Rev. 527, 548 n.139 (1997) (citing sources indicating that the SEC supported the provision only after Congress agreed to the SEC's proposed transaction exclusions).

50. Kripke, *supra* note 47, at 40.

51. *See* Homer Kripke, *The SEC, the Accountants, Some Myths and Some Realities.* 45 N.Y.U. L. Rev. 1151, 1199 (1970).

52. *See* Safe Harbor for Forward-Looking Statements, Exchange Act Release No. 33-7101, 59 Fed. Reg. 52,723, 52,728–29 (Oct. 19, 1994), *available in* 1994 WL 562021, at *7.8.

53. *See* Private Securities Litigation Reform Act of 1995, Pub. L. No. 104-67, § 102, 109 Stat. 737, 749–56 (codified at 15 U.S.C.A. §§ 77z-2, 78u-5 (West 1997)).

54. *See, e.g., Panelists Dispute Reform Laws Impact on Private Class Securities Fraud Litigation,* 29 Sec. Reg. & L. Rep. (BNA) 1134 (Aug. 15, 1997); Matteson, *supra* note 49, at 550–51. A recent study, however, finds that forecasts by a sample of high-technology firms increased after the act. *See* Marilyn Johnson et al., The Impact of Securities Litigation Reform on the Disclosure of Forward-Looking Information by High Technology Firms (Jan. 2, 1998) (unpublished manuscript, on file with the *Yale Law Journal*).

55. If disclosure reduces the frequency of fraud and fraudulent issues are generally of high risk, then one explanation of the finding that the 1933 act reduced the variance of stock returns could be that the act eliminated fraudulent issues. *See* Jarrell, *supra* note 38, at 649. Jarrell sought to test this hypothesis by examining the performance of pre-SEC new issues but excluding from the pre-1934 sample the firms that would have been screened out by the SEC's regulation (the riskiest issues) had the act been in effect in the earlier years. *See id.* at 650. He found that the screened sample performed no better than the entire pre-SEC sample. *See id.* Jarrell concludes that the reduction in variance after the act is not due to effective deterrence of fraud, because high variance is not connected to poor performance in the unregulated period. *See id.*

56. *See* Easterbrook & Fischel, *supra* note 16, at 277.

57. *See* Benston, *Evaluation, supra* note 28, at 135; *cf.* Seligman, *supra* note 20, at 34–35.

58. Bierman, *supra* note 27, at 133–45.

59. *See* Paul G. Mahoney, *The Stock Pools and the Securities Exchange Act,* J. Fin. Econ. (V.51: 343–369 1999).

60. Seligman, for example, asserts that there is a need for mandatory national securities laws because of the history of state corporate law "chartermongering." Seligman, *supra* note 20, at 53–54.

61. *See* Michael Bradley & Cindy A. Schipani, *The Relevance of the Duty of Care Standard in Corporate Governance,* 75 Iowa L. Rev. 1, 66–67 (1989) (significant positive returns on the event date and approximately one month before); Peter Dodd & Richard Leftwich, *The Market for Corporate Charters: "Unhealthy Competition" versus Federal Regulation,* 53 J. Bus. 259, 272–75 (1980) (significant positive returns two years before the event date); Allen Hyman, *The Delaware Controversy—The Legal Debate,* 4 Del. J. Corp. L. 368, 385 (1979) (positive returns four days before the event date); Jeffry Netter & Annette Paulsen, *State Corporation Laws and Shareholders: The Recent Experience,* 18 Fin. Mgmt. 29, 35–37 (1989) (positive returns roughly one month around the event date that were significant at the 10 percent level only); Romano, *supra* note 19, at 270–71 (significant positive returns at three-day, one-week, and one-month intervals around the event date); Wang, *supra* note 19, at 14–18, 21 (significant positive returns for the full sample over a three-day event interval and significant positive returns for Delaware firms over forty days before the event date and over a three-day interval if the shareholder meeting date is used as the event date).

62. In an attempt to explain away the nonnegative stock price effects of reincorporation, Lucian Bebchuk asserts that stock price studies are not probative

of whether state competition benefits shareholders because stale competition may produce some provisions that are harmful to shareholders even if the overall package of provisions is not. *See* Lucian Arye Bebchuk, *Federalism and the Corporation: The Desirable Limits on State Competition in Corporate Law,* 105 Harv. L. Rev. 1435, 1449–50 (1992). This is not a particularly damaging contention against competition and in favor of a federal monopolist for several reasons. First, it is the net wealth effect of a code on investors that is important, and that effect is positive for state corporate law. Second, because state corporation codes are enabling statutes, firms can avoid any such harmful provisions by customizing their charters or bylaws. *See infra* text accompanying note 67 (discussing numerous firms' opting out of the Pennsylvania takeover statute). Indeed, Bebchuk does not identify specific mandatory (hence, unavoidable) provisions in state codes that he believes benefit managers over shareholders. Third, Bebchuk offers no support for the prediction that a federal corporation code would contain fewer harmful provisions than state codes. An examination of the lobbying process in the corporate context indicates that the differences between federal and state politics are, in fact, minimal. *See infra* notes 69–74 and accompanying text. Bebchuk offers two other speculations to refute the validity of the empirical research, but they are incorrect. His contention (offered to explain insignificant price effects of reincorporation) that both the original and the destination states' laws are equally harmful to shareholders (*see* Bebchuk, *supra,* at 1449–50) is not borne out by the evidence. Not only do some studies find significant positive results (*see supra* note 76), but more important, the legal regimes of the destination states differ significantly from those of the states of origin: The destination states are more responsive to reincorporating firms' demands than the originating states in enacting code innovations, and reincorporating firms perceive significant differences between the legal regimes of the two states and offer them as a reason for moving (*see* Romano, *supra* note 19, at 246–47, 258–60). Bebchuk's other contention (offered to explain positive stock price effects) that any price effects of reincorporation are due to changes in the firm's business accompanying or anticipated by the move rather than a reflection of investors' assessment of the new regime (*see* Bebchuk, *supra,* at 1449), while plausible, is not supported by the data. I tested for significant differences in abnormal returns across reincorporating firms grouped according to such potentially confounding transactions, where some transactions would be hypothesized to be negative and others positive, for shareholder wealth, and found none. *See* Romano, *supra* note 19, at 272. This finding is strong evidence that the positive price effects for the full sample in my study were due to investors' positive assessments of the domicile change and not to the accompanying or anticipated transactions.

63. *See, e.g.,* Easterbrook & Fischel, *supra* note 16, at 220–22. Some commentators contended, however, that takeover defenses benefited shareholders by solving a coordination problem created by dispersed stock ownership and thereby enabling managers to negotiate higher bid prices. *See, e.g.,* Lucian Arye Bebchuk, *The Sole Owner Standard for Takeover Policy,* 17 J. Legal Stud. 197 (1988); William J. Camey, *Shareholder Coordination Costs, Shark Repellents, and Takeout Mergers: The Case against Fiduciary Duties,* 1983 Am. B. Found. Res. J. 341.

64. For an analysis of these statutes, see Roberta Romano, *What Is the Value of Other Constituency Statutes to Shareholders?* 43 U. Toronto L. J. 533 (1993).

I found these statutes had no significant stock price effect on the specific legislative event dates and within two-day event intervals. *See id.* at 537. John C. Alexander et al., however, found a significant negative price effect (for firms without poison pills or antitakeover charter amendments) for two of the statutes that I examined when a longer event interval of two days before and three days after was used, and for a third statute, enacted by Indiana in 1989, that was improperly included in their sample because Indiana had had another constituency statute in effect since 1986. *See* John C. Alexander et al., *Nonshareholder Constituency Statutes and Shareholder Wealth: A Note,* 21 J. Banking & Fin. 417, 427 (1997). In fact, I found a negative effect for the earlier Indiana statute (*see* Romano, *supra,* at 539), but it is not a "clean" statute in that it was passed with another antitakeover provision. I did not find any difference for firms with or without defensive tactics in place, but the sample was not subdivided by firm characteristics for each state statute separately, and therefore the results cannot be compared. In addition, my sample consisted of larger firms, as it was constructed solely from NYSE listings, while Alexander et al. include firms traded on the American Stock Exchange and NASD's Automated Quotation System (NASDAQ). Because at least one study has found that it is small firms that experience negative price effects from takeover statutes (*see* M. Andrew Fields & Janet M. Todd, *Firm Size, Antitakeover Charter Amendments, and the Effect of State Antitakeover Legislation,* 21 Managerial Fin. 35 (1995)), the difference in the studies' samples may explain the difference in the results.

65. The most comprehensive study, which finds a small but significant negative stock price effect, is Jonathan M. Karpoff & Paul H. Malatesta, *The Wealth Effects of Second-Generation State Takeover Legislation,* 25 J. Fin. Econ. 291 (1989), which assesses forty statutes. Romano, *supra* note 4, at 60–69, reviews the empirical research on takeover statutes and shareholder wealth.

66. Correspondingly, in contrast to the antitakeover statutes of other states, the Delaware statute did not have a negative stock price effect. *See* John S. Jahera, Jr. & William Pugh, *State Takeover Legislation: The Case of Delaware,* 7 J. L. Econ. & Org. 410, 416–19 (1991) (finding insignificant or positive returns over eight two-day event intervals); Karpoff & Malatesta, *supra* note 65, at 315 (finding an insignificant price effect over a two-day event interval).

67. *See* Romano, *supra* note 4, at 68–69.

68. *See id.* at 70.

69. *See* Roberta Romano, *The Future of Hostile Takeovers: Legislation and Public Opinion,* 57 U. Cin. L. Rev. 457, 485 (1988). Only witnesses employed by the government participated in a greater number of takeover legislation hearings than corporate managers. *See id.*

70. *See id.* at 482–84; Kenneth Lehn & James W. Jones, The Legislative Politics of Hostile Corporate Takeovers (1987) (unpublished manuscript, on file with the *Yale Law Journal*).

71. *See* Henry N. Butler, *Corporation-Specific Anti-Takeover Statutes and the Market for Corporate Charters,* 1988 Wis. L. Rev. 365 *passim*; Romano, *supra* note 69, at 461.

72. Pub. L. No. 90–439, 82 Stat. 454 (1968) (amending Securities Exchange Act of 1934 § 14(d), (e), 15 U.S.C. § 78n(d), (e) (1994)).

73. *See* Romano, *supra* note 69, at 470–74.

74. *See* Romano, *supra* note 4, at 48–49. This explains why Congress did not amend the Williams Act to restrict takeovers further in the 1980s. Over the course of its lengthy deliberative process on takeover legislation, the Supreme Court upheld state takeover regulation (*see* CTS Corp. v. Dynamics Corp. of Am., 481 U.S. 69, 94 (1987)) and firms redirected their lobbying efforts from Congress to the states, which could provide a target with relief more quickly than Congress (*see* sources cited *supra* note 71).

75. In other words, while a social planner would set quality by the average consumer's valuation because he looks at all consumers' welfare, the monopolist, concerned with profits and not social surplus, sets quality by the marginal consumer's valuation because the price increase for higher quality can be passed on to all inframarginal consumers. As the marginal consumer is not likely to be representative of the population, the monopolist's product quality choice will differ from that of the social planner (i.e., it will undersupply quality if the average valuation exceeds the marginal valuation). The bias in quality introduced by the monopolist can be identified only if output will be the same in both cases; this is generally not the case because a monopolist tends to produce less output for a given quality. *See* Jean Tirole, The Theory of Industrial Organization 100–102 (MIT Press: 1988).

76. When the monopolist can produce only one product because the monopolist cannot appropriate the net consumer surplus from introducing a new product design, there may be too few products under monopoly compared to the social optimum; when the monopolist can offer multiple products that are substitutes, it may introduce "too many" products compared to the social optimum because if it charges an above-marginal price for one good it can create demand for a second good, which would not exist if the first good was competitively priced. *See id.* at 104–5. The analysis concerning the monopolist's choice for product diversity is substantially the same as that for product innovation.

77. *See* William P. Albrecht et al., *Regulatory Regimes: The Interdependence of Rules and Regulatory Structure, in* The Industrial Organization and Regulation of the Securities Industry 9, 27, Andrew W. Lo, ed. (University of Chicago Press: 1996).

78. *See* Romano, *supra* note 4, at 45–48.

79. The figures in appendix table I (Editor's Note: these figures can be found in Romano, R. 1998. Empowering Investors. *The Yale Law Journal* 107 (8): 2359–430) provide a conservative estimate of the profitability of Delaware's chartering business because they overstate its expenditures by including, in addition to the appropriations for the Division of Corporations in the Office of the Secretary of State, which administers the corporate registration process, the total appropriations for the Chancery Court and Delaware Supreme Court, which hear corporate law cases at trial and on appeal, respectively, although such cases are a fraction of their caseload. For example, only 30 percent of Chancery Court cases are corporate law cases. *See Chancery Court High Stakes in Delaware,* Nat'l L. J., Feb. 13, 1984, at 32. In addition, the outlays for the Division of Corporations were separately itemized only after 1972; for the years before 1972, the table includes the entire appropriation for the Secretary's Office, although in the subsequent years the ratio of the budget for the division to the budget for the office was slightly under 80 percent.

80. The bulk of the SEC's fee revenue comes from securities' registration. For example, in 1996, securities registered under the 1933 act accounted for 75 percent of the agency's fee revenue, and transactions of covered exchange-listed securities comprised a further 17 percent. *See SEC 1996 Annual Report* (visited Jan. 5, 1998), http://www.sec.gov/asec/annrep96/polas.htm. The figures for fees collected in the 1960s–70s include the fees from the registration of exchanges and brokers as well as securities. *See, e.g.,* 33 SEC Ann. Rep. 149 (1967) (figures for 1965–67); 36 SEC Ann. Rep. 210 (1970) (figures for 1968–70).

81. *See* Congressional Budget Office, 104th Cong., 1st Sess., Memorandum on Growth of Federal User Charges: An Update (Comm. Print 1995). The SEC's revenue is so great that for many years it sought to be self-financing. Congress initially refused its request, preferring to retain a system in which the fees from SEC filings entered into general revenues, and the SEC was allocated a budget far lower than the revenues it produced. In 1996, however, Congress enacted legislation reducing SEC fees over time so that eventually the SEC will collect no more in fees than it costs to run the agency. *See* National Securities Markets Improvement Act of 1996, Pub. L. No. 104-290, §§ 402–5, 110 Stat. 3416, 3441–44 (codified at 15 U.S.C.A. §§ 78a, 77f(b), 78ee (West 1997)). That statute also restricted states' ability to charge filing fees for the registration of securities traded on national exchanges at the same time as it preempted their ability to regulate such issues' registrations. *See id.* § 102(a), 102(c)(2)(D), 110 Stat. at 3417, 3420 (codified at 15 U.S.C.A. § 77r). The change in securities regime advocated in this article would reword this restriction to permit the securities domicile alone to charge such fees. The domicile would be a state, foreign country, or the SEC, depending on the issuer's selection.

82. *See* Romano, *supra* note 19, at 257.

83. *See* Cohn Jamieson, *Stamp Duties in the European Community: Harmonisation by Abolition?* 1991 Brit. Tax Rev. 318–19.

84. *See, e.g.,* Thomas L. Hazen, The Law of Securities Regulation 769, 773 (West Pub. Co.: 3d ed. 1996) (discussing the courts' expansion of statutory scope). While the 1934 act provides the federal courts with exclusive jurisdiction for 1934 act violations (*see* 15 U.S.C. § 78aa (1994)), the 1933 act does not (*see* 15 U.S.C. § 77v), and plaintiffs can bring claims under state securities laws for conduct that would be a 1934 act violation. Nevertheless, the preponderance of securities lawsuits are brought in federal court. *See* Grundfest & Perino, *supra* note 3, at 3–9 (discussing filing trends in securities legislation).

85. *See, e.g.,* Santa Fe Indus. v. Green, 430 U.S. 462, 474–77 (1977) (holding that a breach of fiduciary duty was not a violation of federal securities law); Ernst & Ernst v. Hochfelder, 425 U.S. 185, 201 (1976) (requiring scienter for liability under federal securities fraud statutes).

86. For an overview of the advantages to investors of bringing securities claims in state rather than federal courts, see Marc I. Steinberg, *The Emergence of State Securities Laws: Partly Sunny Skies for Investors,* 62 U. Cin. L. Rev. 395, 418–27 (1993). Grundfest and Perino note the incentives created by the 1995 Reform Act for plaintiffs to use state courts. *See* Grundfest & Perino, *supra* note 3, at 39.

87. *See* sources cited *supra* note 2.

88. *See* Romano, *supra* note 4, at 32–34 (discussing how firms reincorporate to reduce litigation costs); Romano, *supra* note 19, at 249–51 (same).

89. *See* Wilmington City Ry. v. People's Ry., 47 A. 245, 251 (Del. Ch. 1900). For a more recent example of this approach, see *Santa Fe Hills Golf & Country Club v. Safehi Realty Co.,* 349 S.W.2d 27, 34–35 (Mo. 1961).

90. For the details of the argument, see Romano, *supra* note 4, at 38; and Romano, *supra* note 19, at 240–42.

91. *See* Romano, *supra* note 4, at 107.

92. The difference between charter and bylaw amendment is that state corporation codes require shareholder approval of changes to the charter, but not to the bylaws. *See, e.g.,* Del. Code Ann. tit. 8, § 109 (1996) (bylaw amendment); *id.* § 242(b) (charter amendment).

93. *See Some of Surveyed Firms Show Consensus on "Cracker Barrel," Other Issues,* 29 Sec. Reg. & L. Rep. (BNA) 567, 569 (Apr. 25, 1997).

94. A regulatory monopoly affords the SEC the opportunity to implement policies favoring the interests of financial market professionals rather than investors. *See, e.g.,* Phillips & Zecher, *supra* note 35, at 22–23 (discussing disclosure policies); David D. Haddock & Jonathan R. Macey, *Regulation on Demand: A Private Interest Model, with an Application to Insider Trading Regulation,* 30 J. L. & Econ. 311, 318–30 (1987) (discussing insider-trading regulation). Market professionals benefit from receiving free information from firms under the SEC's mandatory disclosure policies and from the absence in the market of more informed traders under the insider-trading prohibition. Regulatory capture by market professionals would be more difficult under the market approach to securities regulation because corporations would opt for the regime more congenial to investors, as the providers of capital direct their funds to firms in those regimes; correspondingly, regulators sensitive to the number of corporations subject to their jurisdiction would adapt their rules to the preferences of investors, rather than to those of market professionals.

95. *See* SEC Derivatives Disclosure, *supra* note 45, at 6054–62 (describing minor changes made in response to comment letters on the proposal and presenting a superficial cost-benefit analysis of the proposal).

96. *See* Roberta Romano, *The Political Dynamics of Derivative Securities Regulation,* 14 Yale J. on Reg. 279, 354–59 (1997) (discussing the shift in the SEC's approach to product innovation). Some might attempt to characterize the SEC's loosening of its holding period for the resale of restricted (unregistered) securities under Rule 144 (*see* Revision of Holding Period Requirements in Rules 144 and 145, 62 Fed. Reg. 9242 (1997) (to be codified at 17 C.F.R. pt. 230)) as evidence of the SEC's responsiveness to competitive pressures, since the reform is a recognition by the agency that compliance costs were too high for small businesses (*see id.* at 9243–44). In my opinion, this action does not provide evidence that the SEC is particularly responsive to competitive pressure. The holding period revision took almost two years to be adopted. Delaware, by contrast, responds to corporate complaints much more quickly. *See* Roberta Romano, *Corporate Governance in the Aftermath of the Insurance Crisis,* 39 Emory L. J. 1155, 1160–61 (1990), at 1160 (discussing the enactment of a limited liability statute within one year of an insurance crisis and a controversial judicial opinion). Moreover, the change has had no effect on the disclosure obligations of the public companies that are the focus of this article's proposal, as it is directed at easing 1933 act offering requirements for small firms and not at easing the continuing reporting obligations of the 1934 act. The 1934 act disclo-

sure obligations have, in contrast to the SEC's moves to limit 1933 act coverage, significantly increased over time, as the SEC has come to view the 1934 act as the centerpiece of its regulatory authority rather than the 1933 act, in a policy referred to as "integrated disclosure." *See, e.g.,* David L. Ratner & Thomas L. Hazen, Securities Regulation 129–34 (West Pub. Co.: 5th ed. 1996). Finally, and most important, the SEC has sought to eliminate competition and establish its regime internationally by identifying harmonization of regulatory standards as a central goal of its policy toward international securities regulation. *See* Policy Statement of the Securities and Exchange Commission on Regulation of International Securities Markets. Exchange Act Release No. 6807, 53 Fed. Reg. 46,963, (1988) (stating that regulators should "seek to minimize differences between systems"). Although the SEC's policy statement also asserted that regulators should be "sensitive to cultural differences and national sovereignty concerns" (*id.*), this is belied by the SEC's implementation of the policy at home, where it requires foreign firms to reconcile their financial statements with GAAP in order to list in the United States (*see infra* notes 190–91 and accompanying text).

97. Jeffrey Gordon has advanced this argument in the corporate law context. *See* Jeffrey N. Gordon, *The Mandatory Structure of Corporate Law,* 89 Colum. L. Rev. 1549, 1573–75 (1989). I remain skeptical, however, of a justification for mandatory rules involving promoters' needs for a commitment device concerning the stability of the initial domicile choice. *See* Roberta Romano, *Answering the Wrong Question: The Tenuous Case for Mandatory Corporate Laws,* 89 Colum. L. Rev. 1599 (1989) (responding to Gordon's argument). A shareholder vote would be required for a change in securities domicile, as it is for a change in incorporation state (*see infra* subsection II.B.2), and, accordingly, the need for mandatory rules as a commitment device would be minimal because the successful occurrence of an opportunistic relocation would be extremely remote.

98. For a recent article advocating this approach, see Paul G. Mahoney, *The Exchange as Regulator,* 83 Va. L. Rev. 1453 (1997).

99. *See* Benston, *Evaluation, supra* note 28, at 133. Paul Mahoney provides a detailed description of the NYSE's pre-SEC disclosure requirements. *See* Mahoney, *supra* note 98, at 1466.

100. *See* Daniel R. Fischel, *Organized Exchanges and the Regulation of Dual Class Common Stock,* 54 U. Chi. L. Rev. 119 (1987), at 125; Mahoney, *supra* note 98, at 1459. Amihud and Mendelson argue that exchanges would provide trading rules that benefit investors only if firms, and not exchanges, choose where a security is listed (in the context of multiple listing of shares or the trading of derivative securities). *See* Yakov Amihud & Haim Mendelson, *A New Approach to the Regulation of Trading across Securities Markets,* 71 N.Y.U. L. Rev. 1411 (1996), at 1442–46. The issues of interest here, however, involve issuer-shareholder transactions and not trading rules. The concerns of Amihud and Mendelson and other critics of exchange self-regulation (which focus on exchanges' mismatched incentives regarding trading rules that can exploit investors (*see, e.g.,* Mahoney, *supra* note 98, at 1462–63)) are thus not relevant to the discussion.

101. The transaction cost savings would obviously be reduced if a firm's shares were traded on more than one exchange. Even if the secondary exchange were to adopt a regime that recognized the primary exchange's rules as govern-

ing all issuer shares regardless of transaction location, investors still would have to know which exchange was the primary one.

102. The hybrid use of courts and arbitrators in class arbitration suggests some of the difficulties. *See, e.g.,* Keating v. Superior Court, 645 P.2d 1192, 1214–18 (Cal. 1982) (Richardson, J., dissenting) (describing problems with class arbitration). For a discussion of these and other difficulties by proponents of arbitration, see G. Richard Shell, *Arbitration and Corporate Governance,* 67 N.C. L. Rev. 517, 551, 553–55, 561 (1989); and Note, *Classwide Arbitration. Efficient Adjudication or Procedural Quagmire?* 67 Va. L. Rev. 787, 799, 805–6 (1981).

103. *See Keating,* 645 P.2d at 1209–10 (holding that judicial involvement in class arbitration includes determination of certification and notice to class, supervision of the adequacy of counsel, dismissal or settlement, and remanding to the trial court to determine the feasibility of the class); Lewis v. Prudential Bache Sec., 235 Cal. Rptr. 69, 75–76 (Ct. App. 1986) (finding class arbitration feasible, and leaving to the trial court the determination of all issues necessary to certify the class and to provide proper notice); Izzi v. Mesquite Country Club, 231 Cal. Rptr. 315, 322 & n.6 (Ct. App. 1986) (remanding to the trial court to determine certifiability of the arbitration class and noting the preferability of court determination of any class-action problems involving notice and discovery). None of the cases permitting classwide arbitration has involved securities law claims.

104. *See* Ronald J. Daniels, *Should Provinces Compete? The Case for a Competitive Corporate Law Market,* 36 McGill L. J. 130, 182–84 (1991).

105. *See infra* section II.A; subsection III.A.2.

106. *Cf.* Mahoney, *supra* note 98, at 1498–99 (discussing the need for government assistance in deterring exchange-regulation fraud).

107. *See* National Securities Markets Improvement Act of 1996, Pub. L. No. 104-290, § 105, 110 Stat. 3416, 3423 (codified at 15 U.S.C.A. §§ 77z-3, 78mm (West 1997)).

108. For an analysis of the SEC's failed effort to expand its jurisdiction to include derivative securities, see Romano, *supra* note 96, at 355–80.

109. *See* National Securities Markets Improvement Act § 102, 110 Stat, at 3417 (codified at 15 U.S.C.A. § 77r).

110. I adopt here terminology more commonly used in the international, as opposed to domestic, law setting: Legislative or prescriptive jurisdiction is "the authority of a state to make its laws applicable to particular conduct, relationships or status" (whether or not that state is the forum state) (Gary B. Born, International Civil Litigation in United States Courts 491 (Kluwer Law International: 3d ed. 1996), as distinct from judicial jurisdiction, the power of a court to adjudicate a dispute, which, for U.S. courts, requires both personal jurisdiction and subject matter jurisdiction (*see id.* at 1–2). The federal securities laws confer both prescriptive and subject matter jurisdiction on federal courts.

111. *See* Unif. Sec. Act § 414, 7B U.L.A. 672 (1985); *see also, e.g.,* Cal. Corp. Code § 25008 (Deering 1997) (codifying section 414).

112. *See, e.g.,* Orman v. Charles Schwab & Co., 676 N.E.2d 241, 246 (Ill. App. Ct. 1996) (refusing to apply state law to claims against a broker because such application would frustrate, if not destroy, the goal of federal uniformity, and stating that "if uniformity is not to prevail, neither rule 10b-b nor the SEC would serve any function or purpose in regulating disclosure").

113. *See* Restatement (Second) of Conflicts of Law § 302 (1971).

114. Robert A. Leflar et al., American Conflicts Law 700 (Michie Co.: 4th ed. 1986). For a similar analysis by a choice-of-law scholar who specializes in corporate law issues, see P. John Kozyris, *Some Observations on State Regulation of Multistate Takeovers—Controlling Choice of Law through the Commerce Clause,* 14 Del. J. Corp. L. 499, 509–11 (1989).

115. Restatement (Second) of Conflicts of Law § 302 cml. e.

116. CTS Corp. v. Dynamics Corp. of Am., 481 U.S. 69, 89 (1987). For an analysis of the relation of the *CTS* decision to the corporate choice-of-law rule, see Kozyris, *supra* note 114, *passim.*

117. *See* Vincent E. O'Brien, *A Study of Class Action Securities Fraud Cases 1988–1996,* at 4 (visited Dec. 28, 1997), http://www.lecg.com/study2.htm#att; *see also* Grundfest & Perino, *supra* note 3, at 9, 31.

118. *Cf.* Amehem Prods., Inc. v. Windsor, 117 S. Ct. 2231, 2249–50 (1997) (affirming the appellate court's rejection of an asbestos class-action settlement for failing to meet statutory class requirements, and suggesting that the predominance of common issues that is a problem in mass tort litigation may not be a problem in securities fraud). In a small number of securities cases, the courts have referred to the class certification issue in passing and largely ignored it when certifying the federal class, adding, on occasion, the proviso that the class could be decertified or divided up at a later date if individual state law issues presented a problem. *See, e.g.,* Lubin v. Sybedon Corp., 688 F. Supp. 1425, 1460–61 (S.D. Cal. 1988) (holding that for purposes of the state securities claim, the federal class, if certified, would need to be divided into subclasses of California and non-California investors); Weinberger v. Jackson, 102 F.R.D. 839, 847 (N.D. Cal. 1984) (certifying a class despite the assertion that a need for individual determinations of state law applicable to members' claims would overwhelm the commonality of the class, by finding the assertion of a conflicts problem premature as the defendants did not show that there was a true conflict among states' interests). Moreover, when the federal ʔuit thereafter settled, there was either no mention of the individual state law determination issue (*see, e.g.,* Weinberger v. Jackson, No. C-89-2301-CAL, 1991 U.S. Dist., LEXIS 3938 (N.D. Cal. Mar. 19, 1991)), or the federal class was certified without any mention of the need to subdivide it for the state claims (*see, e.g., In re* U.S. Grant Hotel Assoc. Sec. Litig., 740 F. Supp. 1460, 1464 (S.D. Cal. 1990) (declaring settlement of the *Lubin v. Sybedon Corp.* litigation). *Matsushita Electric Industrial Co. v. Epstein* (116 S. Ct. 873 (1996)), in which a state court settlement disposed of federal securities claims, did not raise the multijurisdictional issue because the state class action was a corporate law claim for breach of fiduciary duty, and thus only one state's law applied to the class members. *See id.* at 882.

119. *See supra* notes 1–3 and accompanying text (discussing the impact of the 1995 act on filings).

120. *See* Marcel Kahan & Linda Silberman, *Matsushita and Beyond: The Role of State Courts in Class Actions Involving Exclusive Federal Claims,* 1996 Sup. Ct. Rev. 219, 234–48 (discussing use of state courts to settle federal claims).

121. *Cf.* Clay Harris, *European Regulators Probe Defunct 'Virtual' Brokerage,* Fin. Times, Dec. 22, 1997, at 16 (reporting that an Internet broker that sold U.S. over-the-counter shares globally was being investigated by four nations' regulators after operations ceased).

122. *See, e.g.,* Restatement (Second) of Conflicts of Law § 302 cmt. e (1971); Kozyris, *supra* note 114, at 520–21.

123. See Kozyris, *supra* note 114, at 521.

124. *See, e.g.,* Born, *supra* note 110, at 654–55 (stating that the contemporary approach in U.S. law regards choice-of-law provisions as presumptively enforceable); Leflar et al., *supra* note 114, at 415–19 (noting that authorities generally both approve of the right of parties to determine themselves what law governs contracts and prefer this basis for contract choice of law (citing Restatement (Second) of Conflicts of Law § 187)).

125. *See, e.g.,* Born, *supra* note 110, at 655, 661; Leflar et al., *supra* note 114, at 416–17; *cf.* The Bremen v. Zapata Off-Shore Co., 407 U.S. 1, 12–13, 15–16 (1972) (expressing similar concerns in enforcing a choice-of-forum clause).

126. *See* discussion *infra* subsection II.B.1.

127. *See* Roby v. Corporation of Lloyd's, 996 F.2d 1353, 1365–66 (2d Cir. 1993) (upholding a U.K. choice-of-law contract provision over federal securities law claims, while noting the adequacy of remedies in English law). The adequacy-of-the-remedy prong of the Supreme Court's exemptions from upholding contractual choice-of-law clauses has been raised in securities law cases because the federal securities laws prohibit waiver of compliance. *See* 15 U.S.C. §§ 77n, 78cc(a) (1994). Were the federal statutes optional, the antiwaiver provisions would not apply to firms opting out of the federal regime, and the argument against enforcing a choice-of-law clause would be even more attenuated than it is at present.

128. *See* Leflar et al., *supra* note 114, at 417 n.18 (discussing the relationship between the "reasonable relation" requirement and the public policy limitation on choice-of-law clauses under the Uniform Commercial Code).

129. *See supra* subsection I.B.2.

130. *See* discussion *infra* subsection II.B.1.

131. The Restatement (*see* Restatement (Second) of Conflicts of Law § 187 cmt. f (1971)), the Uniform Commercial Code (*see* U.C.C. § 1–105 (1996)), and many states (*see, e.g.,* N.Y. Gen. Oblig. Law § 5–1401 (Consol. Supp. 1997)), recognize that geographic contacts may be unnecessary for parties' effective choice. *See, e.g.,* Leflar et al., *supra* note 114, at 417–18 (discussing the implications of the New York provision).

132. *See* Romano, *supra* note 4, at 132–33.

133. Indeed, two Supreme Court cases interpreting the federal securities law illustrate the difficulties created by the two regimes' being distinct. In *Basic Inc. v. Levinson* (485 U.S. 224, 232–34 (1988)), while imposing disclosure duties on managers regarding merger negotiations, the Court rejected as a valid concern the acquirer's desire for secrecy when nondisclosure for such reasons would not obviously be a breach of fiduciary duty at state law. In *Virginia Bankshares, Inc. v. Sandberg* (501 U.S. 1083, 1102–6 (1991)), a case involving proxy statement misstatements, the Court did not find the requisite causation for a private right of action under section 14(a) of the 1934 act (15 U.S.C. § 78n(a) (1994)) where the complaining shareholders' votes were not required by state law to authorize the action subject to the proxy solicitation. The Court left open the question of whether there would be sufficient causation if the shareholders lost a state remedy otherwise available because of the misstatement. *See Virginia Bankshares,* 501 U.S. at 1107–8.

134. *Compare* 17 C.F.R. § 240.14a-8(c)(l) & (7) (1997) (stating that firms can exclude proposals that are "not a proper subject for action by security holders" and involving "ordinary business operations") *with* Adoption of Amendments Relating to Proposals by Security Holders, Exchange Act Release No. 12999, 41 Fed. Reg. 52,994 (1976) (permitting, where the subject is not proper for shareholder action, proposals couched in precatory language because recommendations to the board are not improper actions at state law, and permitting proposals involving ordinary business, such as employment practices, where they implicate social policy).

135. Such clauses are presumptively enforced at federal common law and by most states. *See* Carnival Cruise Lines, Inc. v. Shute, 499 U.S. 585, 593–95 (1991); Michael E. Solimine, *Forum-Selection Clauses and the Privatization of Procedure,* 25 Cornell Int'l L. J. 51, 63, 69 (1992).

136. *See, e.g.,* Revlon, Inc. v. MacAndrews & Forbes Holdings, Inc., 506 A.2d 173, 182 (Del. 1985) (finding that a board breached its fiduciary duty to shareholders by engaging in a takeover defensive tactic that protected noteholders, whose rights are a matter of contract); Harff v. Kekorian, 324 A.2d 215, 219–20 (Del. Ch. 1974) (stating that bondholders cannot bring a derivative suit), *rev'd on other grounds,* 347 A.2d 133, 134 (Del. 1975). A corporate code would be relevant for a bond contract only when a corporation is close to insolvency, for at that point some states might hold that the board's fiduciary duty encompasses creditors. *See* Credit Lyonnais Bank Nederland, NV. v. Pathe Communications Corp., No. 12150, 1991 Del. Ch. LEXIS 215, at *108 (Del. Ch. Dec. 30, 1991) (suggesting that a board's duty shifts away from shareholders when the company enters the "vicinity of insolvency").

137. *See, e.g.,* Cal. Corp. Code § 25008 (West 1997) (codifying Unif. Sec. Act § 414, 7B U.L.A. 672 (1985)).

138. *See, e.g.,* Del. Code Ann. tit. 6, § 2708(c)(ii) (1993) (requiring a $100,000 minimum contractual amount); N.Y. Gen. Oblig. Law § 5–1401 (Consol. Supp. 1997) (requiring a $250,000 minimum contractual amount).

139. *See* Leflar et al., *supra* note 114, at 6. They note: "[A]ssuming that the local law of a particular American state permits one of its courts to act in a given instance, the only authority which can effectively say that the court may not apply the law that it chooses is that of the federal government, under the powers delegated to it by the Federal Constitution." *Id.* Although there is a well-established judicial tradition upholding forum clauses in commercial contexts, including securities transactions (*see, e.g.,* Scherk v. Alberto-Culver Co., 417 U.S. 506, 519–20 (1974); The Bremen v. Zapata Off-Shore Co., 407 U.S. 1, 18–19 (1972)), to the extent there might be a question of whether firms opting out of the federal regime can also opt out of the federal court system, the congressional legislation establishing the market approach should specify that federal courts are to enforce forum clauses selecting a state court.

140. *See* Solimine, *supra* note 135, at 75–76.

141. *See* cases cited *supra* note 139.

142. *See* Solimine, *supra* note 135, at 55, 63 & n.84 ("[A]t least four states explicitly reject . . . such clauses.").

143. Bruce Hay has criticized adopting a nonbuyer-state approach to product liability litigation, contending that state competition in choice-of-law rules is a more promising alternative approach to substantive law competition regarding

such torts. *See* Bruce L. Hay, *Conflicts of Law and State Competition in the Product Liability System,* 80 Geo. L. J. 617 (1992). He asserts that states' policies of choice-of-law rules and substantive laws are inversely correlated. Thus, when states can follow a choice of law rule favorable to their citizen-plaintiffs under what is referred to in choice of law as the "governmental interests" approach, they can adopt promanufacturer substantive laws to protect in-state firms without harming instate consumers. He concludes that this scenario indicates that competition over choice-of-law rules would produce the optimal level of substantive product liability law, because it would enable states to favor consumers in the choice-of-law rule and manufacturers in the substantive law. *See id.* at 651–52.

Hay's analysis is, however, mistaken. The governmental interest approach looks to the state's substantive policy to determine a state's "interest" in a lawsuit. If a state's law favored defendant-manufacturers, then a court applying the governmental interest standard would not be able to find that the state has expressed an interest in protecting its citizen-plaintiffs. It would therefore not be able to choose a proplaintiff state's law to govern the dispute, as Hay expects. As a consequence, Hay's crucial assumption, that the policy underlying a state's choice-of-law rule would be the inverse of the state's substantive law, is incorrect; the two policies must be positively correlated. Hence, competition in choice-of-law rules cannot substitute for substantive law competition in the product liability setting of concern to Hay, nor in any other substantive law setting. The operation of conflicts-of-law interest analysis prevents opportunistic choices of inconsistent substantive policies and choice-of-law rules. States can, of course, compete on both choice-of-law and substantive dimensions, but the choice-of-law rule that benefits investors in the securities context, an issuer securities domicile rule, is straightforward because it fosters substantive competition, which aids investors since their preferences dictate the competitive outcome. States would thus have an incentive to choose the issuer domicile conflicts rule. But to achieve the full benefits from competition, one state's use of the internal affairs rule must be recognized by all the other states to assure that one state's law governs all of a firm's transactions with investors. This means that the same choice-of-law rule must be uniformly applied as the choice-of-law rule across the states. Over time, states would probably do so. *See supra* text accompanying notes 140–142.

144. Albert Breton's theory of competitive federalism offers a rationale for requiring such provisions, even though competitive securities regimes would most likely adopt the disclosure and voting requirements on their own, as a means to ensure the vitality of competition. Breton maintains that a central government can play a useful role in stabilizing competitive federalism by monitoring state activity to prevent collusion or "races to the bottom" that would undermine the benefits of competition. *See* Albert Breton, Competitive Governments: An Economic Theory of Politics and Public Finance 251 (Cambridge University Press: 1996). The two statutory requirements would obviate the need for the central government to monitor actively the competition over securities regimes. But, because a race for the bottom will not occur in the securities context given the dynamics of capital markets exemplified by the corporate charter market, it is not obvious that monitoring by the central government is necessary in this context.

145. Of course, not every investor needs to know a stock's domicile; the informed investors set the price. This is the meaning of an efficient market. The best available evidence indicates that the U.S. stock market is efficient regarding publicly available information, which includes an issuer's securities domicile. *See* Fama, *supra* note 46, at 1577, 1607 (stating that event studies, which test the "adjustment of prices to public announcements," provide the "cleanest evidence on market efficiency"). For general models of information aggregation through prices with heterogeneously informed investors, see Alan Schwartz & Louis Wilde, *Competitive Equilibria in Markets for Heterogeneous Search Goods under Imperfect Information: A Theoretical Analysis with Policy Implications,* 13 Bell J. Econ. 181 (1982); and sources cited *supra* note 21.

146. *See, e.g.,* Del. Code Ann. tit. 8, § 202(a) (1996).

147. A change in incorporation state (the firm's statutory domicile) requires a shareholder vote because it is effected by a merger of the corporation into a subsidiary incorporated in the new domicile state. Under all state corporation codes, a merger requires shareholder approval. *See, e.g., id.* §§ 251–52.

148. *See, e.g.,* Gordon, *supra* note 97, at 1575.

149. In particular, it can be shown that, under plausible assumptions concerning the breakdown of stock ownership among insiders, outside blockholders, and dispersed investors, a rational strategy for an uninformed shareholder concerned about the possibility of opportunism would not be the strategy of always supporting management with "yes" votes, the strategy emphasized by commentators critical of shareholder voting, but rather a mixed strategy of voting randomly against management's proposals, or a strategy of not voting at all, leaving the decision to the informed voters. Both of these latter strategies are better than always voting "no," as well as always voting "yes." *See* Romano, *supra* note 97, at 1607–10.

150. Mutual funds, for instance, do not outperform the stock market. *See, e.g.,* Stephen A. Ross et al., Corporate Finance 348 (Irwin: 4th ed. 1996). This fact shows that these institutions do not have access to, or a comparative advantage in processing, private information, and there is little reason to think this circumstance would change with the switch to a competitive regime. The criticism leveled at relational investing, in which institutional investors engage in active monitoring of managers, that such investors may obtain private benefits that generate a conflict between their and other shareholders' interests, thereby reducing the value of their activism (*see* Jill E. Fisch, *Relationship Investing: Will It Happen? Will It Work?* 55 Ohio St. L. J. 1009, 1040–41 (1994); Edward B. Rock, *Controlling the Dark Side of Relational Investing,* 15 Cardozo L. Rev. 987, 989 (1994)), is not applicable in our context. The posited private benefits of such investors arise most frequently from the institutions' holding preferred securities (*see, e.g.,* Rock, *supra,* at 1022), but preferred stockholders do not select the regime for common stock. More important, the number of institutions that are able to attain such preferred relational positions is quite small (there are few outside investors equal to Warren Buffett whom managements are willing to trust with the rights of relational positions), and thus they will not be the marginal investor whose tastes dictate regime choices. Accordingly, the possibility of a divergence between institutional and retail investors' preferred securities regimes is remote.

151. *See* 17 C.F.R. § 230.144A note (1997).

152. *See* Luis F. Moreno Trevino, *Access to U.S. Capital Markets for Foreign Issuers: Rule 144A Private Placements,* 16 Hous. J. Int'l L. 159, 195 (1993).

153. *See* 17 C.F.R. § 230.144A (Preliminary Notes).

154. *See, e.g.,* Del. Code Ann. tit. 8, § 262 (1996) (providing appraisal rights in conjunction with mergers, which require shareholder approval); Model Bus. Corp. Act § 13.02 (1992) (providing appraisal rights in conjunction with mergers, asset sales, amendments of articles of incorporation that materially and adversely affect shares by specified impact, and any actions taken pursuant to a shareholder vote where charter, bylaws, or board resolution provide for such rights).

155. *E.g.,* Del. Code. Ann. tit. 8, § 262(h) (providing that for merger dissenters entitled to appraisal, the court should determine "fair value exclusive of any element of value arising from" the merger).

156. In the course of over a decade of research requiring examination of hundreds of corporate charters, I have not come across such a provision.

157. Although investors favor their home countries in their portfolio allocations (*see* Kenneth French & James Poterba, *Investor Diversification and International Equity Markets,* 81 Am. Econ. Rev. 222 (1991)), cross-border flows of capital have dramatically increased over time and are expected to continue to do so (*see* Alan C. Shapiro, Multinational Financial Management 403–4 (Allyn and Bacon: 4th ed. 1991)). As financial markets have been deregulated globally, international market capitalizations have increased, and the benefits of international diversification are becoming widely recognized. *See* Solnik, *supra* note 10, at v–vi. For concise reviews in the legal literature of such investment trends, see Macintosh, *supra* note 8, at 6–10; and Merritt Fox, *Securities Disclosure in a Globalizing Market: Who Should Regulate Whom?* 95 Mich. L. Rev. 2498, 2523–25 (1997).

158. *See* Registration of Foreign Offerings by Domestic Issuers, Exchange Act Release No. 33–4708, 29 Fed. Reg. 9828 (1964) (stating that requirements of the 1933 act are "intended to protect American investors"); *see also* Stephen J. Choi & Andrew T. Guzman, *The Dangerous Extraterritoriality of American Securities Law,* 17 NW. J. Int'l L. & Bus. 207, 221 (1997) (discussing the SEC's adoption of Regulation 5, governing overseas transactions, which changed the regulatory emphasis from "the protection of U.S. investors, wherever they may be located, to the protection of American capital markets").

159. *See* James L. Cochrane, *Are U.S. Regulatory Requirements for Foreign Firms Appropriate?* 17 Fordham Int'l L. J. S58, S61 (1994) (noting that there are "2,000 foreign companies eligible to go on [NYSE's] list . . . were it not for SEC regulations"); James A. Fanto & Roberta S. Karmel, *A Report on the Attitudes of Foreign Companies Regarding a U.S. Listing,* 3 Stan. J. L. Bus. & Fin. 51, 70 (1997).

160. *See* Fanto & Karmel, *supra* note 159, at 71. William Baumol and Burton Malkiel point out that beyond the time and expense entailed in the translation process for GAAP reconciliation, there are difficulties arising from the fact that GAAP requirements are not adapted to the "circumstances of the foreign firm," such as the fact that GAAP rules are tailored to U.S. corporate tax rules, which vary significantly from other nations' taxation. Baumol & Malkiel, *supra* note 33, at 41.

161. *See* Baumol & Malkiel, *supra* note 33, at 41.

162. *See* Edwards, *supra* note 7, at 63.

163. *See id.* at 58–59, 63–64.

164. *See* Multijurisdictional Disclosure and Modifications to the Current Registration and Reporting System for Canadian Issuers, Exchange Act Release No. 6902, 56 Fed. Reg. 30,036 (July 1, 1991).

165. *See* Richard W. Jennings et al., Securities Regulation: Cases and Materials 1581 (Foundation Press: 7th ed. 1992).

166. *See* Fanto & Karmel, *supra* note 159, at 56.

167. *See, e.g.,* Baumol & Malkiel, *supra* note 33, at 46–50; Edwards, *supra* note 7, at 65–66 (noting, however, that more studies must be done before definite conclusions can be reached).

168. *See supra* text accompanying note 33.

169. *See* Jorg Baetge, The Role of Disclosure and Auditing as Affecting Corporate Governance, Presentation at the Symposium on Comparative Corporate Governance at the Max-Planck-Institut, Hamburg, Germany (May 16, 1997).

170. Firms currently respond to such incentives. *See supra* text accompanying notes 29–32.

171. For signaling explanations of foreign firm listings in the United States, see C. Sherman Cheung & Jason Lee, *Disclosure Environment and Listing on Foreign Stock Exchanges,* 19 J. Banking & Fin. 347 (1995); Oren Fuerst, A Theoretical Analysis of the Investor Protection Regulations: Argument for Global Listing of Stocks (Feb. 17, 1998) (unpublished manuscript, on file with the *Yale Law Journal*); and Edward B. Rock, Mandatory Disclosure as Credible Commitment: Going Public, Opting In, Opting Out, and Globalization (1998) (unpublished manuscript, on file with the *Yale Law Journal*).

172. To the extent that the SEC requirement for deregistration of fewer than 300 shareholders (*see* Rock, *supra* note 171, at 11–13 (discussing exit routes under SEC rules)) would no longer be applicable under the market regime because it would impede effective jurisdictional competition, firms could duplicate such an exit barrier by placing a similarly worded provision in their charters. Where the firm's home nation does not recognize a domicile approach and the firm is listed both domestically and in the United States, the firm could craft a supermajority charter amendment limited to the choice of domicile for U.S.-traded shares. In the common case in which the foreign firm uses depositary receipts for its U.S. issue (*see generally* Joseph Velli, *American Depositary Receipts: An Overview,* 17 Fordham Int'l L. J. S38 (1994) (providing an overview of the depositary receipts market)), it might be possible for the firm to place a provision in the service contract entered into with the sponsor of the receipts (which the sponsor would enforce) either prohibiting a domicile change or requiring a supermajority vote of the American depositary receipt holders to effect such a change.

173. *See* Romano, *supra* note 4, at 132 (noting that, with the exception of the United Kingdom and the Netherlands, European nations follow the real seat rule).

174. *See generally* John C. Coffee, Jr., *The Unfaithful Champion: The Plaintiff as Monitor in Shareholder Litigation,* Law & Contemp. Probs., Summer 1985, at 5 (discussing the collective action problem in shareholder litigation).

175. *See* Rodriguez v. Shearson/Am. Express, Inc., 490 U.S. 477 (1989); Shearson/Am. Express, Inc. v. McMahon, 482 U.S. 220 (1987); Scherk v. Al-

berto-Culver Co., 417 U.S. 506 (1974) (overruling Wilko v. Swan, 346 U.S. 427 (1953)).

176. The Supreme Court's forum selection clause jurisprudence has especially emphasized the needs of parties engaged in international commercial transactions when sustaining parties' contractual choices. *See, e.g.,* The Bremen v. Zapata Off-Shore Co., 407 U.S. 1, 8–18 (1972).

177. *See id.* at 17–18; *see also supra* note 135 and accompanying text.

178. *See* Born, *supra* note 110, at 395.

179. *See* Daniels, *supra* note 104, at 182–84; *see also supra* text accompanying note 104.

180. Under current law, U.S. courts have imposed U.S. standards on foreign issuers, instead of applying non-U.S. law in their role as a forum court, in a misguided attempt to protect U.S. investors. *See, e.g.,* Consolidated Gold Fields PLC v. Minorco, SA, 871 F.2d 252 (2d Cir.), *modified,* 890 F.2d 569 (2d Cir. 1989) (applying U.S. law to a takeover contest between foreign firms where the bid permitted U.S. residents to tender only if they did so from outside the United States); Leasco Data Processing Equip. Corp. v. Maxwell, 468 F.2d 1326 (2d Cir. 1972) (applying U.S. law to a purchase of stock in a British corporation by a U.S. corporation on the London Stock Exchange). The danger of such conduct continuing under the proposed regime is probably low, given that Congress will have expressly authorized the applicability of non-U.S. law to the transactions.

181. *See* Born, *supra* note 110, at 4. The critical differences in litigation procedures could lead some foreign issuers to consider an alternative approach to the selection of a convenient forum for disputes, such as the use of an international arbitration clause. But it is problematic whether investors would place sufficient value on this approach to make it worthwhile for the issuer to offer arbitration, unless some features of U.S. litigation practices are retained in the arbitration agreement, such as the use of representative actions. Although arbitration is less costly than litigation to pursue an individual claim, the profitability of most securities cases comes from the ability of an attorney to aggregate claims. Despite potential difficulties in claims aggregation, in the international securities context, there is a significant advantage to arbitration over litigation that may make it highly attractive to U.S. investors: It is easier to enforce arbitration awards worldwide because virtually all nations (including the United States) are signatories to the United Nations Convention recognizing arbitration awards, while there is no global treaty concerning the enforcement of judgments. *See* Andreas F. Lowenfeld, International Litigation and Arbitration 332 (West: 1993).

182. *See, e.g.,* Cochrane, *supra* note 159, at 561, S63–65; Fox, *supra* note 157, at 2582; Merritt Fox, The Political Economy of Statutory Reach: U.S. Disclosure Rules in a Globalizing Market for Securities 14–15 (1997) (unpublished manuscript, on file with the *Yale Law Journal*).

183. *See, e.g.,* Cochrane, *supra* note 159, at S61, S63–65 (criticizing applicability of SEC disclosure requirements for NYSE listing); Jill E. Fiach, *Imprudent Power: Reconsidering U.S. Regulation of Foreign Tender Offers,* 87 NW. U. L. Rev. 523, 573–74 (1993) (criticizing applicability of the Williams Act); Pinto, *supra* note 5, at 73 (same).

184. *See, e.g.,* Choi & Guzman, *supra* note 158, at 241 (reviewing possible jurisdictional rules, including site of sale and firms' choice of domicile, and concluding, "This [strict rule of territorial jurisdiction based on the connection the transaction has with the capital markets of the country] is the rule we advocate"); Stephen J. Choi & Andrew T. Guzman, *National Laws, International Money: Regulation in a Global Capital Market,* 65 Fordham L. Rev. 1855, 1895 (1997) [hereinafter Choi & Guzman, *National Laws*] ("[w]e propose a clear and simple rule: all transactions that occur through an exchange or organized market should be considered within the exclusive jurisdictional reach of the country within which the exchange or organized market operates"). In a recent essay, Choi and Guzman's position has evolved from advocating a strict territorial (site-of-sale) approach to an approach similar to this article's issuer securities domicile approach. *See* Stephen J. Choi & Andrew T. Guzman, *Portable Reciprocity: Rethinking the International Reach of Securities Regulation,* 71 S. Cal. L. Rev., 903 (1998).

Choi and Guzman seek to encourage regulatory competition across nations because they believe that different rules are appropriate for different issuers and investors. One reason for their refusal in their earlier articles to advocate the logical implication of regulatory competition, an issuer domicile rather than site-of-sale approach, was that they finessed the question of whether regulatory competition is for the "top" or "bottom" with respect to investor protection. They asserted that the question was complicated and did not need to be resolved because different rules were appropriate for different clienteles. *See, e.g.,* Choi & Guzman, *National Laws, supra,* at 1876. This is an unsatisfactory position because if the competitive race to diversity produced laws disadvantageous to investors (i.e., it was a race for the bottom), there would be no demand for such differentiated regimes. Notwithstanding their contention, it only makes sense to advocate a policy of regulatory diversity if the competition results in regimes that benefit investors (i.e., it is a race for the top).

The inconsistency in Choi and Guzman's initial position becomes more apparent when they sidestep the implications of a policy of regulatory competition for domestic regulation. Relying on the existing practice of a monopolist SEC, they contend that either investors and issuers within a single nation have homogeneous preferences regarding securities regulation or domestic markets do not value diversity produced by competition, and they conclude that the desirability of international regulatory competition is distinguishable from the domestic context. *See id.* at 1882–83. Their justification of local regulatory monopolies stems from a mistaken understanding of the dynamics of competitive federalism: Competition can lead to uniformity, as well as diversity, in substantive law. Moreover, uniformity produced by regulatory competition is more likely to be of benefit to investors than uniformity derived from a noncompetitive regime. *See* William J. Carney, *Federalism and Corporate Law: A Non-Delaware View of the Results of Competition,* in International Regulatory Competition and Coordination: Perspectives on Economic Regulation in Europe and the United States 153, William Bratton et al., eds. (Oxford University Press: 1996), at 169–72 (comparing uniform corporate law produced competitively in the United States with that produced by noncompetitive European harmonization process). There is, finally, little evidence that diverse securities regimes are appropriate for U.S. and non-U.S. multinationals, or for U.S. investors holding such firms, notwithstanding Choi and Guzman's conjecture. Similar product diversity arguments were hypothesized to explain the benefits of state charter competition, yet the data do not support such claims. *See* Romano, *supra* note 4, at 45–48. There is, then, simply no theoretical or empirical basis for distinguishing between domestic and international securities' regulatory competition.

185. *See* Fox, *supra* note 157, at 2580–83; Fox, *supra* note 182, at 14–15.

186. *See, e.g.,* Fox, *supra* note 182, at 34–35.

187. *See supra* Section I.B.

188. *See supra* text accompanying notes 29–32. One study of foreign stock exchange listings found an inverse relation between listings and disclosure requirements, but the exchanges with the lowest level of disclosure did not have the most foreign listings (although the United States, with the highest disclosure level, did have the fewest foreign listings); more important, the inverse relation was not significant when domestic and foreign exchange disclosure levels were compared. *See* Shahrokh M. Saudagaran & Gary C. Biddle, *Financial Disclosure Levels and Foreign Stock Exchange Listing Decisions, in* International Capital Markets in a World of Accounting Differences 159, 181, 184, Frederick D. S. Choi & Richard M. Levich, eds. (Irwin Professional Pub.: 1994). That is, the data do not support the race-for-the-bottom hypothesis that the probability of a firm listing on a given foreign exchange is inversely related to the exchange's disclosure level when its disclosure level is higher than the disclosure level of the firm's domestic exchange. *See id.*

PART VI

PATENTS WITHOUT MONOPOLY

13

Patent Buyouts

A Mechanism for Encouraging Innovation

MICHAEL KREMER

Economic growth ultimately depends on the production of new ideas, but competitive markets do not provide appropriate incentives for the production of ideas. If consumers pay only the marginal cost of transmitting ideas, revenues will be insufficient to cover the cost of producing ideas. Historically, societies have used a wide variety of mechanisms to encourage production of ideas. Some, such as patents and copyrights, provide inventors with monopolies over goods produced using their ideas. Others, such as the National Science Foundation (NSF) and the synthetic fuels program, directly subsidize research. The United States uses both types of mechanisms; for example, government and industry each spent about $13 billion on health research in 1992 (National Science Board 1993).

Creating monopolies in ideas and directly subsidizing research both lead to serious problems. Patents and copyrights create insufficient incentives for original research because inventors cannot fully capture consumer surplus or spillovers of their ideas to other researchers. Patents and copyrights also create static distortions from monopoly pricing and encourage socially wasteful expenditures on reverse engineering to invent around patents.

Under symmetric information and full commitment, the first-best solution to underprovision of ideas is subsidizing research, rather than creating a new set of monopoly price distortions through the patent system (Spence 1984). However, before research is conducted, the government may not know the costs and expected benefits of research, and it may not even be able to conceive of some inventions. Allowing government officials wide discretion to set payments to inventors ex post may lead to rent seeking and to expropriation of investors after their research costs are sunk.

245

In 1839, the government of France combined elements of the patent system and of direct government support of research by purchasing the patent for daguerreotype photography and placing the technique in the public domain. After the patent was bought out, daguerreotype photography was rapidly adopted worldwide and was subject to myriad technical improvements. Such patent buyouts have the potential to eliminate monopoly price distortions and incentives for wasteful reverse engineering, while encouraging original research.

A major challenge for any system of patent buyouts is determining the price. This chapter examines a mechanism through which the private value of patents would be determined using an auction. The government would offer to buy out patents at this private value times a fixed markup that would roughly cover the difference between the social and private values of inventions. Inventors could decide whether to sell or retain their patents. Patents purchased by the government would typically be placed in the public domain. However, in order to provide auction participants with an incentive to truthfully reveal their valuations, the government would randomly select a few patents that would be sold to the highest bidder. Encouraging innovation through such a mechanism would require more discretion by government officials than the current patent system but substantially less discretion than that exercised by, say, the National Institutes of Health.

As discussed by Dutton (1984) and Shavell and Ypserle (1998), the relative merits of rewards and patents were widely debated in the nineteenth century. Macfie (1869), a member of the British Parliament in the nineteenth century, proposed replacing the patent system with a reward system. In this century, Polanyi (1943) suggested replacing patents with rewards based on ex-post estimates of the value of inventions. Guell and Fischbaum (1995) suggest that the government use its power of eminent domain to purchase pharmaceutical patents. They propose that judges determine the buyout price. One problem with allowing broad administrative discretion over the patent buyout price is that this may lead to purchases at confiscatory prices and thus reduce incentives for innovation. Allowing broad discretion may also lead to wasteful expenditures on rent seeking, and if some groups in society are better able to organize politically than others, this rent seeking may distort the pattern of research (Cohen and Noll 1991). This chapter describes how a market mechanism could be used to determine the value of patents. As a safeguard against confiscation of inventions, patent holders could choose whether to sell their patents. Patent buyouts would thus supplement, rather than replace, the existing patent system. Inventors would receive a markup over the private value of the patents to bring incentives for invention closer to the social value. This chapter also differs from Guell and Fischbaum in addressing the problem of creating proper incentives for the development of complementary and substituting inventions. Shavell and Ypserle (1998) argue that a system in which inventors could choose between rewards and patents would be superior to a pure patent system. One problem with a fixed reward is that people could claim rewards for trivial inventions. General Motors could stick a useless piece of metal onto a Chevrolet, and as long as the automobile sold due to other attractive features, the company could argue it deserved the reward. More generally, this chapter is related to a broader literature on the potential of various mechanisms to encourage innovation (Johnston and Zeckhauser 1991; Romer 1993; Taylor 1995; Baker 1996; Lichtman 1997;[1] Scotchmer 1997).

The chapter is organized as follows. Section I argues that the distortions associated with both patents and direct government support of research are severe enough that other methods of encouraging research should be explored. Section II discusses the historical experience of patent buyouts. Section III explains how an auction could be used to estimate the value of patents and thus determine the buyout price. Section IV discusses equilibrium behavior in the auction when inventors have private information about the value of patents or are the low-cost producers of the patented good. Section V discusses incentives for marketing and development of inventions under patent buyouts. Section VI outlines rules that would be necessary to deal with substituting and complementary patents. Perhaps the chief problem with patent buyouts is that they are potentially vulnerable to collusion, because inventors could bribe auction participants to submit high bids. Section VII discusses several ways the government could control collusion. Section VIII argues that patent buyouts should focus on the pharmaceutical industry. It suggests that a limited trial of patent buyouts could be conducted first, perhaps by a private foundation. If the buyouts seem successful, the program could be tried on a larger scale.

I. Mechanisms for Encouraging Innovation

This section argues that the distortions associated with encouraging research through patents and through direct government support of research are sufficiently severe that it is worth investigating additional mechanisms for encouraging innovation.

I.A. Patents

Encouraging research through patents creates static distortions, underinvestment in research, and distortion of research toward duplicating existing inventions.

Static distortions arise as people who value the good above the marginal cost of production do not consume it at the monopoly price. To take a particularly dramatic example, monopoly pricing of the drug AZT makes it impossible for HIV-positive pregnant women in developing countries to prevent transmission to their children, leading to hundreds of thousands, if not millions, of cases of pediatric AIDS. To see that financing research with monopoly profits not only is not first best, but is generically less efficient than financing research through tax revenue, consider the problem of a social planner choosing a tax to finance research. The principles of Ramsey taxation should clearly guide the planner's decision, and it is highly unlikely that the optimal tax will be a several thousand percent tax on the patented good. Yet, financing research by giving monopoly rights to inventors is equivalent to such a tax.

Patents create far too little incentive for original research because potential inventors will not take consumer surplus into account when deciding whether to undertake research. To take another dramatic example, Michael Milken would presumably pay hundreds of millions of dollars for an effective drug to fight prostate cancer, but pharmaceutical companies do not take this into account in setting their research budgets because they will not be able to extract Milken's consumer surplus. Under the crude assumption that willingness to pay for drugs is proportional to income, calculations using U.S. household income distribution data from the 1995 Current Population Survey (CPS) suggest that the social value of new pharmaceuticals is 2.7 times the profits that would be extracted by a monopolist who could not price discriminate. The deadweight loss due to monopoly pricing would be one-quarter of the sum of profits and consumer surplus.[2]

Another reason patents create insufficient research incentives is that they do not reward researchers for the externalities they create for other researchers. Theoretically, these externalities could either be positive, through knowledge spillovers, or negative, through patent races. However, the available empirical evidence suggests that, on balance, researchers usually create positive externalities for other researchers. Jaffe (1986) finds that, controlling for technological opportunities, firms whose neighbors invest more in research and development have more patents per dollar of research and development (R&D) and a higher return to R&D. Cockburn and Henderson (1993, 1994) find similar results for pharmaceutical firms, even after controlling for measures of technical opportunity. They conclude that, "far from 'mining out' opportunities, competitors' research appears to be a complementary activity to own R&D."

An extensive empirical literature suggests that social returns to innovation far exceed the private returns. Nadiri (1993) summarizes this literature and finds that social rates of return to R&D average close to 50 percent. Mansfield et al. (1977) examine seventeen innovations in detail and find an average social rate of return of 56 percent, compared with a 25 percent private rate of return. In his exhaustive study of the CT scanner industry, Trajtenberg (1990) finds that the social return to R&D was 270 percent, orders of magnitude above the private return.

The available evidence thus suggests that the social rate of return on R&D is at least twice the private rate of return, *given the quantities consumed under monopolistic pricing*. The social rate of return would be even greater if inventions were priced at marginal cost so that the deadweight loss due to monopoly pricing was avoided. If deadweight loss due to monopoly pricing is one-quarter of profits plus consumer surplus (as would be the case, given the U.S. income distribution, if willingness to pay were proportional to income), the social return to research under marginal cost pricing would be $2 \times 5/4 = 2.5$ times the private rate of return on research under the current patent system.

Patents also distort the direction of research by creating too much incentive to develop substitutes for patented goods and too little to create complements. By developing substitute inventions, firms can steal rents from existing patent holders. The limited available evidence suggests that this problem may be severe. Mansfield (1981) finds that 60 percent of a sample of patented innovations were imitated within four years, and the average imitation cost was two-thirds the original cost of invention. Potential developers of complementary inventions will have too little incentive to develop these inventions if they must sink costs into developing the complementary inventions before concluding licensing agreements with owners of original patents (Green and Scotchmer 1982). Sometimes, agreements are not reached, perhaps because of asymmetric information, and developments remain unused. For example, the development of the high-pressure steam engine was blocked by Watt's patent covering all steam engines, Watt's steam engine was long blocked by a previous patent until he found a way to invent around it, and Edison's improved version of the telegraph was blocked by Bell's prior patent for many years (Mokyr 1990). In the analysis below, I will generally make the conservative assumption that the social value of patents is on average only twice the private value.

I.B. Direct Government Support of Research

Since ideas are nonrival goods, standard public goods arguments suggest that research should be publicly financed. However, governments' efforts to finance research are plagued by asymmetric information between researchers and governments. When the government pays for research input, rather than output, it is difficult to prevent researchers from shirking, either by applying little effort or by focusing on areas of purely scientific interest. The work of Nadiri (1993), Nadiri and Mamuneas (1994), and Bernstein and Nadiri (1988, 1991) suggests that the rate of return on privately financed R&D is much higher than that on publicly financed R&D. Lichtenberg (1992) makes the extreme estimate that the within-country social return to private R&D is seven times as large as the return to investment in equipment and structures, but the social return to government-funded R&D is insignificantly different from zero.[3]

Paying for research output through prizes creates much stronger incentives for researchers than paying for research inputs through grants. Prizes were more frequently used in the past than they are today, and they stimulated inventions ranging from food canning to the chronometer (Wright 1983). Wright (1983) and Scotchmer (1997) argue, however, that the potential of prizes is limited because governments lack information on the benefits (or even possibility) of many inventions before they have been invented. This would be less of a problem if government could specify prizes ex post, but in this case, the authority awarding prizes may be tempted to expropriate inventors by offering inadequate prizes. This may be a problem even for prizes ostensibly specified ex ante if the rules governing prize awards are not clear. Sobel (1995) relates the difficulties the inventor of the chronometer encountered in claiming the British government's £20,000 prize for a method of determining longitude at sea.[4]

Another problem with direct government support of research is that small groups who are strongly affected by particular government decisions may lobby to influence these decisions, distorting research expenditures (Cohen and Noll 1991; Romer 1993). For example, some argue that lobbying by defense contractors and AIDS activists has distorted the pattern of military and medical research expenditures.

II. Historical Experience of Patent Buyouts

During the early nineteenth century, when both patents and prizes were used to encourage invention, there were at least two cases in which governments combined the patent and prize systems by buying out patents. Such patent buyouts are attractive since they offer the opportunity to eliminate monopoly pricing distortions and incentives for duplicate research, while raising rewards for original research. It is worth exploring how they functioned in practice.

In 1837, Louis Jacques Mande Daguerre invented photography by developing the daguerreotype process. He exhibited images created using the process, and he offered to sell detailed instructions to a single buyer for 200,000 francs or to 100 to 400 subscribers at 1,000 francs each. Daguerre was not able to find a buyer, but he obtained the backing of Francois Arago, a politician and member of the Académie des Sciences, who argued that it was "indispensable that the government should compensate M. Daguerre direct, and that France should then nobly give to the whole world this discovery which could contribute so much to the progress of art and science."[5] In July 1839, the French government purchased the patent in exchange for pensions of 6000 francs per year to Daguerre, 4000 francs to his partner, and half amounts to their widows upon their deaths. The French government then put the rights to Daguerre's patent in the public domain (except in England, where the French government allowed Daguerre's original patent to remain in force). The invention was rapidly adopted and subjected to technological improvements. Within months, Daguerre's instruction manual was translated into a dozen languages. Many complementary inventions improved the chemistry and lenses used in Daguerre's process.

In England, William Fox Talbot had developed the calotype process independently, and when he heard of Daguerre's process, he patented his own system in 1841 (Nelson 1996). The Daguerre process became the standard and the English process was abandoned, perhaps in part because Talbot charged high fees for use of his process. However, twenty years later, a new process was developed, which also involved making prints from negatives, as had Talbot's process. The subsequent development of photography followed this colloidotype process.

Like Daguerre, Eli Whitney was unable to make much money from his patent (Green 1956). The cotton gin could be easily replicated by local carpenters and blacksmiths, and southern juries were creative in finding technicalities on which to rule against Whitney in the many patent infringement suits that he filed. In 1802, facing bankruptcy, Whitney sold the South Carolina rights to the cotton gin to the state government for $50,000, a tiny fraction of the millions of dollars in surplus generated by the invention. In 1803, on rather flimsy pretexts, South Carolina suspended payment on the unpaid balance of its debt to Whitney, sued to recover the money Whitney had already been paid, and even had him arrested. However, the legislature of 1804 reversed the annulment of 1803. Later, Whitney sold the rights to the cotton gin in North Carolina and Tennessee to the state governments in exchange for an agreement that the states would tax cotton gins and pay the proceeds to Whitney.

Rewards have also been used in more modern times. The U.S. Patent Compensation Board compensates developers of innovations of military value relating to atomic energy. The former Soviet Union rewarded process innovators with a percentage of the cost savings created by their invention (Sinnot 1988). It is worth trying to draw a few lessons from the experience of the cotton gin and daguerreotype patent buyouts. In both cases, the government purchased important patents. The political economy problem with patent buyouts does not seem to be that unscrupulous rent seekers bribe government officials to purchase patents for useless inventions but, rather, as Whitney's experience suggests, that once a good is invented, governments may be tempted to expropriate the inventor.

Both the daguerreotype and the cotton gin were adopted rapidly after the patents were bought out, and they were subject to further technological development afterward. Although we do not have evidence on the counterfactual, it seems plausible that the free availability of the inventions led to wider adoption and that this increased incentives and opportunity for the development of technological improvements.

The daguerreotype example indicates that buying patents may increase inventors' incentive to patent discoveries rather than rely on trade secrecy. The release of information on Daguerre's techniques led to positive externalities for other researchers, helping create scientific advances in chemical reactivity and solar spectrum analysis (Barger and White 1991).

A final, cautionary lesson is that buying out patents and putting them in the public domain will reduce adoption of substitute innovations that remain under patent. It seems possible that the daguerreotype process was too widely adopted because it was free, whereas the Talbot process was costly. It is unclear which process was superior, but it is possible that selectively putting patents in the public domain could lead to the adoption of inferior technology.

III. A Mechanism for Buying Out Patents

A key problem in designing any system of patent buyouts is developing a mechanism for determining the price at which patents would be bought out. Ideally, the patent buyout price would be the social value of the invention, because this would provide incentives to invest in research only if the expected social benefit exceeded the cost.[6]

Scotchmer (1997) argues that patents are an optimal way of rewarding research if the value of inventions is private information of the researcher. Although the value of potential inventions may be private information of the researcher before research is conducted, other firms in the industry are likely to have at least some information on the private value of the invention after inventions are patented. This chapter explores one way to use this information to determine a patent buyout price.

A standard way of eliciting information on the value of indivisible goods, such as patents, is through auctions. Figure 13.1 shows how an auction could be used to determine the price at which the government would offer to buy out patents. Under the mechanism, the market value of patents would be determined through a sealed-bid, second-price auction,[7] and the government would then offer to buy patents at this private value times some constant markup which would reflect the typical ratio of social to private value. Most of the patents that the government would buy would be placed in the public domain. However, in order to give auction participants an incentive to reveal their true valuations, a small proportion of patents, chosen randomly, would be sold to the high bidder. Patent holders would have the right to accept or reject the government's offer. Although the government might require a waiting period following either patenting or Food and Drug Administration (FDA) approval of a drug before it would buy out patents, patent holders would be free to postpone patent buyouts. Inventors who wished to sell their patents to the government would be responsible for paying for the administrative costs of the auction.

Based on the empirical estimates of the social return to innovation discussed above, it seems likely that the government should offer to buy patents at a markup of at least twice their estimated private value. This will

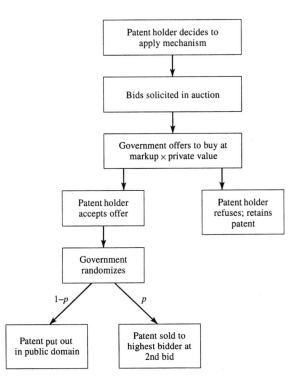

Fig. 13.1 Auction mechanism for patent buyouts.

not match the social value of inventions, but it is likely to be a better approximation than the private value of patents, which is what inventors receive in the absence of patent buyouts.

Under a sealed-bid, second-price auction, auction participants will bid
their expectation of the patent's value, given their information, conditional
on their making the winning bid. It will be efficient for the government to
estimate the private value using information from the entire distribution of
bids, rather than only the highest bid, since there is no reason to throw
away the information provided by the other bids. If the government knew
the prior distribution of valuations, it would be able to aggregate the information of all bidders to estimate the private value of the patent. In practice,
the government does not know the bidders' prior distribution of valuations.
Therefore, it might be best for the government to use a simple rule, such as
offering the original patent holder some multiple of the third highest bid.[8]

The next sections consider the operation of the patent buyout mechanism in several different environments: with inventor cost or informational
advantages, with complementary or substituting inventions, and with the
threat of collusion. As discussed in section VIII, this analysis suggests that

pharmaceuticals may be particularly well suited to patent buyouts. However, before considering these more complicated cases, it is worth first reviewing the advantages of patent buyouts in a perfectly competitive, collusion-free environment.

1. The markup would raise private incentives for original research closer to the social benefit created by the invention.
2. Deadweight losses due to monopoly pricing would be eliminated if patents were put in the public domain.
3. Since monopoly profits would be eliminated, researchers would not have excessive incentives to invent substitutes for existing drugs to steal profits.

IV. Inventor Cost or Informational Advantages

If inventors have private information about the value of the patent or are the low-cost producers of the patented good, they will be more likely to reject the government's offer to buy their patents. This section argues, however, that unless these cost or informational advantages are extreme, the markup will still lead most inventors to sell their patents. In those cases in which inventors do refuse to sell their patents, the system of patent buyouts would be equivalent to the current patent system.

It is useful to consider two polar extremes of auction environments. Subsection IV.A examines the case of a common value auction in which the original inventor is better informed about the patent's value than other bidders are. Subsection IV.B examines the case of a private value auction in which the inventor has the highest value for the patent and there is some dispersion of valuations among bidders.

IV.A. Inventor Informational Advantage

If the inventor has private information about the value of the patent, the winner's curse will lead bidders to make low bids (Milgrom and Weber 1982; Hendricks and Porter 1988; Hendricks, Porter and Wilson 1994). However, the winner's curse may be greatly mitigated by the markup.

Consider an example in which the patent has a common value, the inventor knows this value, and, conditional on the information revealed by the FDA drug-approval process, potential bidders know only that the value is distributed uniformly in (L,U). The bidders will know that if a bid of B leads to the good being sold by the inventor, then the true private value of the patent is uniformly distributed in $(L, \min(U,MB))$, where M is the markup. In equilibrium, auction participants will bid the expected value of the patent, conditional on their bid being accepted, or $(L + \min (U,MB))/2$. This implies that

$$B = \min\left(\frac{L+U}{2}, \max\left[0, \frac{L}{2-M}\right]\right).$$

The markup mitigates an adverse selection problem that could otherwise shut down the market for patents. If $M = 1$, so there is no government markup, auction participants will bid L, and patent owners will never sell their patents. For a markup of 2, auction participants will bid $(L + U)/2$, the government will offer to buy out patents for $L + U$, and patents will always be sold.

This extreme result depends on the assumption that the value of the patent is uniformly distributed. If the distribution of the value of patents conditional on the information available to bidders is skewed, then although adverse selection will be reduced by the markup, it may not be eliminated. The unconditional distribution of the realized value of FDA-approved drugs is extremely skewed (Grabowski and Vernon 1990), but there is likely to be much less variance and skewness in the distribution of the expected value conditional on the information available to bidders, including the number of people suffering from the disease, the availability of competing drugs, and the efficacy and side effects of the drug as revealed during the FDA approval process. Moreover, a skewed distribution of realized values of patents does not necessarily imply a skewed distribution of beliefs about the *expected* value of the patent. After all, the skewness of realized values of lottery tickets is extremely high, but there would be only minor problems of asymmetric information in selling lottery tickets. Note also that inventors will have an incentive to reveal as much information as possible about the invention to reduce adverse selection in bidding. As a referee has pointed out, asymmetric information about the value of inventions makes sales of pharmaceutical patents by small biotech firms to larger pharmaceutical firms complicated, and it sometimes blocks them entirely. Nonetheless, because such transactions frequently take place currently without any government markup, it seems likely that many patents would be sold in the presence of a 100 percent markup.

IV.B. Inventors Who Are Low-Cost Producers

Inventors are often the low-cost producers of their inventions because they own complementary assets, such as marketing networks or unpatented intangible information on production techniques. However, inventors will still typically sell their patents because the government will offer a markup and because the inventor will still be able to produce the good if the patent is placed in the public domain.

To focus on the effect of differences in cost among potential producers, suppose that the inventor can produce at a cost c_0, that the ith lowest cost producer can produce at cost c_i, and that demand for the good is given by

$Q = P^{\alpha}$, where $\alpha < -1$. For a patent holder with cost c_i, the optimal price is $c_i\,\alpha/(\alpha + 1)$, which yields profits of

$$\pi_i = c_i^{1+\alpha}\left(\frac{\alpha}{\alpha + 1}\right)^{\alpha}\left(\frac{-1}{\alpha + 1}\right).$$

Under a second-price, sealed-bid auction, each auction participant will bid its valuation, π_i. Suppose that the government offers to buy out the patent at $MZ\pi_j$, where π_j denotes the value of the jth highest bid, Z is some multiplier, such as the historical ratio of the jth highest bid to the highest bid, and $M > 1$ is the markup. Inventors will sell their patents to the government if $\pi_0 < MZ\pi_j + (1 - p)\pi_{\text{COMP}}$, where π_0 is the value to the inventor of a monopoly on the good, p is the probability that patents purchased by the government will be transferred to the high bidder, and π_{COMP} is the value to the original inventor of producing the good in competition with other firms. If the patent is placed in the public domain and if $c'/c < \alpha/(\alpha + 1)$, so the inventor's cost advantage is not too large relative to the monopoly markup, then under Bertrand competition, the inventor will limit price and obtain profits $\pi_{\text{COMP}} = c_1^{\alpha} + (c_1 - c_0)$.

Given the drastic markups in pharmaceuticals, and the ease of manufacturing most pharmaceuticals, this condition for limit pricing is likely to be fulfilled. However, if the patent is placed in the public domain, if $c_1/c_0 > \alpha/(\alpha + 1)$, so the inventor's cost advantage is drastic, then the inventor will sell the good at the monopoly price and obtain profits π_0. In this case, patent buyouts will not ameliorate monopoly price distortions. This suggests that patent buyouts are likely to be most desirable in industries in which prices would be considerably lower in the absence of patents, such as the pharmaceutical industry. Patent buyouts are also more desirable in industries where cost differences are small, because they would occasionally entail transferring the patent to higher-cost producers. (As discussed in section VII, patent buyers would not be allowed to resell the patent to the original owner because this could facilitate collusion.)

To see why inventors will typically sell their patents, note that if $c_j/c_0 < (MZ)^{-1/(1+\alpha)}$, so the cost advantage is not too great relative to the markup, then $MZ\pi_j > \pi_0$. On the other hand, if $c_1/c_0 > \alpha/(\alpha + 1)$, inventors will sell the patent for sufficiently small p because their monopoly price will not be constrained by competition and, hence, π_0 will equal π_{COMP}.

If potential bidders differ in their valuations but must spend some resources to learn their valuation, the costs of processing information are likely to reduce entry into the auction and hence reduce the average winning bid in equilibrium. Presumably, bidding costs will be smaller relative to the value of the patent for more valuable patents, so bidding costs will be less likely to deter bidding on pharmaceuticals, which have already undergone FDA approval and thus are likely to be valuable.

Despite the markup, there will be cases in which asymmetric infrastructure, cost advantages, or bidding costs lead bids to be so low that the inventor will refuse to sell the patent. In such cases, existing patent rules will remain in force and (abstracting from administrative costs) nothing will have been gained or lost by the procedure. Because inventors who wish to sell their patents would be responsible for covering the administrative costs of the auction, they would not use the mechanism in those cases in which they anticipated bids would less than half the value of the invention. Hence, the administrative costs of the auction would not be incurred in those cases in which it is clear that the mechanism would not succeed.

V. Incentives for Product Development

Incentives for marketing and development are likely to be enhanced by patent buyouts. Suppose that the private value of a patent is $\pi(E)$, where E denotes expenditures on development and marketing. In the absence of patent buyouts, patent owners will invest in development until $\partial\pi/\partial E = 1$. Patent owners who expect to sell their patent at a markup of M will invest until $\partial\pi/\partial E = 1/M$. Inventors would be free to delay patent sales to first undertake development and marketing if they wished.

Some opportunities for further development may appear only after patents have been sold. For example, technological advances in related fields may open up new opportunities for development after the patent has been bought out. Patent buyouts will strengthen incentives for this further development if it can be patented or appropriated in some other way. This is because the market for a complementary invention will be larger if the original invention is sold at marginal cost. Moreover, the developer of the complementary invention will not have to split its value with the original inventor or take the risk that unresolved patent disputes with the original inventor will block new complementary products.

Although patent buyouts increase inventors' incentive to conduct development prior to the buyout and increase others' incentives to conduct development after the buyout, they reduce inventors' incentives to conduct unpatentable development after patent buyouts. For example, pharmaceutical firms have much less incentive to test for new uses for generic drugs than for patented drugs. In practice, there may be other ways of appropriating investment in marketing and development. For example, some aspirin manufacturers have sufficient market power that even without patent protection they advertise aspirin's effectiveness in preventing heart attacks. The substantial technological improvements to the daguerreotype process and the cotton gin after the patents were bought out provide at least some suggestion that patent buyouts do not greatly discourage further technological development. In any case, pharmaceuticals typically need little new development after they have been approved by the FDA.[9]

VI. Substitute and Complementary Patents

Anticipation that future substitute patents will be bought out will reduce current research incentives in two ways. As subsection VI.A shows, patent buyouts act as a subsidy to research, increasing the chance that future substitutes will be developed quickly. To attain the socially optimal level of research, the markup must therefore be greater than the ratio of the social value of inventions to their private value *given the current level of research*. Subsection VI.B shows that anticipated buyouts of substitute patents also deter current research by causing future patents to be placed in the public domain and thus to be more formidable competitors. In order to preserve incentives for current research, patent buyouts would incorporate a rule that if a patent remains in private hands and a substitute patent is put up for auction, the holder of the original patent could have it jointly randomized with the new patent. Either both patents would be placed in the public domain or both patents would be transferred to their respective high bidders. Complementary patents would also be jointly randomized, as discussed in subsection VI.C.

VI.A. Patent Buyouts as Research Subsidies

The expectation that future patent buyouts will encourage research on substitutes will partially offset the tendency for the markup to spur research. The optimal markup will therefore be greater than the current ratio of the social value of inventions to their private value. To see this, consider models of creative destruction, such as those of Aghion and Howitt (1992) and Grossman and Helpman (1991), in which each invention is eventually subject to competition from future inventions. Under these models, research at time t, x_t, can be written as $x_t = \varphi(M_t, x_{t+1})$, where M_t is the subsidy to research at time t, $\varphi_1 > 0$, and $\varphi_2 < 0$. Suppose that there is a constant markup M. Denote the research effort that would be chosen by a social planner as x^s. I assume that x^s is greater than x^p, the level of research undertaken in the absence of patent buyouts.[10] The optimal markup M^s solves $x^s = \varphi(M^s, x^s)$. The optimal markup will be the typical ratio of the social value of inventions to their private value, given that the socially optimal amount of research will be conducted in the future. M^s is greater than the markup needed to induce research x^s given the expectation that future patents will not be bought out, M^p, since M^p solves $x^s = \varphi(M^p, x^p)$. To see the intuition, note that the expected lifetime of patents, and hence their private value, will be lower if more research is expected in the future. Hence, the ratio of social to private value under patent buyouts will be greater than the ratio of social to private value without patent buyouts. This implies that the optimal markup is even larger than the figure of 2 to 3.33 suggested by section II.

VI.B. Joint Randomization for Substitute Patents

Patent buyouts at time $t + 1$ may reduce incentives for research at time t not only by encouraging research at time $t + 1$, but also by causing inventions at time $t + 1$ to be placed in the public domain and sold at marginal cost and thus to be more formidable competitors for inventions developed at time t.[11] As explained below, incentives for current research can be preserved by holding a joint randomization to determine whether substitute patents would each be put into the public domain or transferred to their respective high bidders.

To see why anticipated patent buyouts with separate randomization could weaken current research incentives, note that bids for a new patent would be reduced by the likelihood that future substitutes will be put in the public domain. For example, people would bid less for a patent on Prozac if they expected that the patent on Zoloft would be put in the public domain. (This point is shown formally in an unpublished version of this chapter [Kremer 1998].)

Joint randomization could preserve incentives for current research. It would work as follows: If the patent on one invention was in private hands, and a substitute was invented and put up for auction, the holder of the original patent could ask for it to be re-auctioned at the same time as the substitute patent. Prospective buyers would bid on each patent separately, but the government would conduct a single randomization to determine whether the original and substitute patents would be put in the public domain or whether each would be sold to the high bidder in its auction.[12]

Note that joint randomization does not require a bureaucracy to judge whether goods are substitutes. Any patent holder could claim that his patent was a substitute for a new patent and request that it be jointly randomized with the new patent. Even if the new patent was not, in fact, a substitute for the old patent, jointly randomizing the old patent together with an unrelated new patent would create no harm and would have the advantage of possibly transferring another patent to the public domain.

Under joint randomization, each patent will be valued based on the contingency that both it and a possible future substitute stay in private hands, as discussed in Kremer (1998). Joint randomization or reversion to the existing patent system would occur only if the original patent remained in private hands. Presumably, these cases would be rare because most patents would be sold to the government and placed in the public domain.

The analysis above assumes that demand for the original invention is affected only by the contemporaneous price of the substitute, not the expected future price. This assumption seems appropriate for nondurable goods—that is, goods that are destroyed when they are consumed, such as most pharmaceuticals. However, as discussed in Kremer [1998], demand for durable, nonrentable goods will be reduced by anticipated buyouts of future substitute patents, even under joint randomization. Patent buyouts along the lines discussed in this chapter may therefore be less appropriate for such patents.

VI.C. Joint Randomization for Complementary Patents

Whereas anticipation that substitute patents will be put in the public domain reduces the price at which patents are bought out, anticipation that complementary patents will be bought out increases the buyout price. Under separate patent buyouts, inventors are paid the marginal value of their inventions, conditional on the other complementary patents being bought out. The sum of these marginal values may be greater than the total value of a set of complementary inventions.

To see this in a simple case, consider an example in which two complementary inventions each have private value 0.1π individually but have value π together, and suppose that the social value of the patents alone or together is twice their private value. If one patent is put in the public domain, then the reward for invention of the other patent will be 0.9π times the markup. This implies that under separate patent buyouts the developers of *each* patent can expect to receive approximately 0.9π times the markup, because bidders for the first patent will anticipate that the second patent is likely to be put in the public domain, and by the time the second patent has been invented, the first patent will probably be in the public domain. This will create excessive incentives for creation of the pair of inventions because the social value of the pair is only 2π. (It would also create an incentive for inventors to divide up inventions into multiple complementary patents.)

To reduce the possibility that the government pays more than the social value of complementary patents, and to avoid creating incentives for inventors to split up inventions into multiple patents, the government should not separately purchase complementary patents. Patent owners who do not wish to sell jointly would not have to sell their patents, but they would not be eligible for future, separate patent buyouts. Inventors who sell one patent to the government would not be eligible to sell future complementary patents to the government until after a waiting period elapsed.

If a set of drugs were complementary, the government would offer to buy out the set together, and if the offer were refused, the government would then offer to buy out only a (randomly selected) single member of the set. A markup of two suffices to ensure that a single owner of an arbitrary number of complementary patents will always prefer to sell all the patents to the government rather than sell one patent and retain the others.[13]

If complementary patents were held by different owners, the government would solicit bids both on those patents belonging to each owner and on the entire set of complementary patents. If the owners could not agree to a joint sale, the government would offer to buy the patents controlled by one owner picked randomly, with probability proportional to the estimated value of his patents.

The government could determine whether the patents were very strong complements by looking at the pattern of bids. If a set of patents are complements, the sum of the bids for subsets will be less than the bids for the entire set (assuming that the bidders anticipate that they will not perfectly cooperate in pricing the goods after buying out the patents). If the government mistakenly classified patents as complements and refused to buy out each patent separately, patent owners would not be harmed if they agreed to sell jointly, and even if they could not agree to sell jointly, they would still be better off than under the current patent system, so long as at least one member of the set of complementary patents was put in the public domain.

One of the advantages of buying out patents for pharmaceuticals is that complementary patents are considerably less common in pharmaceuticals than in other industries. Whereas in many fields inventions are typically protected by several patents, pharmaceuticals are much more often protected by a single patent.[14] This is in part because a new drug is often a particular molecule and in part because the FDA approval process is so expensive that it does not make sense to break a drug into two separate drugs, each of which would have to be approved separately. Of course, some drugs are complements. For example, a chemotherapy drug may create side effects, and another drug may alleviate those side effects.

VII. Preventing Collusion

The auction mechanism is potentially vulnerable to collusion because patent holders would have an incentive to bribe auction participants to bid high. The bidder would only have to pay the government with probability p. However, with 100 percent probability, the patent holder would receive an inflated payment. It is impossible to eliminate collusion, but, as subsection VII.A explains, a variety of mechanisms could be used to minimize collusion. Subsection VII.B discusses how the prices paid by the government for patents could be limited by ceiling prices based on actual sales of the patented pharmaceutical.

VII.A. Mechanisms for Preventing Collusion

The government could make collusion more difficult using standard procedures such as requiring bids to be sealed, punishing companies and individuals found guilty of collusion, and rewarding whistle-blowers. This would make collusion more difficult and more dangerous. Several additional methods specific to patent buyouts could also be used:

1. The government would base the price it offers the inventor on the third highest bid. The original patent holder would therefore have

to bribe three companies instead of one to ensure a substantial increase in the buyout price. This should significantly increase both the difficulty of collusion and the chance of detection.

2. The agency purchasing patents could have authority to call the bluff of suspected overbidders by reducing the markup and selling to the high bidder without randomization in a set percentage of cases. For example, suppose that, based on the other bids and any knowledge of the industry, the government's best estimate of the patent's value was π. If a bidder offered $\pi + x$ and the agency suspected collusion,[15] the government could offer to buy out the patent at $\pi + \$1$ and then require the suspected colluding bidder to purchase the patent at its bid of $\pi + x$. The government would make a profit of $x - 1$ from the attempted collusion.

3. The government could develop lists of suspect bidders by checking whether winning bidders made money, since systematic overbidders would incur big losses.

4. To prevent inventors from forming front companies and having them submit high bids, bidders would have to provide information on any ties they had with the inventor. Bidders who lied about financial ties with the inventor would be subject to prosecution.

5. Bidders could be required to pay a licensing fee or deposit allowing them to participate in a number of auctions. This would make it unprofitable for patent holders to set up dummy companies simply to bid on their own patents.

Excluding bidders will be costly if there are only a few potential bidders, but there will often be many potential bidders because it is straightforward to manufacture most drugs, as evidenced by the fact that there are often many different producers of generic drugs. (For example, fourteen firms produce oral albuterol sulfate.) Any system of patent buyouts that relies on auctioning patents should focus on drugs that are easy to produce, rather than those that require complicated manufacturing facilities.

6. To prevent inventors from developing a reputation for buying back their patents at inflated prices, inventors would be prohibited from buying back the patent from the winning bidder or making other payments to bidders. Preventing these side payments might be one of the most difficult aspects of preventing collusion.

At least in the early years of any program of patent buyouts, the government agency administering the program would presumably have a budget for patent buyouts and would not be able to afford all the patents that were available for purchase. One option would be to allow the agency to choose which patents to purchase, so that if the price for a particular patent was too high, it could decline to purchase the patent and cancel the randomization. This would tend to reduce collusion because raising the patent buyout price would reduce the chance that the patent would be bought out.

VII.B. Ceiling Prices

Because patent sales are voluntary, the private value of the patent acts as a
floor on the patent buyout price. If the mechanisms for limiting collusion
discussed in the previous subsection were thought inadequate, there are
several ways that governments could establish ceiling prices and thus reduce the risk of paying vastly inflated sums for patents.

1. A waiting period of several years could be required before patents
   were bought by the government, and ceiling prices could be set as
   a multiple of annual revenues prior to the patent buyout. A waiting period would also make it easier for bidders to assess the value
   of patents and would further guarantee that inventors would have
   incentives for marketing and development. Of course, setting ceiling prices as a multiple of prebuyout revenue would lead firms to
   artificially boost sales, for example, by offering hospitals discounts
   on other drugs in exchange for purchasing the patented drug or
   even by paying outright kickbacks. Tied sales would have to be
   prohibited. A second ceiling could be established based on the
   prebuyout price times postbuyout consumption.
2. The amount paid for patents could be capped by total sales of the
   drug following the patent buyout times an administrative estimate
   of the social value of the drug per dose or per patient. International
   estimates of the cost in disability-adjusted life years of various diseases are already available. These could be combined with information on drug effectiveness from FDA trials to estimate a ceiling
   price per dose. Setting these ceilings requires administrative discretion, but the associated rent seeking may be limited by the fact
   that setting a ceiling only requires a fairly transparent decision
   about the social value of the drug per dose. Public interest groups
   could monitor attempts to set outrageous prices per dose more easily than they can monitor whether the National Institutes of Health
   (NIH) are subsidizing pure science in the guise of developing an
   AIDS vaccine or whether national laboratories and breeder reac-
   tors are being created for pork barrel or scientific reasons. The historical record suggests that the political economy problem in setting patent buyout prices is more that governments have an
   incentive to expropriate inventors ex post than that inventors
   wrangle huge sums for unimportant products.
3. It also might be worth considering a mechanism like that in figure
   13.2, with a ceiling price based on the actual profits obtained from
   the new drug. Inventors who wished to participate would have
   their patents randomized. The patent would be randomized to the
   high bidder with some probability p and placed in the public domain with probability $1 - p$. Inventors would be paid only if the
   patent was randomized to the high bidder. In this case, they would
   receive $(M/p) \min(\text{bid}, \pi)$, where M is the markup, bid is the estimated value of the patent based on the bids, and π is the realized

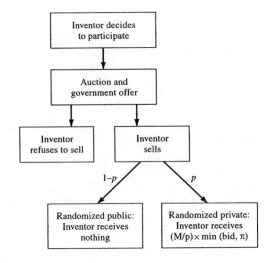

Fig. 13.2 Patent buyouts with ceiling price.

revenue (or, ideally, profits) from the drug. The expected payment received by the inventor is thus M min (bid, π).[16]

Inventors could try to manipulate the ceiling price by bribing the high bidder to boost sales artificially through tie-ins with other products. The government would have to monitor bidders carefully to minimize such tie-ins. Although tie-ins will cost the government money, they will not necessarily reduce efficiency, since by increasing sales they may counteract the static distortions created by monopoly pricing. The majority of patents would be put in the public domain so the issue would not arise, and in any case, it is likely to be difficult for firms to greatly increase demand artificially for drugs covering serious sharply defined diseases, such as cystic fibrosis.

It is easy to dream up scenarios under which people could evade rules designed to discourage collusion, but it is also important to remember that many institutions that are theoretically vulnerable to collusion operate relatively well. For example, peer review is highly vulnerable to collusion, yet the NSF and NIH seem relatively effective. Moreover, limited collusion is not necessarily that harmful. Collusion itself is not a problem; deadweight losses due to collusion are a problem, and there is little reason to think that these deadweight losses would exceed the deadweight losses due to insufficient original research, monopoly-price distortions, and the diversion of effort to "me too" research in the absence of patent buyouts. Even if collusion raises patent prices above their social value, the social value of inventions may be approximated better by the collusive price than by the existing patent system, under which private incentives for developing new inventions are likely to be less than half the social value of the inventions. Finally, if implicit collusion were expected to significantly raise patent prices, then the markup over the private value could be reduced accordingly. For example, if the optimal markup were three (as seems plausible), and if collusion were thought to raise prices by up to 50 percent, then the government could simply offer a markup of two.

The auction mechanism described in this chapter may be appropriate for many pharmaceuticals, but it would not be appropriate in industries where markets are too thin for auctions or patents are not an effective means of protecting inventions. In such industries, the government could simply offer to buy out patents for an amount equal to postbuyout sales times an administratively determined estimate of the average consumer surplus per unit of the good consumed.

VIII. Conclusion: Trial Patent Buyouts

Previous sections have examined the potential of patent buyouts to supplement our current system of promoting innovations through patents and direct government support of research. The government could offer to buy out patents at their private value, as revealed by an auction, times a markup designed to cover the difference between the private and social values of inventions. This mechanism involves more government discretion than the current patent system but substantially less discretion than government funding of research through the NSF or NIH. Patent buyouts could potentially increase incentives for original invention closer to their social value, reduce incentives for wasteful "me too" research, and eliminate monopoly pricing distortions. On the other hand, patent buyouts could also cause a number of problems, including collusion to raise buyout prices.

When new institutions are proposed, there is a natural tendency to focus on their potential risks and shortcomings. However, it is also important to recognize that existing mechanisms of encouraging innovation have serious flaws. In an 1851 editorial (cited by Dutton [1984]) urging that patents be abolished, *The Economist* wrote that the granting of patents "inflames cupidity, excites fraud, stimulates men to run after schemes . . . begets disputes and quarrels betwixt inventors, provokes endless lawsuits [and] makes men ruin themselves for the sake of getting the privilege of a patent. . . . " All this is true, and yet it seems clear that the world is much better off with patents than without them. The same may be true for patent buyouts.

Because it is difficult to gauge the effects of patent buyouts based on theory alone, and because large-scale patent buyouts would be risky, it might be useful to first try patent buyouts on a limited basis. Such a trial could help determine whether inventors would sell their patents and whether bids would be substantially greater than realized profits or revenues, as would be the case if collusion were severe. This would help policymakers judge whether patent buyouts should be abandoned, redesigned, or used more widely.

Pharmaceuticals are a natural area to try patent buyouts because markets would be relatively competitive in the absence of patents, patent protection is effective, monopoly markups are large, drugs are nondurable, "me too" inventions are widespread, and considerable information is generated during FDA trials so potential bidders could make informed bids.[17] Moreover, because many pharmaceutical patents are valuable, the administrative costs of the system are likely to be small relative to the benefits of patent buyouts. Once FDA approval has been granted, little new development is typically required.

Finally, buying out pharmaceutical patents is likely to have benign distributional consequences, whereas buying out, say, patents for improved yachts will not. Financing pharmaceutical research through patents places the financing burden on disease victims. If disease incidence is random, and not fully insurable, people will prefer ex ante to insure themselves by funding the research out of general tax revenue.

The system could initially be applied to treatments for a few specific diseases considered to be particularly important or particularly subject to problems resulting from the patent system. Orphan drug legislation provides a precedent for establishing special rules for drugs designed to treat particular diseases.

A private foundation could conduct an initial trial of patent buyouts. If the experience of the foundation patent buyout was positive, the government could consider appropriating, say, $100 million from general revenue or from the NIH budget for patent buyouts.

One precedent for innovative philanthropic support of research is the million dollar prize established by the Rockefeller Foundation for invention of a diagnostic test for gonorrhea and chlamydia suitable for use in developing countries. The social value of such a diagnostic test is likely to far exceed the private value, since gonorrhea and chlamydia are believed to increase the likelihood of HIV transmission three- to fivefold (Rockefeller Foundation 1997). Although gonorrhea and chlamydia are easily treated, millions of people go untreated because tests suitable for use in developing countries are not available. The prospect of patents does not seem to have encouraged sufficient research on diagnostic tests and, in any case, monopoly pricing of such diagnostic tests might dramatically reduce the number of people tested and treated, spurring the spread of HIV.

A shortcoming of prizes, including the Rockefeller Foundation Prize, is that they do not allow for trade-offs among various performance criteria. To be eligible for the Rockefeller Foundation Prize, diagnostic tests must be 99 percent accurate, take less than twenty minutes, require no more power than can be delivered by a nine-volt battery, be storable for six months in tropical conditions, cost less than U.S. $0.25 per device to manufacture, and be usable by health workers with only primary education after two hours of training (Rockefeller Foundation 1997). Ideally, the specifications would be much more flexible, since it is possible that it would be very hard to design a test that would exactly meet the Rockefeller Foundation's specifications but easy to create a test that was slightly less accurate, but much cheaper, faster, and simpler to use.

Perhaps the Rockefeller Foundation should consider announcing that if the prize has not been claimed by the date the offer expires (March 1, 1999), it would consider using the funds to buy out a patent on a diagnostic test that does not completely fulfill the prize criteria. The foundation might want to buy only part of the patent rights, given the limited funds it is making available. For example, the foundation might buy out the last ten years of the patent. In such an auction, the auction participants would bid for the full rights to the patent, with probability $1 - p$ the foundation would offer to buy out the last ten years of the patent for its estimated full value, and with probability p the foundation would buy out the patent fully, at twice its estimated full value, and then sell the patent rights to the highest bidder at the second highest bid.

This chapter has examined the use of auctions to determine patent buyout prices, but the general approach to limiting government discretion through public auctions may be more widely applicable. Optimal mechanism design often requires decisions tailored either to individuals or to small numbers of agents. However, government rules typically restrict the use of some types of information. For example, civil service rules limit discretion over pay and promotion decisions. Similarly, there are extensive rules restricting what types of evidence are admissible in trials, even though other information could shift priors. This chapter has considered a system that allows governments to tailor decisions to individuals without allowing unlimited government discretion over small numbers of people. To induce people to reveal the information needed by the government, an auction is held in which bidders need only be awarded the item with a small probability. I am currently exploring whether a similar mechanism can be used to determine a price at which taxpayers would be allowed to purchase exemption from distortionary taxation.

Notes

I thank Susan Athey, Edward Drozd, Glenn Ellison, Sara Ellison, Edward Glaeser, Zvi Grilliches, Rebecca Henderson, Bengt Holmstrom, Eric Maskin, John Matsuzaka, Atif Mian, Rob Porter, Paul Romer, Andrei Sarychev, Steven Shavell, Kenneth Sokoloff, two anonymous referees, and the editor for comments and discussions, and Elizabeth Beasley and Sarah Jatko for research assistance.

1. Lichtman (1997) has suggested that the government subsidize low-valuation consumers to avoid distortions from monopoly pricing through a form of price discrimination. Note that targeting subsidies to low-valuation consumers

requires that the government have lots of information, and that if the patent owner had this information, he could price discriminate. Moreover, Lichtman's proposal does not bring private research incentives in line with social incentives.

2. Price discrimination may reduce this deadweight loss, but it is unlikely to allow pharmaceutical companies to capture much of the consumer surplus from the tail of high-income, high-valuation customers.

3. However, see Toole (1997) for an alternative view.

4. However, others are more sympathetic to the prize administrators (Paul David, personal communication).

5. Cited in Nelson (1996).

6. Many readers may think that this rule needs to be modified to take account of the deadweight loss associated with taxation; for an argument that such adjustment should not be made, see Kaplow (1996).

7. Sealing the bids may make collusion more difficult.

8. Because this type of rule is robust to outliers, it makes the system less prone to disruption by a few crazy bidders or, as discussed in section V, by collusion. For example, if it were thought that the social value of inventions was typically M times the private value, the private value was Y times the value of the highest bid, and the highest bid was typically Z times the third highest bid, then the government would offer MYZ times the third highest bid.

9. If complete patent buyouts prevented development, the mechanism could be modified to allow some market power in newly invented goods. For example, the government could offer to buy out the last ten years of a patent after it had been in private hands for seven years. Alternatively, rather than placing patents in the public domain, the government could sell a limited number of licenses to produce the good, converting what would have been a monopoly into an oligopoly.

10. Although equilibrium research effort may be either greater or less than optimal in models of creative destruction, the empirical evidence suggests that the current patent system produces too little research and development (Jones and Williams 1995).

11. This effect does not arise in the Aghion and Howitt model because they assume that all inventions are drastic.

12. If the original inventor had not previously sold the original patent to the government, then the government would pay a markup on the original patent, but if the original had been through a previous patent buyout, the government would not pay a second markup.

13. To see this, note that the patent owner will receive $M\pi$ in exchange for a set of patents that are worth π together and zero alone. The owner would receive a maximum of $M\pi/2$ in exchange for all but one of the patents. The remaining patent will be worth π with probability $1 - p$ and a maximum of $\pi/2$ with probability p. The owner will therefore prefer to sell all the patents as long as $M\pi > M\pi/2 + (1 - p)\pi + p\pi/2$, or equivalently, if $2 - p < M$.

14. Sometimes a new drug will be protected both by a product patent and by process patents on techniques manufacturing. The government could refuse to buy process patents separately and only agree to buy product patents when sold together with any associated process patents.

15. Collusion could be indicated by an abnormally high variance of bids, entry of companies that had not participated in the past, or high bids by suspected colluders relative to those from a known group of "honest" bidders.

16. This mechanism does not require the inventor to bear nearly as much risk as it may seem at first glance. Inventors should be able to insure themselves at rates that are close to actuarially fair against the possibility that the patent will be randomized to the high bidder, since this probability is objective and known to all (unlike the value of patents, about which inventors may have private information). Inventors would sign contracts under which they would receive x in every state of the world and pay x/p if their patents were sold to the high bidder. Risk-averse inventors would like to buy enough insurance to receive $ME[\min (\text{bid},\pi)]$ in every state of the world, where the expectation is taken conditional on the inventors' information.

17. Distortions in the market for health care may actually strengthen the case for buying out pharmaceutical patents. Although people may consume too much health care due to subsidies, subsidies for pharmaceuticals are generally smaller than for alternative, more expensive, treatments, such as surgery, so pharmaceutical subsidies may be desirable on second-best grounds.

References

Aghion, Philippe, and Peter Howitt, "A Model of Growth through Creative Destruction," *Econometrica*, LX (March 1992) 323–51.

Baker, Dean, "The High Cost of Protectionism: The Case of Intellectual Property Claims," mimeo, 1996.

Barger, M. Susan, and William B. White, *The Daguerreotype* (Washington, D.C., and London: Smithsonian Institute Press, 1991).

Bernstein, J., and M. I. Nadiri, "Interindustry R&D, Rates of Return, and Production in High-Tech Industries," *American Economic Review*, LXXVIII (1988), 429–34.

———, "Product Demand, Cost of Production, Spillovers, and the Social Rate of Return to R&D," NBER Working Paper No. 3625, January 1991.

Cockburn, Ian, and Rebecca Henderson, "Racing to Invest: The Dynamics of Competition in Ethical Drug Discovery," Massachusetts Institute of Technology, Sloan School of Management, September 1993.

———, "Racing or Spilling? The Determinants of Research Productivity in Ethical Drug Discovery," Massachusetts Institute of Technology, Sloan School of Management, 1994.

Cohen, Linda R., and Roger G. Noll, *The Technology Pork Barrel* (Washington, D.C.: Brookings, 1991).

Dutton, H. I., *The Patent System and Inventive Activity During the Industrial Revolution 1750–1852* (Manchester: Manchester University Press, 1984).

Grabowski, Henry, and John Vernon, "A New Look at the Returns and Risks to Pharmaceutical R&D," *Management Science*, XXXVI, No. 7 (July 1990).

Green, Constance M., *Eli Whitney and the Birth of American Technology* (Boston: Little, Brown and Company, 1956).

Green, Jerry R., and Susanne Scotchmer, "Antitrust Policy, the Breadth of Patent Protection and the Incentive to Develop New Products," Harvard Institute for Economic Research Discussion Paper No. 1467, Cambridge, Mass., 1982.

Grossman, Gene M., and Elehanan Helpman, *Innovation and Growth in the Global Economy* (Cambridge, Mass.: MIT Press, 1991).

Guell, Robert C., and Fischbaum, Marvin, "Toward Allocative Efficiency in the Prescription Drug Industry," *The Milbank Quarterly*, LXXIII (1995), 213–29.

Hendricks, Kenneth, and Robert H. Porter, "An Empirical Study of an Auction with Asymmetric Information," *American Economic Review*, LXXVIII (1988), 865–83.

Hendricks, Kenneth, Robert H. Porter, and Charles A. Wilson, "Auctions for Oil and Gas Leases with an Informed Bidder and a Random Reservation Price," *Econometrica*, LXII (November 1994), 1415–44.

Jaffe, Adam, "Technological Opportunity and Spillovers of R&D: Evidence from Firms' Patents, Profits, and Market Value," *American Economic Review*, LXXVI (December 1986), 984–1001.

Johnston, Mark, and Richard Zeckhauser, "The Australian Pharmaceutical Subsidy Gambit: Transmuting Deadweight Loss and Oligopoly Rents to Consumer Surplus," NBER Working Paper No. 3783, July 1991.

Jones, Charles I., and John Williams, "Too Much of A Good Thing? The Economics of Investment in R&D," Working Paper, August 1995.

Kaplow, Louis, "The Optimal Supply of Public Goods and the Distortionary Cost of Taxation," *National Tax Journal*, XLIX (December 1996), 513–33.

Kremer, Michael, "Patent Buyouts: A Mechanism for Encouraging Innovation," available from the author or the Massachusetts Institute of Technology, 1998.

Lichtenberg, Frank R., "R&D Investment and International Productivity Differences," National Bureau of Economic Research Working Paper No. 4161, 1992.

Lichtman, Douglas G., "Pricing Prozac," Yale Law School Working Paper, 1997.

Macfie, R. A., *Recent Discussions on the Abolition of Patents for Inventions* (London: Longmans, Green, Reader, and Dyer, 1869).

Mansfield, Edwin, et al., *The Production and Application of New Industrial Technology* (New York: W. W. Norton & Company, 1977).

Mansfield, Edwin, Mark Schwartz, and Samuel Wagner, "Imitation Costs and Patents: An Empirical Study," *Economic Journal*, XCI (December 1981), 907–18.

Milgrom, Paul, and Robert Weber, "The Value of Information in a Sealed-Bid Auction," *Journal of Mathematical Economics*, X (June 1982), 105–14.

Mokyr, Joel, *The Lever of Riches: Technological Creativity and Economic Progress* (New York: Oxford University Press, 1990).

Nadiri, M. Ishaq, "Innovations and Technological Spillovers," NBER Working Paper No. 4423, 1993.

Nadiri, M. Ishaq, and Theofanis P. Mamuneas, "The Effects of Public Infrastructure and R&D Capital on the Cost Structure and Performance of U.S. Manufacturing Industries," *Review of Economics and Statistics*, LXXVI (February 1994), 22–37.

National Science Board, *Science and Engineering Indicators* (Washington, D.C.: U.S. Government Printing Office, 1993).

Nelson, Kenneth E., *A Thumbnail Sketch of Daguerreotypes*, The Daguerrian Society, 1996, http://java.austinc.edu/dag/resources/history/.

Polanyi, Michael, "Patent Reform," *Review of Economic Studies*, XI (1943), 61–76.

The Rockefeller Foundation, *The STD Diagnostics Challenge: Rules and Regulations* (New York: The Rockefeller Foundation, February 1997).

Romer, Paul, "Implementing a National Technology Strategy with Self-Organizing Industry Investment Boards," National Bureau of Economic Research, reprint No. 1870, 1993.

Scotchmer, Suzanne, "On the Optimality of the Patent System," University of California, Berkeley Working Paper No. 236, October 1997.

Shavell, Steven, and Tanguy van Ypserle, "Rewards versus Intellectual Property Rights," mimeo, Harvard Law School, 1998.

Sinnot, John P., *World Patent Law and Practice*, Volume 2M (New York: Matthew Bender, 1998).

Sobel, Dava, *Longitude* (New York: Walker and Company, 1995).

Spence, Michael, "Cost Reduction, Competition and Industry Performance," *Econometrica*, LII (January 1984), 101–21.

Taylor, Curtis R., "Digging for Golden Carrots: An Analysis of Research Tournaments," *American Economic Review*, LXXXV (September 1995), 872–90.

Toole, Andrew, "The Impact of Federally Funded Basic Research on Industrial Innovation: Evidence from the Pharmaceutical Industry," mimeo, Christensen Associates, Madison, Wis., 1997.

Trajtenberg, Manuel, *Economic Analysis of Product Innovation: The Case of CT Scanners* (Cambridge, Mass.: Harvard University Press, 1990).

Wright, Brian D., "The Economics of Invention Incentives: Patents, Prizes, and Research Contracts," *American Economic Review*, LXXIII (September 1983), 691–707.

PART VII

URBAN TRANSIT

14

Curb Rights

Eliciting Competition and Entrepreneurship
in Urban Transit

DANIEL B. KLEIN, ADRIAN T. MOORE, AND BINYAM REJA

Urban transit in the United States has long been dominated by government ownership and regulation, and it has been declining steadily in ridership and productivity (APTA 1995). An economist-cum-policymaker would seek to inject competition and entrepreneurship into the sector by privatizing it. The two types of privatization often advocated are contracting out and "free competition" (Department of Transportation 1984; Lave 1985; Gomez-Ibanez and Meyer 1993). Experience has shown, however, that each approach has serious shortcomings.

Contracting out allows government officials to set routes, fares, and the types of vehicles to be used, while putting production and operations in the hands of cost-conscious private companies. Small cities and counties have increasingly contracted out bus service. Larger transit agencies have a harder time establishing major contracting programs, in part because of privileges granted to transit unions. Contracting has reduced costs significantly (Teal 1988, 218–19; Perry, Babitsky, and Gregersen 1988, 134–35), but contracts, even when competitively let, preserve transit monopoly and service regimentation. Transit agencies use various contracting schemes, which Williamson (1976) and Goldberg (1976) have criticized because the methods tend in practice to resemble regulated monopoly.

The second proposal, "free competition," promises on-the-road competition, perhaps in the form of freewheeling jitneys, which are small vehicles that pick up and drop off passengers along a route but do not necessarily follow a schedule. The deregulation or "free competition" precept is incomplete, however, when applied to a service that operates on government property, namely, the roadway, curbspace, and sidewalk areas where pas-

275

sengers congregate in waiting. Bus operators must invest in cultivating passenger congregations and must be able to appropriate the returns on their investment. Depending on how "free competition" is governed, it might give rise to parasitic interloping on routes, where jitneys run ahead of scheduled buses to pick up waiting passengers. Such interloping might undermine any scheduled service and inhibit the development of transit markets. All this activity takes place on public property where market mechanisms are lacking.

Calls to merely privatize the buses and to deregulate bus operations have neglected crucial issues rooted in the management and utilization of the public domain. They ignore curbspaces as a fundamental resource of the industry. In fact, the rules—property rights—governing passenger pickup areas are a determining feature of transit markets. Variations in curb rights explain the differences in transit markets seen in the United States and elsewhere. An appreciation of curb-rights issues leads to a better understanding of transit markets.

We proceed by first examining four case studies of transit markets with deficient property rights: the jitney episode in the United States, 1914 to 1916; jitneys and route associations in less-developed countries (LDCs); illegal jitneys in New York City; and the British experience of bus privatization and deregulation. These case studies help us to develop a logic of transit operations and to formulate a theory of transit markets. Finally, we propose a system of "curb rights" that promises to improve transit markets.

Transit Markets with Deficient Property Rights

The U.S. Jitney Episode of 1914 to 1916

When the automobile came on the scene, so did freewheeling competition in urban transit. Jitneys charging a nickel per ride picked up waiting passengers along the routes of the electric streetcars. The jitneys were usually just the sedans of the day, serving as shared-ride taxicabs along loosely defined routes. They quickly became popular because of their flexibility and speed—almost twice that of the streetcars. They were more comfortable and less crowded, and sometimes they would deviate from the main route to make courtesy dropoffs. By 1915, jitneys operated in most major cities and reportedly numbered 62,000 nationally (Eckert and Hilton 1972, 295–96; Saltzman and Solomon 1973, 63).

Streetcar companies immediately reported losses due to jitney competition, and many began laying off employees and cutting service. But jitneys did not just interlope on streetcar routes; they also filled important market niches. For the most part, jitneys made short trips and provided transportation to many people who otherwise would not have been served by the streetcars. Although jitneys charged no more than the streetcars, their gross revenues far exceeded the streetcars' loss of revenue (Eckert and Hilton 1972, 296; Rosenbloom 1972, 5).

The jitneys were loosely organized and highly spontaneous. Most jitney drivers were independent, some between jobs or working part-time to supplement their income. Many were simply working people who picked up fares on the way to their regular job. Others were teenagers who borrowed their parents' car to earn money after school (Eckert and Hilton 1972, 294). Jitneys adapted flexibly as demand changed with the weather, time of day, day of the week, special events, and so on. Despite the decentralized nature of jitney transport, customs, voluntary associations, and company fleets began to emerge. The associations helped drivers obtain insurance and share maintenance services and protected the drivers from hostile lawmaking; sometimes the group members coordinated routes and schedules (Eckert and Hilton 1972, 295–97).

The electric streetcar companies saw the jitneys as an infringement on their exclusive franchises and lobbied the government to regulate the jitneys. The municipalities went along with streetcar demands, in part because the streetcars afforded them tax revenue and free movement of police and fire department personnel (Hilton 1985, 37). Municipalities required jitney drivers to obtain substantial liability bonds and operating permits. These measures and other antijitney ordinances proved fatal. The jitneys had largely disappeared by 1917, after just two years of rapid growth and experimentation.

The jitney situation posed a fundamental question of property rights: Is interloping on scheduled service a form of theft or a form of legitimate competition? The authorities decided it was "thievery", plain and simple, and instead of developing a framework that could accommodate competitive coexistence, they stamped out freewheeling transit in favor of large-scale monopoly.

Jitneys and Route Associations in the Less-Developed Countries

Transit services similar to the U.S. jitneys of 1915 still operate on the streets of hundreds of cities throughout the less-developed world. Takyi (1990) describes the jitney's appeal to riders:

> They charge relatively low fares and provide wide coverage across a city, often serving poor areas that get no other service. Their operations are flexible so they can add service at peak times and quickly cover new neighborhoods. Their small size and cheap labor enables them to profitably provide frequent service in smaller neighborhoods and along narrow streets, as well as work the main thoroughfares. With fewer passengers, they often make fewer stops and faster time (171).

The American jitneys of 1915 had these advantages until regulations blunted their competitive edge. In the LDCs, laws have been passed to prevent jitneys from interloping on official service and from establishing competing routes, but the enforcement is lax, and, as Takyi (1990) says, the jitneys "never operate legally" (175). Takyi tells of "the loss of passengers at transit stops to jitneys during lean as well as peak periods."

As jitney service develops in thick transit markets, various curbside conflicts and confusions start to occur. Any operator who attempts to establish scheduled service will face interloping. Some operators will run ahead of the scheduled service; others will linger at the curb to fill up, disrupting traffic and taking ridership from the arriving vehicle (Roth and Shephard 1984, 4; Diandas and Roth 1995, 27–28; Takyi 1990, 167, 175). Consumers may be reasonably well served, but discoordination and lack of trust are often severe (Grava 1980, 285).

Often, the jitney operators form a route association, an informal organization to bring order and regularity to service by means of extralegal norms and explicit rules. The jitney literature suggests that route associations have in large measure governed transit services in Lima (De Soto 1989), Hong Kong, Istanbul, Buenos Aires, Manila, Calcutta, and Caracas (Roth and Shephard 1984; Takyi 1990). The route association becomes a regulatory body, similar to government but more local and entrepreneurial. The association lays down rules against interloping and deviating from schedules. It also fixes fares on the route, which may vary with time of day. Associations create enough order to control destructive conflict, but they also operate as cartels. Roth and Shephard (1984, 42), De Soto (1989, 99), Grava (1980, 282), and Cervero (1997, 130, 142) report that associations limit entry.

Thus, we arrive again at the issue of rights to waiting passengers—or curb rights. Jitneys initially transgressed the curb rights of the official bus operators, yet eventually they organized to establish curb rights for themselves. How, then, do they prevent new interlopers from transgressing their rights? Mainly, it seems, by employing physical intimidation and strong-arm tactics. Roth (1987) notes that "the methods used by route associations to protect their territory can become criminal, unlawful, perhaps even homicidal" (224–25). Grava (1980) describes route enforcement by means "considerably beyond the law" by "district strongmen, . . . local bosses, criminal gangs, powerful families, brotherhoods of operators or otherwise legal associations" (282). As is common in black markets everywhere, outlaw entrepreneurs employ violence to maintain their territory. De Soto (1989) tells of route associations in Lima appointing "dispatchers" to monitor compliance with rules and bribing the police to accost and harass "pirates" trying to invade their route (102).

Once route associations have organized their operations, they often seek official recognition. By lobbying, bribery, petition gathering, and other means, the route associations often acquire official status, receiving permits or licenses. Along with official recognition, however, come political obligations and regulations. Transit history in Colombo (Diandas and Roth 1995) and Lima (De Soto 1989) shows a cycle of transit governance: Once the decentralized private operators gain official recognition, they are hamstrung by regulation and suffer invasion by a new generation of interlopers. Without curb rights, established officially or otherwise, orderly, scheduled fixed-route service does not last.

Illegal Jitney Vans in New York City

Black-market jitneying is not restricted to the LDCs. In New York City and Miami, jitney vans have operated extensively, interloping at public bus stops and establishing routes of their own. People who ride the illegal vans give a number of reasons for preferring them to the city buses.[1] By far, the most often-mentioned reason is that the jitneys are faster and even cheaper than the city buses. Jitneys also provide a more comfortable ride, with no standing, and many riders enjoy having a driver who speaks their native language. Finally, many riders say that the jitney is safer than the public bus. Because jitneys come more often, riders do not have to wait as long at the bus stop, where one runs a risk of being mugged (Levine and Wachs 1986). Also, jitney drivers will not pick up passengers who are drunk and disorderly or who otherwise bother or threaten the other passengers. Jitney riders, who are mostly members of minority groups, appreciate being able to escape the forced association with all comers that a public bus entails.

Extreme cases of interloping jitneys may develop where market conditions are favorable and enforcement efforts not yet mobilized. To persist once enforcement begins, interloping must expand to a point at which the individual illegal operator finds safety in numbers. Such a jitney outbreak either continues as a significant force or disappears. In most U.S. cities, either market conditions have not favored illegal jitneys or enforcement has been effective.[2] A notable instance of such a jitney outbreak has occurred in New York City. (On Miami's jitneys, see Klein, Moore, and Reja 1997).

The transit strike in 1980 prompted modern jitney operation in New York City. Illegal jitneys emerged to provide local service and feeder service to the Long Island Rail Road station in Jamaica (southeast Queens). As Boyle (1993) explains, "[T]he jitneys thrived along busy bus routes . . . because of the high numbers of people congregated at the bus stops along these routes" (3). Boyle reasons that jitney service has developed especially in neighborhoods of Caribbean immigrants because those riders had become accustomed to relying on jitneys in their native lands. After the strike ended and regular bus service resumed, enforcement against the jitneys was only "sporadic" (Boyle 1993, 3). Jitneys had reached the "takeoff" point to self-sustained operation. The authorities now faced the dilemma of cracking down on services that were well regarded by paying customers and treated sympathetically by reporters and news commentators.

To operate legally, the vans would have to obtain special permits and a special insurance policy and undergo multiple inspections each year, and the driver would need a special license. The vans could then pick up and discharge passengers only by prearranged appointment; of course, they could not use city bus stops. It is estimated that between 2,500 and 5,000 vans flout these laws (Boyle 1993, 4).

A public transit executive claimed that, each year, the jitney vans were diverting $30 million of revenue from public transit (Machalaba 1991). Transit police had been assigned to areas near bus stops to crack down on the interlopers. The *New York Times* reported: "In the 18 months ended December 1991, a special task force issued 6,542 civil notices of violation against the vans and 11773 criminal summonses, . . . [and made] 251 arrests" (Mitchell 1992). Still, the vans were thought to be uncontrollable. A police officer remarked that two or three vans sail by for every one he tickets, and van drivers paid small regard to the summonses. The *Wall Street Journal* (Machalaba 1991) reported that, over a one-year period, the van drivers had been assessed fines of more than $4 million, but the city collected only $150,000. Fear of racial flare-ups dampened the will to go beyond current enforcement measures, which amount to random delay and hassles for the drivers and their patrons.

The New York jitney experience shows again that unsubsidized private enterprise can supply fixed-route transit, even when having to cope with enforcement efforts against the jitneys. We see also that the property right to waiting bus passengers, as well as the degree of enforcement, is a fundamental component in such operations.

Bus Privatization and Deregulation in Britain

The 1985 Transport Act deregulated the British bus industry everywhere except London.[3] (In London, competition is required only as competitive contracting; there is no on-the-road competition.) All publicly owned bus companies were reorganized as private corporations. The law requires operators to register the commencement of, or changes to, bus service at least forty-two days in advance. The only grounds for local government to refuse to allow a service are serious safety or traffic congestion problems. Local authorities can supplement privately registered routes by putting unserved routes out for competitive tender.

Deregulation permits only scheduled services, not unscheduled services such as jitneys. This restriction, along with the strength of law enforcement in Britain, precludes freewheeling jitney activity and the sort of interloping seen in the LDCs.

On-the-road competition was initially strong, but it has tapered off to a rather low level (Dodgson 1991, 125; Hibbs 1993, 52). However, one must also consider the question of contestability, or the ability of potential entry to disciplined incumbent firms. Mackie, Preston, and Nash (1995, 232) and Dodgson and Katsoulacos (1991, 265–66) suggest that contestability is constrained by the sunk costs of establishing a scheduled service and by the "economies of experience" held by incumbent operators. Another constraint of contestability, which they do not mention, is the ability of an incumbent firm to react quickly to a competitive challenge. Contestability theory suggests that if an incumbent firm can quickly and easily reduce its fares when a competitor challenges it, would-be entrants might be reluctant to enter, even in a market with high fares (Bailey 1981; Bailey and Friedlander 1982). The challenger can no longer expect to grab market share by offering a lower price, and the incumbent has the advantage of experience, reputation, and, in most cases, size.

In fact, British firms have rarely competed by offering lower fares (Dodgson and Katsoulacos 1991, 271–72). Real bus fares increased 17 percent between 1987 and 1994 (White 1995, 198). Instead of competing by offering lower fares, firms chose to offer more frequent service than their competitors. Free competition does not necessarily generate price cutting, as has also been found in deregulated taxi markets (Frankena and Paulter 1986; Teal and Berglund 1987). It seems that information and coordination problems between drivers and potential riders may push transit markets toward a single, or focal, fare rate.

Under the British reforms, registering a scheduled service does not secure one a right to the congregating passengers at the curb. One bus operator can interlope, in a manner of speaking, by registering his own *scheduled* service, to be provided just minutes before the scheduled service of another. As the law does not proscribe schedule matching, local authorities must allow it. Many British bus operators adopt this strategy, which we call "schedule jockeying" (Dodgson 1991, 126; Dodgson and Katsoulacos 1991, 269; Savage 1993, 146; Gomez-Ibanez and Meyer 1990, 13). Because the established firm has no period secure from schedules of competitors, congregations of passengers waiting at the curb can be snatched up by competitors offering comparable fares. Waiting time so dominates passengers' travel decisions that any reputation and amenity advantages an incumbent may offer are not likely to keep waiting travelers from taking the first bus to arrive (Weisman 1981; Wachs 1992; Dobson and Nicolaidis 1974).

Incumbent bus companies, however, quickly learned to monitor the registration of new services by competitors using this strategy, and they often respond promptly in kind. The forty-two-day registration period makes it easy for firms to monitor each other's changes in service and to respond in a potentially endless regress. In the face of a mutually destructive battle, the incumbent has often responded simply by scheduling service so frequently that the challenger cannot expect to get enough riders to survive. The practice, known as "route swamping," has been very common (Dodgson 1991, 126; Dodgson and Katsoulacos 1991, 269; Savage 1993, 146; Gomez-Ibanez and Meyer 1990, 13). The technique has a strategic effect in the immediate contest and in signaling the willingness to use route swamping against future challenges. The ability of incumbent firms to quickly and easily change their schedules in reaction to entry, by virtue of the forty-two-day registration period, constrains contestability in the same way that easily and quickly adjustable prices do in standard contestability theory.

Large incumbent firms often conclude a route-swamping conflict by buying out small rival firms. Also common are mergers between firms that do not compete directly against each other (Mackie, Preston, and Nash 1995, 235; Savage 1993, 147). Many of the latter mergers have taken the form of holding companies, with their subsidiaries often geographically dispersed (Gomez-Ibanez and Meyer 1990, 12–13). The result has been a clear trend toward oligopolistic and even monopolistic operations in the industry, another important unexpected outcome of deregulation (Banister and Pickup 1990, 81; Savage 1993, 147). In many counties, just a few firms control over 80 percent of the market (Banister and Pickup 1990, 81). Small operators have been progressively squeezed out of the competitive market, while finding more success in the tendered contract market.

The literature offers a plethora of explanations for the concentration of the industry. Hibbs (1991, 4) suggests economies of scope and management efficiencies. Mackie, Preston, and Nash (1995, 235–36) and White (1995, 202–3) point to financial advantages of larger firms, managerial economies of scale, and purchasing power. Gomez-Ibanez and Meyer (1990, 12–13) argue that holding companies offer many advantages, including very low costs and the ability to move vehicles and managers from subsidiary to subsidiary as market conditions dictate. They add that firms with large networks have a distinct advantage in the growing use of single-rate, unlimited-travel fare cards. Nash (1988, 110) indicates that larger firms enjoy considerable economies of scope in scheduling buses and avoiding long layovers between runs. Finally, Dodgson and Katsoulacos (1991, 267) point out that, to some extent, the managers of formerly public firms may have retained their old habit of output maximization despite its inappropriateness for achieving the new goal of profit maximization. The issue of integration might suggest yet another explanation. Dodgson (1991, 124) and Nash (1988) note a steady decline in interoperator ticket availability. White (1992, 56) mentions one case in which the removal of schedule coordination and interoperator ticketing led to a 20 percent reduction in ridership.[4]

Although many of these theories have merit, curb rights are fundamental to the peculiar form of deregulation in Britain. Recognizing that the ability to swamp a route is necessary to combat schedule jockeying, one understands the advantages of larger firms with broader networks. As Gomez-Ibanez and Meyer (1990, 13) point out, a larger company has more supervisors, drivers, and buses at its disposal, which it can shift about to swamp a route where a competitor has commenced schedule jockeying. A larger firm will also have greater financial flexibility to maintain such "fighting fleets" (Dodgson and Katsoulacos 1991, 267, 270). Indeed, the very largeness of the firm presents a formidable warning, signaling potential entrants that entry can and will be met by swamping. Although British deregulation of buses has led to large reductions in costs and public subsidization (White

1995, 194; Mackie, Preston, and Nash 1995, 238; White 1992, 50), it has also yielded a surprising degree of industry concentration, with lackluster competition. Our theory of schedule jockeying and route swamping, rooted in an appreciation of curb rights, helps to explain these developments.

A Theory of Transit Services

The Market Advantages of Jitneys

The American experience from 1914 to 1916 and that of transit markets in some LDCs today suggest jitneys have market advantages over scheduled bus service on both the supply side and the demand side. Because jitney operators follow a route but not necessarily a schedule, they enjoy efficiencies in flexibility with respect to their schedules and to changes in weather, congestion, time of day, day of week, and so on. They enjoy flexibility in responding to traffic conditions and can make small deviations from the route. Under a free-entry policy for jitneys, one could expect a cascade of irregular, short-term participants on heavily traveled routes.

On the demand side, passengers waiting for a scheduled bus are generally quite happy to ride a jitney that charges a comparable fare and goes to the same destination. The jitney running ahead offers several advantages. It is available "now," whereas the bus is yet to arrive. It is smaller and faster; its driver is perhaps more courteous; and it may offer deviations from its route, perhaps at an extra charge. The bus is cumbersome and dreary; the jitney is entrepreneurial, more personalized, and even somewhat charming (Takyi 1990, 165). Still, patrons may prefer to wait for the scheduled bus because it offers more certainty and trustworthiness and perhaps because it is more comfortable than the jitney (Grava 1980, 285). In what follows, we posit that passengers generally prefer to ride in the preceding jitney that charges the same fare as the scheduled service.

Appropriability of the Returns on Investment in Scheduled Service

If, in the presence of scheduled service, jitneys enjoy inherent market advantages, the fate of scheduled service hinges on whether jitneys have free run of the streets. The specification and enforcement of curb rights determine whether jitneying will flourish. In the experience of America in 1915, of illegal jitneys in America today, and of jitneying in some LDC cities, scheduled services do not enjoy fully established and exclusive curb rights, either because jitneying is legally permitted or because legal prohibitions are not effectively enforced.

Where interloping is both prohibited and effectively controlled, bus companies will invest in establishing routes and schedules, publicizing the information, and running the service in an incipient market because they can appropriate the value of these efforts to bring people out to the curb. Although transportation economists have identified no economies of scale in merely expanding bus service (Viton 1981; Shipe 1992; Hensher 1988), they have neglected the appropriability of the returns on investment in setting up and cultivating a route. But firms make specific investments in cultivating a route and schedule, and the appropriability of returns on this investment depends on curb rights. We assume that, because jitneys enjoy inherent market advantages, if they are free to interlope, they will dissolve any scheduled service. Without the "anchor" of scheduled service, however, fewer riders congregate at the curb and thus fewer jitneys ply the route.

Thick and Thin Transit Markets in the Absence of Curb Rights

Another distinction of fundamental importance is whether ridership on the transit route is potentially heavy enough to sustain the cascade of jitneys in the absence of scheduled service. If the market is potentially thick, a situation may develop in which there is no scheduled service, jitneys ply the route spontaneously because they have confidence in finding passengers, and passengers congregate at the curb because they have confidence in finding jitneys plying the route. The emergence of conventions that coordinate vehicle services and congregating passengers occurs in America today in the cases of some commuter shuttle vans and carpooling practices (Walder 1985; Cervero 1996, 97).

In an inherently thin market, this outcome, even if it occurs, cannot be sustained: There will not be enough passengers for jitney service to be frequent, so waiting times for unscheduled service will be too long to induce passengers to congregate. Because the coordination problem of unscheduled service is severe in thin markets, service might disappear altogether.

The Thick Market: The Jitney Cascade Is Sustained

Consider the case of the potentially thick market with no exclusive curb rights and thus no scheduled service. The horizontal axis of figure 14.1 counts the number of jitneys per hour that ply the route. The vertical axis counts the number of passengers who congregate at the curb per hour. The thick line shows the number of jitneys that would come out to serve the route, given the number of congregating passengers. This jitneying function shows that no jitneys serve the route when there are no congregating passengers; beyond a threshold point, however, as congregation grows, more jitneys offer service. In the figure, the jitneying response is shown as linear,

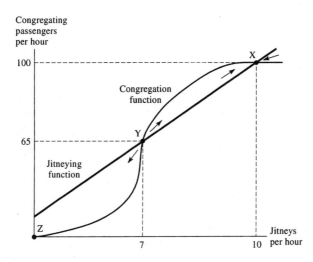

Fig. 14.1 Interactions between congregating passengers and cruising jitneys in a potentially thick market.

but it might plausibly be shown as rising at a declining rate because of congestion among jitneys. The thin curve shows the number of people who would congregate at the curb, given the number of jitneys serving the route. It starts at zero, then rises at an increasing rate, but because only so many people have any demand at all for jitney service, the curve eventually flattens out.

The curves show the mutual dependence of the two sides of the market. If only 60 people congregate per hour over the course of a week, about 6.7 jitneys an hour will respond. The next week, people expect about 6.7 jitneys an hour, and therefore only about 50 people will congregate. The next week, jitney operators expect only 50 people per hour, and the jitney function shows that the jitneys will come out in even smaller numbers, and so on. For a point to the lower left of point Y, the system degenerates to no market at all, point Z. At point Z, a stable equilibrium, it would make no sense for any jitneys to ply the route or for anyone to wait for a jitney.

Suppose that a critical mass were to develop beyond point Y, perhaps due to a transit strike, a coordinated effort by jitney operators, or an unusual event such as the Olympics or a hurricane. In that case, the system would maintain its life. If, for example, 8 jitneys per hour were to ply the route, that would induce significant congregations, which would induce even more jitneys, and the system would bounce up to the other stable equilibrium at point X. Ten jitneys per hour induce exactly 100 congregating passengers, and 100 congregating passengers induce exactly 10 jitneys. This condition is the realization of potential in a thick market.

The Thin Market: The Dissolving Anchor

Figure 14.2 presents the thin market but also posits that the market begins with scheduled bus service. This is the case of the "dissolving anchor." The scheduled service begins to operate and builds up a market. At first, no jitneys participate, perhaps because jitney operators have not seen an opportunity before the development of this market or because they have not tested the powers of enforcement against interloping. With scheduled service and no jitneys, the number of passengers corresponding to point A wait for the bus. This passenger congregation is the "anchor" provided by scheduled service. Assume that, for some reason, jitneying suddenly becomes possible, perhaps because operators come to recognize that enforcement against interloping is weak or nonexistent. They begin to run ahead of the scheduled service, and many passengers are willing to take whichever vehicle comes first. The relationship between the upper congregation function (with scheduled service) and the jitneying function implies that the system will be driven to point B, where 9 jitneys ply the route and 100 passengers wait for service. Passengers and jitneys like this outcome, but because the scheduled bus is now not getting enough riders, it pulls out. The anchor dissolves. Now passengers are less enthusiastic about congregating at curbside for two reasons. First, they do not have the guarantee of anchor service, so they may have to wait longer or with more uncertainty for a carrier. Second, without scheduled service, there is no longer a focal schedule for arrival times at the stops. Jitney arrival times become less predictable. Hence, when people go to the curb, they go with less certainty of when a jitney will arrive, and they wait longer at the curb.[5] The decrease in passenger enthusiasm is shown by the shift downward of the congregation function. Nine jitneys per hour now attract fewer passengers. This reduc-

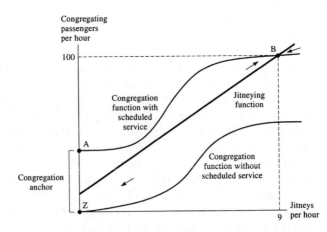

Fig. 14.2 Interloping jitneys dissolve the scheduled service and destroy the market.

tion in turn reduces the number of jitneys, which in turn reduces the number of passengers, and so on. Finally, the system settles at point Z, for zilch. Thus, the progression is as follows: We begin at point A with scheduled service; jitneys come to interlope and the system moves to point B; the anchor is dissolved; and then the system moves to point Z, or market disintegration. In a thin market, the jitney cascade cannot be sustained.

A Typology of Route-Based Transit Markets

In figure 14.3, we suggest a typology of fixed-route urban transit. The top-left cell represents unsubsidized buses with exclusive monopolies on routes with moderate to thin patronage. Exclusive rights are established; there is no interloping and no competition. Therefore, the scheduled service is preserved. But potential problems include inadequate competition and inert monopoly: The incumbent knows that entry is unlikely and consequently skimps on service or increases fares. Moreover, potential operators will waste resources seeking the "rent" associated with the monopoly privilege (Tullock 1967).

In the bottom-left cell, the story is not much different. Again, scheduled service is preserved because interloping is not tolerated. Because the mar-

	Exclusive Route for the Scheduled Service Provider	No Exclusive Rights for Scheduled Service	No Exclusive Rights and Scheduled Service is Subsidized (and Charges Low Fares)
Thin Market	Scheduled Service Preserved *Possible Problems:* inadequate competition, inert monopoly	Interlopers Dissolve Any Anchor *Possible Problems:* market destroyed	Scheduled Service Monopolizes Market *Possible Problems:* franchising problems, subsidy inefficiencies, political conflict, limited discovery, limited flexibility
Thick Market (Potentially)	Scheduled Service Preserved *Possible Problems:* inadequate competition, inert monopoly	Interlopers Dissolve Scheduled Service, But a Cascade of Jitneys Offers Low-Cost, Unscheduled Service *Possible Problems:* low quality, irregularity, unreliability, untrustworthiness	Scheduled Services Preserved, but Jitneys May Serve Excess Demand *Possible Problems:* franchising problems, subsidy inefficiencies, political conflict

Fig. 14.3 A typology of fixed-route urban transit.

ket is thick, it would be better able to support multiple scheduled services, more frequent service, and more consumer choice, but, still, competition is not tolerated. The problem of inert monopoly is more severe.

The middle cells present conditions without exclusive rights, because they are not granted or not enforced. The entire route is essentially a pure commons. With no impediment to running ahead or interloping, in a thin transit market, shown in the top-middle cell, interlopers will run ahead on any scheduled service and collect the waiting passengers. This is the case of the dissolving anchor. The lack of property rights in the waiting passengers results in the "tragedy of the commons" (Hardin 1968). The entire market may be destroyed, for once the anchor has dissolved, people no longer wait and jitneys no longer ply the route.

The case of the thick market is shown in the bottom-middle cell. Here, the lack of curb rights may not be a serious problem. Indeed, any scheduled service will be dissolved, but in a thick market, scheduled service does not necessarily function as an "anchor." Combining elements of figures 14.1 and 14.2, visualize the lower congregation function (without scheduled service) in figure 14.2 as intersecting the jitneying function, as does the congregation function in figure 14.1. The market is thick enough to sustain the cascade of jitneys, and riders will be satisfied by flexible, low-cost, and frequent service. This outcome has sometimes occurred: in the American jitney experience of 1915, a few markets in America today (both illegal and legal), and many of the LDC transit markets. In any place, however, possible problems with the jitney cascade outcome include low quality, irregularity of service, high uncertainty of terms, and lack of trust.

A case that does *not* fit into the typology but which would go between the first and second columns can be imagined. In the British deregulation experience, bus operators neither enjoy exclusive monopolies (column 1) nor operate on a pure commons (column 2). Rather, free competition is permitted among providers who register schedules in advance. The situation is not that of the pure commons because freewheeling is not permitted. The British example suggests that nuanced approaches can be fashioned to fit between the two extremes of exclusive monopoly and pure commons. We will pursue this idea and propose a property-rights framework that avoids monopoly by refining rights along a route.

In the cases considered so far, we have assumed that any scheduled provider could enter the market and would receive no subsidies. Now, consider the case in which scheduled service does receive subsidies (notably government subsidies, but much of the reasoning applies also to cross-subsidies). Subsidies usually lead to very low fares. When subsidized service is combined with exclusive curb rights, conditions are similar to those described in the first column of figure 14.3. The scheduled service, because it charges low fares, is now even more immune to interloping, so again it is preserved. Inadequate competition and the familiar problems attendant to government subsidization characterize this case.

The third column of figure 14.3 depicts the results of subsidized, low-fare service without exclusive curb rights. Interlopers are free to run ahead of the scheduled service, but doing so would be futile because patrons decide they will wait for the scheduled bus, which offers a lower fare. For example, in Los Angeles in 1983, private jitneys were allowed to operate on thirty public transit routes. Matching the 85¢ public bus fare, they succeeded initially, but they promptly withdrew when the city lowered bus fares to 50¢ (Teal and Nemer 1986).

In a thick market, shown in the bottom-right cell, the low fares of the scheduled service again will attract riders, but demand might exceed supply. One of the present authors has witnessed transit operations in Shanghai, where low-fare buses are packed sardine-style and jitneys and taxis cater to the excess demand. In this case, jitneys survive because of excess demand and because they offer superior quality (less crowding, speedier service), even though they charge higher fares. Further, jitneys charge according to trip distance, so someone traveling a short distance might find the jitney fare more appealing than the undifferentiated bus fare.

Now, imagine a decision to privatize and deregulate. If public transit subsidies are eliminated, only the first two columns of figure 14.3 remain. These two options represent the horns of a dilemma. In one case, a provider of scheduled service has an exclusive monopoly over the entire route. Without competition, the provider has little incentive for service improvement and innovation, and fares will be higher. In the other case, no exclusive rights exist. The anchor of scheduled service would be dissolved by jitneys, and markets may never emerge. If policymakers are confined to choosing between these two horns, they should choose on the basis of whether the market is thin or thick. If the market is thin, they should choose monopoly, because the alternative results in no service at all. If the market is potentially thick, they should choose not to grant exclusive rights to the route and simply allow the jitney cascade to burgeon. This option will bring freewheeling service and competitive energy to the market, whereas the alternative would be inert monopoly.

Even better, however, would be an option that avoids both horns of the dilemma, one with limited exclusive rights, to prevent the anchor from dissolving, and with freewheeling competition on the route.

Governance for Bus and Jitney Services: Curb Rights

The answer lies in a system of curb rights that both guarantees some exclusivity to those who successfully cultivate passenger congregations *and* fosters the jitney cascade. No specific system of curb rights is necessarily best for all transit conditions. Because each case is unique, local officials ought to use their knowledge of local conditions to create a suitable curb-rights system.[6]

Spatial Demarcation of Curb Rights

A simple case would combine a scheduled service provider with the jitney cascade. Figure 14.4 is a schematic diagram showing curb rights demarcated in space and time. Consider first just the spatial component, where exclusionary zones are separated by a distance. The 8:00 A.M. column shows four curb zones. When we speak of "curb zones" or "curb rights," it should be understood that we mean not only the curb but also the adjoining space on the sidewalk and road—in other words, a complete bus stop. The column shows how Company A is granted two exclusionary curb zones where no other operators may pick up passengers. Think of each exclusionary zone as being 200 feet in length, with the bus stop situated at the midpoint. Company A has an incentive to invest in creating passenger congregations at its bus stops. It would establish a route and schedule and be free from interloping. Yet, along the same route, jitneys meeting minimal safety and insurance requirements would operate, picking up passengers at nonexclusive zones, or commons. At the commons, passengers have an alternative to Company A, because others (including Company A) may stop and offer service.

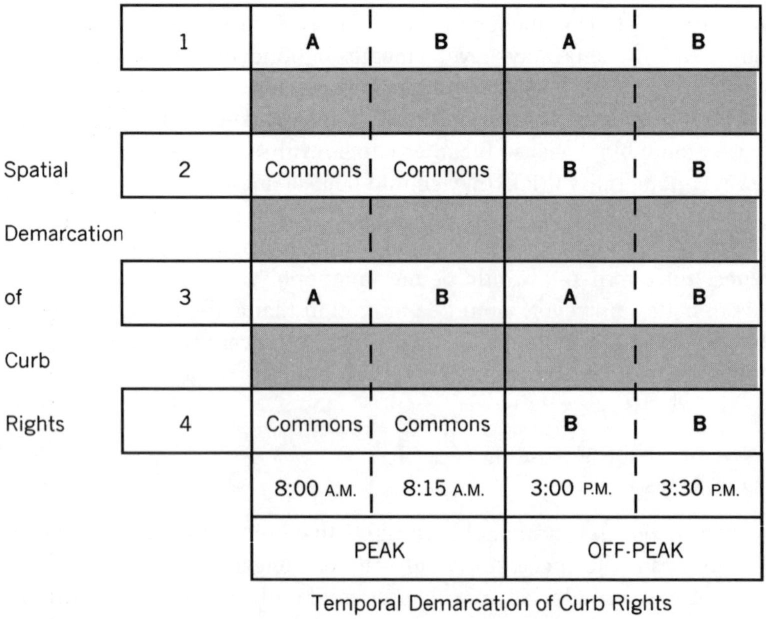

	1	A	B	A	B
Spatial	2	Commons	Commons	B	B
Demarcation					
of	3	A	B	A	B
Curb					
Rights	4	Commons	Commons	B	B
		8:00 A.M.	8:15 A.M.	3:00 P.M.	3:30 P.M.
		PEAK		OFF-PEAK	

Temporal Demarcation of Curb Rights

Fig. 14.4 Property-rights assignment to curb zones. "A" denotes a curb right held by Company A; "B" denotes a curb right held by Company B.

Temporal Demarcation of Curb Rights

Exclusionary zones may also be defined according to time intervals. Consider the two peak-period columns, at 8:00 A.M. and 8:15 A.M. These illustrate that curb zones may be exclusive for Company A during a fifteen-minute interval and then become the "property" of Company B. This system may make enforcement more difficult, but time-elapsed video evidence could show curb-rights violations. This principle of exclusionary intervals responds to the central failing of the British bus deregulation: the ability of one company to insert its service just ahead of the competitor's. Hence, schedule jockeying and route swamping are present, which disrupt service and diminish competitiveness in the industry.

In a thin market, giving free play to the jitney cascade might dissipate all service. Off-peak periods often present thin markets. The off-peak times in figure 14.4 show an arrangement that precludes jitneys but accommodates competition on the route by granting exclusionary zones first to Company A and then to Company B. Instead of temporal alternation, local authorities might deem it better to have spatial alternation of A and B in the same column. Either way, this competitive arrangement would avoid monopoly, unless the two providers were to collude, and would give each provider an incentive to invest in building its ridership. It forgoes, however, the creative and highly efficient input of the freewheelers.

Auctioning Curb Zones

Now, look at figure 14.4 and envision dollar signs in place of the As and Bs. The authorities could define exclusive curb zones and simply put them up for sale, perhaps in the form of five-year leases. The leases could be sold at a set price or auctioned. Auctioning the curb rights would avoid the hazard of monopoly power arising from a maldistribution of initial rights (Hahn 1984). The curbspace holder could then have its buses make stops in its leased zones. Under this plan, individuals with local advantages and knowledge of local opportunities could negotiate to make the most of the resource, and the one with the highest valuation would get the curbspace. Further possibilities emerge if the curb rights may be sublet or resold, which we think should be permitted. The holder may then wish to authorize other carriers to pick up in its curbspace in exchange for a monthly rental payment. Or it could sell the lease rights to a provider with a higher valuation of the curbspace.

One can imagine the emergence of professional curb-zone entrepreneurs who lease available zones, sublet pickup rights to carriers, stage passengers and carriers, and monitor and police the curb rights. Such leaseholders could even sublet to jitney associations, but they would manage this competition to protect their interest in their dealings with scheduled buses. Leaseholders could also profit by using the advertising opportunities on transit benches and shelters (Weisman 1984). Our visualization of a curb-rights system includes at least four categories of participants: local officials, curb-zone leaseholders, transit operators (bus companies, jitneys, and so forth), and passengers.

The scenario of a market in curb rights might raise the specter of holding companies or "robber barons" buying all the curb zones and exercising monopoly power over the route. The local authorities could preclude this outcome, however, in a variety of ways. In a thick market, the most powerful method is for them to reserve certain curb zones as jitney commons, giving the jitney cascade a potential to compete with scheduled service. In a thin market with a monopoly problem, the authorities could ensure that competing service providers each have their own curb rights.

Enforcement of Curb Rights

Any curb-rights scheme depends crucially on the enforceability of curb rights. Enforceability may not be feasible, but we have good grounds for optimism. In the United States today, only in very exceptional instances, as in New York City and Miami, are the curb rights of official services transgressed at all. In Britain, where the scheduled service is typically unsubsidized, no interloping occurs. Most Americans are law abiding, and local governments can protect curb rights.

Demsetz (1967) has explained how one's effort to establish and enforce one's own property rights depends on the costs and benefits of doing so. Local authorities ought to take measures to reduce the costs and increase the benefits of enforcing curb rights. The holder of the curb rights should be encouraged to monitor the "property." Violation of the rights should be treated as private torts, as well as municipal violations. Therefore, in addition to depending on municipal enforcement efforts by traffic or transit police, holders of curb rights could, for instance, set up enclosed video cameras to watch for repeated trespass. The video footage of trespassing jitneys would simplify their identification and apprehension and serve as evidence. Technology and official practice are advancing the photographic enforcement of traffic laws (Turner 1995; Blackburn and Gilbert 1995). Furthermore, the drivers of scheduled vehicles could provide eyewitness accounts of running ahead. Suits could also be brought against riders of trespassing jitneys. The holders of curb rights could put up signs at its bus stops: "Boarding an unauthorized vehicle in this zone is a trespass and subject to civil suit." Travelers would find this reasonable because they could simply walk away from the exclusionary zone to wait legally for a jitney. With a sense of curbspace proprietorship and fair competition, both jitney operators and passengers would be likely to respect curb rights.

Emergence of Staging Areas on Private Property

Jitney commons zones are designated in figure 14.4, but it might not be necessary to preestablish such zones. It might be sufficient to prohibit jitneys from picking up passengers in the A zones, allowing their own curb zones and staging areas to emerge spontaneously. Local officials may wish to manage the emergence of such pickup spots to avoid sidewalk congestion or to provide transit focal points, but if certain places seem to be emerging as workable jitney spots, the officials ought to smile on the development. They may wish to alter parking or standing rules at such spots and perhaps even provide turnouts, benches, and shelters. Imagine a McDonald's restaurant emerging as a jitneying point, where travelers can buy breakfast and organize shared rides on innovative McTransit (Rehmke 1991). If the McDonald's began to charge for daytime parking or to cooperate in announcing or arranging jitney departures, this activity ought to be regarded as legitimate private enterprise. Throughout the city, entrepreneurs may find it profitable to develop jitney staging areas on private property, and jitney associations may want to negotiate a system of such spots with local businesses. In our scheme, local officials are not primarily regulators; they are creators and enforcers of property rights. Provided that jitney operators and staging entrepreneurs do not tread on the property rights of others, they should be allowed to operate unencumbered.

Conclusion

We have developed a theory of scheduled bus service that recognizes the importance of generating passenger congregations. Furthermore, the returns on investments in cultivating passenger congregations must be appropriable or protected from interloping. Transit markets tend to be gored by one of the two horns of a dilemma. In some markets, scheduled operators can appropriate the value of passenger congregations, but only by means of a grant of exclusive rights not only to the waiting passengers but also to the entire route. Thus, the first horn is transit monopoly. The other horn is the pure commons, which gives rise to freewheeling competition like that found in some LDC cities. In this case, no one cultivates passenger congregations for scheduled service because interlopers will expropriate the investment. In consequence, thin markets receive especially poor service.

A nuanced approach based on property rights can maneuver between the horns of this dilemma. We can have the best of both cases: scheduled service and freewheeling jitneys. Figure 14.5 revises figure 14.3 by inserting our solution between exclusive monopoly and the pure commons (and by eliminating the case of subsidized service).

	Exclusive Route for the Scheduled Service Provider	Refined System of Curb Rights for Scheduled Service	No Exclusive Rights for Scheduled Service
Thin Market	**Scheduled Service Preserved** *Possible Problems:* inadequate competition, inert monopoly	**Scheduled Service Preserved; Potential for Competing Scheduled Services; Commons Provides Jitneying Opportunities**	**Interlopers Dissolve Any Anchor** *Possible Problems:* market destroyed
Thick Market (Potentially)	**Scheduled Service Preserved** *Possible Problems:* inadequate competition, inert monopoly	**Scheduled Services Preserved *and* Cascade of Jitneys Offers Low-Cost, Unscheduled Service**	**Interlopers Dissolve Any Scheduled Service, but a Cascade of Jitneys Offers Low-Cost, Unscheduled Service** *Possible Problems:* low quality, irregularity, unreliability, untrustworthiness

Fig. 14.5 A typology of unsubsidized fixed-route urban transit incorporating curb rights.

The type of governance suggested here rests on the creation of exclusive and transferable curb rights, leased by auction. Scheduled service providers would have exclusive protection where their passengers congregate, and jitneys would pick up passengers at curb zones designated as commons. Within the property-rights framework of curb rights, entrepreneurs would be free, able, and driven to introduce ever better service, revise schedules and route structures, establish connections among transit providers, introduce new vehicles, and use new pricing strategies. Once the system of curb rights was sensibly implemented, the market process would operate. One feature of this process is competition; another is the discovery of new opportunities for service resulting from entrepreneurial insight into changing local conditions. Within a suitable framework of property rights, the invisible hand will be able to do in urban transit markets what it does so well in other parts of the economy.

Notes

This chapter is a condensation of the authors' book *Curb Rights: A Foundation for Free Enterprise in Urban Transit* (Washington, D.C.: Brookings Institution, 1997). The authors would like to thank Pete Fielding, Pia Koskenoja, Charles Lave, James Nolan, and Ken Small for valuable comments. For financial support, the authors thank the California Department of Transportation (contract RTA-65V450) and the University of California Transportation Center.

1. This paragraph is drawn from news reports about jitney riders. See Bonapace (1993), Fried (1994), Garvin (1992), Machalaba (1991), and Onishi (1994).

2. Boyle (1993) states: "Transit and planning personnel in Chicago, Los Angeles, Atlanta, and Houston indicate that jitneys were not operating in any extensive or arranged fashion in their cities" (1).

3. Gomez-Ibanez and Meyer (1990), Banister and Pickup (1990), and White (1995) provide summaries of the 1985 Transport Act.

4. Indeed, many trips using more than one carrier are more expensive than a trip of the same length on one carrier. Hibbs (1991, 5) argues, however, that only a small number of trips involve a change of carrier. Yet, if firms really cannot negotiate interoperable ticket agreements, and thereby lose ridership, they have an incentive to expand their network to minimize the inconvenience to riders.

5. It might be thought that once the scheduled service pulls out, the jitneying function would shift outward, because jitneys pick up passengers that had been taking scheduled service. This shift may not occur, however, because passengers are now more randomly dispersed over the course of the hour due to the loss of schedule focus.

6. The hope that local government officials will carry out this task diligently, honestly, and competently must take heed of public choice considerations. But the realm of hope is one of relatives, not absolutes. The public choice pitfalls of government action do not undermine the merit of our proposal when placed in comparison to the status quo or other schemes for government management, because in those other arrangements, the same public choice pitfalls apply with equal or greater force. The curb-rights proposal does suffer from public choice pitfalls in comparison to full privatization of not only curb zones and bus stops but also the entire system of streets and sidewalks. On the viability of such a plan, see Klein (1998).

References

APTA (American Public Transit Association). 1995. *Fact Book 1995*. Washington, D.C.: American Public Transit Association.

Bailey, Elizabeth. 1981. "Contestability and the Design of Regulatory and Antitrust Policy." *American Economic Association Papers and Proceedings* 71 (2):178–83.

Bailey, Elizabeth E., and Ann Friedlander. 1982. "Market Structure and Multiproduct Industries." *Journal of Economic Literature* 20:1024–48.

Banister, David, and Laurie Pickup. 1990. "Bus Transport in the Metropolitan Areas and London." In *Deregulation and Transport: Market Forces in the Modern World*, edited by P. Bell and P. Cloke. London: David Fulton Publishers, 67–83.

Blackburn, Robert, and Daniel Gilbert. 1995. *Photographic Enforcement of Traffic Laws*. Washington, D.C.: Transportation Research Board (TE7.N36 #219).

Bonapace, Ruth. 1993. "Commuter War: Vans Battle Buses for Riders." *New York Times*, 14 February, XIII, NJ1.

Boyle, D. 1993. "Jitney Enforcement Strategies in New York City." Paper No. 940642, presented at the 73rd Annual Meeting of Transportation Research Board.

Cervero, Robert. 1997. *Paratransit in America: Redefining Mass Transportation.* Westport, Conn.: Praeger.

Demsetz, Harold. 1967. "Toward a Theory of Property Rights." *American Economic Review* (papers and proceedings) 57:347–59.

Department of Transportation, Urban Mass Transportation Administration. 1984. "Private Enterprise Participation Program." *Federal Register* 49.

De Soto, Hernando. 1989. *The Other Path: The Invisible Revolution in the Third World.* Translated by June Abbott. New York: Harper & Row.

Diandas, John, and Gabriel Roth. 1995. "Alternative Approaches to Improving Route Bus Services in Sri Lanka." Fourth International Conference on Competition and Ownership in Land Passenger Transport, July, Rotorua, New Zealand.

Dobson, Ricardo, and Gregory C. Nicolaidis. 1974. "Preferences for Mass Transit Service by Homogeneous Groups of Individuals." General Motors Research Publication. GMR-1616.

Dodgson, J. S. 1991. "The Bus Industry and the Cases of Australia, the USA, and the UK." In *Transportation Deregulation: An International Movement*, edited by K. Button and D. Pitfield. London: Macmillan.

Dodgson, John S., and Y. Katsoulacos. 1991. "Competition, Contestability and Predation: The Economics of Competition in Deregulated Bus Markets." *Transportation Planning and Technology* 15:263–75.

Eckert, Ross D., and George W. Hilton. 1972. "The Jitneys." *Journal of Law and Economics* 15:293–325.

Frankena, Mark, and Paul Paulter. 1986. "Taxicab Regulation: An Economic Analysis." *Research in Law and Economics* 9:129–65.

Fried, Joseph P. 1994. "A New Law Escalates the War against Unlicensed Vans." *New York Times*, 13 February, I, 43:1.

Garvin, Glenn. 1992. "Van Ban." *Reason* 24 (December):53–55.

Goldberg, Victor P. 1976. "Regulation and Administered Contracts." *Bell Journal of Economics* 7:426–48.

Gomez-Ibanez, Jose A., and John R. Meyer. 1990. "Privatizing and Deregulating Local Public Services: Lessons from Britain's Buses." *American Planning Association Journal* 9 (Winter):9–21.

———. 1993. *Going Private: The International Experience with Transport Privatization.* Washington, D.C.: Brookings Institution.

Grava, Sigurd. 1980. "Paratransit in Developing Countries." In *Transportation and Development around the Pacific.* New York: American Society of Civil Engineers.

Hahn, Robert W. 1984. "Market Power and Transferable Property Rights." *Quarterly Journal of Economics* 753–65.

Hardin, Garret. 1968. "The Tragedy of the Commons." *Science* 13 December, 1243–48.

Hensher, David A. 1988. "Productivity in Privately Owned and Operated Bus Firms in Australia." In *Bus Deregulation and Privatization: An International Perspective*, edited by J. S. Dodgson and N. Topham. Aldershot, U.K.: Avebury.

Hibbs, John. 1991. *An Evaluation of Urban Bus Deregulation in Britain: A Survey of Management Attitudes.* Oxford: Pergamon Press.

———. 1993. *On the Move: A Market for Mobility on the Roads.* London: Institute of Economic Affairs.

Hilton, George W. 1985. "The Rise and Fall of Urban Transit." In *Urban Transit: The Private Challenge to Public Transportation,* edited by C. Lave. San Francisco: Pacific Institute.

Klein, Daniel B. 1998. "Planning and the Two Coordinations, with Illustration in Urban Transit." *Planning and Markets* (http://www-pam.usc.edu/v1i1a1s1. html).

Klein, Daniel B., Adrian T. Moore, and Binjam Reja. 1997. *Curb Rights: A Foundation for Free Enterprise in Urban Transit.* Washington, D.C.: Brookings Institution.

Lave, Charles A., ed. 1985. *Urban Transit: The Private Challenge to Public Transportation.* San Francisco: Pacific Institute.

Levine, Ned, and Martin Wachs. 1986. "Bus Crime in Los Angeles: II. Victims and Public Impact." *Transportation Research* 20:285–93.

Machalaba, David. 1991. "Opportunistic Vans Are Running Circles around City Buses." *Wall Street Journal,* VII, 24.

Mackie, Peter, John Preston, and Chris Nash. 1995. "Bus Deregulation: Ten Years On." *Transport Reviews* 15 (3):229–51.

Mitchell, Alison. 1992. "Vans Fighting a Strong Guerrilla War for New York's Streets." *New York Times,* 24 January, A16.

Nash, Christopher A. 1988. "Integration of Public Transport: An Economic Assessment." In *Bus Deregulation and Privatization: An International Perspective,* edited by J. S. Dodgson and N. Topham. Aldershot, U.K.: Avebury.

Onishi, Norimitsu. 1994. "Bus Fare Dips $1 to Attract Livery Riders." *New York Times,* 25 September, XII CY, 10:6.

Perry, J., T. Babitsky, and H. Gregersen. 1988. "Organizational Form and Performance in Urban Mass Transit." *Transportation Reviews* 8:125–43.

Rehmke, Gregory F. 1991. "McTransit for the 1990s." *Econ Update* (March):3f.

Rosenbloom, Sandra. 1972. "Taxis and Jitneys." *Reason* (February):4–16.

Roth, Gabriel. 1987. *The Private Provision of Public Services in Developing Countries.* New York: Oxford University Press.

Roth, Gabriel, and Anthony Shepherd. 1984. *Wheels within Cities: New Alternatives for Passenger Transport.* London: Adam Smith Institute.

Saltzman, Arthur, and Richard Solomon. 1973. "Jitney Operations in the United States." *Highway Research Record* 449:63–71.

Savage, Ian. 1993. "Deregulation and Privatization of Britain's Local Bus Industry." *Journal of Regulatory Economics* 143–58.

Shipe, Richard Thomas. 1992. "Cost and Productivity in the U.S. Urban Bus Transit Sector, 1978–1989." Ph.D. diss., University of California, Berkeley.

Takyi, Isaac K. 1990. "An Evaluation of Jitney Systems in Developing Countries." *Transportation Quarterly* (January):163–77.

Teal, Roger. 1988. "Public Transit Service Contracting: A Status Report." *Transportation Quarterly* 42 (2):207–22.

Teal, Roger, and Mary Berglund. 1987. "The Impacts of Taxi Deregulation in the USA." *Journal of Transport Economics and Policy* 21 (January):37–56.

Teal, Roger, and T. Nemer. 1986. "Privatization of Urban Transit: The Los Angeles Jitney." *Transportation* 13:5–22.

Tullock, Gordon. 1967. "The Welfare Costs of Tariffs, Monopolies and Theft." *Western Economic Journal* 5:224–32.

Turner, Daniel S. 1995. "Video Evidence for Highway Tort Trials." *Transportation Research Record* 1464:86–91.

Viton, P. A. 1981. "A Translog Cost Function for Urban Bus Transit." *Journal of Industrial Economics* 29:287–304.

Wachs, Martin. 1992. "Can Transit Be Saved? Of Course It Can!" Keynote address at Metropolitan Conference on Public Transportation Research, Chicago.

Walder, Jay. 1985. "Private Commuter Vans in New York." In *Urban Transit*, edited by C. Lave. San Francisco: Pacific Institute.

Weisman, Mark. 1981. "Variables Influencing Transit Use." *Traffic Quarterly* 35: 371–83.

———. 1984. "Advertising Transit Shelter Program." *Transportation Quarterly* 38 (July):361–74.

White, Peter R. 1992. "Three Years' Experience of Bus Service Deregulation in Britain." In *Privatization and Deregulation in Passenger Transportation*, edited by A. Talvite, D. Hensher, and M. Beesley. Helsinki: The University of Tampere.

———. 1995. "Deregulation of Local Bus Services in Great Britain: An Introductory Review." *Transport Reviews* 15:185–209.

Williamson, Oliver E. 1976. "Franchise Bidding for Natural Monopolies—In General and with Respect to CATV." *Bell Journal of Economics* 7:73–104.

Index

Page numbers in italic refer to pages with figures.

About The Independent Institute

THE INDEPENDENT INSTITUTE is a non-profit, non-partisan, scholarly research and educational organization that sponsors comprehensive studies of the political economy of critical social and economic issues.

The politicization of decision-making in society has too often confined public debate to the narrow reconsideration of existing policies. Given the prevailing influence of partisan interests, little social innovation has occurred. In order to understand both the nature of and possible solutions to major public issues, The Independent Institute's program adheres to the highest standards of independent inquiry and is pursued regardless of prevailing political or social biases and conventions. The resulting studies are widely distributed as books and other publications, and are publicly debated through numerous conference and media programs.

In pursuing this uncommon independence, depth, and clarity, The Independent Institute seeks to push at the frontiers of our knowledge, redefine the debate over public issues, and foster new and effective directions for government reform.

The INDEPENDENT INSTITUTE

100 Swan Way, Oakland, California 94621-1428, U.S.A. Telephone: 510-632-1366 · Facsimile: 510-568-6040. E-mail: info@independent.org · Website: http://www.independent.org

Other Titles Available through The Independent Institute

THE ACADEMY IN CRISIS
The Political Economy of Higher
  Education
Edited by John W. Sommer
Foreword by Nathan Glazer
AGRICULTURE AND THE STATE
Market Processes and Bureaucracy
E. C. Pasour, Jr.
Foreword by Bruce L. Gardner
ALIENATION AND THE SOVIET ECONOMY
The Collapse of the Socialist Era
Paul Craig Roberts
Foreword by Aaron Wildavsky
AMERICAN HEALTH CARE
Government, Market Processes and the
  Public Interest
Roger D. Feldman
Foreword by Mark V. Pauly
ANTITRUST AND MONOPOLY
Anatomy of a Policy Failure
D. T. Armentano
Foreword by Yale Brozen
ARMS, POLITICS, AND THE ECONOMY
Historical and Contemporary
  Perspectives
Edited by Robert Higgs
Foreword by William A. Niskanen
BEYOND POLITICS
Markets, Welfare and the Failure of
  Bureaucracy
William C. Mitchell and Randy T.
  Simmons
Foreword by Gordon Tullock
THE CAPITALIST REVOLUTION IN LATIN
  AMERICA
Paul Craig Roberts and Karen LaFollette
  Araujo
Foreword by Peter T. Bauer
CUTTING GREEN TAPE
Toxic Pollutants, Environmental
Regulation and the Law
Edited by Richard Stroup and Roger E.
  Meiners
Foreword by W. Kip Viscusi
THE DIVERSITY MYTH
Multiculturalism and Political
  Intolerance on Campus
David O. Sacks and Peter A. Thiel
Foreword by Elizabeth Fox-Genovese
FREEDOM, FEMINISM AND THE STATE
Edited by Wendy McElroy
Foreword by Lewis Perry
HAZARDOUS TO OUR HEALTH?
FDA Regulation of Health Care Products
Edited by Robert Higgs
Foreword by Joel J. Nobel
HOT TALK, COLD SCIENCE
Global Warming's Unfinished Debate
S. Fred Singer
Foreword by Frederick Seitz

LIBERTY FOR WOMEN
Freedom and Feminism in the Twenty-
  First Century
Edited by Wendy McElroy
Foreword by Wendy Kaminer
MONEY AND THE NATION STATE
The Financial Revolution, Government
  and the World Monetary System
Edited by Kevin Dowd and Richard H.
  Timberlake, Jr.
Foreword by Merton H. Miller
OUT OF WORK
Unemployment and Government in
  Twentieth-Century America
Richard K. Vedder and Lowell E.
  Gallaway
Foreword by Martin Bronfenbrenner
PRIVATE RIGHTS & PUBLIC ILLUSIONS
Tibor R. Machan
Foreword by Nicholas Rescher
REGULATION AND THE REAGAN ERA
Politics, Bureaucracy and the Public
  Interest
Edited by Roger Meiners and Bruce
  Yandle
Foreword by Robert W. Crandall
TAXING CHOICE
The Predatory Politics of Fiscal
  Discrimination
Edited by William F. Shughart II
Foreword by Paul W. McCracken
TAXING ENERGY
Oil Severance Taxation and the
  Economy
Robert Deacon, Stephen DeCanio, H. E.
  Frech, III, and M. Bruce Johnson
Foreword by Joseph P. Kalt
THAT EVERY MAN BE ARMED
The Evolution of a Constitutional Right
Stephen P. Halbrook
TO SERVE AND PROTECT
Privatization and Community in
  Criminal Justice
Bruce L. Benson
Foreword by Marvin E. Wolfgang
THE VOLUNTARY CITY
Choice, Community and Civil Society
Edited by David T. Beito, Peter Gordon
  and Alexander Tabarrok
Foreword by Paul Johnson
WINNERS, LOSERS & MICROSOFT
Competition and Antitrust in High
  Technology
Stan J. Liebowitz and Stephen E.
  Margolis
Foreword by Jack Hirshleifer
WRITING OFF IDEAS
Taxation, Foundations, and
  Philanthropy in America
Randall G. Holcombe

For further information and a catalog of publications, please contact
The Independent Institute